# THE NONPROFIT ALMANAC
## 2012

Also of interest from the Urban Institute Press:

*Nonprofits and Business,* edited by Joseph J. Cordes and
C. Eugene Steuerle

*Nonprofits and Government: Collaboration and Conflict,* second
edition, edited by Elizabeth T. Boris and C. Eugene Steuerle

*Property-Tax Exemption for Charities: Mapping the Battlefield,*
edited by Evelyn Brody

# THE NONPROFIT ALMANAC
## 2012

Katie L. Roeger,
Amy S. Blackwood, and
Sarah L. Pettijohn

Foreword by
Robert D. Reischauer

**THE URBAN INSTITUTE PRESS**
WASHINGTON, DC

**THE URBAN INSTITUTE PRESS**
2100 M Street, N.W.
Washington, D.C. 20037

ISBN 978-0-87766-773-5 (paper, alk. paper)
ISSN 1949-8187

Printed in the United States of America

16  15  14  13  12          1  2  3  4  5

**THE URBAN INSTITUTE** is a nonprofit, nonpartisan policy research and educational organization established in Washington, D.C., in 1968. Its staff investigates the social, economic, and governance problems confronting the nation and evaluates the public and private means to alleviate them. The Institute disseminates its research findings through publications, its web site, the media, seminars, and forums.

Through work that ranges from broad conceptual studies to administrative and technical assistance, Institute researchers contribute to the stock of knowledge available to guide decisionmaking in the public interest.

Conclusions or opinions expressed in Institute publications are those of the authors and do not necessarily reflect the views of officers or trustees of the Institute, advisory groups, or any organizations that provide financial support to the Institute.

# Contents

## Figures

## Tables

# Foreword

The world has changed greatly since the 2008 edition of the *Nonprofit Almanac*, which provided information on the sector up to the onset of the Great Recession. The severe contraction and subsequent period of slow economic growth continued to affect not only businesses but also governments and many nonprofits in 2009 and 2010, the most recent years covered by the 2012 *Almanac*. While the data reveal that the U.S. nonprofit sector continued to grow, adding jobs while business and government shed them, growth has been uneven. Health care and hospitals expanded more strongly than most other components, notably social services and the arts. Fees for services remain the largest component of revenues.

This year's *Nonprofit Almanac* features data for 2000 to 2010, providing solid trend information on the state of the nonprofit sector in the United States, a sector that continues to contribute an estimated 5.5 percent of GDP and employ about 9 percent of the labor force. The 10-year picture reveals both the continuity of nonprofit growth over time as well as year-to-year variations in the sector's financial and employment situation. What is particularly striking is the decline in numbers of individuals making contributions and bequests during the recession as well as the precipitous decline in interest and dividend income. These trends clearly reveal the effect of the recession on resources available to nonprofits, but they underestimate the full impact because they do not capture the surge in demand for services that many social services nonprofits experienced in the wake of job losses and foreclosures.

Another noteworthy trend is the gap between income and expenditures, which was negative for 8 of the 10 years covered, rising to −$65 billion by 2010. It appears that the growth of the sector is being financed by borrowing or drawing down of reserves, trends that are likely to weaken affected parts of the sector over the long haul.

The *Nonprofit Almanac 2012* is the latest in a series that the National Center for Charitable Statistics (NCCS) at the Urban Institute began in 1997. An almanac of this scope is a significant achievement, especially since the raw material is often not available in a usable form. During the past 15 years, NCCS has refined the data and estimation methods and worked diligently to improve the information available on nonprofit organizations.

The authors of this volume pull together data from various government and nonprofit sources and make estimates where necessary to provide the most comprehensive statistical picture of the nonprofit sector available. Their methods are described in detail for the readers of this volume.

NCCS, in collaboration with the IRS, state charity regulators, and nonprofit partners, deserves credit for helping improve the major nonprofit data source, the annual IRS Form 990. NCCS has also taken the lead in creating research-quality databases from Form 990 information and making them accessible online, thereby encouraging additional study. Regretfully, basic information on employment and the economic contributions of nonprofits is still not well identified in government data sources, and some important sources are not made available for analysis. The lag time for getting Form 990 data is also problematic for those who rely on it for policy decisions and planning.

The utility of the *Nonprofit Almanac* is evident. It deepens understanding of the nonprofit sector's role in society and opens it up to further analysis. Both are important contributions.

**Robert Reischauer**
*President Emeritus*
The Urban Institute

# 1

# The Nonprofit Sector and Its Place in the National Economy

The nonprofit sector has faced many challenges since the publication of the 2008 *Almanac*: an ailing economy that threatens contributions; stock market declines that reduce endowments or other investments; increased demands for many services such as job training, mortgage assistance, or food; and new IRS filing regulations that promote transparency and accountability. Even amid these challenges, the nonprofit sector as a whole has continued to grow in numbers, employees, wages, and assets. This growth was largely driven by hospitals and other health care organizations because of increased health care spending.

These trends, however, should not mask the cutbacks and hardships that nonprofit organizations, especially small ones, have experienced these past few years. Some organizations closed their doors during the recession; others cut staff, wages, or program activities to stay afloat; and some that relied heavily on one type of funding experienced greater hardships. Still, the nonprofit sector continues to show its resilience and has become a larger and more important part of the U.S. economy since 2008.

This book explores the nonprofit sector, its finances, and its role in the national economy. Specifically, the *Almanac* examines wages and employment trends, financial trends, giving and volunteering, and the size, scope, and finances of public charities. Chapters 1–4 present statistics on the entire nonprofit sector, while chapter 5 focuses exclusively on the finances of 501(c)(3) public charities. This first chapter presents empirical estimates of the size of the nonprofit sector in relation to the national economy.

The nonprofit sector is large and diverse and made up of small and large organizations. These organizations encourage civic participation; allow for expression of religious, social, and artistic values; provide basic social services; and strengthen communities. Nonprofit organizations have different board and management styles, and some organizations use professional staff while other organizations use all-volunteer labor. Different organizations rely on different streams of funding as well. Some organizations within the sector depend on individual contributions, while others rely on government funds or fees for services.

The differences between organizations in the nonprofit sector make it easier to define the sector by what it is not: it is not part of government nor is it a part of the business sector. More descriptively, it is also referred to as the charitable, voluntary, tax-exempt, independent, third, social, or philanthropic sector. These additional names suggest the importance of the nonprofit sector in our society: it is a resource for those in need as well as the voluntary foundation of civil society.

In this chapter and throughout the *Almanac,* we use two primary sources of data: Internal Revenue Service (IRS) records and Bureau of Economic Analysis (BEA) estimates. We therefore use IRS and BEA definitions of the sector in most of our analyses.

## The Nonprofit Landscape

In 2012, nearly 1.6 million nonprofit organizations were registered with the Internal Revenue Service, meaning they had applied for and received tax-exempt recognition. This figure does not include congregations or their auxiliary groups, or smaller organizations that earn less than $5,000 in revenue annually. If religious congregations and smaller organizations were taken into account, the estimated number of nonprofits would be closer to 2.3 million.[1] Nonprofit groups that generate more than $50,000 in gross receipts are required to file a tax return with the IRS known as the Form 990 or Form 990-EZ; these organizations are referred to as reporting nonprofits or filers.

This vast and varied assembly—about 1 nonprofit for every 175 Americans—operates all across the United States but tends to be located in urban areas or near large cities (figure 1.1). Large metropolitan areas, such as Los Angeles, Chicago, and New York City, have the highest concentration of nonprofit organizations. The three counties with the most registered nonprofits in 2012 are Los Angeles County, California, with a total of 36,735 organizations; Cook County, Illinois, with 24,216; and New York County, New York, with 19,454. Just 1 percent of counties nationwide have 5,000 or more registered nonprofits. Counties with smaller populations have fewer nonprofit organizations. Nearly 60 percent of counties have fewer than 100 registered nonprofit organizations.

The nonprofit sector includes many diverse organizations. Under the Internal Revenue Code, more than 30 types of legal entities are classified as 501(c) organizations; all are exempt from corporate income taxes, but not all are charitable. Table 1.1 displays the number, expenses, and assets by type of tax exemption. The 501(c)(3) category, which can receive tax-deductible contributions, includes public charities and private foundations. It accounts for approximately three-quarters of the nonprofit sector in number of organizations, expenses, and assets (see the shaded rows in table 1.1). As the range of organizations classified as tax exempt under section 501(c) is quite large, we also categorize nonprofits by the type of services they provide or the types of activities they conduct. These organization types, or subsectors, are explained further below.

1. There are roughly 300,000 religious congregations based on data from the American Church List and an estimated 400,000 smaller organizations based on data extrapolated from select state registers.

Figure 1.1. Number of Registered Nonprofit Organizations by County, 2012

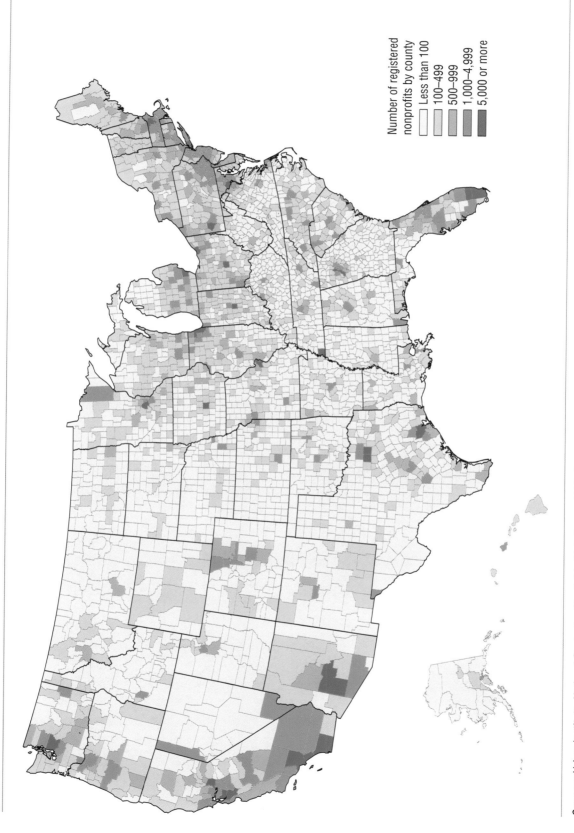

Number of registered
nonprofits by county

Less than 100
100–499
500–999
1,000–4,999
5,000 or more

*Sources:* Urban Institute, National Center for Charitable Statistics; and U.S. Census Bureau, 2010 Census.
*Notes:* Locations are based on an organization's address on file with the Internal Revenue Service and do not include multiple locations or satellite offices. P.O. boxes are excluded.

**Table 1.1.** Types of Tax-Exempt Organizations and Number, Expenses, and Assets by Type

| Section of 1986 IRC | Description of organization | Entities registered with the IRS, 2012 | Entities reporting to the IRS, 2010 | Expenses of reporting entities, 2010 ($ millions) | Assets of reporting entities, 2010 ($ millions) |
|---|---|---|---|---|---|
| 501(c)(1) | Corporations organized under acts of Congress | 237 | 8 | 11 | 237 |
| 501(c)(2) | Title-holding corporations for exempt organizations | 4,581 | 3,001 | 1,197 | 12,487 |
| 501(c)(3) | Religious, charitable, and similar organizations | 1,057,486 | 467,776 | 1,515,587 | 3,335,334 |
| | *501(c)(3) Public charities* | *958,740* | *366,086* | *1,454,753* | *2,708,905* |
| | *501(c)(3) Private foundations* | *98,746* | *101,690* | *60,834* | *626,429* |
| 501(c)(4) | Civic leagues and social welfare organizations | 86,916 | 30,255 | 83,932 | 89,438 |
| 501(c)(5) | Labor, agriculture, and horticulture organizations | 46,812 | 22,327 | 22,355 | 33,577 |
| 501(c)(6) | Business leagues, chambers of commerce, real estate boards, and trade boards | 63,988 | 36,442 | 39,031 | 65,582 |
| 501(c)(7) | Social and recreational clubs | 47,210 | 19,835 | 12,587 | 25,625 |
| 501(c)(8) | Fraternal beneficiary societies and associations | 50,711 | 9,994 | 17,175 | 114,594 |
| 501(c)(9) | Voluntary employee-beneficiary associations | 7,163 | 6,686 | 161,158 | 201,254 |
| 501(c)(10) | Domestic fraternal societies and associations | 15,527 | 2,356 | 403 | 2,771 |
| 501(c)(11) | Teachers' retirement fund associations | 7 | 7 | 35 | 300 |
| 501(c)(12) | Benevolent life insurance associations, mutual ditch or irrigation companies, mutual or cooperative telephone companies, etc. | 5,202 | 3,901 | 53,701 | 124,843 |
| 501(c)(13) | Cemetery companies | 8,173 | 2,635 | 905 | 9,819 |
| 501(c)(14) | State-chartered credit unions and mutual reserve funds | 2,472 | 2,861 | 22,949 | 435,246 |
| 501(c)(15) | Mutual insurance companies or associations | 822 | 306 | 70 | 349 |
| 501(c)(16) | Cooperative organizations to finance crop operations | 13 | 9 | 15 | 406 |
| 501(c)(17) | Supplemental unemployment benefit trusts | 130 | 101 | 394 | 232 |
| 501(c)(18) | Employee-funded pension trusts created before June 25, 1959 | 2 | 1 | 163 | 1,153 |
| 501(c)(19) | War veterans organizations | 32,286 | 8,449 | 1,351 | 3,077 |

*(continued)*

**Table 1.1.** Types of Tax-Exempt Organizations and Number, Expenses, and Assets by Type *(continued)*

| Section of 1986 IRC | Description of organization | Entities registered with the IRS, 2012 | Entities reporting to the IRS, 2010 | Expenses of reporting entities, 2010 ($ millions) | Assets of reporting entities, 2010 ($ millions) |
|---|---|---|---|---|---|
| 501(c)(20) | Legal service organizations | 5 | 4 | 1 | 1 |
| 501(c)(21) | Black lung benefits trusts | 28 | 0 | 0 | 0 |
| 501(c)(22) | Withdrawal liability payment funds | 0 | 0 | 0 | 0 |
| 501(c)(23) | Veterans organizations created before 1880 | 3 | 3 | 308 | 3,333 |
| 501(c)(24) | Trusts described in section 4049 of the Employment Retirement Security Act of 1974 | 1 | 0 | 0 | 0 |
| 501(c)(25) | Title-holding corporations or trusts with multiple parents | 825 | 688 | 1,045 | 22,327 |
| 501(c)(26) | State-sponsored organizations providing health coverage for high-risk individuals | 11 | 10 | 391 | 170 |
| 501(c)(27) | State-sponsored workers' compensation reinsurance organizations | 9 | 3 | 1,187 | 6,644 |
| 501(c)(40) | Religious and apostolic organizations | 218 | 0 | 0 | 0 |
| 501(c)(50) | Cooperative hospital service organizations | 10 | 9 | 505 | 516 |
| 501(c)(60) | Cooperative service organizations or operating educational organizations | 1 | 0 | 0 | 0 |
| Other | Organizations not classified above, including charitable risk pools | 126,461 | 395 | 1,225 | 345 |
| | Total | 1,557,310 | 618,062 | 1,937,681 | 4,489,660 |

*Sources:* Urban Institute, National Center for Charitable Statistics, Core Files (2010); and Internal Revenue Service, Exempt Organizations Business Master File (2012).

*Notes:* Not all Internal Revenue Code (IRC) Section 501(c)(3) organizations are included because certain organizations, such as churches (and their integrated auxiliaries or subordinate units) and conventions or associations of churches, need not apply for recognition of tax exemption unless they specifically request a ruling. Organizations that had their tax-exempt status revoked for failing to file a financial return for three consecutive years are excluded. Registered organizations have applied for and received their tax-exempt status from the Internal Revenue Service (IRS). Reporting organizations had more than $50,000 in gross receipts in 2010 and were therefore required to file a financial return (either the Form 990 or the Form 990-EZ) with the IRS. Because of lags in filing and processing Forms 990, financial information on nonprofit organizations is two years behind registration information.

# Nonprofit Sector Classification Systems

There are two classification systems for nonprofit activities. The first is the National Taxonomy of Exempt Entities (NTEE), designed specifically to group tax-exempt entities by similarity of mission or primary purpose, activity, type, and major function. The 26 major categories of the NTEE are shown in table 1.2, along with the number of

**Table 1.2.** Organizations, Expenses, and Assets in the Nonprofit Sector by Type, 2010

| Nonprofit category | Organizations reporting to the IRS | % of organizations reporting to the IRS | Reported expenses ($ millions) | % of total expenses | Reported assets ($ millions) | % of total assets |
|---|---|---|---|---|---|---|
| Arts, culture, and humanities | 46,538 | 7.5 | 38,620 | 2.0 | 122,079 | 2.7 |
| Education | 86,188 | 13.9 | 250,875 | 12.9 | 857,864 | 19.1 |
| Environmental quality, protection, and beautification | 11,085 | 1.8 | 9,993 | 0.5 | 27,424 | 0.6 |
| Animal-related | 9,975 | 1.6 | 6,239 | 0.3 | 15,565 | 0.3 |
| Health | 27,425 | 4.4 | 888,487 | 45.9 | 1,172,128 | 26.1 |
| Mental health and crisis intervention | 10,161 | 1.6 | 28,804 | 1.5 | 23,718 | 0.5 |
| Diseases, disorders, and medical disciplines | 12,792 | 2.1 | 16,241 | 0.8 | 23,910 | 0.5 |
| Medical research | 2,728 | 0.4 | 9,786 | 0.5 | 35,622 | 0.8 |
| Crime and legal-related | 10,058 | 1.6 | 8,847 | 0.5 | 9,221 | 0.2 |
| Employment and job-related | 18,470 | 3.0 | 34,549 | 1.8 | 41,398 | 0.9 |
| Food, agriculture, and nutrition | 8,095 | 1.3 | 11,033 | 0.6 | 10,241 | 0.2 |
| Housing and shelter | 22,485 | 3.6 | 23,062 | 1.2 | 83,315 | 1.9 |
| Public safety, disaster preparedness, and relief | 12,262 | 2.0 | 3,298 | 0.2 | 9,554 | 0.2 |
| Recreation, sports, leisure, and athletics | 52,577 | 8.5 | 29,863 | 1.5 | 52,333 | 1.2 |
| Youth development | 9,638 | 1.6 | 6,886 | 0.4 | 14,215 | 0.3 |
| Human services—multipurpose and other | 47,894 | 7.7 | 122,325 | 6.3 | 171,246 | 3.8 |
| International, foreign affairs, and national security | 8,658 | 1.4 | 30,262 | 1.6 | 34,154 | 0.8 |
| Civil rights, social action, and advocacy | 3,232 | 0.5 | 4,123 | 0.2 | 5,198 | 0.1 |
| Community improvement and capacity building | 55,625 | 9.0 | 38,752 | 2.0 | 124,833 | 2.8 |
| Philanthropy, voluntarism, and grantmaking foundations | 90,206 | 14.6 | 75,734 | 3.9 | 664,827 | 14.8 |
| Science and technology research institutes and services | 3,619 | 0.6 | 14,902 | 0.8 | 20,603 | 0.5 |
| Social science research institutes and services | 1,096 | 0.2 | 2,402 | 0.1 | 4,425 | 0.1 |

*(continued)*

**Table 1.2.** Organizations, Expenses, and Assets in the Nonprofit Sector by Type, 2010 *(continued)*

| Nonprofit category | Organizations reporting to the IRS | % of organizations reporting to the IRS | Reported expenses ($ millions) | % of total expenses | Reported assets ($ millions) | % of total assets |
|---|---|---|---|---|---|---|
| Other public and societal benefit | 22,525 | 3.6 | 92,116 | 4.8 | 630,711 | 14.0 |
| Religion-related | 26,145 | 4.2 | 12,947 | 0.7 | 33,978 | 0.8 |
| Mutual/membership benefit organizations | 17,885 | 2.9 | 177,227 | 9.1 | 300,638 | 6.7 |
| Unknown | 700 | 0.1 | 308 | 0.0 | 460 | 0.0 |
| Total | 618,062 | 100.0 | 1,937,681 | 100.0 | 4,489,660 | 100.0 |

*Source:* Urban Institute, National Center for Charitable Statistics, Core Files (2010).
*Notes:* Only organizations required to file annually with the IRS (all private foundations, public charities, and 501(c) other organizations that receive at least $50,000 in gross receipts annually) are included in these figures. Expenses include both operating expenses and grants or transfer payments made to individuals and other organizations.

entities that reported to the IRS in each category and the share of reported expenses and assets. In 2010, health organizations, which include hospitals, community health systems, and primary care facilities, accounted for 46 percent of the nonprofit sector expenses and over a quarter of its assets. Education, the second-largest subsector, accounted for 13 percent of expenses and 19 percent of total assets.

The second way of classifying nonprofit activity is with the North American Industry Classification System (NAICS), which groups organizations into industries based on similarities in producing goods or services. Table 1.3 displays the nonprofit sector according to NAICS. The first two columns show the numerical code assigned to the industry and the industry description. To provide a measure of the size of each NAICS industry, the third column reports estimated nonprofit wages (adjusting for unreported wages), and the fourth column shows the percentage of all nonprofit wages that fall under that NAICS code. Again, health care, especially hospitals, accounts for the largest share of wages (49 percent). Chapter 2 provides more detailed information on wages in the nonprofit sector.

The estimated nonprofits wages reported in table 1.3 do not take into account volunteer labor, an important component of nonprofit sector resources. Many nonprofit organizations rely on volunteers to help run their programs. In fact, the dollar value of volunteer labor is almost equal to the value of donations. In 2010, the value of volunteers, calculated using average private wages, was $283.8 billion. The combination of nonprofit wages and volunteer labor exceeded $871.5 billion in 2010, and volunteers accounted for nearly 50 percent of nonprofit wages (table 1.4).

The number and value of volunteers has changed between 2003, the first year data are available, and 2010. The wage value of volunteers increased 39.4 percent between 2003 and

**Table 1.3.** Scope of the Nonprofit Sector as Classified by the North American Industry Classification System, 2010

| NAICS code | Industry | Estimated nonprofit wages ($ millions) | % of nonprofit wages |
|---|---|---|---|
| 11 | Agriculture, forestry, fishing, and hunting | 396 | 0.1 |
| 22 | Utilities | 2,505 | 0.4 |
| 48–49 | Transportation and warehousing | 105 | 0.0 |
| 51 | Information | 2,836 | 0.5 |
| 52 | Finance and insurance | 7,070 | 1.2 |
| 53 | Real estate and rental and leasing | 158 | 0.0 |
| 54 | Professional, scientific, and technical services | 15,997 | 2.7 |
| 56 | Administrative and support and waste management and remediation services | 1,128 | 0.2 |
| 61 | Educational services | 94,016 | 16.0 |
| 62 | Health care and social assistance | 329,196 | 56.0 |
| | *Hospitals, nursing and residential care facilities, and ambulatory health care services* | *285,616* | *48.6* |
| | *Social assistance* | *43,580* | *7.4* |
| 71 | Arts, entertainment, and recreation | 14,984 | 2.5 |
| 72 | Accommodation and food services | 374 | 0.1 |
| 81 | Other services, except public administration | 96,629 | 16.4 |
| | Industry subtotal | 565,394 | 96.2 |
| | *Less nonprofits serving business* | *10,765* | *1.8* |
| | Equals NPISH portion of industry subtotal | 554,629 | 94.4 |
| | Plus other industry wages | 22,271 | 3.8 |
| | BEA NPISH wages | 576,900 | 98.2 |
| | Total nonprofit wages | 587,665 | 100.0 |

*Source:* Authors' estimates, largely based on the tax-exempt share of wages from U.S. Census Bureau, Economic Census (2002, 2007); U.S. Department of Commerce, Bureau of Economic Analysis, National Income and Product Accounts, table 1.13 (2011); private wages from U.S. Department of Labor, Bureau of Labor Statistics, Quarterly Census of Employment and Wages (2011); and wages from Urban Institute, National Center for Charitable Statistics, Core Files (Public Charities, 2010).
BEA = Bureau of Economic Analysis
NPISH = nonprofit institutions serving households
*Notes:* Industries are listed as classified by the North American Industry Classification System (NAICS). These figures only include actual wages paid; they do not reflect volunteer labor. The industry subtotal is the sum of the industry-by-industry estimates in the rows above it. Because those estimates include nonprofits serving business, but the BEA NPISH estimates do not, we subtract our estimated wages for nonprofits serving business from the industry subtotal, yielding the NPISH portion of our industry subtotal. The difference between that estimate and the BEA's NPISH estimate is the wages of nonprofits whose industry classification is unknown. The total nonprofit wages are the BEA NPISH number plus our estimate for nonprofits serving business. See chapter 2 for a detailed description of the authors' methodology.

**Table 1.4.** Nonprofit Wages and the Wage Value of Volunteer Work, 2003–10

|  | 2003 | 2004 | 2005 | 2006 | 2007 | 2008 | 2009 | 2010 |
|---|---|---|---|---|---|---|---|---|
| Wage value of volunteering ($ billions)[a] | 193.9 | 215.4 | 217.9 | 215.6 | 270.2 | 259.6 | 277.7 | 283.8 |
| Nonprofit wages ($ billions)[b] | 429.6 | 450.7 | 467.7 | 495.8 | 524.7 | 554.8 | 573.6 | 587.7 |
| **Total ($ billions)** | **623.5** | **666.1** | **685.6** | **711.4** | **794.9** | **814.4** | **851.3** | **871.5** |
| Wage value of volunteers as % of nonprofit wages | 45.1 | 47.8 | 46.6 | 43.5 | 51.5 | 46.8 | 48.4 | 48.3 |

*Sources:*
a. Authors' calculations based on U.S. Department of Labor, Bureau of Labor Statistics, American Time Use Survey (2010); Current Employment Statistics (2010); and Volunteering in the United States (2005–10).
b. Authors' calculations based on U.S. Census Bureau, Economic Census (2002, 2007); U.S. Department of Commerce, Bureau of Economic Analysis, National Income and Product Accounts, table 1.13 (2011); private wages from U.S. Department of Labor, Bureau of Labor Statistics, Quarterly Census of Employment and Wages (2011); and wages from Urban Institute, National Center for Charitable Statistics, Core Files (Public Charities, 2010).
*Notes:* See table 3.14, this volume, for the authors' calculations for the wage value of volunteering; see chapter 2 for authors' calculations of nonprofit wages. The values shown here differ from those in table 1.3 because of rounding.

2007. The value of volunteer labor decreased 3.9 percent between 2007 and 2008 with the start of the recession. However, in 2009 the value of volunteer labor exceeded the pre-recession value. Chapter 3 provides more details on trends in giving and volunteering.

# The Nonprofit Sector in Comparison with Other Sectors

The Bureau of Economic Analysis at the Department of Commerce measures the size of the U.S. economy. It divides the economy into four sectors: government, business, households, and nonprofit institutions serving households (NPISH). The BEA definition of nonprofits organizations varies from the IRS definition. The BEA's NPISH definition does not include all tax-exempt organizations. It excludes organizations that serve businesses, such as chambers of commerce, and nonprofits such as credit unions and university presses that are also counted as serving business because they sell goods and services in the same ways as for-profit businesses. Nonprofits that fall under the NPISH definition include those that provide services in one of the following five categories: religious and welfare (social services, grantmaking foundations, political organizations, museums, and libraries), medical care, education and research, recreation (cultural, sports, and civic and fraternal organizations), and personal business (labor unions, legal aid, and professional associations).

In 2010, NPISHs contributed $804.8 billion to the gross domestic product (GDP). As displayed in figure 1.2, this equates to 5.5 percent of GDP. This is down slightly from the 2009 percentage of 5.7 percent. In general, though, the proportion of the GDP attributed to NPISHs has been steadily increasing over the past 60 years (table 1.5).

**Figure 1.2.** Nonprofit Organizations' Share of U.S. Gross Domestic Product, 2010 (percent)

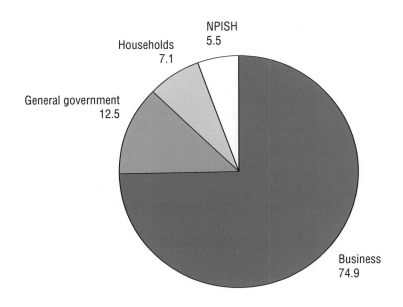

*Source:* Authors' calculations based on U.S. Department of Commerce, Bureau of Economic Analysis, National Income and Product Accounts, table 1.3.5 (2011).
NPISH = nonprofit institutions serving households
*Note:* See table 1.5, this volume, for source data.

**Table 1.5.** Gross Value Added to the U.S. Economy by Sector, 1929–2010 ($ billions)

| Year | GDP | Business | Households | NPISH | General government |
|------|------|----------|------------|-------|--------------------|
| 1929 | 103.6 | 89.4 | 7.4 | 1.5 | 5.2 |
| 1930 | 91.2 | 77.3 | 6.9 | 1.6 | 5.4 |
| 1931 | 76.5 | 63.4 | 6.1 | 1.5 | 5.5 |
| 1932 | 58.7 | 47.0 | 5.2 | 1.4 | 5.2 |
| 1933 | 56.4 | 45.1 | 4.5 | 1.3 | 5.5 |
| 1934 | 66.0 | 53.8 | 4.4 | 1.3 | 6.5 |
| 1935 | 73.3 | 60.6 | 4.5 | 1.3 | 6.9 |
| 1936 | 83.8 | 69.4 | 4.7 | 1.4 | 8.4 |
| 1937 | 91.9 | 77.3 | 5.0 | 1.5 | 8.1 |
| 1938 | 86.1 | 70.7 | 5.0 | 1.5 | 8.8 |
| 1939 | 92.2 | 76.6 | 5.2 | 1.5 | 8.9 |
| 1940 | 101.4 | 85.3 | 5.4 | 1.6 | 9.1 |
| 1941 | 126.7 | 108.1 | 5.7 | 1.7 | 11.2 |

*(continued)*

**Table 1.5.** Gross Value Added to the U.S. Economy by Sector, 1929–2010 ($ billions) *(continued)*

| Year | GDP | Business | Households | NPISH | General government |
|------|-----|----------|-----------|-------|--------------------|
| 1942 | 161.9 | 135.2 | 6.5 | 1.9 | 18.4 |
| 1943 | 198.6 | 157.9 | 7.1 | 2.1 | 31.6 |
| 1944 | 219.8 | 168.8 | 7.9 | 2.3 | 40.8 |
| 1945 | 223.0 | 166.9 | 8.6 | 2.5 | 45.1 |
| 1946 | 222.2 | 177.7 | 8.8 | 2.9 | 32.8 |
| 1947 | 244.1 | 203.1 | 9.7 | 3.5 | 27.8 |
| 1948 | 269.1 | 227.2 | 10.6 | 4.0 | 27.2 |
| 1949 | 267.2 | 222.9 | 11.6 | 4.4 | 28.3 |
| 1950 | 293.7 | 247.3 | 13.0 | 4.8 | 28.6 |
| 1951 | 339.3 | 283.5 | 14.6 | 5.3 | 35.8 |
| 1952 | 358.3 | 295.7 | 16.4 | 5.7 | 40.4 |
| 1953 | 379.3 | 312.6 | 18.3 | 6.3 | 42.2 |
| 1954 | 380.4 | 310.1 | 20.0 | 6.8 | 43.5 |
| 1955 | 414.7 | 339.5 | 22.0 | 7.4 | 45.8 |
| 1956 | 437.4 | 356.3 | 23.9 | 8.1 | 49.1 |
| 1957 | 461.1 | 374.0 | 25.8 | 8.9 | 52.4 |
| 1958 | 467.2 | 373.8 | 27.8 | 9.7 | 55.8 |
| 1959 | 506.6 | 407.7 | 30.1 | 10.6 | 58.3 |
| 1960 | 526.4 | 419.9 | 32.6 | 12.0 | 62.0 |
| 1961 | 544.8 | 431.4 | 34.6 | 12.8 | 66.0 |
| 1962 | 585.7 | 463.9 | 37.0 | 14.0 | 70.7 |
| 1963 | 617.8 | 488.0 | 39.1 | 15.2 | 75.5 |
| 1964 | 663.6 | 524.9 | 41.2 | 16.5 | 81.1 |
| 1965 | 719.1 | 570.7 | 43.6 | 18.2 | 86.6 |
| 1966 | 787.7 | 624.3 | 46.2 | 20.4 | 96.8 |
| 1967 | 832.4 | 653.6 | 49.1 | 22.7 | 107.0 |
| 1968 | 909.8 | 713.5 | 51.9 | 25.6 | 118.8 |
| 1969 | 984.4 | 769.1 | 56.0 | 29.4 | 130.0 |
| 1970 | 1,038.3 | 802.2 | 59.8 | 32.8 | 143.5 |
| 1971 | 1,126.8 | 868.3 | 65.5 | 36.7 | 156.4 |
| 1972 | 1,237.9 | 957.1 | 70.8 | 40.5 | 169.4 |
| 1973 | 1,382.3 | 1,077.4 | 76.5 | 45.2 | 183.2 |

*(continued)*

**Table 1.5.** Gross Value Added to the U.S. Economy by Sector, 1929–2010 ($ billions) *(continued)*

| Year | GDP | Business | Households | NPISH | General government |
|---|---|---|---|---|---|
| 1974 | 1,499.5 | 1,164.5 | 83.0 | 50.6 | 201.3 |
| 1975 | 1,637.7 | 1,265.8 | 90.8 | 56.7 | 224.5 |
| 1976 | 1,824.6 | 1,420.7 | 98.7 | 61.8 | 243.5 |
| 1977 | 2,030.1 | 1,590.0 | 107.9 | 67.6 | 264.6 |
| 1978 | 2,293.8 | 1,809.4 | 121.3 | 75.6 | 287.5 |
| 1979 | 2,562.2 | 2,028.5 | 136.0 | 84.8 | 313.0 |
| 1980 | 2,788.1 | 2,186.1 | 156.5 | 97.0 | 348.5 |
| 1981 | 3,126.8 | 2,454.0 | 177.8 | 109.7 | 385.3 |
| 1982 | 3,253.2 | 2,514.9 | 196.7 | 122.7 | 419.0 |
| 1983 | 3,534.6 | 2,741.1 | 212.5 | 135.6 | 445.4 |
| 1984 | 3,930.9 | 3,065.5 | 231.0 | 149.3 | 485.1 |
| 1985 | 4,217.5 | 3,283.9 | 250.3 | 159.8 | 523.4 |
| 1986 | 4,460.1 | 3,461.5 | 268.0 | 174.3 | 556.3 |
| 1987 | 4,736.4 | 3,662.0 | 288.0 | 194.8 | 591.5 |
| 1988 | 5,100.4 | 3,940.2 | 313.1 | 216.6 | 630.6 |
| 1989 | 5,482.1 | 4,235.7 | 337.2 | 237.0 | 672.2 |
| 1990 | 5,800.5 | 4,453.9 | 363.3 | 260.6 | 722.7 |
| 1991 | 5,992.1 | 4,558.6 | 383.7 | 282.2 | 767.6 |
| 1992 | 6,342.3 | 4,829.2 | 405.3 | 305.9 | 801.9 |
| 1993 | 6,667.4 | 5,084.1 | 428.3 | 323.8 | 831.2 |
| 1994 | 7,085.2 | 5,425.2 | 461.3 | 338.7 | 859.9 |
| 1995 | 7,414.7 | 5,677.8 | 492.2 | 359.9 | 884.8 |
| 1996 | 7,838.5 | 6,030.2 | 519.8 | 377.2 | 911.3 |
| 1997 | 8,332.4 | 6,442.8 | 550.9 | 398.3 | 940.3 |
| 1998 | 8,793.5 | 6,810.8 | 583.9 | 426.3 | 972.5 |
| 1999 | 9,353.5 | 7,249.0 | 628.4 | 454.5 | 1,021.6 |
| 2000 | 9,951.5 | 7,715.5 | 673.5 | 483.7 | 1,078.8 |
| 2001 | 10,286.2 | 7,913.6 | 719.5 | 513.4 | 1,139.6 |
| 2002 | 10,642.3 | 8,132.8 | 746.0 | 552.1 | 1,211.4 |
| 2003 | 11,142.2 | 8,502.8 | 762.7 | 584.5 | 1,292.2 |
| 2004 | 11,853.3 | 9,070.1 | 806.0 | 617.7 | 1,359.3 |
| 2005 | 12,623.0 | 9,680.1 | 864.4 | 642.0 | 1,436.5 |

*(continued)*

**Table 1.5.** Gross Value Added to the U.S. Economy by Sector, 1929–2010 ($ billions) *(continued)*

| Year | GDP | Business | Households | NPISH | General government |
|------|-----|----------|------------|-------|--------------------|
| 2006 | 13,377.2 | 10,262.4 | 924.8 | 678.1 | 1,512.0 |
| 2007 | 14,028.7 | 10,738.3 | 968.1 | 717.8 | 1,604.6 |
| 2008 | 14,291.5 | 10,787.8 | 1,042.8 | 762.9 | 1,698.0 |
| 2009 | 13,939.0 | 10,338.8 | 1,046.9 | 789.1 | 1,764.1 |
| 2010 | 14,526.5 | 10,879.1 | 1,033.6 | 804.8 | 1,809.1 |

*Source:* U.S. Department of Commerce, Bureau of Economic Analysis, National Income and Product Accounts, table 1.3.5 (2011).

GDP = gross domestic product

NPISH = nonprofit institutions serving households

*Notes:* Value added by the business sector equals GDP excluding gross value added by households, NPISHs, and general government. Government enterprises are classified as part of the business sector, as are nonprofits serving business. Value added by NPISHs equals compensation of employees of nonprofit institutions, the rental value of nonresidential fixed assets owned and used by NPISHs, and rental income of persons for tenant-occupied housing owned by nonprofit institutions. Value added by the general government equals compensation of general government employees plus general government consumption of fixed capital. Figures are shown in constant dollars and are not adjusted for inflation.

Figure 1.2 shows the relative size of all four sectors as defined by the BEA; keep in mind that government enterprises (congressionally established private corporations that fulfill a public purpose) are classified as part of the business sector and not general government. Additionally, while the GDP and business sector decreased, households, NPISHs, and the general government sector experienced an increase from 2008 to 2009 when the recession hit.

The contributions of NPISHs are underestimated. The BEA definition of NPISHs excludes nonprofit organizations that serve business, such as chambers of commerce, trade associations, and homeowners associations. In addition, some nonprofits that sell goods and services in the same way as for-profit organizations—such as tax-exempt cooperatives, credit unions, mutual financial institutions, and tax-exempt manufacturers like university presses—are also excluded from the NPISH definition. These types of nonprofits are included in the business sector estimates. Despite these limitations, however, the BEA's estimates of NPISHs are the best data available for comparing the different sectors' economic contributions.

Even with the BEA data, placing a value on the economic product of nonprofits is difficult because economic contributions of nonprofits are measured not by the value of what they produce, but by the cost of the resources they consume. This leads to an undervaluation of the output of the nonprofit sector because the value of volunteer labor is not included in the estimates. Also, except for employee wages and salaries, data on the costs of the resources nonprofits consume are a bit questionable because cost reporting is not practiced uniformly throughout the sector. Given these constraints, the amount of wages and salaries paid by each sector provides a reasonable basis for comparison. Interestingly, while government and business wages and salaries fell in 2009 during the recession, wages and salaries in NPISHs did not. This growth of wages and salaries by NPISHs during the recession was due in part to the health care industry, which indicators suggest continued growing despite the difficult economic times.

In 2010, NPISHs paid $576.9 billion in wages and salaries (table 1.6), excluding nonprofits serving business.[2] Figure 1.3 shows the share of wage and salary accruals in the U.S. economy by sector in 2010. The business sector accounts for the greatest share in the economy at about 74 percent, followed by government at 17 percent and NPISHs at 9 percent.

2. The figures in table 1.6 differ from those in table 1.3 because the wages of nonprofit organizations serving business are included in the business column in table 1.6 but are separated from NPISH wages in table 1.3. The breakdown could not be completed for table 1.6 because data are not available before 1990.

**Table 1.6.** Wage and Salary Accruals by Economic Sector, 1948–2010 ($ billions)

| Year | Total | Business | Households | NPISH | General government | Government enterprises |
|------|-------|----------|------------|-------|--------------------|------------------------|
| 1948 | 135.6 | 113.2 | 2.4 | 3.2 | 16.8 | 2.2 |
| 1949 | 134.7 | 110.5 | 2.4 | 3.5 | 18.3 | 2.5 |
| 1950 | 147.2 | 120.8 | 2.6 | 3.8 | 20.0 | 2.6 |
| 1951 | 171.4 | 138.4 | 2.6 | 4.1 | 26.3 | 2.9 |
| 1952 | 185.7 | 148.6 | 2.6 | 4.5 | 30.0 | 3.4 |
| 1953 | 199.0 | 160.4 | 2.7 | 5.0 | 30.9 | 3.4 |
| 1954 | 197.4 | 158.0 | 2.6 | 5.4 | 31.4 | 3.5 |
| 1955 | 212.2 | 170.4 | 3.0 | 5.9 | 32.9 | 3.7 |
| 1956 | 229.1 | 184.5 | 3.2 | 6.4 | 35.0 | 3.8 |
| 1957 | 240.0 | 192.7 | 3.3 | 7.0 | 37.0 | 4.0 |
| 1958 | 241.4 | 190.5 | 3.5 | 7.7 | 39.7 | 4.4 |
| 1959 | 259.8 | 206.5 | 3.5 | 8.4 | 41.4 | 4.7 |
| 1960 | 273.1 | 215.6 | 3.8 | 9.6 | 44.1 | 5.1 |
| 1961 | 280.7 | 219.6 | 3.7 | 10.2 | 47.2 | 5.3 |
| 1962 | 299.5 | 233.8 | 3.8 | 11.2 | 50.7 | 5.7 |
| 1963 | 314.9 | 245.1 | 3.8 | 12.1 | 53.9 | 6.1 |

*(continued)*

**Table 1.6.** Wage and Salary Accruals by Economic Sector, 1948–2010 ($ billions) *(continued)*

| Year | Total | Business | Households | NPISH | General government | Government enterprises |
|---|---|---|---|---|---|---|
| 1964 | 337.9 | 262.5 | 3.9 | 13.1 | 58.4 | 6.5 |
| 1965 | 363.8 | 282.6 | 3.9 | 14.4 | 62.9 | 7.1 |
| 1966 | 400.3 | 309.5 | 4.0 | 16.1 | 70.7 | 7.7 |
| 1967 | 429.1 | 328.8 | 4.1 | 17.9 | 78.3 | 8.2 |
| 1968 | 471.9 | 359.9 | 4.3 | 20.3 | 87.4 | 9.3 |
| 1969 | 518.2 | 395.1 | 4.4 | 23.3 | 95.4 | 10.2 |
| 1970 | 551.5 | 415.7 | 4.4 | 25.9 | 105.5 | 11.7 |
| 1971 | 584.6 | 437.2 | 4.5 | 28.6 | 114.3 | 12.5 |
| 1972 | 638.8 | 478.6 | 4.6 | 31.3 | 124.3 | 13.5 |
| 1973 | 708.7 | 535.6 | 4.7 | 34.5 | 133.9 | 14.9 |
| 1974 | 772.2 | 585.7 | 4.5 | 38.3 | 143.7 | 16.8 |
| 1975 | 814.9 | 610.1 | 4.6 | 42.5 | 157.7 | 18.5 |
| 1976 | 899.7 | 679.2 | 5.3 | 46.1 | 169.1 | 19.8 |
| 1977 | 994.2 | 756.6 | 5.8 | 50.1 | 181.7 | 20.9 |
| 1978 | 1,120.6 | 860.9 | 6.4 | 56.2 | 197.1 | 22.9 |
| 1979 | 1,253.4 | 972.1 | 6.3 | 62.9 | 212.1 | 25.0 |
| 1980 | 1,373.5 | 1,062.5 | 6.0 | 71.8 | 233.2 | 28.2 |
| 1981 | 1,511.5 | 1,170.4 | 6.0 | 80.9 | 254.2 | 31.7 |
| 1982 | 1,587.7 | 1,217.0 | 6.1 | 90.2 | 274.4 | 33.1 |
| 1983 | 1,677.6 | 1,283.4 | 6.2 | 98.5 | 289.5 | 35.3 |
| 1984 | 1,845.0 | 1,421.2 | 7.1 | 106.7 | 310.0 | 38.1 |
| 1985 | 1,982.7 | 1,527.9 | 7.2 | 114.6 | 333.0 | 40.8 |
| 1986 | 2,104.2 | 1,616.8 | 7.6 | 125.0 | 354.8 | 42.5 |
| 1987 | 2,257.8 | 1,730.4 | 7.6 | 141.6 | 378.2 | 45.0 |
| 1988 | 2,440.7 | 1,869.7 | 8.2 | 159.0 | 403.8 | 48.3 |
| 1989 | 2,584.3 | 1,971.6 | 8.8 | 173.4 | 430.5 | 50.6 |
| 1990 | 2,743.6 | 2,079.0 | 9.2 | 191.0 | 464.4 | 54.7 |
| 1991 | 2,817.4 | 2,110.4 | 9.0 | 206.3 | 491.7 | 57.1 |
| 1992 | 2,960.8 | 2,215.5 | 10.0 | 223.4 | 511.9 | 60.1 |

*(continued)*

**Table 1.6.** Wage and Salary Accruals by Economic Sector, 1948–2010 ($ billions) *(continued)*

| Year | Total | Business | Households | NPISH | General government | Government enterprises |
|------|-------|----------|------------|-------|--------------------|------------------------|
| 1993 | 3,086.3 | 2,312.8 | 10.5 | 234.7 | 528.3 | 60.7 |
| 1994 | 3,252.4 | 2,448.7 | 10.9 | 246.7 | 546.1 | 63.3 |
| 1995 | 3,438.5 | 2,599.9 | 11.7 | 262.9 | 564.0 | 65.1 |
| 1996 | 3,624.1 | 2,755.1 | 11.8 | 276.3 | 580.9 | 67.2 |
| 1997 | 3,878.0 | 2,971.5 | 11.9 | 292.2 | 602.4 | 69.4 |
| 1998 | 4,185.5 | 3,231.2 | 13.8 | 311.3 | 629.2 | 72.0 |
| 1999 | 4,470.3 | 3,469.4 | 12.5 | 329.3 | 659.1 | 74.6 |
| 2000 | 4,832.3 | 3,767.4 | 13.4 | 351.7 | 699.8 | 79.9 |
| 2001 | 4,957.5 | 3,830.6 | 12.8 | 374.4 | 739.7 | 82.2 |
| 2002 | 5,002.8 | 3,802.6 | 12.5 | 400.0 | 787.7 | 85.4 |
| 2003 | 5,160.2 | 3,898.6 | 13.9 | 421.3 | 826.4 | 86.9 |
| 2004 | 5,416.8 | 4,098.9 | 14.8 | 441.9 | 861.2 | 91.6 |
| 2005 | 5,712.4 | 4,340.5 | 15.0 | 458.4 | 898.5 | 93.0 |
| 2006 | 6,076.7 | 4,635.8 | 16.1 | 485.9 | 938.9 | 96.2 |
| 2007 | 6,422.5 | 4,901.2 | 17.7 | 514.3 | 989.3 | 99.7 |
| 2008 | 6,556.7 | 4,952.2 | 18.6 | 543.8 | 1,042.1 | 102.0 |
| 2009 | 6,284.3 | 4,630.7 | 16.8 | 562.9 | 1,073.9 | 101.3 |
| 2010 | 6,417.6 | 4,735.8 | 14.8 | 576.9 | 1,090.1 | 100.8 |

*Source:* U.S. Department of Commerce, Bureau of Economic Analysis, National Income and Product Accounts, table 1.13 (2011).
NPISH = nonprofit institutions serving households
*Notes:* Government enterprises are shown for information only; they are included in the totals for business. Wage and salary accruals for nonprofits serving business are also included in business. Business includes domestic business only and excludes wages and salary accruals for the rest of the world, which are not available separately. The business total is the sum of the BEA's wage and salary accruals for corporate business and noncorporate business. Figures are shown in constant dollars and are not adjusted for inflation.

Looking at the economic contribution of the sectors by wages (excluding volunteers), both NPISH and general government increase as a share of the total over time. NPISH increases from 2.4 percent to 9 percent, and government increases from 12.4 percent to 17 percent, between 1948 and 2010.

Figure 1.4 shows how the share of the national wage bill by sector has changed since 1948. The share of wages and salaries attributed to NPISHs has been increasing

**Figure 1.3.** Nonprofit Organizations' Share of Wage and Salary Accruals in the U.S. Economy, 2010 (percent)

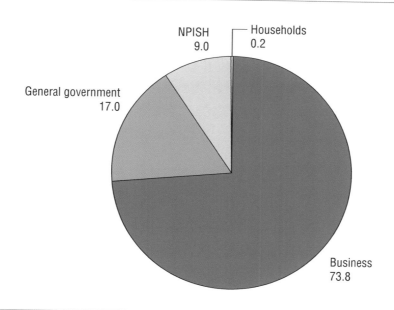

*Source:* Authors' calculations based on U.S. Department of Commerce, Bureau of Economic Analysis, National Income and Product Accounts, table 1.13 (2011).
NPISH = nonprofit institutions serving households
*Note:* See table 1.6, this volume, for source data.

**Figure 1.4.** Wage and Salary Accruals by Economic Sector, 1948–2010 (percent)

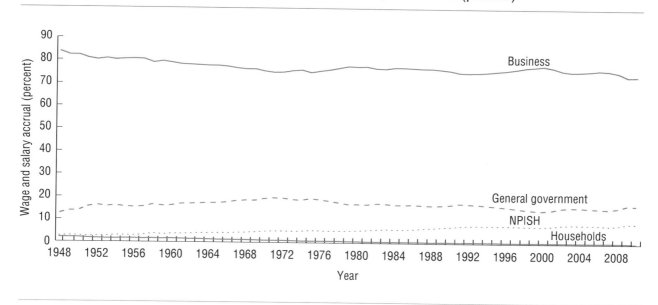

*Source:* Authors' calculations based on U.S. Department of Commerce, Bureau of Economic Analysis, National Income and Product Accounts, table 1.13 (2011).
NPISH = nonprofit institutions serving households
*Note:* See table 1.6, this volume, for source data.

steadily over this period, while the shares attributed to business and government have shown greater fluctuation. As displayed, the business share of wages dropped steadily from 1948 to 1975, then rose until 2000, and has been declining since. The share attributed to government peaked around the mid-1970s, declined until around 2000, and has been on a general upward trend since. Between 2000 and 2010, NPISH wages grew faster than any other sector. NPISH wages grew 30 percent, while government wages increased 23 percent and business wages decreased by 1 percent (adjusting for inflation).

The share of the economy also changes slightly if supplements to salaries are included in the wage estimate (table 1.7). Supplements to salaries consist of employer

**Table 1.7.** Wage and Salary Accruals and Supplements to Salaries by Economic Sector, 1948–2010 ($ billions)

| Year | Total | Business | Households | NPISH | General government | Government enterprises |
|------|-------|----------|------------|-------|--------------------|------------------------|
| 1948 | 141.9 | 118.2 | 2.4 | 3.2 | 18.1 | 2.3 |
| 1949 | 141.9 | 115.8 | 2.4 | 3.6 | 20.1 | 2.5 |
| 1950 | 155.3 | 127.6 | 2.6 | 3.9 | 21.2 | 2.6 |
| 1951 | 181.5 | 146.8 | 2.7 | 4.3 | 27.7 | 2.9 |
| 1952 | 196.1 | 157.4 | 2.6 | 4.6 | 31.5 | 3.4 |
| 1953 | 210.2 | 170.0 | 2.7 | 5.1 | 32.4 | 3.5 |
| 1954 | 209.1 | 168.0 | 2.6 | 5.5 | 33.0 | 3.5 |
| 1955 | 225.8 | 181.8 | 3.1 | 6.1 | 34.8 | 3.8 |
| 1956 | 244.6 | 197.5 | 3.3 | 6.6 | 37.2 | 3.9 |
| 1957 | 257.7 | 207.3 | 3.3 | 7.3 | 39.8 | 4.2 |
| 1958 | 259.6 | 205.2 | 3.5 | 8.0 | 42.9 | 4.6 |
| 1959 | 281.2 | 223.8 | 3.6 | 8.9 | 44.9 | 5.0 |
| 1960 | 296.6 | 234.6 | 3.8 | 10.1 | 48.1 | 5.5 |
| 1961 | 305.4 | 239.4 | 3.7 | 10.7 | 51.6 | 5.7 |
| 1962 | 327.3 | 256.2 | 3.8 | 11.8 | 55.5 | 6.1 |
| 1963 | 345.2 | 269.3 | 3.8 | 12.8 | 59.3 | 6.6 |
| 1964 | 370.8 | 288.5 | 3.9 | 14.0 | 64.4 | 7.1 |
| 1965 | 399.5 | 310.9 | 4.0 | 15.3 | 69.3 | 7.6 |
| 1966 | 442.5 | 342.9 | 4.0 | 17.2 | 78.4 | 8.3 |

*(continued)*

**Table 1.7.** Wage and Salary Accruals and Supplements to Salaries by Economic Sector, 1948–2010 ($ billions) *(continued)*

| Year | Total | Business | Households | NPISH | General government | Government enterprises |
|------|-------|----------|------------|-------|--------------------|------------------------|
| 1967 | 475.1 | 364.3 | 4.2 | 19.2 | 87.4 | 8.8 |
| 1968 | 524.3 | 400.4 | 4.4 | 21.7 | 97.8 | 9.9 |
| 1969 | 577.6 | 440.7 | 4.4 | 25.0 | 107.5 | 11.0 |
| 1970 | 617.2 | 465.4 | 4.5 | 27.9 | 119.4 | 12.8 |
| 1971 | 658.9 | 492.4 | 4.6 | 31.0 | 130.9 | 14.0 |
| 1972 | 725.1 | 543.1 | 4.6 | 34.3 | 143.1 | 15.2 |
| 1973 | 811.2 | 612.8 | 4.8 | 38.2 | 155.4 | 16.8 |
| 1974 | 890.2 | 673.3 | 4.6 | 42.6 | 169.7 | 19.3 |
| 1975 | 949.2 | 707.7 | 4.6 | 47.3 | 189.6 | 22.2 |
| 1976 | 1,059.4 | 796.0 | 5.4 | 51.6 | 206.4 | 24.0 |
| 1977 | 1,180.6 | 893.3 | 5.9 | 56.4 | 225.0 | 25.9 |
| 1978 | 1,335.5 | 1,021.3 | 6.5 | 63.0 | 244.7 | 28.3 |
| 1979 | 1,498.4 | 1,155.4 | 6.4 | 70.5 | 266.1 | 31.4 |
| 1980 | 1,647.7 | 1,265.7 | 6.1 | 80.4 | 295.5 | 35.8 |
| 1981 | 1,819.9 | 1,397.8 | 6.2 | 90.7 | 325.2 | 40.6 |
| 1982 | 1,919.9 | 1,459.8 | 6.3 | 101.1 | 352.7 | 42.8 |
| 1983 | 2,035.7 | 1,542.3 | 6.3 | 111.8 | 375.3 | 46.0 |
| 1984 | 2,245.6 | 1,705.3 | 7.3 | 122.6 | 410.4 | 49.3 |
| 1985 | 2,411.9 | 1,828.7 | 7.3 | 132.2 | 443.7 | 53.4 |
| 1986 | 2,559.4 | 1,936.7 | 7.7 | 144.4 | 470.6 | 55.6 |
| 1987 | 2,736.9 | 2,066.4 | 7.7 | 163.3 | 499.5 | 58.9 |
| 1988 | 2,955.0 | 2,231.9 | 8.3 | 182.5 | 532.3 | 64.0 |
| 1989 | 3,132.6 | 2,356.3 | 9.0 | 200.2 | 567.1 | 67.3 |
| 1990 | 3,328.6 | 2,488.1 | 9.4 | 221.4 | 609.7 | 73.5 |
| 1991 | 3,441.1 | 2,544.3 | 9.2 | 240.1 | 647.5 | 77.2 |
| 1992 | 3,634.4 | 2,685.8 | 10.2 | 261.1 | 677.3 | 81.8 |
| 1993 | 3,800.5 | 2,813.7 | 10.8 | 275.3 | 700.7 | 83.0 |
| 1994 | 4,002.5 | 2,977.8 | 11.2 | 289.4 | 724.1 | 86.8 |
| 1995 | 4,199.2 | 3,135.7 | 12.0 | 308.0 | 743.5 | 89.0 |
| 1996 | 4,395.6 | 3,293.6 | 12.2 | 323.0 | 766.8 | 91.7 |

*(continued)*

**Table 1.7.** Wage and Salary Accruals and Supplements to Salaries by Economic Sector, 1948–2010 ($ billions) *(continued)*

| Year | Total | Business | Households | NPISH | General government | Government enterprises |
|------|-------|----------|------------|-------|-------------------|-----------------------|
| 1997 | 4,670.1 | 3,524.5 | 12.2 | 341.2 | 792.2 | 94.8 |
| 1998 | 5,027.8 | 3,827.5 | 14.1 | 365.5 | 820.7 | 98.0 |
| 1999 | 5,359.1 | 4,093.2 | 12.9 | 389.9 | 863.1 | 101.6 |
| 2000 | 5,793.6 | 4,452.4 | 13.8 | 415.4 | 912.0 | 108.3 |
| 2001 | 5,984.5 | 4,563.3 | 13.1 | 441.0 | 967.1 | 112.2 |
| 2002 | 6,116.3 | 4,592.9 | 12.8 | 476.5 | 1,034.1 | 116.3 |
| 2003 | 6,388.3 | 4,758.3 | 14.2 | 506.4 | 1,109.4 | 116.5 |
| 2004 | 6,699.6 | 4,982.9 | 15.2 | 535.6 | 1,165.9 | 125.2 |
| 2005 | 7,071.5 | 5,272.6 | 15.3 | 555.8 | 1,227.8 | 128.1 |
| 2006 | 7,483.7 | 5,592.9 | 16.5 | 587.0 | 1,287.3 | 133.0 |
| 2007 | 7,863.0 | 5,867.0 | 18.1 | 616.5 | 1,361.4 | 137.7 |
| 2008 | 8,079.1 | 5,969.2 | 19.1 | 652.4 | 1,438.4 | 141.1 |
| 2009 | 7,815.4 | 5,628.0 | 17.5 | 676.3 | 1,493.6 | 140.7 |
| 2010 | 7,980.6 | 5,743.4 | 15.5 | 691.2 | 1,530.5 | 140.6 |

*Source:* U.S. Department of Commerce, Bureau of Economic Analysis, National Income and Product Accounts, table 1.13 (2011).
NPISH = nonprofit institutions serving households
*Notes:* Government enterprises are shown for information only; they are included in the totals for business. Wage and salary accruals for nonprofits serving business are also included in business. Business includes domestic business only and excludes wages and salary accruals for the rest of the world, which are not available separately. The business total is the sum of the BEA's wage and salary accruals for corporate business and noncorporate business. Figures are shown in constant dollars and are not adjusted for inflation.

contributions for employee pension and insurance funds and employer contributions for government social insurance. When considering these benefits, the government share increases 2 percent and both NPISH and business decline slightly.

Figure 1.5 displays NPISH wages as a percentage of general government wages. Looking at wages and salaries only, NPISH wages have grown significantly over the past 60 years. While NPISH wages were only 15 percent of general government wages in 1952, they were 53 percent in 2010. However, if we consider benefits and wages and

**Figure 1.5.** Wages and Salaries of Nonprofit Institutions Serving Households Compared with Government Wages and Salaries, 1948–2010 (percent)

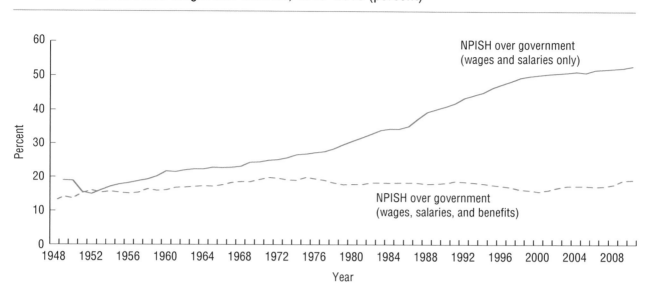

*Source:* Authors' calculations based on U.S. Department of Commerce, Bureau of Economic Analysis, National Income and Product Accounts, table 1.13 (2011).
*Note:* See table 1.6, this volume, for source data.

salaries, NPISH wages have grown at a much smaller rate—by about 6 percent over the past 60 years. This indicates that while NPISH salaries have been increasing, the benefits and other supplements to income are not at the same level as those of the government sector.

## Nonprofit Employment

In 2010, the nonprofit sector employed 13.7 million people. Between 2000 and 2010, nonprofit employment grew an estimated 18 percent, faster than the overall U.S. economy. Excluding nonprofits, U.S. nonfarm employment declined roughly 3 percent between 2000 and 2010. As a result, the share of nonprofit employment to nonfarm employment grew from 8.8 percent in 2000 to 10.6 percent in 2010 (see figure 1.6 and table 1.8). See chapter 2 for more details on how the employment estimates and the industry totals were created.

**Figure 1.6.** Nonprofit Employees and Nonprofit Employment as a Percentage of U.S. Nonfarm Employment, 1998–2010

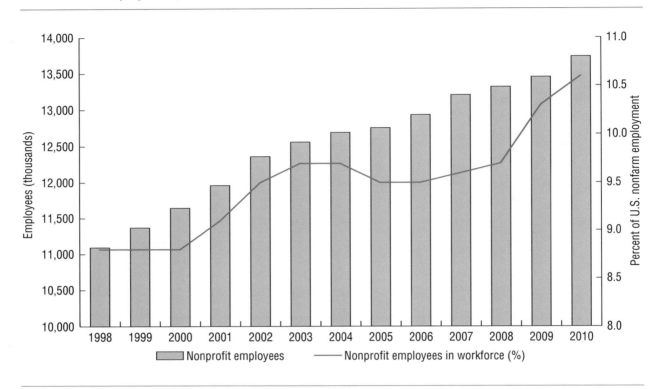

Nonprofit employees    —— Nonprofit employees in workforce (%)

*Source:* Authors' calculations based on U.S. Census Bureau, Economic Census (2002, 2007); U.S. Department of Labor, Bureau of Labor Statistics; and Urban Institute, National Center for Charitable Statistics, Core Files (Public Charities, 1998–2009); nonfarm employment from U.S. Department of Labor, Bureau of Labor Statistics, Current Employment Statistics (1998–2010).
*Notes:* See table 2.2, this volume, for authors' estimate of nonprofit employment. See table 1.8, this volume, for source data. The nonfarm employment figures have been seasonally adjusted.

**Table 1.8.** U.S. Employment in the Nonprofit Sector, 1998–2010

| Year | Nonprofit employees (thousands)[a] | Nonfarm employees (thousands)[b] | Nonprofit employees in workforce (%) |
|------|-----------------------------------|----------------------------------|--------------------------------------|
| 1998 | 11,092 | 125,930 | 8.8 |
| 1999 | 11,370 | 128,993 | 8.8 |
| 2000 | 11,659 | 131,785 | 8.8 |
| 2001 | 11,971 | 131,826 | 9.1 |
| 2002 | 12,348 | 130,341 | 9.5 |
| 2003 | 12,538 | 129,999 | 9.6 |
| 2004 | 12,660 | 131,435 | 9.6 |
| 2005 | 12,723 | 133,703 | 9.5 |
| 2006 | 12,900 | 136,086 | 9.5 |
| 2007 | 13,164 | 137,598 | 9.6 |
| 2008 | 13,272 | 136,790 | 9.7 |
| 2009 | 13,418 | 130,807 | 10.3 |
| 2010 | 13,699 | 129,818 | 10.6 |

*Sources:*

a. Authors' calculations based on U.S. Census Bureau, Economic Census (2002, 2007); U.S. Department of Labor, Bureau of Labor Statistics; and Urban Institute, National Center for Charitable Statistics, Core Files (Public Charities, 1998–2009). Nonfarm employment is from U.S. Department of Labor, Bureau of Labor Statistics, Current Employment Statistics (1998–2010).

b. U.S. Department of Labor, Bureau of Labor Statistics, Current Employment Statistics (1998–2010).

*Notes:* See table 2.2, this volume, for authors' estimate of nonprofit employment. The nonfarm employment figures have been seasonally adjusted.

# Conclusion

The nonprofit sector plays a vital role in the quality of life in the United States, and its role in the national economy has been increasing. In 2010, nonprofits (NPISH) accounted for an estimated 5.5 percent of GDP and 9 percent of the economy's wages. In the remaining chapters of this *Almanac,* we analyze both the financial and human resources of the nonprofit sector. Chapter 2 focuses on wage and employment trends in the overall sector, while chapter 3 discusses the critical role of donors, foundations, and volunteers. Chapter 4 "follows the money" to portray the nonprofit sector's revenues and outlays, and chapter 5 looks in depth at public charities and their finances.

# Sources

Mead, Charles Ian, Clinton P. McCully, and Marshall B Reinsdorf. 2003. "Income and Outlays of Households and of Nonprofit Institutions Serving Households." *Survey of Current Business* 83(4): 13–17.

The Urban Institute, National Center for Charitable Statistics. 1998–2010. "IRS Business Master Files, Exempt Organizations (2010)." Washington, DC: The Urban Institute.

———. 2010. "Core Files." Washington, DC: The Urban Institute.

U.S. Census Bureau. 2002. "2002 Economic Census." http://www.census.gov/econ/census02/ (accessed May 17, 2012).

———. 2007. "2007 Economic Census." http://www.census.gov/econ/census07/ (accessed May 17, 2012).

———. 2010. "2010 Census." http://2010.census.gov/2010census/ (accessed May 17, 2012).

U.S. Department of Commerce, Bureau of Economic Analysis. 2011. "National Income and Product Accounts Tables." http://www.bea.gov/iTable/iTable.cfm?ReqID=9&step=1 (accessed May 17, 2012).

U.S. Department of Labor, Bureau of Labor Statistics. 1998–2011. "Employment, Hours, and Earnings from the Current Employment Statistics Survey (National)." http://www.bls.gov/ces/home.htm (accessed May 17, 2012).

———. 2005–10. "American Time Use Survey." http://www.bls.gov/tus/home.htm (accessed May 17, 2012).

———. 2005–10. "Current Population Survey." http://www.bls.gov/cps/home.htm (accessed May 17, 2012).

# *2*

# Wage and Employment Trends

Many nonprofit organizations operating in the United States rely on paid employees to deliver programs and services. Doctors, teachers, musicians, counselors, researchers, child care providers, executives, and many others have careers in the nonprofit sector. This chapter estimates nonprofit employment and wages for the sector and its varied industries and subsectors. Unfortunately, wage and employment data by industry are not currently collected comprehensively and annually by any government agency. The numbers presented here are the authors' estimates drawn from various nonprofit and government sources. These estimates are subject to revision as better data and methods become available.

Nonprofit organizations paid $587.7 billion in wages in 2010, 9.2 percent of all wages paid that year. Nonprofit wages grew an estimated 64 percent from 2000, when they totaled $359.2 billion. Actual wage growth was 29 percent after adjusting for inflation. Table 2.1 displays nonprofit wages by industry using the North American Industry Classification System. These figures include religious organizations and other nonprofit groups that may not be registered with the Internal Revenue Service (IRS). Industries not listed have either no nonprofits or too few employees to report separately and are therefore combined in the "other" industry wages category. The wage estimates also include both full-time and part-time employees but exclude such benefits as health insurance and employer contributions to retirement.

In 2010, the health care and social assistance sector accounted for most nonprofit wages. Health and social assistance includes hospitals, mental health centers, crisis hotlines, blood banks, soup kitchens, senior centers, and similar organizations. Wages for the health care and social assistance sector account for 56 percent of all nonprofit wages in 2010 (figure 2.1). Hospitals, residential care facilities, and ambulatory health care services drive wage levels in the sector, accounting for nearly half of all nonprofit wages. Much of the wage growth in the industry reflects recent increases in health care spending. If hospitals are removed from the employment trend, nonprofit

**Table 2.1.** Nonprofit Wages by Industry, 2000–10 (millions of current dollars)

| NAICS code | Industry | 2000 | 2001 | 2002 | 2003 | 2004 | 2005 | 2006 | 2007 | 2008 | 2009 | 2010 |
|---|---|---|---|---|---|---|---|---|---|---|---|---|
| 11 | Agriculture, forestry, fishing, and hunting | 278 | 308 | 310 | 314 | 325 | 327 | 375 | 390 | 393 | 399 | 396 |
| 22 | Utilities | 1,019 | 1,135 | 1,159 | 1,269 | 1,346 | 1,431 | 1,586 | 1,712 | 2,264 | 2,424 | 2,505 |
| 48–49 | Transportation and warehousing | 53 | 59 | 62 | 68 | 78 | 81 | 84 | 90 | 93 | 96 | 105 |
| 51 | Information | 2,222 | 2,286 | 2,266 | 2,314 | 2,409 | 2,531 | 2,627 | 2,714 | 2,878 | 2,920 | 2,836 |
| 52 | Finance and insurance | 3,633 | 3,903 | 4,343 | 5,651 | 5,851 | 6,327 | 6,508 | 6,551 | 6,455 | 6,935 | 7,070 |
| 53 | Real estate and rental and leasing | 88 | 95 | 100 | 104 | 114 | 121 | 140 | 153 | 159 | 153 | 158 |
| 54 | Professional, scientific, and technical services | 7,624 | 7,900 | 8,604 | 9,085 | 9,864 | 11,398 | 12,668 | 14,036 | 15,082 | 15,223 | 15,997 |
| 56 | Administrative and support and waste management and remediation services | 685 | 709 | 758 | 803 | 773 | 810 | 857 | 901 | 954 | 990 | 1,128 |
| 61 | Educational services | 50,051 | 53,926 | 58,980 | 62,585 | 66,442 | 69,742 | 70,041 | 75,233 | 86,355 | 91,604 | 94,016 |
|  | *Colleges, universities, professional schools, and junior colleges* | *33,785* | *35,958* | *38,780* | *41,108* | *43,827* | *46,425* | *46,336* | *49,699* | *57,233* | *60,913* | *62,622* |
|  | *Other education* | *16,266* | *17,968* | *20,200* | *21,478* | *22,615* | *23,316* | *23,705* | *25,534* | *29,122* | *30,691* | *31,394* |
| 62 | Health care and social assistance | 184,255 | 197,319 | 212,477 | 228,704 | 240,904 | 253,321 | 269,719 | 286,424 | 306,468 | 320,393 | 329,196 |

| | | | | | | | | | | | |
|---|---|---|---|---|---|---|---|---|---|---|---|
| *Hospitals, nursing and residential care facilities, and ambulatory health care services* | 157,207 | 169,368 | 182,250 | 196,716 | 207,753 | 219,303 | 233,522 | 248,204 | 265,755 | 278,352 | 285,616 |
| *Social assistance* | 27,048 | 27,952 | 30,227 | 31,988 | 33,152 | 34,018 | 36,196 | 38,220 | 40,713 | 42,041 | 43,580 |
| 71 Arts, entertainment, and recreation | 9,467 | 10,624 | 10,940 | 11,534 | 12,166 | 12,757 | 13,894 | 14,871 | 14,922 | 14,905 | 14,984 |
| 72 Accommodation and food services | 215 | 245 | 266 | 277 | 291 | 307 | 328 | 362 | 370 | 364 | 374 |
| 81 Other services, except public administration | 63,964 | 66,553 | 72,331 | 75,727 | 79,092 | 80,588 | 84,719 | 90,352 | 95,540 | 95,708 | 96,629 |
| Industry subtotal | 323,554 | 345,065 | 372,294 | 398,435 | 419,655 | 439,741 | 463,545 | 493,790 | 531,931 | 552,115 | 565,394 |
| *Less nonprofit serving business* | 7,503 | 7,632 | 7,903 | 8,333 | 8,837 | 9,295 | 9,924 | 10,446 | 11,024 | 10,743 | 10,765 |
| Equals NPISH portion of industry subtotal | 318,076 | 338,063 | 363,334 | 389,651 | 411,159 | 431,203 | 455,076 | 485,567 | 524,032 | 542,262 | 554,629 |
| Plus nonprofit wages not classified by NAICS | 33,624 | 36,337 | 36,666 | 31,649 | 30,741 | 27,197 | 30,824 | 28,733 | 19,768 | 20,638 | 22,271 |
| BEA NPISH wages | 351,700 | 374,400 | 400,000 | 421,300 | 441,900 | 458,400 | 485,900 | 514,300 | 543,800 | 562,900 | 576,900 |
| Total nonprofit wages | 359,203 | 382,032 | 407,903 | 429,633 | 450,737 | 467,695 | 495,824 | 524,746 | 554,824 | 573,643 | 587,665 |

*Source:* Authors' estimates based on U.S. Census Bureau, Economic Census (1997, 2002, 2007); U.S. Department of Commerce, Bureau of Economic Analysis, National Income and Product Accounts (2011); U.S. Department of Labor, Bureau of Labor Statistics, Quarterly Census of Employment and Wages (2000–11); and Urban Institute, National Center for Charitable Statistics, Core Files (Public Charities, 2000–10).

BEA = Bureau of Economic Analysis

NPISH = nonprofit institutions serving households

*Notes:* Industries are listed as classified by the North American Industry Classification System (NAICS). These figures include only actual wages paid; they do not reflect volunteer labor. The industry subtotal is the sum of the industry-by-industry estimates in the rows above it. Because those estimates include nonprofits serving business but the BEA NPISH estimates do not, the authors subtract estimated wages for nonprofits serving business from the industry subtotal, yielding the NPISH portion of industry subtotal. The difference between that estimate and the BEA's NPISH estimate is the wages of nonprofits whose industry classification is unknown. Total nonprofit wages are the sum of the BEA NPISH number plus the authors' estimate for nonprofits serving business. Please see the methodology section of this chapter for a detailed description of the calculations.

**Figure 2.1.** Distribution of Nonprofit Wages by Industry, 2010 (percent)

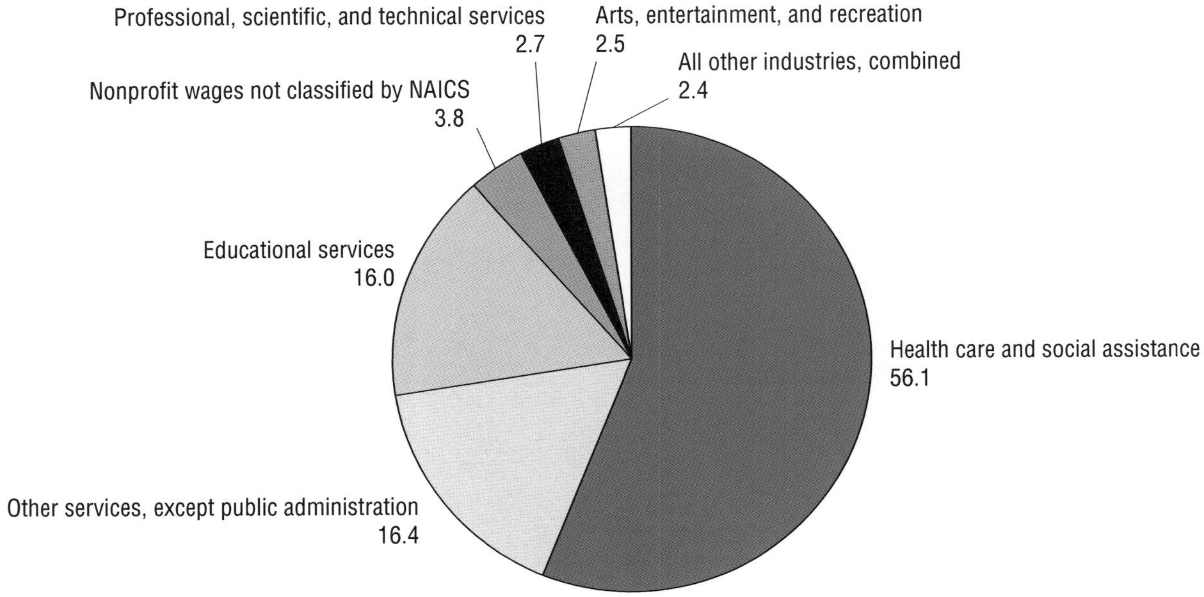

Professional, scientific, and technical services 2.7
Arts, entertainment, and recreation 2.5
All other industries, combined 2.4
Nonprofit wages not classified by NAICS 3.8
Educational services 16.0
Health care and social assistance 56.1
Other services, except public administration 16.4

*Source:* Authors' estimates based on U.S. Census Bureau, Economic Census (2007); U.S. Department of Commerce, Bureau of Economic Analysis, National Income and Product Accounts (2010); U.S. Department of Labor, Bureau of Labor Statistics, Quarterly Census of Employment and Wages (2010); and Urban Institute, National Center for Charitable Statistics, Core Files (Public Charities, 2010).

wages would have grown more slowly from 2000 to 2010, 50 percent compared with 64 percent.

The "other services" sector accounts for 16.4 percent of total nonprofit wages, making it the second-largest industry. This category includes grantmaking foundations, fundraising or other supporting organizations, professional societies or associations, groups promoting or administering religious activities, cemeteries, human rights organizations, advocacy organizations, conservation and wildlife organizations, and others. Educational services such as colleges, elementary and technical schools, exam preparation, hockey camps, and dance instruction make up the third-largest segment of wages at 16.0 percent. Higher education accounts for two-thirds of educational services wages and nearly 11 percent of nonprofit sector wages.

Wages in the utilities industry grew the most over the decade, although it is a small part of the nonprofit sector (see table 2.1). The utilities industry includes nonprofits that provide gas, electricity, water, and sanitary services as well as installation, maintenance, and repair of necessary equipment. Wages nearly doubled from 2000 through 2010 after adjusting for inflation, but most of the growth occurred from 2008 to 2010 because of increased funding for energy efficiency and renewable energy grants. The Energy Policy Act of 2005 significantly altered energy policy in the United States by offering tax incentives and loan guarantees to companies that produced various types of energy (i.e., nuclear power, fossil fuel production, alternative fuels). Additional employees may have been hired to increase companies' capacity to provide alternative energy. The Energy Independence and Security Act passed in 2007 further changed energy policy and established new efficiency standards, which may have led to an increase in the number of employees needed. In addition, the Energy Efficiency and Conservation Block Grant program designated more than $3.2 billion in 2009 to support clean energy technologies. This initiative is one of many that helped increase wages in the utility industry.

In 2010, the nonprofit sector employed nearly 13.7 million people (table 2.2). The number of employees increased 17 percent from the 2000 level of just over 11.6 million employees. The health care and social assistance industry accounts for the greatest number of employees, 54 percent. The "other services" industry employs the second-largest number of employees and accounts for 22 percent of the sector's paid workers. As with wages, the number of employees in the utilities sector grew more than any other industry between 2000 and 2010, increasing 73 percent. The number of workers employed in the information industry and in the agriculture, forestry, fishing, and hunting industry declined 2 percent between 2000 and 2010.

Table 2.3 and figure 2.2 show the annual average nonprofit compensation per nonprofit employee by industry. Across all industries, average annual nonprofit compensation increased from $27,751 in 2000 to $41,274 in 2010, a 49 percent increase (17 percent after adjusting for inflation). These data, however, do not take into account differences in nonprofit wages between staff and executives. Average annual compensation per nonprofit employee varies widely by industry. In 2010, the utilities and finance and insurance industries had the highest average compensation, nearly $89,000. Professional, scientific, and technical services followed closely at $81,000. Accommodation and food services had the lowest annual average compensation at about $20,000. This industry is lower in part because it includes camps, which hire many seasonal employees. It is also one of the lowest paid in the for-profit sector. The industry with the next-lowest compensation is the "other education" industry, with annual average compensation of about $24,000. This industry also includes many part-time or seasonal positions, such as yoga instructors, sports camp instructors, and driver's education teachers.

During the 2007–09 economic recession, the unemployment rate hit an 18-year high. Since 2008, the overall number of employees in the U.S. economy has been declining. Employment in the nonprofit sector, however, continued to increase throughout the recession. In fact, the nonprofit sector grew faster—in terms of employees and wages—than business and government (tables 2.4 and 2.5). From 2000 to 2010, the number of employees in the nonprofit sector increased 17 percent while the government sector increased 8 percent and the business sector declined about 6 percent. Wages in the nonprofit sector grew 29 percent over the decade, after adjusting for inflation. This growth rate was faster than that of business, which declined about 1 percent, and government, which increased 23 percent.

Even before the recession, the nonprofit sector was growing faster than the other sectors. Between 2000 and 2007, employment in the nonprofit sector grew 13 percent compared with 7 percent in government and 3 percent in the business sector.

**Table 2.2.** Nonprofit Employment by Industry, 2000–10

| NAICS code | Industry | 2000 | 2001 | 2002 | 2003 |
|---|---|---|---|---|---|
| 11 | Agriculture, forestry, fishing, and hunting | 12,499 | 13,560 | 13,369 | 13,553 |
| 22 | Utilities | 16,322 | 17,140 | 17,214 | 18,554 |
| 48–49 | Transportation and warehousing | 1,314 | 1,462 | 1,502 | 1,619 |
| 51 | Information | 38,109 | 39,236 | 40,087 | 39,508 |
| 52 | Finance and insurance | 57,934 | 58,721 | 66,462 | 83,010 |
| 53 | Real estate and rental and leasing | 2,595 | 2,766 | 2,813 | 2,808 |
| 54 | Professional, scientific, and technical services | 122,689 | 127,046 | 144,951 | 150,234 |
| 56 | Administrative and support and waste management and remediation services | 28,772 | 28,446 | 29,335 | 29,612 |
| 61 | Educational services | 2,099,986 | 2,143,728 | 2,229,313 | 2,266,095 |
| | *Colleges, universities, profession schools, and junior colleges* | *833,291* | *853,736* | *873,141* | *895,342* |
| | *Other education* | *1,266,695* | *1,289,992* | *1,356,172* | *1,370,753* |
| 62 | Health care and social assistance | 6,168,100 | 6,362,231 | 6,555,309 | 6,667,525 |
| | *Hospitals, nursing and residential care facilities, and ambulatory health care services* | *4,928,887* | *5,061,023* | *5,207,243* | *5,308,471* |
| | *Social assistance* | *1,239,213* | *1,301,208* | *1,348,067* | *1,359,053* |
| 71 | Arts, entertainment, and recreation | 437,971 | 452,120 | 460,296 | 471,677 |
| 72 | Accommodation and food services | 14,412 | 15,759 | 16,725 | 17,075 |
| 81 | Other services, except public administration | 2,658,507 | 2,708,783 | 2,770,701 | 2,776,604 |
| | Total | 11,659,210 | 11,970,999 | 12,348,079 | 12,537,871 |

*Source:* Authors' estimates based on U.S. Census Bureau, Economic Census (1997, 2002, 2007); U.S. Department of Commerce, Bureau of Economic Analysis, National Income and Product Accounts (2011); U.S. Department of Labor, Bureau of Labor Statistics, Quarterly Census of Employment and Wages (2000–11); and Urban Institute, National Center for Charitable Statistics, Core Files (Public Charities, 2000–10).
*Notes:* Industries are listed as classified by the North American Industry Classification System (NAICS).
Please see the methodology section of this chapter for a detailed description of the authors' calculations.

| 2004 | 2005 | 2006 | 2007 | 2008 | 2009 | 2010 |
|---|---|---|---|---|---|---|
| 13,120 | 12,832 | 13,340 | 13,076 | 12,755 | 12,623 | 12,254 |
| 18,515 | 18,801 | 19,883 | 20,382 | 26,285 | 27,894 | 28,202 |
| 1,764 | 1,794 | 1,822 | 1,881 | 1,910 | 1,975 | 2,091 |
| 38,822 | 39,605 | 39,113 | 38,424 | 39,905 | 40,186 | 37,380 |
| 80,980 | 82,306 | 79,399 | 75,345 | 73,654 | 82,700 | 79,636 |
| 2,890 | 2,924 | 3,174 | 3,354 | 3,477 | 3,420 | 3,386 |
| 150,500 | 164,867 | 171,165 | 176,540 | 179,882 | 193,142 | 197,451 |
| 28,404 | 28,043 | 28,575 | 28,297 | 28,534 | 29,111 | 32,406 |
| 2,323,434 | 2,300,587 | 2,340,577 | 2,393,771 | 2,255,159 | 2,301,139 | 2,350,982 |
| *912,080* | *922,572* | *941,573* | *962,774* | *986,474* | *1,014,607* | *1,026,686* |
| *1,411,354* | *1,378,015* | *1,399,003* | *1,430,998* | *1,268,685* | *1,286,532* | *1,324,296* |
| 6,724,131 | 6,803,446 | 6,890,905 | 7,019,679 | 7,221,943 | 7,354,835 | 7,460,825 |
| *5,355,211* | *5,416,285* | *5,483,096* | *5,580,917* | *5,732,665* | *5,831,997* | *5,898,865* |
| *1,368,921* | *1,387,162* | *1,407,809* | *1,438,763* | *1,489,278* | *1,522,838* | *1,561,961* |
| 488,167 | 498,444 | 514,061 | 533,318 | 542,337 | 528,034 | 524,332 |
| 17,340 | 17,761 | 18,277 | 18,796 | 19,438 | 19,500 | 18,965 |
| 2,771,528 | 2,751,202 | 2,780,207 | 2,841,077 | 2,867,112 | 2,823,575 | 2,950,798 |
| 12,659,596 | 12,722,612 | 12,900,499 | 13,163,942 | 13,272,392 | 13,418,136 | 13,698,709 |

**Table 2.3.** Average Annual Compensation per Nonprofit Employee by Industry, 2000–10 (current dollars)

| NAICS code | Industry | 2000 | 2001 | 2002 | 2003 | 2004 | 2005 | 2006 | 2007 | 2008 | 2009 | 2010 |
|---|---|---|---|---|---|---|---|---|---|---|---|---|
| 11 | Agriculture, forestry, fishing, and hunting | 22,244 | 22,743 | 23,182 | 23,139 | 24,793 | 25,494 | 28,090 | 29,839 | 30,779 | 31,599 | 32,314 |
| 22 | Utilities | 62,423 | 66,243 | 67,327 | 68,379 | 72,700 | 76,123 | 79,772 | 84,014 | 86,132 | 86,911 | 88,830 |
| 48–49 | Transportation and warehousing | 40,604 | 40,456 | 41,387 | 42,281 | 44,049 | 44,884 | 46,230 | 47,947 | 48,730 | 48,657 | 50,264 |
| 51 | Information | 58,313 | 58,272 | 56,536 | 58,571 | 62,052 | 63,911 | 67,166 | 70,627 | 72,119 | 72,675 | 75,881 |
| 52 | Finance and insurance | 62,707 | 66,468 | 65,350 | 68,076 | 72,252 | 76,872 | 81,966 | 86,951 | 87,635 | 83,852 | 88,779 |
| 53 | Real estate and rental and leasing | 34,025 | 34,513 | 35,698 | 36,967 | 39,301 | 41,215 | 44,120 | 45,465 | 45,605 | 44,839 | 46,776 |
| 54 | Professional, scientific, and technical services | 62,138 | 62,184 | 59,358 | 60,472 | 65,543 | 69,136 | 74,012 | 79,509 | 83,842 | 78,819 | 81,017 |
| 56 | Administrative and support and waste management and remediation services | 23,801 | 24,937 | 25,827 | 27,130 | 27,213 | 28,886 | 29,982 | 31,825 | 33,451 | 34,003 | 34,797 |
| 61 | Educational services | 23,834 | 25,155 | 26,456 | 27,618 | 28,597 | 30,315 | 29,925 | 31,429 | 38,292 | 39,808 | 39,990 |
| | *Colleges, universities, profession schools, and junior colleges* | *40,544* | *42,119* | *44,414* | *45,913* | *48,052* | *50,322* | *49,211* | *51,621* | *58,017* | *60,036* | *60,994* |
| | *Other education* | *12,841* | *13,929* | *14,895* | *15,669* | *16,024* | *16,920* | *16,944* | *17,844* | *22,954* | *23,856* | *23,706* |

| |  | | | | | | | | | | | |
|---|---|---|---|---|---|---|---|---|---|---|---|---|
| 62 | Health care and social assistance | 29,872 | 31,014 | 32,413 | 34,301 | 35,827 | 37,234 | 39,141 | 40,803 | 42,436 | 43,562 | 44,123 |
| | *Hospitals, nursing and residential care facilities, and ambulatory health care services* | 31,895 | 33,465 | 34,999 | 37,057 | 38,794 | 40,490 | 42,590 | 44,474 | 46,358 | 47,728 | 48,419 |
| | *Social assistance* | 21,827 | 21,481 | 22,423 | 23,537 | 24,217 | 24,524 | 25,711 | 26,565 | 27,338 | 27,607 | 27,901 |
| 71 | Arts, entertainment, and recreation | 21,615 | 23,498 | 23,768 | 24,453 | 24,922 | 25,593 | 27,027 | 27,885 | 27,514 | 28,228 | 28,576 |
| 72 | Accommodation and food services | 14,887 | 15,560 | 15,881 | 16,234 | 16,803 | 17,299 | 17,954 | 19,267 | 19,020 | 18,691 | 19,733 |
| 81 | Other services, except public administration | 24,060 | 24,569 | 26,106 | 27,273 | 28,537 | 29,292 | 30,472 | 31,802 | 33,323 | 33,896 | 32,747 |
| | Total | 27,751 | 28,825 | 30,150 | 31,779 | 33,149 | 34,564 | 35,932 | 37,511 | 40,078 | 41,147 | 41,274 |

*Source:* Authors' estimates based on U.S. Census Bureau, Economic Census (1997, 2002, 2007); U.S. Department of Commerce, Bureau of Economic Analysis, National Income and Product Accounts (2011); U.S. Department of Labor, Bureau of Labor Statistics, Quarterly Census of Employment and Wages (2000–11); and Urban Institute, National Center for Charitable Statistics, Core Files (Public Charities, 2000–10).

*Notes:* Industries are listed as classified by the North American Industry Classification System (NAICS). Please see the methodology section of this chapter for a detailed description of the authors' calculations. Values are not adjusted for inflation.

**Figure 2.2.** Average Annual Compensation per Nonprofit Employee by Industry, 2010 (current dollars)

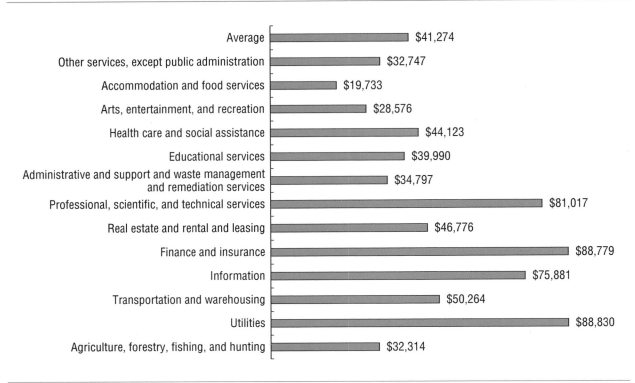

*Source:* Authors' estimates based on U.S. Census Bureau, Economic Census (2007); U.S. Department of Commerce, Bureau of Economic Analysis, National Income and Product Accounts (2010); U.S. Department of Labor, Bureau of Labor Statistics, Quarterly Census of Employment and Wages (2010); and Urban Institute, National Center for Charitable Statistics, Core Files (Public Charities, 2010).
*Note:* Values are not adjusted for inflation.

Nonprofit wages grew 21 percent between 2000 and 2007 versus 17 percent for government and 8 percent for the business sector, after adjusting for inflation.

Grouping NAICS industries at the two-digit level masks some differences in specific organizations that are not faring well in the current economic climate. When looking at the six-digit NAICS code, a fuller picture emerges of the recession's impact on nonprofit organizations. For example, musical groups and artists (NAICS code 711130) have seen declines of over 10 percent in both wages and salaries between 2007 and 2010. Organizations in this group organize, promote, and/or manage concerts for musicians, chamber orchestras, vocalists, and other music performers. Likewise, employment has declined for law offices, museums, musical groups and artists, computer training, labor unions, theater companies and dinner theaters, fundraising, residential care facilities, and others (see supplemental tables 2.12–2.17).

While employment in the nonprofit sector as a whole grew during the economic recession, not all industries were immune to the recession's effects. The number of employees in the real estate and rental and leasing category has been declining since 2008. Employment in the finance and insurance industry and in "other education" declined in 2008. Employment and wage growth slowed in the social assistance category in 2009 and

**Table 2.4.** Number of Employees by U.S. Economic Sector, 2000–10 (thousands)

| Year | Total U.S. workers[a] | Business | Nonprofits[b] | Government |
|---|---|---|---|---|
| 2000 | 131,785 | 99,336 | 11,659 | 20,790 |
| 2001 | 131,826 | 98,737 | 11,971 | 21,118 |
| 2002 | 130,341 | 96,480 | 12,348 | 21,513 |
| 2003 | 129,999 | 95,878 | 12,538 | 21,583 |
| 2004 | 131,435 | 97,154 | 12,660 | 21,621 |
| 2005 | 133,703 | 99,176 | 12,723 | 21,804 |
| 2006 | 136,086 | 101,212 | 12,900 | 21,974 |
| 2007 | 137,598 | 102,216 | 13,164 | 22,218 |
| 2008 | 136,790 | 101,009 | 13,272 | 22,509 |
| 2009 | 130,807 | 94,834 | 13,418 | 22,555 |
| 2010 | 129,818 | 93,637 | 13,699 | 22,482 |

*Sources:*
a. U.S. Department of Labor, Bureau of Labor Statistics, Current Employment Statistics (2000–10).
b. Authors' calculations based on U.S. Census Bureau, Economic Census (1997, 2002, 2007); U.S. Department of Labor, Bureau of Labor Statistics; and Urban Institute, National Center for Charitable Statistics, Core Files (Public Charities, 2000–10).
*Notes:* See table 2.2, this volume, for authors' estimate of nonprofit employment. Nonfarm employment figures have been seasonally adjusted.

**Table 2.5.** Total Annual Wages by U.S. Economic Sector, 2000–10 (billions of current dollars)

| Year | Total | Business | NPISH | General government | Households |
|---|---|---|---|---|---|
| 2000 | 4,832.3 | 3,759.9 | 359.2 | 699.8 | 13.4 |
| 2001 | 4,957.5 | 3,823.0 | 382.0 | 739.7 | 12.8 |
| 2002 | 5,002.8 | 3,794.7 | 407.9 | 787.7 | 12.5 |
| 2003 | 5,160.2 | 3,890.3 | 429.6 | 826.4 | 13.9 |
| 2004 | 5,416.8 | 4,090.1 | 450.7 | 861.2 | 14.8 |
| 2005 | 5,712.4 | 4,331.3 | 467.6 | 898.5 | 15.0 |
| 2006 | 6,076.7 | 4,625.9 | 495.8 | 938.9 | 16.1 |
| 2007 | 6,422.5 | 4,890.8 | 524.7 | 989.3 | 17.7 |
| 2008 | 6,556.7 | 4,941.2 | 554.8 | 1,042.1 | 18.6 |
| 2009 | 6,284.3 | 4,620.0 | 573.6 | 1,073.9 | 16.8 |
| 2010 | 6,417.6 | 4,725.0 | 587.7 | 1,090.1 | 14.8 |

*Source:* Authors' estimates based on U.S. Census Bureau, Economic Census (1997, 2002, 2007); U.S. Department of Commerce, Bureau of Economic Analysis, National Income and Product Accounts (2011); U.S. Department of Labor, Bureau of Labor Statistics, Quarterly Census of Employment and Wages (2000–11); and Urban Institute, National Center for Charitable Statistics, Core Files (Public Charities, 2000–10).
NPISH = nonprofit institutions serving households
*Notes:* These figures only include actual wages paid; they do not reflect volunteer labor. The NPISH wage includes authors' estimates of nonprofits serving business. Please see the methodology section of this chapter for a detailed description of the authors' calculations. Values are not adjusted for inflation.

**Figure 2.3.** Annual Growth Rate in Total Nonprofit Wages and Employment by Industry, 2000–10 (percent)

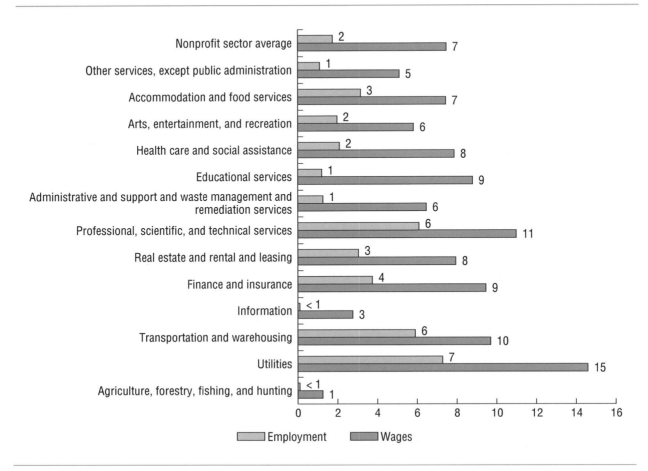

*Source:* Authors' estimates based on U.S. Census Bureau, Economic Census (1997, 2002, 2007); U.S. Department of Commerce, Bureau of Economic Analysis, National Income and Product Accounts (2011); U.S. Department of Labor, Bureau of Labor Statistics, Quarterly Census of Employment and Wages (2000–11); and Urban Institute, National Center for Charitable Statistics, Core Files (Public Charities, 2000–10).

2010. This is consistent with findings from a national study of nonprofit human service providers with government grants or contracts where 50 percent of providers froze or reduced salaries (Boris et al. 2010).

To get a sense of the relative growth of nonprofits in different industries, figure 2.3 shows the compound annual growth rates in wages and employment from 2000 to 2010. The utilities sector has the highest growth rate in any industry, although it is not a large segment of the nonprofit sector. Growth is also faster than average in professional, scientific, and technical services, and in transportation and warehousing. Wages and employment at nonprofits in the information and agriculture, forestry, fishing, and hunting fields remained steady.

Finally, figure 2.4 shows the compound annual growth rate of average annual nonprofit compensation per employee by industry. Compensation in most industries has

**Figure 2.4.** Annual Growth Rate of Average Annual Compensation per Nonprofit Employee by Industry, 2000–10 (percent)

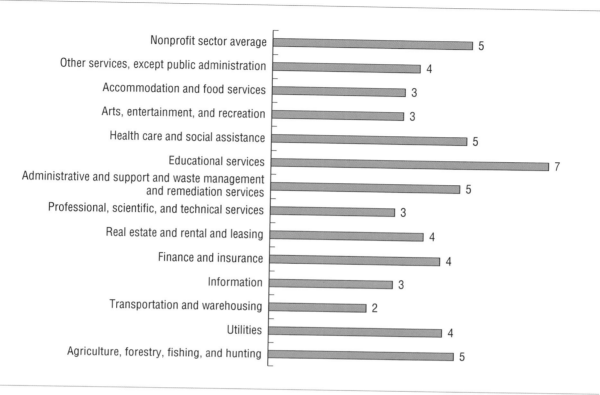

*Source:* Authors' estimates based on U.S. Census Bureau, Economic Census (1997, 2002, 2007); U.S. Department of Commerce, Bureau of Economic Analysis, National Income and Product Accounts (2011); U.S. Department of Labor, Bureau of Labor Statistics, Quarterly Census of Employment and Wages (2000–11); and Urban Institute, National Center for Charitable Statistics, Core Files (Public Charities, 2000–10).

been increasing between 4 and 5 percent a year. Transportation and warehousing; information; professional, scientific, and technical services; arts, entertainment, and recreation; and accommodation and food services have been somewhat below that rate, but still about 3 percent a year. The educational services industry has experienced the highest growth at 7 percent a year.

## Conclusion

In 2010, nonprofit organizations paid $587.7 billion in wages and employed nearly 13.7 million people. Employment and wages in the nonprofit sector continued to grow even during the economic recession. Wages in the nonprofit sector grew almost 30 percent over the decade, after adjusting for inflation, and employment increased 17 percent. Nonprofit sector growth, in both wages and employees, outpaced both the government and business sectors.

This chapter presents the authors' estimates of nonprofit employment and wages using available data. While these estimates attempt to capture nonprofit sector employment and wages by combining estimates from both government and nonprofit sources, there is still no single source for nonprofit salary and employment data. While researchers at the John Hopkins University's Center for Civil Society Studies have been able to work with Bureau of Labor Statistics microdata, their estimates still underreport actual wages because the data represent only a single slice of the sector—organizations tax-exempt under 501(c)(3)—and are based on unemployment filings, which exclude many religious and religiously affiliated organizations. In addition, five states are missing from the Hopkins dataset.

Nonprofit employment data are among the most significant and largest areas of missing data on the nonprofit sector. This chapter and its supplementary tables contain the most detailed and comprehensive estimates of nonprofit wages and employment currently available by industry. The authors hope they form the base for further comparative analysis among industries within the nonprofit sector, and between for-profit and nonprofit organizations in the same industry.

## Supplementary Tables

The estimates presented in this chapter attempt to capture nonprofit sector employment and wages by combining estimates from both government and nonprofit sources. The methodology details how nonprofit wages and employment information was compiled, but tables 2.6–2.19 show much of the data behind the estimates presented in this chapter.

The data for these estimates come from three main sources: Bureau of Economic Analysis wage and salary accruals by industry; Bureau of Labor Statistics, Quarterly Census of Employment and Wages (QCEW); and wage and salary data from the National Center for Charitable Statistics based on IRS Form 990 data. The data from the QCEW are based on unemployment insurance data collected from states. Unemployment data are the most comprehensive available data on wages and salaries paid by establishments in the United States, including nonprofit organizations. Drawn from reports filed by employers under the Federal Unemployment Insurance Tax Act and the Federal Unemployment Tax Act (FUTA), the data contain the total wages paid during the calendar year for establishments that employ four or more workers. For more information on how the estimates were created and how the data in these tables were combined and modified to yield the estimates in tables 2.1 and 2.2, please refer to the methodology section of this chapter. The supplementary tables include the following:

■  Table 2.6 lists the wages of nonprofit employees covered by unemployment insurance in NAICS 61 (educational services), 62 (health care and social assistance), 71 (arts, entertainment, and recreation), and 81 (other services, except public administration). These industries have a nonprofit breakdown in the Economic Census. For most industries, wages covered by unemployment insurance are the same as total reported wages.

- Since many nonprofit employees in educational institutions and religious organizations are not covered by unemployment insurance, table 2.7 compares covered wages to total reported wages for those industries.
- For industries not covered in table 2.6, table 2.8 shows the wages reported to the IRS. Two-digit industries missing from both table 2.6 and table 2.8 had zero wages reported to the IRS. This table includes all public charities as well as 501(c) other nonprofits that report to the IRS.
- Tables 2.9, 2.10, and 2.11 are analogous to tables 2.6, 2.7, and 2.8, but for employment rather than wages.
- Tables 2.12–2.14 provide wages covered by unemployment insurance at the six-digit NAICS level for industries making up NAICS 61, 62, 71, and 81.
- Tables 2.15–2.17 list the number of employees covered by unemployment insurance at the six-digit NAICS level for industries making up NAICS 61, 62, 71, and 81.
- Table 2.18 shows the calculation of estimated wages for nonprofits serving business as reported in table 2.1.
- Table 2.19 shows the National Taxonomy of Exempt Entities (NTEE) codes comprising each two-digit NAICS industry reported in tables 2.8 and 2.11.

# Methodology

Nonprofit employment data are among the most significant and largest area of missing data on the nonprofit sector. Data on nonprofit wages or employment by industry are not published annually, and what data are available are limited. The estimates presented in this chapter attempt to capture nonprofit sector employment and wages by combining estimates from both government and nonprofit sources.

## Sources of Nonprofit Wages and Employment

Data for the wage and salary estimates are drawn from five sources: BEA wage and salary accruals by industry, BLS's Quarterly Census of Employment and Wages, the Census Bureau's Economic Census, the Census Bureau's County Business Patterns, and wage and salary data from the National Center for Charitable Statistics based on IRS Form 990 data.

Estimated nonprofit wages are based on BEA data. The BEA publishes an annual series on wage and salary accruals in its National Income and Project Accounts table 6.3D. The data include a breakdown for nonprofit institutions serving households (NPISH). Unfortunately, NPISHs do not cover the entire nonprofit sector; nonprofits serving business are excluded, but the authors are able to estimate wages and salaries for nonprofits serving business. Nonprofits serving business include portions of NAICS codes 813 (religious, grantmaking, civic, professional, and similar organizations) and 5417 (scientific research and development services). The total nonprofit wages, as reported in table 2.1, are the sum of BEA NPISH wages and the authors' estimates of nonprofit serving business.

The single most comprehensive source of wage and employment data by industry is the QCEW, which is produced by the Bureau of Labor Statistics based on state unemployment insurance filings. Data for the QCEW are drawn from reports filed by employers under the Federal Unemployment Insurance Tax Act and FUTA that document the total wages paid during the calendar year for establishments that employ four or more workers. These data include nonprofit organizations. The QCEW is the BEA's major source for wage data and accounts for about 95 percent of BEA wage estimates. Unfortunately, the QCEW published data do not disaggregate the private ownership category into nonprofit and for-profit. In addition, religious organizations and religiously affiliated organizations (mostly schools) are not required to participate in unemployment insurance, although some choose to; as a result, many are missing from BLS data. The BEA's wage and employment estimates are larger because the BEA estimates wages for workers not covered by unemployment insurance and for wages earned but not reported to the government.

Every five years, the Economic Census publishes nonprofit wage and employment estimates for five industries: NAICS 54 (professional, scientific, and technical services), 61 (educational services), 62 (health care and social assistance), 71 (arts, entertainment, and recreation), and 81 (other services, except public administration). Total nonprofit wages in the 2007 Census were $392.4 billion. That was just 68 percent of the BEA NPISH wages for the same year of $576.9 billion. Total nonprofit wages in the 2002 Census were $299.4 billion. That was just 75 percent of the BEA NPISH wages for the same year of $400.0 billion. The 1997 Census reported nonprofit wages of $186.7 billion, which was 63 percent of the BEA estimate of $294.4 billion for the same year. The wages missing from the census are understated by these comparisons because the industries that the authors believe make up nonprofits serving business are included in the smaller census estimates but excluded from the larger BEA estimates.

A major reason the census estimates are so low is that the census excludes some important nonprofit industries: elementary and secondary schools (NAICS 6111); junior colleges (NAICS 6112); colleges, universities, and professional schools (NAICS 6113); labor unions and similar labor organizations (NAICS 81393); political organizations (NAICS 81394); and religious organizations (NAICS 8131). Even after these (and other) differences are taken into consideration, however, census wages in 2007 for the five two-digit NAICS industries where nonprofits are tracked are less than private wages from the QCEW for the same industries by over $15 billion. This may be because the Economic Census is not a true census; it only samples smaller organizations.

In addition to the Economic Census, the U.S. Census Bureau releases an annual series of county business data by industry, known as the County Business Patterns (CBP). The CBP series includes data on the number of establishments, employment during the week of March 12, first-quarter payroll, and annual payroll. These data are useful for studying the economic activity of small areas, analyzing changes over time, and benchmarking other statistical series to the Economic Census. Data from the CBP are broken down by establishment type (e.g., corporations, sole proprietorships) and include nonprofit organizations. The authors use CBP data for select industries not covered by unemployment insurance.

Nonprofits that file Form 990 or Form 990-EZ report wages to the IRS. However, small nonprofits and religious organizations are not required to file and are therefore missing from the IRS data. The IRS releases two files containing wage data: the Statistics of Income (SOI) sample files and the Return Transaction File (RTF). The SOI files are carefully reviewed by the IRS for data quality. They contain all large organizations and a sample of small ones, weighted to achieve some totals in the overall population, but not wages. As a result, the sampling results in large year-to-year fluctuations in wages by industry, particularly among smaller industries. Although comprehensive for organizations that file the Form 990, the RTF is not checked for accuracy. The authors' review found various errors where wages from a given Form 990 were off by a factor of 1,000 or more. Both IRS files contain the most recent return filed by an organization. Organizations filing late may be represented in these datasets by a prior year return. In addition, employment numbers are requested on Form 990 but not Form 990-EZ.

Drawing from both files, which are available from the National Center for Charitable Statistics, the authors constructed a dataset consisting of the wages and salaries paid by 501(c)(3) and 501(c) other tax-exempt organizations by NAICS industry code. To construct the file, the authors used the sum of lines 25 (officers' compensation) and 26 (other wages and salaries) from the schedule of functional expenses for organizations filing Form 990 and the compensation line from Form 990-EZ. The RTF was cleaned by replacing all RTF records with the same record from SOI where available. Wage outliers were identified, individually investigated, and manually corrected by reference to the original Form 990 where available, or by interpolation between other years when not available.

NCCS developed the National Taxonomy of Exempt Entities (NTEE) classification system, which is used to group organizations according to their primary purpose or mission. The NTEE codes were mapped to the NAICS codes. Before assigning the NAICS code, the NTEE industry classification codes were carefully reviewed. During this process, the authors uncovered a few discrepancies that change the estimates from the previous version of the *Almanac*. First, a number of large organizations were misclassified and should have been included under the utilities industry. Also, over 10 large organizations were incorrectly coded as K99 (food, agriculture, and nutrition n.e.c.) when they should have been coded Y34 (voluntary employees' beneficiary association). These organizations totaled more than $30 million in wages each year. Second, NTEE code C20 (pollution abatement & control) was missing from NAICS 56 (administrative and support and waste management and remediation services), and A40 (visual arts) was missing from NAICS 54 (professional, scientific, and technical services).

While each dataset mentioned above sheds some light on nonprofit wages and employment, no single dataset is sufficient to produce estimates of nonprofit wages and employment by industry. The method developed largely by Kennard T. Wing for *The*

*Nonprofit Almanac 2008* attempts to use the strengths of each, while minimizing its weaknesses. The basic approach is to determine the share of nonprofit wages by industry using the Economic Census, CBP, and IRS data and then multiply the tax-exempt share by the value for the whole private industry from QCEW. The authors then attempt to measure total wages, including the imputation for wage not covered by unemployment insurance, by multiplying the nonprofit percentages by wages for each industry.

## Calculating Tax-Exempt Share of Wages by Industry

The first step in calculating nonprofit wages by industry is to determine what proportion of total wages is paid by the nonprofit sector for each industry. The authors used the Economic Census, when available, to determine the nonprofit share of wages by industry. When Economic Census data were not available or were questionable, the authors turned to CBP estimates or IRS data.

The Economic Census breaks down wage and employment data for the nonprofit sector for select industries. The industries with a nonprofit breakout in the Economic Census are NAICS 54, 61, 62, 71, and 81. The first step for these industries was to calculate the tax-exempt share of wages from the Economic Census at the six-digit NAICS level.

The Economic Census is conducted every five years, so percentages from the 2002 Census were used for 2002. Percentages from the 2007 Census were used for 2007 and forward. Percentages for 2000 and 2001 were calculated using linear interpolation between the 1997 and 2002 Census percentages. Likewise, percentages for 2003 and 2006 were interpolated using the 2002 and 2007 Census.

For general medical and surgical hospitals (NAICS 6221), psychiatric and substance abuse hospitals (NAICS 6222), and specialty (except psychiatric and substance abuse) hospitals (NAICS 6223), government hospitals were backed out of the census totals before calculating the nonprofit percentage. For the 1997 Census, there was no way to break out government hospitals in NAICS 6223, so they are included in the nonprofit percentages for 2000–01.

Important parts of the educational services and other services industries are excluded from the census, requiring the authors to identify alternative sources for the tax-exempt share. This includes junior colleges (NAICS 6112); colleges, universities, and professional schools (NAICS 6113); elementary and secondary schools (NAICS 6111); labor unions and similar labor organizations (NAICS 81393); political organizations (NAICS 81394); and religious organizations (NAICS 8131). The tax-exempt share for these industries is based on the County Business Patterns annual payroll for nonprofit organizations.

The remaining industries have no nonprofit breakout in the Economic Census. For these, the authors used the NCCS wage dataset based on IRS SOI and RTF files. Wages were totaled by two-digit NAICS industries by reclassifying the NTEE core codes according to the scheme shown in table 2.19. This resulted in the numbers reported in table 2.6.

## Creating Wage Estimates

After the tax-exempt shares of wages by industry were calculated, the authors applied these percentages to the QCEW private wages. The authors obtained QCEW private wages at the six-digit NAICS level. In general, calculations were carried out at the six-digit NAICS level and then aggregated. In 1997, however, data suppressed to protect the identity of individual organizations required the authors to combine cosmetology and barber schools (NAICS 611511) and flight training (NAICS 611512). Also, calculations using IRS Form 990 data were performed at the two-digit NAICS level. Estimated wages covered by unemployment insurance at the six-digit NAICS levels are shown in tables 2.12–2.14.

Examination of the results of these calculations revealed an implausible discontinuity in two NAICS industries: 541710 and 541720, both concerned with research establishments. As a result, the authors elected to substitute CBP estimates for these industries.

For most industries in tables 2.12–2.14, the wages covered by unemployment insurance represent the total reported wages for the industry. In a few industries, however, a significant number of nonprofit employees are not covered by unemployment insurance. For these, the authors estimated total reported wages by replacing the QCEW private wages by wage estimates from County Business Patterns. The four main industries in which replacement occurred were elementary and secondary schools; junior colleges; colleges, universities, and professional schools; and religious organizations. These results are shown in table 2.7.

Finally, the authors attempted to measure total wages, including BEA's imputation for unreported wages, by multiplying the nonprofit share of wages by BEA wages by industry. These calculations were carried out at the two-digit NAICS level. These are the wage estimates reported in table 2.1.

## Employment Estimates

Employment estimates were developed similarly to wage estimates, with two differences. First, for industries available from the Economic Census, the nonprofit share of employment was used instead of the share of wages, and the share was multiplied by private employment in the industry, rather than wages. Second, because BEA does not provide an estimate of NPISH employment, only two employment estimates were calculated: nonprofit employment covered by unemployment insurance, and total reported nonprofit employment.

For the remaining industries, the authors multiplied the nonprofit share of wages by QCEW private employment. This method is limited because it assumes that wage levels in the nonprofit and for-profit portions within a given industry are similar. If nonprofit wage levels are significantly lower, for example, nonprofit employment will be underestimated.

The authors explored using IRS data on employment as an alternative approach. Comparisons of the wages and employment reported on the same Forms 990 suggested that employment was being underreported to the IRS. Employment numbers reported to the IRS also resulted in lower estimated employment than the estimates from the wage-share method, so this method offered no correction for the suspected under-estimation problem. Recognizing its limitations, the authors chose the wage-share approach as the best available at this time. Nonprofit employment data remain the largest missing piece in nonprofit data.

## Alternative Wages and Employment Estimates

The Johns Hopkins Center for Civil Society Studies recently released a brief on nonprofit employment based on access to QCEW microdata. The Center estimated that organizations exempt under section 501(c)(3) of the Internal Revenue Code employed 10.7 million people in 2010 (Salamon, Sokolowski, and Geller 2012), lower than the estimates reported in this chapter. Among the reasons for the differences in estimates:

- Five states are missing from the Hopkins data reported: Massachusetts, Mississippi, New Hampshire, Oregon, and Wyoming.
- 501(c)(3) organizations are a subset of the total number of nonprofits in the sector, albeit the largest portion. The employment and wage estimates presented in this chapter encompass the entire nonprofit sector.
- Religious organizations and religiously affiliated organizations (mostly schools) are not required to participate in unemployment insurance, so many are missing from the QCEW data. When creating estimates of nonprofit employment, the authors incorporate data from the QCEW, BEA, Economic Census, and IRS Form 990s to ensure that all industries are included. The BEA's wage and employment estimates are larger than QCEW figures because BEA includes wages for workers not covered by unemployment insurance; BEA also estimates wages earned but not reported to the government.

## Limitations to the Estimates

There are also some limitations with the wage-share method for estimating nonprofit wages and employment:

- Nonprofit wages may be much lower in some industries than for-profit wages, resulting in significant underestimates.
- IRS data are based on legal entities, while QCEW data are based on establishments. A single entity may have multiple establishments, and a single establishment may have multiple legal entities. Where there are multiple establishments or entities, they may be classified into different industry categories. As a result, the IRS and QCEW could be classifying the same organization in different industries.
- IRS data are coded according to the NTEE classification system. QCEW are coded according to NAICS. The authors' conversion from NTEE to NAICS maps one

NTEE code into one NAICS code. This may have reduced the size of some NAICS industries and inflated others.

■ A BLS analyst reported that many small organizations use a professional accounting firm to do all reporting and filing on their behalf, and that these businesses end up being counted in the same NAICS industry as the accounting firm, which is industry 54. The authors have no data on the extent of this problem.

Ideally, the Bureau of Labor Statistics would modify its data collection and reporting for QCEW to distinguish private nonprofits from private for-profits in all industries. Such an approach would provide an excellent basis for estimating nonprofit wages and employment. Then, researchers would need only to correct for the organizations not covered by unemployment insurance and for unreported wages.

## Sources

Boris, Elizabeth T., Erwin de Leon, Katie L. Roeger, and Milena Nikolova. 2010. "Human Service Nonprofits and Government Collaboration: Findings from the 2010 National Survey of Nonprofit Government Contracting and Grants." Washington, DC: The Urban Institute.

Salamon, Lester M., S. Wojciech Sokolowski, and Stephanie L. Geller. 2012. *Holding the Fort: Nonprofit Employment during a Decade of Turmoil.* Nonprofit Employment Bulletin 39. Baltimore, MD: Johns Hopkins University Center for Civil Society Studies. http://ccss.jhu.edu/wp-content/uploads/downloads/2012/01/NED_National_2012.pdf.

The Urban Institute, National Center for Charitable Statistics. 1998–2010. "Core Files." Washington, DC: The Urban Institute.

———. 1998–2008. "Internal Revenue Service Statistics of Income Files." Washington, DC: The Urban Institute.

———. 2011. NCCS NTEE/NAICS Crosswalk. Washington, DC: The Urban Institute.

U.S. Census Bureau. 1991–2009. County Business Patterns.

———. 2002. "2002 Economic Census." http://www.census.gov/econ/census02/ (accessed May 17, 2012).

———. 2007. "2007 Economic Census." http://www.census.gov/econ/census07/ (accessed May 17, 2012).

U.S. Department of Commerce, Bureau of Economic Analysis. 2009. "Updated Summary of NIPA Methodologies." Washington, DC: U.S. Department of Commerce, Bureau of Economic Analysis. http://www.bea.gov/scb/pdf/2009/11%20November/1109_nipa_method.pdf.

———. 2011. "National Income and Product Accounts Tables." http://www.bea.gov/iTable/iTable.cfm?ReqID=9&step=1 (accessed May 17, 2012).

U.S. Department of Education, National Center for Education Statistics. 2008. Integrated Postsecondary Education Data System. Washington, DC: U.S. Department of Education, National Center for Education Statistics.

U.S. Department of Labor, Bureau of Labor Statistics. 1998–2011. Quarterly Census of Employment and Wages. Washington, DC: U.S. Department of Labor, Bureau of Labor Statistics.

———. 2011. "Employment and Wages Online Annual Averages, 2010." http://www.bls.gov/cew/cewbultn10.htm.

**Table 2.6.** Nonprofit Wages Covered by Unemployment Insurance for Industries with Tax Status Identified in the Economic Census, 1990–2010 (millions of current dollars)

| | NAICS Code and Industry Description | | | | |
|---|---|---|---|---|---|
| Year | 61 Educational services | 62 Health care and social assistance | 71 Arts, entertainment, and recreation | 81 Other services, except public administration | Total |
| 1990 | 23,430 | 97,407 | 5,705 | 16,949 | 143,491 |
| 1991 | 25,168 | 106,716 | 5,779 | 17,646 | 155,309 |
| 1992 | 26,785 | 117,053 | 5,658 | 18,790 | 168,286 |
| 1993 | 28,327 | 123,052 | 5,686 | 19,534 | 176,598 |
| 1994 | 29,917 | 129,369 | 5,926 | 20,705 | 185,916 |
| 1995 | 31,714 | 136,297 | 6,202 | 21,802 | 196,014 |
| 1996 | 33,668 | 143,072 | 6,657 | 23,003 | 206,400 |
| 1997 | 36,147 | 151,053 | 6,928 | 24,571 | 218,699 |
| 1998 | 39,310 | 160,643 | 7,585 | 25,501 | 233,039 |
| 1999 | 41,653 | 167,775 | 8,143 | 27,207 | 244,778 |
| 2000 | 44,681 | 177,193 | 8,898 | 29,511 | 260,283 |
| 2001 | 48,395 | 191,572 | 9,481 | 31,888 | 281,337 |
| 2002 | 51,994 | 206,375 | 9,780 | 33,806 | 301,955 |
| 2003 | 55,823 | 220,471 | 10,318 | 35,012 | 321,624 |
| 2004 | 59,101 | 233,614 | 10,829 | 36,578 | 340,122 |
| 2005 | 62,210 | 245,078 | 11,269 | 37,916 | 356,473 |
| 2006 | 66,189 | 260,247 | 12,048 | 40,085 | 378,569 |
| 2007 | 71,159 | 276,472 | 12,800 | 42,790 | 403,221 |
| 2008 | 76,361 | 296,157 | 13,478 | 45,686 | 431,681 |
| 2009 | 80,197 | 310,228 | 13,025 | 45,733 | 449,183 |
| 2010 | 82,288 | 319,147 | 12,956 | 46,517 | 460,909 |

*Sources:* Authors' estimates based on private wages from U.S. Department of Labor, Bureau of Labor Statistics, Quarterly Census of Employment and Wages (1990–2011). The tax-exempt share of wages is from U.S. Census Bureau, Economic Census (1997, 2002, and 2007).
*Notes:* Industries are listed as classified by the North American Industry Classification System (NAICS). The professional, scientific, and technical services sector is also included in the Economic Census, but the authors believe these data are flawed.

**Table 2.7.** Nonprofit Wages Reported to the Census Bureau or Covered by Unemployment Insurance for Select Industries with Many Employees Exempt from Unemployment Insurance, 1990–2010 ($ millions)

| | NAICS Code and Industry Description | | | | | | | | | |
| | 611110 | | 611210 | | 611310 | | 611210+611310 | | 813110 | |
| | Elementary and secondary schools | | Junior colleges | | Colleges, universities, and professional schools | | Junior colleges, colleges, universities, and professional schools | | Religious organizations | |
| Year | Reported | Covered | Reported | Covered | Reported | Covered | Reported | Covered | Reported | Covered |
|---|---|---|---|---|---|---|---|---|---|---|
| 1990 | 5,817.2 | 5,479.1 | — | 182.1 | — | 16,775.5 | 18,177.0 | 16,957.6 | 10,077.4 | 1,297.7 |
| 1991 | 6,347.2 | 6,028.1 | — | 230.5 | — | 17,871.9 | 19,673.8 | 18,102.4 | 11,000.7 | 1,317.1 |
| 1992 | 7,375.1 | 6,299.9 | — | 242.4 | — | 19,144.6 | 21,351.1 | 19,387.0 | 11,947.6 | 1,410.6 |
| 1993 | 7,661.7 | 6,739.4 | — | 249.8 | — | 20,192.7 | 23,195.3 | 20,442.5 | 12,806.4 | 1,486.7 |
| 1994 | 8,283.7 | 7,214.6 | — | 257.9 | — | 21,244.2 | 24,330.8 | 21,502.1 | 13,636.1 | 1,576.7 |
| 1995 | 9,053.4 | 7,836.2 | — | 267.5 | — | 22,330.0 | 25,504.4 | 22,597.5 | 15,341.4 | 1,693.3 |
| 1996 | 9,808.4 | 8,485.0 | — | 287.1 | — | 23,431.2 | 26,587.2 | 23,718.3 | 16,266.5 | 1,839.8 |
| 1997 | 10,606.9 | 9,313.7 | — | 303.8 | — | 24,898.6 | 28,174.2 | 25,202.5 | 17,529.7 | 2,281.9 |
| 1998 | 11,478.6 | 9,999.8 | 583.8 | 304.7 | 29,043.8 | 27,215.0 | 29,627.6 | 27,519.8 | 18,853.5 | 2,261.3 |
| 1999 | 12,633.5 | 10,949.4 | 599.3 | 293.2 | 30,888.5 | 28,267.8 | 31,487.8 | 28,561.0 | 20,390.6 | 2,506.7 |
| 2000 | 13,676.8 | 11,997.2 | 627.8 | 294.2 | 32,713.7 | 30,014.0 | 33,341.5 | 30,308.2 | 22,089.5 | 2,793.3 |
| 2001 | 14,998.3 | 13,172.4 | 645.6 | 281.3 | 34,823.8 | 32,215.8 | 35,469.4 | 32,497.2 | 23,294.6 | 3,048.3 |

*(continued)*

**Table 2.7.** Nonprofit Wages Reported to the Census Bureau or Covered by Unemployment Insurance for Select Industries with Many Employees Exempt from Unemployment Insurance, 1990–2010 ($ millions) *(continued)*

| | 611110 Elementary and secondary schools | | 611210 Junior colleges | | 611310 Colleges, universities, and professional schools | | 611210+611310 Junior colleges, colleges, universities, and professional schools | | 813110 Religious organizations | |
|---|---|---|---|---|---|---|---|---|---|---|
| Year | Reported | Covered | Reported | Covered | Reported | Covered | Reported | Covered | Reported | Covered |
| 2002 | 16,714.9 | 14,376.5 | 682.9 | 256.3 | 37,188.0 | 34,350.0 | 37,870.9 | 34,606.3 | 24,843.7 | 3,311.1 |
| 2003 | 17,482.8 | 15,463.7 | 778.0 | 258.0 | 38,799.7 | 36,905.9 | 39,577.7 | 37,164.0 | 25,714.8 | 3,554.1 |
| 2004 | 18,219.1 | 16,516.0 | 818.5 | 266.0 | 41,090.9 | 38,912.4 | 41,909.4 | 39,178.4 | 26,305.7 | 3,739.7 |
| 2005 | 18,327.4 | 17,553.2 | 856.5 | 269.5 | 43,007.1 | 40,685.4 | 43,863.6 | 40,954.9 | 27,114.6 | 3,914.0 |
| 2006 | 19,669.0 | 18,865.1 | 934.4 | 256.4 | 45,461.2 | 43,001.1 | 46,395.6 | 43,257.5 | 28,146.6 | 4,169.7 |
| 2007 | 21,157.1 | 20,462.6 | 984.1 | 228.6 | 48,866.7 | 46,012.4 | 49,850.7 | 46,241.0 | 30,250.5 | 4,518.8 |
| 2008 | 22,535.1 | 22,133.0 | 1,033.6 | 230.4 | 52,803.7 | 49,138.1 | 53,837.2 | 49,368.5 | 31,425.6 | 4,806.8 |
| 2009 | 23,356.6 | 23,166.6 | 1,088.7 | 243.1 | 55,179.5 | 51,792.6 | 56,268.2 | 52,035.7 | 31,689.5 | 4,667.8 |
| 2010 | 24,149.9 | 23,352.8 | 1,192.9 | 261.4 | 57,898.2 | 53,356.9 | 59,091.1 | 53,618.3 | 31,953.4 | 4,856.3 |

NAICS Code and Industry Description

*Sources:* Reported wages are authors' estimates based on multiplying tax-exempt shares by national total private wages from U.S. Census Bureau, County Business Patterns (1991–2009). Covered wages are authors' estimates based on multiplying tax-exempt shares by private wages from U.S. Department of Labor, Bureau of Labor Statistics, Quarterly Census of Employment and Wages (1991–2010).
*Note:* The NAICS 611210+611310 column is the sum of the two columns to its left, except for 1990–97 reported wages, when the more detailed breakout was not available.
— = not available

**Table 2.8.** Wages Reported to the Internal Revenue Service for Two-Digit Industries with Tax Status Not Identified in the Economic Census, 2000–10 ($ millions)

| NAICS code | Industry | 2000 | 2001 | 2002 | 2003 | 2004 | 2005 | 2006 | 2007 | 2008 | 2009 | 2010 |
|---|---|---|---|---|---|---|---|---|---|---|---|---|
| 11 | Agriculture, forestry, fishing, and hunting | 249.1 | 273.8 | 279.3 | 289.6 | 293.1 | 296.7 | 321.9 | 329.4 | 331.5 | 328.6 | 326.4 |
| 22 | Utilities | 1,007.6 | 1,123.8 | 1,159.8 | 1,273.8 | 1,340.5 | 1,414.0 | 1,557.3 | 1,676.9 | 2,212.0 | 2,367.6 | 2,447.7 |
| 48–49 | Transportation and warehousing | 47.7 | 52.9 | 55.3 | 60.6 | 68.5 | 70.9 | 74.4 | 80.2 | 82.0 | 84.6 | 92.4 |
| 51 | Information | 2,210.6 | 2,247.7 | 2,249.0 | 2,291.5 | 2,357.4 | 2,488.5 | 2,578.7 | 2,656.6 | 2,824.7 | 2,860.8 | 2,780.9 |
| 52 | Finance and insurance | 3,476.3 | 3,739.8 | 4,171.3 | 5,392.0 | 5,679.1 | 6,038.6 | 6,236.9 | 6,400.8 | 6,280.3 | 6,598.9 | 6,730.7 |
| 53 | Real estate and rental and leasing | 83.8 | 90.9 | 95.4 | 98.4 | 107.8 | 115.2 | 133.1 | 145.7 | 150.3 | 144.6 | 148.3 |
| 54 | Professional, scientific, and technical services | 6,607.5 | 7,464.6 | 8,504.6 | 8,995.6 | 9,413.3 | 10,761.7 | 11,719.5 | 12,716.8 | 13,377.2 | 14,441.3 | 15,266.5 |
| 56 | Administrative and support and waste management and remediation services | 670.5 | 695.3 | 741.5 | 771.6 | 773.5 | 789.1 | 838.2 | 874.3 | 915.9 | 948.7 | 1,078.3 |
| 72 | Accommodation and food services | 189.7 | 215.5 | 233.2 | 242.9 | 255.0 | 269.3 | 287.0 | 307.5 | 324.5 | 325.5 | 325.8 |

*Sources*: Urban Institute, National Center for Charitable Statistics, Core Files (Public Charities and Others, 1990–2010), with error corrections and missing-data interpolations performed by the authors.
*Note*: Industries are listed as classified by the North American Industry Classification System (NAICS).

**Table 2.9.**  Nonprofit Employees Covered by Unemployment Insurance for Industries with Tax Status Identified in the Economic Census, 1990–2010

| Year | NAICS Code and Industry Description | | | | Total |
|------|------|------|------|------|------|
| | 61 Educational services | 62 Health care and social assistance | 71 Arts, entertainment, and recreation | 81 Other services, except public administration | |
| 1990 | 1,096,456 | 4,743,144 | 467,990 | 1,044,464 | 7,352,055 |
| 1991 | 1,103,775 | 4,914,286 | 447,666 | 1,022,204 | 7,487,931 |
| 1992 | 1,112,223 | 5,099,150 | 398,349 | 1,040,952 | 7,650,674 |
| 1993 | 1,128,628 | 5,258,231 | 377,885 | 1,055,754 | 7,820,498 |
| 1994 | 1,160,831 | 5,380,798 | 380,729 | 1,082,886 | 8,005,243 |
| 1995 | 1,188,070 | 5,511,127 | 380,543 | 1,105,635 | 8,185,374 |
| 1996 | 1,231,017 | 5,650,303 | 382,535 | 1,127,386 | 8,391,242 |
| 1997 | 1,275,924 | 5,785,640 | 388,798 | 1,152,111 | 8,602,474 |
| 1998 | 1,331,349 | 5,941,902 | 403,242 | 1,167,192 | 8,843,685 |
| 1999 | 1,374,691 | 6,060,531 | 415,481 | 1,199,868 | 9,050,571 |
| 2000 | 1,420,498 | 6,168,100 | 437,971 | 1,240,964 | 9,267,532 |
| 2001 | 1,474,205 | 6,362,231 | 452,120 | 1,272,986 | 9,561,542 |
| 2002 | 1,526,325 | 6,555,309 | 460,296 | 1,298,571 | 9,840,501 |
| 2003 | 1,572,083 | 6,667,525 | 471,677 | 1,294,493 | 10,005,778 |
| 2004 | 1,608,525 | 6,724,131 | 488,167 | 1,297,155 | 10,117,978 |
| 2005 | 1,643,074 | 6,803,446 | 498,444 | 1,296,363 | 10,241,328 |
| 2006 | 1,682,303 | 6,890,905 | 514,061 | 1,312,405 | 10,399,675 |
| 2007 | 1,731,168 | 7,019,679 | 533,318 | 1,333,573 | 10,617,737 |
| 2008 | 1,787,797 | 7,221,943 | 542,337 | 1,364,724 | 10,916,801 |
| 2009 | 1,828,603 | 7,354,835 | 528,034 | 1,327,561 | 11,039,034 |
| 2010 | 1,844,522 | 7,460,825 | 524,332 | 1,313,679 | 11,143,358 |

*Sources:* Authors' estimates based on private employment from U.S. Department of Labor, Bureau of Labor Statistics, Quarterly Census of Employment and Wages (1990–2011). Tax-exempt share of wages is from U.S. Census Bureau, Economic Census (1997, 2002, and 2007).

*Notes:* Industries are listed as classified by the North American Industry Classification System (NAICS). The professional, scientific, and technical services category is also included in the Economic Census, but the authors believe these data are flawed.

**Table 2.10.** Nonprofit Employees Reported to the Census Bureau or Covered by Unemployment Insurance for Select Industries with Many Employees Exempt from Unemployment Insurance, 1990–2010

| | NAICS Code and Industry Description | | | | | | | | | |
| | 611110 Elementary and secondary schools | | 611210 Junior colleges | | 611310 Colleges, universities, and professional schools | | 611210+611310 Junior colleges, colleges, universities, and professional schools | | 813110 Religious organizations | |
| Year | Reported | Covered | Reported | Covered | Reported | Covered | Reported | Covered | Reported | Covered |
|---|---|---|---|---|---|---|---|---|---|---|
| 1990 | 397,081 | 329,116 | — | 9,484 | — | 703,830 | 1,023,410 | 713,313 | 1,096,313 | 100,138 |
| 1991 | 413,196 | 336,959 | — | 11,295 | — | 703,183 | 1,061,539 | 714,478 | 1,143,374 | 98,731 |
| 1992 | 461,634 | 341,525 | — | 11,229 | — | 706,590 | 1,108,542 | 717,819 | 1,196,396 | 103,009 |
| 1993 | 474,134 | 356,556 | — | 11,293 | — | 706,009 | 1,152,942 | 717,302 | 1,244,083 | 105,878 |
| 1994 | 495,616 | 372,349 | — | 11,365 | — | 720,293 | 1,167,809 | 731,658 | 1,265,938 | 109,514 |
| 1995 | 517,983 | 389,257 | — | 11,138 | — | 728,292 | 1,182,774 | 739,430 | 1,315,906 | 114,076 |
| 1996 | 535,971 | 405,399 | — | 11,270 | — | 750,446 | 1,190,760 | 761,716 | 1,380,975 | 119,772 |
| 1997 | 562,693 | 424,711 | — | 11,666 | — | 771,413 | 1,224,713 | 783,080 | 1,436,546 | 130,366 |
| 1998 | 580,165 | 444,761 | 23,546 | 11,260 | 1,215,115 | 800,408 | 1,238,661 | 811,668 | 1,469,386 | 135,897 |
| 1999 | 611,247 | 468,747 | 22,982 | 10,213 | 1,242,825 | 811,627 | 1,265,808 | 821,840 | 1,517,882 | 145,352 |
| 2000 | 637,294 | 491,787 | 23,663 | 9,574 | 1,259,745 | 823,716 | 1,283,408 | 833,291 | 1,569,353 | 151,810 |
| 2001 | 657,756 | 513,820 | 23,336 | 9,051 | 1,270,559 | 844,685 | 1,293,894 | 853,736 | 1,595,009 | 159,212 |
| 2002 | 698,251 | 536,094 | 24,419 | 7,836 | 1,300,282 | 865,305 | 1,324,701 | 873,141 | 1,638,915 | 166,785 |

*(continued)*

**Table 2.10.** Nonprofit Employees Reported to the Census Bureau or Covered by Unemployment Insurance for Select Industries with Many Employees Exempt from Unemployment Insurance, 1990–2010 *(continued)*

| | NAICS Code and Industry Description | | | | | | | | | |
|---|---|---|---|---|---|---|---|---|---|---|
| | 611110 | | 611210 | | 611310 | | 611210+611310 | | 813110 | |
| | Elementary and secondary schools | | Junior colleges | | Colleges, universities, and professional schools | | Junior colleges, colleges, universities, and professional schools | | Religious organizations | |
| Year | Reported | Covered | Reported | Covered | Reported | Covered | Reported | Covered | Reported | Covered |
| 2003 | 707,586 | 555,470 | 25,547 | 7,589 | 1,331,697 | 887,753 | 1,357,244 | 895,342 | 1,652,741 | 172,669 |
| 2004 | 711,390 | 570,964 | 24,695 | 7,681 | 1,390,059 | 904,399 | 1,414,754 | 912,080 | 1,645,426 | 175,119 |
| 2005 | 687,029 | 590,152 | 30,656 | 7,604 | 1,401,703 | 914,968 | 1,432,359 | 922,572 | 1,625,909 | 177,104 |
| 2006 | 706,455 | 607,855 | 33,326 | 7,037 | 1,427,054 | 934,536 | 1,460,380 | 941,573 | 1,639,099 | 179,417 |
| 2007 | 727,748 | 631,710 | 38,729 | 6,140 | 1,463,842 | 956,634 | 1,502,571 | 962,774 | 1,680,761 | 183,678 |
| 2008 | 741,305 | 655,568 | 39,819 | 6,197 | 1,510,358 | 980,277 | 1,550,176 | 986,474 | 1,688,767 | 186,379 |
| 2009 | 751,392 | 665,890 | 40,879 | 6,681 | 1,547,424 | 1,007,926 | 1,588,303 | 1,014,607 | 1,680,943 | 184,929 |
| 2010 | 761,239 | 663,513 | 43,250 | 7,404 | 1,596,099 | 1,019,282 | 1,639,350 | 1,026,686 | 1,712,400 | 181,449 |

*Sources:* Reported employees are authors' estimates based on multiplying tax-exempt shares by national total private employment from U.S. Census Bureau, County Business Patterns (1991–2009). Covered employees are authors' estimates based on multiplying tax-exempt shares by private employment from U.S. Department of Labor, Bureau of Labor Statistics, Quarterly Census of Employment and Wages (1991–2010).

*Note:* The NAICS 611210+611310 column is the sum of the two columns to its left, except for 1990–97 reported wages, when the more detailed breakout was not available.

— = not available

**Table 2.11.** Estimated Employment for Two-Digit Industries with Tax Status Not Identified in the Economic Census, 2000–10

| NAICS code | Industry | 2000 | 2001 | 2002 | 2003 | 2004 | 2005 | 2006 | 2007 | 2008 | 2009 | 2010 |
|---|---|---|---|---|---|---|---|---|---|---|---|---|
| 11 | Agriculture, forestry, fishing, and hunting | 12,499 | 13,560 | 13,369 | 13,553 | 13,120 | 12,832 | 13,340 | 13,076 | 12,755 | 12,623 | 12,254 |
| 22 | Utilities | 16,322 | 17,140 | 17,214 | 18,554 | 18,515 | 18,801 | 19,883 | 20,382 | 26,285 | 27,894 | 28,202 |
| 48–49 | Transportation and warehousing | 1,314 | 1,462 | 1,502 | 1,619 | 1,764 | 1,794 | 1,822 | 1,881 | 1,910 | 1,975 | 2,091 |
| 51 | Information | 38,109 | 39,236 | 40,087 | 39,508 | 38,822 | 39,605 | 39,113 | 38,424 | 39,905 | 40,186 | 37,380 |
| 52 | Finance and insurance | 57,934 | 58,721 | 66,462 | 83,010 | 80,980 | 82,306 | 79,399 | 75,345 | 73,654 | 82,700 | 79,636 |
| 53 | Real estate and rental and leasing | 2,595 | 2,766 | 2,813 | 2,808 | 2,890 | 2,924 | 3,174 | 3,354 | 3,477 | 3,420 | 3,386 |
| 54 | Professional, scientific, and technical services | 118,444 | 127,046 | 144,951 | 150,234 | 150,500 | 164,867 | 171,165 | 176,540 | 179,882 | 193,142 | 197,451 |
| 56 | Administrative and support and waste management and remediation services | 28,772 | 28,446 | 29,335 | 29,612 | 28,404 | 28,043 | 28,575 | 28,297 | 28,534 | 29,111 | 32,406 |
| 72 | Accommodation and food services | 14,412 | 15,759 | 16,725 | 17,075 | 17,340 | 17,761 | 18,277 | 18,796 | 19,438 | 19,500 | 18,965 |

*Sources*: Authors' estimates based on multiplying the tax-exempt wage share by private employment. Tax-exempt wages by industry are from Urban Institute, National Center for Charitable Statistics, Core Files (Public Charities and Others, 2000–10). Private wages and private employment by industry are from U.S. Department of Labor, Bureau of Labor Statistics, Quarterly Census of Employment and Wages (2000–11).

*Notes*: Industries are listed as classified by the North American Industry Classification System (NAICS). Please see the methodology section of this chapter for a discussion of estimated employment and its limitations.

**Table 2.12.** Nonprofit Wages Covered by Unemployment Insurance for Six-Digit Industries with Tax Status Identified in the Economic Census, 1990–96 ($ millions)

| NAICS code | Industry | 1990 | 1991 | 1992 | 1993 | 1994 | 1995 | 1996 |
|---|---|---|---|---|---|---|---|---|
| 541110 | Offices of lawyers | 607.9 | 621.3 | 663.9 | 677.2 | 694.7 | 713.1 | 743.7 |
| 611110 | Elementary and secondary schools | 5,479.1 | 6,028.1 | 6,299.9 | 6,739.4 | 7,214.6 | 7,836.2 | 8,485.0 |
| 611210 | Junior colleges | 182.1 | 230.5 | 242.4 | 249.8 | 257.9 | 267.5 | 287.1 |
| 611310 | Colleges, universities, and professional schools | 16,775.5 | 17,871.9 | 19,144.6 | 20,192.7 | 21,244.2 | 22,330.0 | 23,431.2 |
| 611410 | Business and secretarial schools | 25.2 | 21.7 | 20.2 | 18.0 | 17.3 | 16.9 | 16.4 |
| 611420 | Computer training | 2.1 | 2.3 | 2.8 | 3.1 | 3.8 | 5.0 | 6.1 |
| 611430 | Professional and management development training | 112.5 | 118.7 | 137.3 | 143.3 | 154.7 | 168.8 | 201.5 |
| 611511 | Cosmetology and barber schools | 6.2 | 6.3 | 6.0 | 5.9 | 5.5 | 5.3 | 5.2 |
| 611512 | Flight training | 7.4 | 7.1 | 6.6 | 6.1 | 6.5 | 6.6 | 6.6 |
| 611513 | Apprenticeship training | 174.2 | 157.4 | 140.5 | 127.0 | 121.8 | 120.2 | 125.9 |
| 611519 | Other technical and trade schools | 118.7 | 131.8 | 139.9 | 148.6 | 150.6 | 160.4 | 180.5 |
| 611610 | Fine arts schools | 119.3 | 120.3 | 127.5 | 134.2 | 150.1 | 162.5 | 182.0 |
| 611620 | Sports and recreation instruction | 26.6 | 27.9 | 31.2 | 35.7 | 39.7 | 43.4 | 48.8 |
| 611630 | Language schools | 19.6 | 22.2 | 25.5 | 27.3 | 29.6 | 31.6 | 36.2 |
| 611691 | Exam preparation and tutoring | 21.8 | 22.7 | 25.1 | 27.5 | 29.9 | 32.8 | 37.9 |
| 611692 | Automobile driving schools | 5.6 | 5.5 | 5.6 | 5.8 | 6.2 | 6.6 | 6.9 |
| 611699 | All other miscellaneous schools and instruction | 86.3 | 95.0 | 100.4 | 114.4 | 125.0 | 133.8 | 152.6 |
| 611710 | Educational support services | 267.6 | 298.1 | 329.5 | 348.0 | 359.6 | 386.4 | 458.4 |
| 621410 | Family planning centers | 233.3 | 264.5 | 326.4 | 359.0 | 384.1 | 408.2 | 425.6 |
| 621420 | Outpatient mental health and substance abuse centers | 1,323.1 | 1,433.7 | 1,563.7 | 1,729.6 | 1,918.0 | 2,087.7 | 2,252.0 |

|  |  | | | | | | |
|---|---|---|---|---|---|---|---|
| 621491 | HMO medical centers | 2,259.0 | 2,359.2 | 2,450.9 | 2,418.4 | 2,570.1 | 2,738.2 | 2,828.8 |
| 621492 | Kidney dialysis center | 87.6 | 104.4 | 124.1 | 140.6 | 153.6 | 172.8 | 193.3 |
| 621493 | Freestanding ambulatory surgical and emergency centers | 223.9 | 305.1 | 337.6 | 338.3 | 359.6 | 399.5 | 410.2 |
| 621498 | All other outpatient care centers | 795.4 | 759.6 | 909.3 | 1,004.3 | 1,134.4 | 1,182.4 | 1,238.6 |
| 621610 | Home health care services | 1,571.1 | 2,017.0 | 2,531.0 | 3,036.5 | 3,505.5 | 4,048.8 | 4,387.2 |
| 621910 | Ambulance services | 133.0 | 150.6 | 164.6 | 177.2 | 199.2 | 224.1 | 260.3 |
| 621991 | Blood and organ banks | 506.0 | 561.5 | 621.1 | 703.4 | 777.3 | 825.7 | 840.3 |
| 621999 | All other miscellaneous ambulatory health care services | 25.2 | 27.7 | 31.7 | 34.7 | 41.7 | 42.8 | 52.1 |
| 622110 | General medical and surgical hospitals | 66,593.5 | 72,642.9 | 79,336.9 | 82,521.6 | 85,654.6 | 89,020.9 | 92,771.0 |
| 622210 | Psychiatric and substance abuse hospitals | 1,092.2 | 1,168.0 | 1,199.6 | 1,153.4 | 1,139.2 | 1,133.4 | 1,089.3 |
| 622310 | Specialty (except psychiatric and substance abuse) hospitals | 1,775.6 | 1,987.7 | 2,242.8 | 2,406.1 | 2,479.1 | 2,627.8 | 2,848.7 |
| 623110 | Nursing care facilities | 4,213.8 | 4,678.5 | 5,192.0 | 5,562.5 | 6,007.1 | 6,500.0 | 6,923.7 |
| 623210 | Residential mental retardation facilities | 1,869.1 | 2,120.3 | 2,302.8 | 2,399.0 | 2,533.1 | 2,750.8 | 2,930.6 |
| 623220 | Residential mental health and substance abuse facilities | 1,003.6 | 1,113.8 | 1,173.1 | 1,255.5 | 1,332.3 | 1,464.0 | 1,558.0 |
| 623311 | Continuing care retirement communities | 1,728.8 | 1,936.6 | 2,055.7 | 2,165.7 | 2,249.1 | 2,366.8 | 2,526.0 |
| 623312 | Homes for the elderly | 554.5 | 617.8 | 677.6 | 722.5 | 778.0 | 829.2 | 978.0 |
| 623990 | Other residential care facilities | 1,221.7 | 1,344.8 | 1,511.8 | 1,636.3 | 1,751.1 | 1,960.5 | 2,129.6 |
| 624110 | Child and youth services | 976.4 | 1,077.9 | 1,221.0 | 1,336.7 | 1,490.1 | 1,651.7 | 1,811.9 |
| 624120 | Services for the elderly and persons with disabilities | 2,085.3 | 2,270.2 | 2,554.6 | 2,712.7 | 2,907.9 | 3,028.3 | 3,161.4 |

*(continued)*

**Table 2.12.** Nonprofit Wages Covered by Unemployment Insurance for Six-Digit Industries with Tax Status Identified in the Economic Census, 1990–96 ($ millions) (*continued*)

| NAICS code | Industry | 1990 | 1991 | 1992 | 1993 | 1994 | 1995 | 1996 |
|---|---|---|---|---|---|---|---|---|
| 624190 | Other individual and family services | 1,992.6 | 2,180.7 | 2,405.7 | 2,653.1 | 2,892.1 | 3,203.4 | 3,453.0 |
| 624210 | Community food services | 269.6 | 346.8 | 380.4 | 398.7 | 424.1 | 426.4 | 415.0 |
| 624221 | Temporary shelters | 268.5 | 318.7 | 389.5 | 418.2 | 474.0 | 532.6 | 557.1 |
| 624229 | Other community housing services | 127.4 | 152.5 | 167.1 | 190.9 | 229.3 | 257.0 | 273.5 |
| 624230 | Emergency and other relief services | 534.3 | 491.1 | 505.5 | 477.4 | 476.1 | 499.0 | 513.2 |
| 624310 | Vocational rehabilitation services | 2,405.5 | 2,548.6 | 2,731.3 | 2,935.8 | 3,109.8 | 3,290.1 | 3,428.4 |
| 624410 | Child day care services | 1,537.3 | 1,736.4 | 1,945.5 | 2,163.8 | 2,398.3 | 2,624.5 | 2,814.7 |
| 711110 | Theater companies and dinner theaters | 1,792.9 | 1,703.2 | 1,302.6 | 1,066.0 | 991.4 | 907.5 | 856.5 |
| 711120 | Dance companies | 132.0 | 141.0 | 147.9 | 157.1 | 160.7 | 181.2 | 183.3 |
| 711130 | Musical groups and artists | 415.4 | 430.1 | 465.1 | 495.1 | 494.2 | 528.5 | 555.6 |
| 711190 | Other performing arts companies | 3.4 | 3.7 | 3.6 | 4.2 | 5.9 | 6.9 | 6.5 |
| 711310 | Promoters of performing arts, sports, and similar events with facilities | 275.3 | 256.5 | 224.2 | 249.3 | 277.3 | 321.2 | 350.2 |
| 711320 | Promoters of performing arts, sports, and similar events without facilities | 44.4 | 38.4 | 43.0 | 44.4 | 48.8 | 56.6 | 60.4 |
| 712110 | Museums | 717.9 | 745.7 | 799.4 | 847.4 | 900.2 | 946.4 | 1,143.1 |
| 712120 | Historical sites | 127.3 | 132.3 | 133.9 | 135.0 | 168.2 | 169.9 | 192.4 |
| 712130 | Zoos and botanical gardens | 220.9 | 228.4 | 271.5 | 294.2 | 304.1 | 328.2 | 351.5 |
| 712190 | Nature parks and other similar institutions | 28.4 | 28.7 | 29.2 | 33.7 | 38.1 | 44.1 | 45.6 |

| NAICS code | Industry | | | | | | | |
|---|---|---|---|---|---|---|---|---|
| 713910 | Golf courses and country clubs | 999.6 | 1,096.3 | 1,191.9 | 1,261.7 | 1,368.9 | 1,471.1 | 1,573.5 |
| 713940 | Fitness and recreational sports centers | 817.6 | 836.2 | 893.5 | 930.2 | 979.9 | 1,042.0 | 1,123.5 |
| 713990 | All other amusement and recreation industries | 129.8 | 139.0 | 152.5 | 167.5 | 188.0 | 198.6 | 215.1 |
| 813110 | Religious organizations | 1,297.7 | 1,317.1 | 1,410.6 | 1,486.7 | 1,576.7 | 1,693.3 | 1,839.8 |
| 813211 | Grantmaking foundations | 594.6 | 640.3 | 702.9 | 781.1 | 824.9 | 905.5 | 991.2 |
| 813212 | Voluntary health organizations | 579.7 | 552.8 | 588.2 | 621.8 | 773.1 | 833.4 | 884.3 |
| 813219 | Other grantmaking and giving services | 737.0 | 761.1 | 836.3 | 857.6 | 896.2 | 944.4 | 1,001.4 |
| 813311 | Human rights organizations | 523.5 | 556.5 | 601.8 | 628.3 | 662.3 | 699.6 | 746.2 |
| 813312 | Environment, conservation, and wildlife organizations | 388.7 | 353.5 | 366.5 | 371.0 | 390.7 | 423.9 | 446.7 |
| 813319 | Other social advocacy organizations | 872.4 | 883.7 | 963.6 | 1,037.9 | 1,129.3 | 1,230.9 | 1,295.1 |
| 813410 | Civic and social organizations | 3,630.6 | 3,823.6 | 4,034.7 | 4,206.4 | 4,490.5 | 4,719.2 | 4,831.2 |
| 813910 | Business associations | 3,004.9 | 3,174.8 | 3,374.5 | 3,526.6 | 3,686.4 | 3,900.3 | 4,096.2 |
| 813920 | Professional organizations | 1,596.8 | 1,694.1 | 1,808.3 | 1,918.2 | 2,030.6 | 2,149.9 | 2,309.6 |
| 813930 | Labor unions and similar labor organizations | 2,367.3 | 2,488.2 | 2,570.1 | 2,603.6 | 2,657.1 | 2,733.0 | 2,851.3 |
| 813940 | Political organizations | 143.9 | 100.8 | 163.5 | 120.7 | 194.0 | 140.0 | 217.4 |
| 813990 | Other similar organizations (except business, professional, labor, and political organizations) | 1,212.2 | 1,299.4 | 1,368.9 | 1,373.6 | 1,393.1 | 1,428.4 | 1,492.1 |

*Sources:* Authors' estimates based on private wages from the U.S. Department of Labor, Bureau of Labor Statistics, Quarterly Census of Employment and Wages (1990–2011). Tax-exempt share of wages is from U.S. Census Bureau, Economic Census (1997, 2002, and 2007).

*Notes:* Industries are listed as classified by the North American Industry Classification System (NAICS). Industries 541710 (physical, engineering, and biological research services) and 541720 (research and development in the social sciences and humanities) are also included in the Economic Census, but the authors believe these data are flawed.

**Table 2.13.** Nonprofit Wages Covered by Unemployment Insurance for Six-Digit Industries with Tax Status Identified in the Economic Census, 1997–2003 ($ millions)

| NAICS code | Industry | 1997 | 1998 | 1999 | 2000 | 2001 | 2002 | 2003 |
|---|---|---|---|---|---|---|---|---|
| 541110 | Offices of lawyers | 791.7 | 848.7 | 892.6 | 968.0 | 1,029.6 | 1,056.5 | 1,104.0 |
| 611110 | Elementary and secondary schools | 9,313.7 | 9,999.8 | 10,949.4 | 11,997.2 | 13,172.4 | 14,376.5 | 15,463.7 |
| 611210 | Junior colleges | 303.8 | 304.7 | 293.2 | 294.2 | 281.3 | 256.3 | 258.0 |
| 611310 | Colleges, universities, and professional schools | 24,898.6 | 27,215.0 | 28,267.8 | 30,014.0 | 32,215.8 | 34,350.0 | 36,905.9 |
| 611410 | Business and secretarial schools | 16.4 | 20.0 | 24.6 | 30.3 | 36.4 | 43.3 | 43.7 |
| 611420 | Computer training | 7.6 | 13.4 | 20.8 | 30.2 | 34.0 | 32.4 | 28.5 |
| 611430 | Professional and management development training | 221.5 | 265.3 | 293.0 | 346.8 | 366.0 | 371.3 | 401.6 |
| 611511 | Cosmetology and barber schools | 4.8 | 5.9 | 7.1 | 8.7 | 10.9 | 13.8 | 12.5 |
| 611512 | Flight training | 7.5 | 8.9 | 9.9 | 11.0 | 11.2 | 9.9 | 12.3 |
| 611513 | Apprenticeship training | 136.6 | 149.9 | 174.6 | 200.1 | 228.3 | 269.1 | 286.5 |
| 611519 | Other technical and trade schools | 208.3 | 238.7 | 256.5 | 273.6 | 308.9 | 336.4 | 356.8 |
| 611610 | Fine arts schools | 187.1 | 202.6 | 230.3 | 256.9 | 291.0 | 323.7 | 319.4 |
| 611620 | Sports and recreation instruction | 49.9 | 58.1 | 67.9 | 82.3 | 99.5 | 121.0 | 129.7 |
| 611630 | Language schools | 40.1 | 46.9 | 52.7 | 59.2 | 66.3 | 65.2 | 71.5 |
| 611691 | Exam preparation and tutoring | 43.8 | 64.3 | 87.3 | 123.2 | 153.6 | 175.5 | 197.1 |
| 611692 | Automobile driving schools | 7.4 | 9.5 | 11.4 | 14.8 | 18.5 | 21.8 | 19.6 |
| 611699 | All other miscellaneous schools and instruction | 176.0 | 199.6 | 247.6 | 299.1 | 366.4 | 413.4 | 413.8 |
| 611710 | Educational support services | 524.2 | 507.7 | 658.8 | 639.2 | 734.4 | 814.3 | 902.5 |
| 621410 | Family planning centers | 449.6 | 457.6 | 459.6 | 472.4 | 494.6 | 523.0 | 494.8 |
| 621420 | Outpatient mental health and substance abuse centers | 2,428.0 | 2,627.7 | 2,706.6 | 2,882.9 | 3,104.7 | 3,338.4 | 3,529.7 |

|  |  | | | | | | | |
|---|---|---|---|---|---|---|---|---|
| 621491 | HMO medical centers | 2,716.7 | 2,581.5 | 2,394.9 | 2,280.9 | 2,304.0 | 2,340.5 | 2,638.5 |
| 621492 | Kidney dialysis center | 223.8 | 243.2 | 245.7 | 263.6 | 292.2 | 308.4 | 322.2 |
| 621493 | Freestanding ambulatory surgical and emergency centers | 413.3 | 398.8 | 376.5 | 402.0 | 420.3 | 444.7 | 494.6 |
| 621498 | All other outpatient care centers | 1,300.3 | 1,425.0 | 1,472.0 | 1,565.5 | 1,711.2 | 1,752.9 | 1,996.3 |
| 621610 | Home health care services | 4,659.6 | 4,445.1 | 4,078.2 | 4,246.3 | 4,520.9 | 5,060.2 | 5,406.9 |
| 621910 | Ambulance services | 291.0 | 342.9 | 388.8 | 454.0 | 528.3 | 615.6 | 674.6 |
| 621991 | Blood and organ banks | 892.3 | 996.3 | 1,049.6 | 1,163.1 | 1,324.8 | 1,486.0 | 1,632.6 |
| 621999 | All other miscellaneous ambulatory health care services | 58.9 | 70.2 | 73.5 | 86.3 | 96.5 | 109.5 | 119.4 |
| 622110 | General medical and surgical hospitals | 97,613.1 | 103,905.7 | 108,306.1 | 113,633.2 | 122,564.8 | 132,413.3 | 142,594.5 |
| 622210 | Psychiatric and substance abuse hospitals | 1,094.1 | 1,161.1 | 1,218.4 | 1,238.8 | 1,367.4 | 1,492.1 | 1,536.5 |
| 622310 | Specialty (except psychiatric and substance abuse) hospitals | 3,048.4 | 3,180.3 | 3,147.4 | 3,155.9 | 3,356.1 | 3,558.4 | 4,000.6 |
| 623110 | Nursing care facilities | 7,311.3 | 7,835.5 | 8,154.4 | 8,692.6 | 9,402.5 | 10,064.8 | 10,233.3 |
| 623210 | Residential mental retardation facilities | 3,161.9 | 3,427.2 | 3,753.1 | 4,114.9 | 4,506.9 | 4,797.6 | 4,950.8 |
| 623220 | Residential mental health and substance abuse facilities | 1,692.6 | 1,886.3 | 2,049.7 | 2,235.6 | 2,459.9 | 2,625.5 | 2,770.8 |
| 623311 | Continuing care retirement communities | 2,635.7 | 2,734.7 | 2,770.8 | 2,971.7 | 3,173.0 | 3,484.1 | 3,904.1 |
| 623312 | Homes for the elderly | 1,034.8 | 1,084.6 | 1,133.7 | 1,202.2 | 1,218.0 | 1,205.3 | 1,244.8 |
| 623990 | Other residential care facilities | 2,324.1 | 2,533.9 | 2,786.5 | 3,030.4 | 3,273.3 | 3,411.6 | 3,485.0 |
| 624110 | Child and youth services | 2,018.7 | 2,182.1 | 2,412.0 | 2,679.4 | 3,001.2 | 3,169.9 | 3,367.2 |
| 624120 | Services for the elderly and persons with disabilities | 3,332.5 | 3,546.0 | 3,919.2 | 4,016.1 | 4,323.3 | 4,722.8 | 5,056.0 |

*(continued)*

**Table 2.13.** Nonprofit Wages Covered by Unemployment Insurance for Six-Digit Industries with Tax Status Identified in the Economic Census, 1997–2003 ($ millions) *(continued)*

| NAICS code | Industry | 1997 | 1998 | 1999 | 2000 | 2001 | 2002 | 2003 |
|---|---|---|---|---|---|---|---|---|
| 624190 | Other individual and family services | 3,732.4 | 4,112.3 | 4,545.4 | 5,102.1 | 5,760.3 | 6,270.7 | 6,511.7 |
| 624210 | Community food services | 391.5 | 431.1 | 460.9 | 513.7 | 565.6 | 546.3 | 556.3 |
| 624221 | Temporary shelters | 608.2 | 696.8 | 776.1 | 853.5 | 959.9 | 1,064.5 | 1,125.4 |
| 624229 | Other community housing services | 304.2 | 343.8 | 387.2 | 431.4 | 456.0 | 529.3 | 576.6 |
| 624230 | Emergency and other relief services | 522.6 | 571.4 | 631.3 | 696.2 | 770.7 | 851.0 | 830.2 |
| 624310 | Vocational rehabilitation services | 3,704.7 | 3,996.2 | 4,305.9 | 4,636.8 | 5,009.1 | 5,255.2 | 5,380.6 |
| 624410 | Child day care services | 3,088.2 | 3,425.9 | 3,771.8 | 4,171.4 | 4,606.9 | 4,933.2 | 5,036.6 |
| 711110 | Theater companies and dinner theaters | 794.2 | 808.2 | 795.5 | 874.8 | 926.3 | 954.4 | 938.5 |
| 711120 | Dance companies | 182.7 | 195.1 | 184.3 | 199.7 | 211.7 | 216.2 | 230.0 |
| 711130 | Musical groups and artists | 602.3 | 646.4 | 729.7 | 839.4 | 881.0 | 866.7 | 1,014.3 |
| 711190 | Other performing arts companies | 7.3 | 8.4 | 8.6 | 11.1 | 11.1 | 10.4 | 11.5 |
| 711310 | Promotors of performing arts, sports, and similar events with facilities | 346.5 | 407.8 | 496.4 | 471.5 | 494.1 | 501.5 | 529.7 |
| 711320 | Promoters of performing arts, sports, and similar events without facilities | 62.4 | 78.0 | 100.8 | 144.1 | 176.5 | 207.5 | 176.2 |
| 712110 | Museums | 1,121.4 | 1,243.2 | 1,350.5 | 1,483.8 | 1,619.4 | 1,677.4 | 1,728.2 |
| 712120 | Historical sites | 199.6 | 205.5 | 234.6 | 268.8 | 285.6 | 273.0 | 279.6 |
| 712130 | Zoos and botancial gardens | 382.3 | 418.9 | 475.8 | 508.0 | 546.9 | 561.1 | 595.4 |

| Code | Organization | | | | | | | |
|---|---|---|---|---|---|---|---|---|
| 712190 | Nature parks and other similar institutions | 49.5 | 55.3 | 61.4 | 70.1 | 80.3 | 86.3 | 94.1 |
| 713910 | Golf courses and country clubs | 1,718.0 | 1,864.8 | 1,995.4 | 2,176.9 | 2,278.2 | 2,399.2 | 2,567.0 |
| 713940 | Fitness and recreational sports centers | 1,229.8 | 1,384.4 | 1,425.6 | 1,540.7 | 1,643.5 | 1,684.7 | 1,772.8 |
| 713990 | All other amusement and recreation industries | 232.5 | 268.8 | 284.0 | 308.8 | 326.7 | 341.9 | 380.7 |
| 813110 | Religious organizations | 2,281.9 | 2,261.3 | 2,506.7 | 2,793.3 | 3,048.3 | 3,311.1 | 3,554.1 |
| 813211 | Grantmaking foundations | 1,077.9 | 1,198.6 | 1,330.7 | 1,476.0 | 1,664.9 | 1,852.2 | 1,870.8 |
| 813212 | Voluntary health organizations | 912.4 | 969.4 | 995.2 | 1,101.5 | 1,254.4 | 1,318.2 | 1,395.3 |
| 813219 | Other grantmaking and giving services | 1,096.3 | 1,053.3 | 1,140.4 | 1,264.0 | 1,389.0 | 1,432.4 | 1,455.8 |
| 813311 | Human rights organizations | 782.6 | 872.5 | 948.9 | 1,018.6 | 1,113.0 | 1,185.3 | 1,240.1 |
| 813312 | Environment, conservation, and wildlife organizations | 486.1 | 528.3 | 587.8 | 658.4 | 732.0 | 821.8 | 952.9 |
| 813319 | Other social advocacy organizations | 1,400.7 | 1,513.6 | 1,675.4 | 1,891.2 | 2,127.5 | 2,340.1 | 2,405.5 |
| 813410 | Civic and social organizations | 5,047.5 | 4,781.5 | 5,050.9 | 5,452.9 | 5,846.9 | 6,060.0 | 6,103.3 |
| 813910 | Business associations | 4,307.3 | 4,612.4 | 4,890.2 | 5,148.7 | 5,468.3 | 5,632.0 | 5,840.2 |
| 813920 | Professional organizations | 2,475.2 | 2,710.1 | 2,906.4 | 3,163.9 | 3,482.7 | 3,697.6 | 3,841.0 |
| 813930 | Labor unions and similar labor organizations | 2,987.9 | 3,098.9 | 3,224.6 | 3,397.5 | 3,571.7 | 3,721.2 | 3,854.4 |
| 813940 | Political organizations | 143.7 | 211.9 | 177.6 | 259.4 | 202.3 | 316.6 | 233.3 |
| 813990 | Other similar organizations (except business, professional, labor, and political organizations) | 1,571.6 | 1,688.8 | 1,772.1 | 1,885.6 | 1,986.9 | 2,118.0 | 2,265.3 |

*Sources*: Authors' estimates based on private wages from the U.S. Department of Labor, Bureau of Labor Statistics, Quarterly Census of Employment and Wages (1990–2011). Tax-exempt share of wages is from U.S. Census Bureau, Economic Census (1997, 2002, and 2007).

*Notes*: Industries are listed as classified by the North American Industry Classification System (NAICS). Industries 541710 (physical, engineering, and biological research services) and 541720 (research and development in the social sciences and humanities) are also included in the Economic Census, but the authors believe these data are flawed.

**Table 2.14.** Nonprofit Wages Covered by Unemployment Insurance for Six-Digit Industries with Tax Status Identified in the Economic Census, 2004–10 ($ millions)

| NAICS code | Industry | 2004 | 2005 | 2006 | 2007 | 2008 | 2009 | 2010 |
|---|---|---|---|---|---|---|---|---|
| 541110 | Offices of lawyers | 1,158.7 | 1,203.7 | 1,263.7 | 1,339.5 | 1,392.9 | 1,351.6 | 1,352.9 |
| 611110 | Elementary and secondary schools | 16,516.0 | 17,553.2 | 18,865.1 | 20,462.6 | 22,133.0 | 23,166.6 | 23,352.8 |
| 611210 | Junior colleges | 266.0 | 269.5 | 256.4 | 228.6 | 230.4 | 243.1 | 261.4 |
| 611310 | Colleges, universities, and professional schools | 38,912.4 | 40,685.4 | 43,001.1 | 46,012.4 | 49,138.1 | 51,792.6 | 53,356.9 |
| 611410 | Business and secretarial schools | 48.3 | 49.0 | 47.0 | 47.4 | 52.4 | 64.1 | 70.1 |
| 611420 | Computer training | 28.7 | 30.2 | 30.1 | 31.5 | 31.3 | 29.2 | 28.6 |
| 611430 | Professional and management development training | 417.9 | 456.7 | 506.4 | 550.9 | 574.0 | 543.2 | 559.5 |
| 611511 | Cosmetology and barber schools | 11.8 | 10.2 | 8.6 | 6.5 | 7.1 | 7.8 | 9.1 |
| 611512 | Flight training | 15.2 | 19.6 | 24.1 | 30.2 | 34.0 | 32.3 | 31.8 |
| 611513 | Apprenticeship training | 313.2 | 333.3 | 357.2 | 403.5 | 438.6 | 427.5 | 429.4 |
| 611519 | Other technical and trade schools | 347.5 | 358.7 | 371.5 | 396.9 | 425.8 | 463.9 | 517.4 |
| 611610 | Fine arts schools | 312.9 | 317.7 | 327.7 | 334.8 | 356.5 | 357.9 | 372.8 |
| 611620 | Sports and recreation instruction | 144.7 | 155.5 | 169.0 | 181.1 | 192.9 | 194.7 | 202.9 |
| 611630 | Language schools | 77.6 | 75.8 | 82.6 | 97.8 | 116.8 | 127.5 | 143.9 |
| 611691 | Exam preparation and tutoring | 223.1 | 260.0 | 292.9 | 331.4 | 367.5 | 377.8 | 407.5 |
| 611692 | Automobile driving schools | 18.6 | 17.4 | 17.2 | 16.4 | 16.7 | 16.4 | 16.8 |
| 611699 | All other miscellaneous schools and instruction | 391.3 | 420.2 | 451.8 | 465.0 | 482.6 | 488.9 | 510.3 |
| 611710 | Educational support services | 1,056.1 | 1,197.8 | 1,380.6 | 1,561.8 | 1,763.1 | 1,863.4 | 2,016.8 |
| 621410 | Family planning centers | 475.9 | 439.3 | 545.1 | 550.2 | 594.8 | 615.7 | 614.7 |

|  |  | | | | | | | |
|---|---|---|---|---|---|---|---|---|
| 621420 | Outpatient mental health and substance abuse centers | 3,736.2 | 3,983.0 | 4,145.9 | 4,396.4 | 4,661.9 | 4,783.6 | 4,966.4 |
| 621491 | HMO medical centers | 2,929.3 | 3,239.1 | 3,648.0 | 3,872.1 | 3,984.4 | 4,203.8 | 7,514.8 |
| 621492 | Kidney dialysis center | 346.4 | 367.5 | 412.7 | 415.1 | 468.7 | 498.2 | 526.3 |
| 621493 | Freestanding ambulatory surgical and emergency centers | 553.8 | 614.1 | 720.7 | 789.5 | 854.4 | 919.6 | 957.0 |
| 621498 | All other outpatient care centers | 2,224.2 | 2,698.2 | 2,940.5 | 3,133.7 | 3,428.5 | 3,678.4 | 3,961.4 |
| 621610 | Home health care services | 5,863.0 | 6,241.7 | 6,728.2 | 7,172.9 | 7,792.2 | 8,580.2 | 9,155.1 |
| 621910 | Ambulance services | 727.9 | 794.5 | 852.3 | 925.2 | 1,000.2 | 1,062.1 | 1,101.1 |
| 621991 | Blood and organ banks | 1,690.2 | 1,772.8 | 1,917.4 | 2,097.1 | 2,347.5 | 2,526.1 | 2,461.1 |
| 621999 | All other miscellaneous ambulatory health care services | 132.2 | 150.9 | 177.5 | 200.8 | 206.7 | 204.1 | 222.5 |
| 622110 | General medical and surgical hospitals | 152,082.3 | 159,899.4 | 169,892.9 | 180,556.1 | 193,581.3 | 202,943.9 | 205,067.3 |
| 622210 | Psychiatric and substance abuse hospitals | 1,586.9 | 1,594.4 | 1,646.6 | 1,683.5 | 1,803.1 | 1,865.4 | 1,897.3 |
| 622310 | Specialty (except psychiatric and substance abuse) hospitals | 4,196.3 | 4,537.3 | 4,952.9 | 5,464.6 | 6,277.5 | 6,751.4 | 7,188.5 |
| 623110 | Nursing care facilities | 10,505.1 | 10,644.6 | 11,017.0 | 11,440.9 | 11,979.6 | 12,327.0 | 12,543.1 |
| 623210 | Residential mental retardation facilities | 5,142.2 | 5,294.1 | 5,589.9 | 5,967.4 | 6,322.2 | 6,517.3 | 6,593.8 |
| 623220 | Residential mental health and substance abuse facilities | 2,874.9 | 2,999.8 | 3,199.3 | 3,436.8 | 3,698.2 | 3,803.4 | 3,871.3 |
| 623311 | Continuing care retirement communities | 4,189.1 | 4,405.5 | 4,646.2 | 4,841.8 | 5,250.4 | 5,721.1 | 5,982.1 |
| 623312 | Homes for the elderly | 1,286.7 | 1,348.7 | 1,415.8 | 1,524.1 | 1,606.0 | 1,646.3 | 1,691.5 |
| 623990 | Other residential care facilities | 3,592.6 | 3,619.3 | 3,723.1 | 3,864.8 | 4,043.0 | 3,998.5 | 3,880.0 |
| 624110 | Child and youth services | 3,453.8 | 3,536.8 | 3,792.5 | 4,092.5 | 4,328.6 | 4,377.4 | 4,462.8 |

(continued)

**Table 2.14.** Nonprofit Wages Covered by Unemployment Insurance for Six-Digit Industries with Tax Status Identified in the Economic Census, 2004–10 ($ millions) *(continued)*

| NAICS code | Industry | 2004 | 2005 | 2006 | 2007 | 2008 | 2009 | 2010 |
|---|---|---|---|---|---|---|---|---|
| 624120 | Services for the elderly and persons with disabilities | 5,304.6 | 5,557.8 | 5,906.3 | 6,158.1 | 6,864.2 | 7,457.5 | 7,952.3 |
| 624190 | Other individual and family services | 6,773.9 | 7,120.6 | 7,557.0 | 8,378.0 | 8,730.4 | 9,082.0 | 9,422.6 |
| 624210 | Community food services | 560.2 | 561.7 | 574.5 | 622.5 | 676.1 | 703.2 | 755.8 |
| 624221 | Temporary shelters | 1,185.2 | 1,240.8 | 1,302.5 | 1,360.5 | 1,431.0 | 1,457.5 | 1,511.9 |
| 624229 | Other community housing services | 602.2 | 641.1 | 698.2 | 749.3 | 816.0 | 874.6 | 968.8 |
| 624230 | Emergency and other relief services | 900.9 | 897.8 | 939.0 | 976.3 | 1,046.1 | 1,032.2 | 1,072.2 |
| 624310 | Vocational rehabilitation services | 5,569.3 | 5,607.0 | 5,829.0 | 6,103.1 | 6,362.5 | 6,505.3 | 6,597.7 |
| 624410 | Child day care services | 5,129.3 | 5,270.0 | 5,475.5 | 5,698.8 | 6,001.3 | 6,092.1 | 6,208.0 |
| 711110 | Theater companies and dinner theaters | 952.9 | 916.6 | 945.3 | 903.2 | 977.7 | 938.3 | 947.7 |
| 711120 | Dance companies | 246.2 | 251.1 | 269.4 | 293.0 | 312.9 | 306.7 | 306.2 |
| 711130 | Musical groups and artists | 954.7 | 959.0 | 1,090.5 | 1,148.0 | 1,241.5 | 1,043.3 | 1,036.8 |
| 711190 | Other performing arts companies | 12.1 | 11.9 | 12.6 | 14.6 | 15.6 | 14.5 | 15.3 |
| 711310 | Promotors of performing arts, sports, and similar events with facilities | 570.4 | 590.7 | 652.5 | 684.1 | 734.1 | 742.5 | 736.2 |
| 711320 | Promotors of performing arts, sports, and similar events without facilities | 165.1 | 174.1 | 165.7 | 167.3 | 176.9 | 167.3 | 174.6 |
| 712110 | Museums | 1,789.2 | 1,878.7 | 1,989.2 | 2,135.8 | 2,308.8 | 2,232.3 | 2,183.0 |
| 712120 | Historical sites | 299.9 | 303.0 | 317.4 | 340.7 | 367.1 | 372.7 | 406.2 |

| NAICS | Industry | | | | | | | |
|---|---|---|---|---|---|---|---|---|
| 712130 | Zoos and botanical gardens | 638.2 | 668.6 | 719.6 | 778.6 | 828.1 | 826.7 | 850.9 |
| 712190 | Nature parks and other similar institutions | 92.9 | 95.8 | 97.6 | 117.7 | 130.0 | 137.7 | 146.0 |
| 713910 | Golf courses and country clubs | 2,793.7 | 2,938.5 | 3,093.4 | 3,300.4 | 3,427.7 | 3,306.4 | 3,294.3 |
| 713940 | Fitness and recreational sports centers | 1,885.7 | 2,009.7 | 2,155.3 | 2,316.1 | 2,350.8 | 2,350.8 | 2,253.4 |
| 713990 | All other amusement and recreation industries | 427.6 | 471.1 | 539.1 | 600.9 | 607.0 | 586.3 | 605.5 |
| 813110 | Religious organizations | 3,739.7 | 3,914.0 | 4,169.7 | 4,518.8 | 4,806.8 | 4,667.8 | 4,856.3 |
| 813211 | Grantmaking foundations | 1,905.5 | 2,036.4 | 2,213.0 | 2,500.4 | 2,795.9 | 2,930.4 | 3,091.3 |
| 813212 | Voluntary health organizations | 1,420.4 | 1,491.0 | 1,591.8 | 1,785.7 | 1,908.8 | 1,941.1 | 1,923.0 |
| 813219 | Other grantmaking and giving services | 1,451.8 | 1,471.1 | 1,499.4 | 1,554.4 | 1,621.4 | 1,600.9 | 1,564.8 |
| 813311 | Human rights organizations | 1,300.7 | 1,334.4 | 1,404.6 | 1,522.8 | 1,660.9 | 1,726.6 | 1,772.3 |
| 813312 | Environment, conservation, and wildlife organizations | 1,071.4 | 1,179.4 | 1,265.7 | 1,512.4 | 1,697.6 | 1,807.5 | 1,871.7 |
| 813319 | Other social advocacy organizations | 2,510.8 | 2,671.2 | 2,806.4 | 3,033.8 | 3,343.0 | 3,471.8 | 3,668.8 |
| 813410 | Civic and social organizations | 6,162.0 | 6,297.6 | 6,525.7 | 6,770.1 | 6,969.0 | 6,754.5 | 6,679.1 |
| 813910 | Business associations | 6,110.1 | 6,464.9 | 6,854.7 | 7,214.8 | 7,570.9 | 7,541.4 | 7,515.0 |
| 813920 | Professional organizations | 4,083.2 | 4,157.4 | 4,349.7 | 4,678.4 | 4,997.2 | 5,135.2 | 5,261.4 |
| 813930 | Labor unions and similar labor organizations | 3,933.2 | 3,968.1 | 4,121.4 | 4,249.8 | 4,474.0 | 4,472.7 | 4,418.0 |
| 813940 | Political organizations | 378.0 | 254.6 | 413.6 | 356.2 | 499.1 | 327.7 | 459.5 |
| 813990 | Other similar organizations (except business, professional, labor, and political organizations) | 2,511.2 | 2,675.8 | 2,869.2 | 3,092.1 | 3,341.2 | 3,355.2 | 3,436.0 |

*Sources:* Authors' estimates based on private wages from the U.S. Department of Labor, Bureau of Labor Statistics, Quarterly Census of Employment and Wages (1990–2011). Tax-exempt share of wages is from U.S. Census Bureau, Economic Census (1997, 2002, and 2007).
*Notes:* Industries are listed as classified by the North American Industry Classification System (NAICS). Industries 541710 (physical, engineering, and biological research services) and 541720 (research and development in the social sciences and humanities) are also included in the Economic Census, but the authors believe these data are flawed.

**Table 2.15.** Nonprofit Employment Covered by Unemployment Insurance for Six-Digit Industries with Tax Status Identified in the Economic Census, 1990–96 (millions)

| NAICS code | Industry | 1990 | 1991 | 1992 | 1993 | 1994 | 1995 | 1996 |
|---|---|---|---|---|---|---|---|---|
| 541110 | Offices of lawyers | 21,966 | 21,648 | 21,771 | 21,962 | 22,038 | 21,946 | 22,070 |
| 611110 | Elementary and secondary schools | 329,116 | 336,959 | 341,525 | 356,556 | 372,349 | 389,257 | 405,399 |
| 611210 | Junior colleges | 9,484 | 11,295 | 11,229 | 11,293 | 11,365 | 11,138 | 11,270 |
| 611310 | Colleges, universities, and professional schools | 703,830 | 703,183 | 706,590 | 706,009 | 720,293 | 728,292 | 750,446 |
| 611410 | Business and secretarial schools | 1,424 | 1,163 | 1,031 | 902 | 856 | 803 | 736 |
| 611420 | Computer training | 129 | 126 | 140 | 157 | 183 | 226 | 260 |
| 611430 | Professional and management development training | 5,429 | 5,301 | 5,664 | 6,007 | 6,098 | 6,417 | 6,857 |
| 611511 | Cosmetology and barber schools | 691 | 653 | 578 | 530 | 500 | 460 | 441 |
| 611512 | Flight training | 441 | 411 | 375 | 347 | 351 | 352 | 336 |
| 611513 | Apprenticeship training | 9,924 | 8,019 | 6,952 | 6,365 | 5,807 | 5,550 | 5,575 |
| 611519 | Other technical and trade schools | 5,923 | 5,839 | 5,840 | 6,038 | 6,142 | 6,365 | 6,833 |
| 611610 | Fine arts schools | 8,514 | 8,504 | 8,846 | 9,236 | 9,931 | 10,395 | 10,949 |
| 611620 | Sports and recreation instruction | 2,791 | 2,823 | 3,050 | 3,446 | 3,886 | 4,128 | 4,357 |
| 611630 | Language schools | 1,964 | 2,212 | 2,444 | 2,606 | 2,761 | 2,869 | 3,138 |
| 611691 | Exam preparation and tutoring | 1,700 | 1,686 | 1,859 | 2,109 | 2,299 | 2,528 | 2,835 |
| 611692 | Automobile driving schools | 287 | 295 | 309 | 326 | 341 | 360 | 370 |
| 611699 | All other miscellaneous schools and instruction | 5,216 | 5,550 | 5,677 | 6,115 | 6,556 | 6,897 | 7,565 |
| 611710 | Educational support services | 9,595 | 9,756 | 10,114 | 10,589 | 11,113 | 12,031 | 13,648 |
| 621410 | Family planning centers | 12,426 | 14,170 | 15,925 | 16,636 | 17,208 | 17,839 | 18,183 |
| 621420 | Outpatient mental health and substance abuse centers | 67,942 | 70,394 | 73,697 | 79,869 | 86,216 | 91,778 | 95,639 |

|  |  | | | | | | |
|------|----------|---|---|---|---|---|---|
| 621491 | HMO medical centers | 64,728 | 63,579 | 61,342 | 62,993 | 64,050 | 65,014 |
| 621492 | Kidney dialysis center | 3,905 | 4,716 | 5,153 | 5,588 | 6,067 | 6,656 |
| 621493 | Freestanding ambulatory surgical and emergency centers | 6,064 | 8,536 | 8,549 | 9,135 | 9,889 | 10,143 |
| 621498 | All other outpatient care centers | 33,145 | 33,376 | 35,409 | 37,580 | 38,298 | 39,176 |
| 621610 | Home health care services | 97,775 | 132,902 | 151,272 | 171,012 | 189,312 | 201,104 |
| 621910 | Ambulance services | 10,452 | 11,707 | 12,375 | 13,420 | 14,490 | 16,215 |
| 621991 | Blood and organ banks | 24,607 | 25,891 | 28,543 | 30,258 | 31,268 | 30,950 |
| 621999 | All other miscellaneous ambulatory health care services | 1,087 | 1,168 | 1,257 | 1,405 | 1,476 | 1,655 |
| 622110 | General medical and surgical hospitals | 2,773,154 | 2,924,663 | 2,972,007 | 2,977,071 | 2,991,660 | 3,049,298 |
| 622210 | Psychiatric and substance abuse hospitals | 45,923 | 45,277 | 43,059 | 41,857 | 39,652 | 37,561 |
| 622310 | Specialty (except psychiatric and substance abuse) hospitals | 64,735 | 73,905 | 76,683 | 77,751 | 79,929 | 84,915 |
| 623110 | Nursing care facilities | 309,098 | 335,935 | 347,769 | 360,773 | 370,478 | 380,673 |
| 623210 | Residential mental retardation facilities | 134,389 | 152,179 | 155,688 | 162,972 | 172,990 | 178,882 |
| 623220 | Residential mental health and substance abuse facilities | 65,079 | 68,441 | 71,624 | 73,681 | 78,304 | 80,551 |
| 623311 | Continuing care retirement communities | 130,789 | 138,398 | 141,377 | 141,793 | 144,261 | 147,885 |
| 623312 | Homes for the elderly | 39,615 | 45,222 | 47,705 | 50,193 | 52,181 | 56,737 |
| 623990 | Other residential care facilities | 77,107 | 87,582 | 92,840 | 97,765 | 106,393 | 111,835 |
| 624110 | Child and youth services | 66,429 | 76,815 | 83,340 | 90,699 | 96,548 | 100,864 |
| 624120 | Services for the elderly and persons with disabilities | 154,189 | 175,504 | 185,678 | 193,956 | 200,822 | 207,651 |

*(continued)*

**Table 2.15.** Nonprofit Employment Covered by Unemployment Insurance for Six-Digit Industries with Tax Status Identified in the Economic Census, 1990–96 (millions) *(continued)*

| NAICS code | Industry | 1990 | 1991 | 1992 | 1993 | 1994 | 1995 | 1996 |
|---|---|---|---|---|---|---|---|---|
| 624190 | Other individual and family services | 133,295 | 136,903 | 144,449 | 156,107 | 167,573 | 180,086 | 188,013 |
| 624210 | Community food services | 21,714 | 25,692 | 26,923 | 27,969 | 28,939 | 28,205 | 27,501 |
| 624221 | Temporary shelters | 19,603 | 22,262 | 26,180 | 27,615 | 30,183 | 32,855 | 33,245 |
| 624229 | Other community housing services | 8,565 | 9,789 | 10,270 | 11,360 | 12,955 | 14,014 | 14,437 |
| 624230 | Emergency and other relief services | 30,906 | 27,212 | 26,690 | 24,760 | 22,770 | 23,181 | 23,120 |
| 624310 | Vocational rehabilitation services | 197,099 | 195,323 | 200,145 | 209,162 | 219,109 | 228,526 | 228,719 |
| 624410 | Child care services | 149,323 | 158,585 | 169,072 | 183,081 | 195,941 | 206,577 | 213,679 |
| 711110 | Theater companies and dinner theaters | 200,771 | 180,382 | 124,457 | 92,607 | 81,483 | 67,841 | 57,630 |
| 711120 | Dance companies | 4,836 | 5,113 | 5,025 | 5,193 | 5,132 | 5,409 | 5,386 |
| 711130 | Musical groups and artists | 27,906 | 25,846 | 24,990 | 26,236 | 27,108 | 27,435 | 27,164 |
| 711190 | Other performing arts companies | 238 | 285 | 285 | 285 | 329 | 316 | 370 |
| 711310 | Promotors of performing arts, sports, and similar events with facilities | 13,503 | 12,538 | 11,267 | 11,269 | 12,143 | 13,188 | 14,012 |
| 711320 | Promoters of performing arts, sports, and similar events without facilities | 3,101 | 2,378 | 2,323 | 2,347 | 2,565 | 2,713 | 2,814 |
| 712110 | Museums | 42,981 | 42,400 | 44,292 | 46,007 | 47,820 | 49,190 | 51,443 |
| 712120 | Historical sites | 8,025 | 8,635 | 8,525 | 8,796 | 9,221 | 9,334 | 9,446 |
| 712130 | Zoos and botanical gardens | 13,512 | 13,489 | 15,024 | 15,817 | 16,087 | 16,922 | 17,810 |

| NAICS | Industry | | | | | | | |
|---|---|---|---|---|---|---|---|---|
| 712190 | Nature parks and other similar institutions | 2,431 | 2,350 | 2,258 | 2,552 | 2,867 | 3,244 | 3,294 |
| 713910 | Golf courses and country clubs | 70,534 | 73,994 | 77,309 | 80,575 | 85,249 | 90,074 | 94,238 |
| 713940 | Fitness and recreational sports centers | 68,100 | 67,752 | 69,280 | 71,935 | 74,967 | 78,176 | 81,503 |
| 713990 | All other amusement and recreation industries | 12,053 | 12,503 | 13,311 | 14,265 | 15,758 | 16,701 | 17,423 |
| 813110 | Religious organizations | 100,138 | 98,731 | 103,009 | 105,878 | 109,514 | 114,076 | 119,772 |
| 813211 | Grantmaking foundations | 26,972 | 26,395 | 27,238 | 28,221 | 28,828 | 30,216 | 32,893 |
| 813212 | Voluntary health organizations | 28,476 | 26,542 | 26,961 | 28,236 | 32,783 | 33,791 | 33,960 |
| 813219 | Other grantmaking and giving services | 38,508 | 36,088 | 37,425 | 37,157 | 37,502 | 38,450 | 38,929 |
| 813311 | Human rights organizations | 30,853 | 31,085 | 32,111 | 32,467 | 33,644 | 34,308 | 35,149 |
| 813312 | Environment, conservation, and wildlife organizations | 23,531 | 21,203 | 20,605 | 20,241 | 20,655 | 21,285 | 21,792 |
| 813319 | Other social advocacy organizations | 59,269 | 55,940 | 57,075 | 59,307 | 61,738 | 64,231 | 64,786 |
| 813410 | Civic and social organizations | 348,733 | 336,883 | 342,977 | 353,242 | 361,468 | 371,331 | 374,021 |
| 813910 | Business associations | 108,835 | 108,530 | 110,222 | 110,278 | 111,864 | 113,867 | 115,012 |
| 813920 | Professional organizations | 51,804 | 52,802 | 53,048 | 54,421 | 55,634 | 57,410 | 58,530 |
| 813930 | Labor unions and similar labor organizations | 137,755 | 140,111 | 139,771 | 139,622 | 139,597 | 139,934 | 141,993 |
| 813940 | Political organizations | 7,641 | 4,846 | 7,685 | 5,213 | 8,827 | 5,600 | 8,695 |
| 813990 | Other similar organizations (except business, professional, labor, and political organizations) | 81,949 | 83,048 | 82,825 | 81,471 | 80,832 | 81,136 | 81,854 |

*Sources*: Authors' estimates based on private employment from the U.S. Department of Labor, Bureau of Labor Statistics, Quarterly Census of Employment and Wages (1990–2011). Tax-exempt share of employment from the U.S. Census Bureau, Economic Census (1997, 2002, and 2007).

*Notes*: Industries are listed as classified by the North American Industry Classification System (NAICS). Industries 541710 (physical, engineering, and biological research services) and 541720 (research and development in the social sciences and humanities) are also included in the Economic Census, but the authors believe these data are flawed.

**Table 2.16.** Nonprofit Employment Covered by Unemployment Insurance for Six-Digit Industries with Tax Status Identified in the Economic Census, 1997–2003 (millions)

| NAICS code | Industry | 1997 | 1998 | 1999 | 2000 | 2001 | 2002 | 2003 |
|---|---|---|---|---|---|---|---|---|
| 541110 | Offices of lawyers | 22,482 | 23,195 | 23,690 | 24,106 | 24,669 | 25,156 | 25,559 |
| 611110 | Elementary and secondary schools | 424,711 | 444,761 | 468,747 | 491,787 | 513,820 | 536,094 | 555,470 |
| 611210 | Junior colleges | 11,666 | 11,260 | 10,213 | 9,574 | 9,051 | 7,836 | 7,589 |
| 611310 | Colleges, universities, and professional schools | 771,413 | 800,408 | 811,627 | 823,716 | 844,685 | 865,305 | 887,753 |
| 611410 | Business and secretarial schools | 738 | 866 | 999 | 1,131 | 1,322 | 1,490 | 1,432 |
| 611420 | Computer training | 307 | 482 | 705 | 918 | 980 | 964 | 904 |
| 611430 | Professional and management development training | 7,302 | 8,076 | 8,822 | 10,071 | 10,372 | 10,614 | 10,515 |
| 611511 | Cosmetology and barber schools | 401 | 437 | 476 | 535 | 629 | 718 | 620 |
| 611512 | Flight training | 354 | 391 | 441 | 489 | 493 | 455 | 530 |
| 611513 | Apprenticeship training | 5,903 | 6,182 | 6,797 | 7,494 | 7,972 | 8,955 | 9,404 |
| 611519 | Other technical and trade schools | 7,255 | 7,922 | 8,503 | 9,330 | 10,105 | 10,746 | 10,769 |
| 611610 | Fine arts schools | 11,407 | 12,312 | 13,449 | 14,632 | 15,914 | 17,174 | 17,370 |
| 611620 | Sports and recreation instruction | 4,512 | 5,098 | 5,827 | 6,729 | 7,947 | 9,410 | 9,808 |
| 611630 | Language schools | 3,395 | 3,856 | 4,321 | 4,680 | 5,193 | 5,139 | 5,415 |
| 611691 | Exam preparation and tutoring | 3,232 | 4,387 | 5,642 | 7,097 | 8,363 | 9,682 | 10,326 |
| 611692 | Automobile driving schools | 394 | 556 | 725 | 925 | 1,141 | 1,357 | 1,189 |
| 611699 | All other miscellaneous schools and instruction | 8,195 | 9,023 | 10,445 | 12,377 | 14,579 | 16,611 | 16,163 |
| 611710 | Educational support services | 14,739 | 15,334 | 16,952 | 19,012 | 21,639 | 23,775 | 26,827 |
| 621410 | Family planning centers | 18,647 | 18,573 | 18,435 | 18,371 | 18,386 | 18,475 | 16,958 |
| 621420 | Outpatient mental health and substance abuse centers | 99,845 | 102,474 | 106,203 | 109,127 | 112,214 | 115,740 | 119,214 |

|  |  | | | | | | |
|---|---|---|---|---|---|---|---|
| 621491 | HMO medical centers | 62,768 | 60,457 | 55,581 | 52,409 | 53,055 | 53,268 | 54,620 |
| 621492 | Kidney dialysis center | 7,478 | 7,660 | 7,671 | 8,115 | 8,512 | 8,640 | 8,798 |
| 621493 | Freestanding ambulatory surgical and emergency centers | 10,026 | 9,989 | 9,282 | 9,350 | 9,313 | 9,626 | 10,141 |
| 621498 | All other outpatient care centers | 39,993 | 42,079 | 42,626 | 44,131 | 45,545 | 46,738 | 50,524 |
| 621610 | Home health care services | 209,433 | 197,168 | 181,675 | 180,117 | 182,336 | 194,771 | 200,033 |
| 621910 | Ambulance services | 17,570 | 19,894 | 21,809 | 24,089 | 26,761 | 29,625 | 30,881 |
| 621991 | Blood and organ banks | 31,341 | 33,475 | 34,283 | 36,489 | 40,195 | 43,217 | 44,657 |
| 621999 | All other miscellaneous ambulatory health care services | 1,819 | 2,071 | 2,200 | 2,522 | 2,795 | 3,139 | 3,307 |
| 622110 | General medical and surgical hospitals | 3,103,347 | 3,191,034 | 3,254,892 | 3,283,586 | 3,364,327 | 3,451,617 | 3,519,099 |
| 622210 | Psychiatric and substance abuse hospitals | 36,060 | 38,814 | 40,555 | 40,492 | 42,843 | 46,345 | 44,579 |
| 622310 | Specialty (except psychiatric and substance abuse) hospitals | 89,041 | 89,559 | 84,467 | 81,525 | 83,229 | 83,408 | 88,139 |
| 623110 | Nursing care facilities | 384,409 | 390,224 | 388,366 | 391,024 | 401,026 | 410,649 | 405,663 |
| 623210 | Residential mental retardation facilities | 185,242 | 189,557 | 199,429 | 206,112 | 216,175 | 225,300 | 229,930 |
| 623220 | Residential mental health and substance abuse facilities | 84,517 | 89,942 | 94,816 | 98,683 | 103,834 | 108,064 | 110,530 |
| 623311 | Continuing care retirement communities | 147,151 | 145,063 | 143,281 | 146,217 | 149,331 | 156,890 | 170,516 |
| 623312 | Homes for the elderly | 60,633 | 62,153 | 63,152 | 64,224 | 63,302 | 62,016 | 62,506 |
| 623990 | Other residential care facilities | 117,640 | 121,905 | 128,973 | 134,302 | 139,843 | 141,715 | 140,378 |
| 624110 | Child and youth services | 104,380 | 109,579 | 116,836 | 124,075 | 133,087 | 133,226 | 136,737 |
| 624120 | Services for the elderly and persons with disabilities | 215,974 | 221,477 | 224,921 | 231,452 | 238,882 | 255,725 | 261,898 |

*(continued)*

**Table 2.16.** Nonprofit Employment Covered by Unemployment Insurance for Six-Digit Industries with Tax Status Identified in the Economic Census, 1997–2003 (millions) *(continued)*

| NAICS code | Industry | 1997 | 1998 | 1999 | 2000 | 2001 | 2002 | 2003 |
|---|---|---|---|---|---|---|---|---|
| 624190 | Other individual and family services | 196,671 | 204,871 | 216,521 | 229,538 | 246,400 | 260,113 | 266,157 |
| 624210 | Community food services | 25,799 | 27,121 | 28,324 | 29,511 | 30,753 | 27,940 | 27,269 |
| 624221 | Temporary shelters | 35,166 | 38,345 | 40,672 | 42,656 | 45,480 | 48,666 | 50,085 |
| 624229 | Other community housing services | 15,521 | 16,530 | 17,685 | 18,663 | 19,002 | 20,925 | 21,316 |
| 624230 | Emergency and other relief services | 22,904 | 23,664 | 24,905 | 25,959 | 27,116 | 27,933 | 26,647 |
| 624310 | Vocational rehabilitation services | 238,753 | 247,782 | 257,504 | 264,297 | 271,434 | 273,857 | 274,404 |
| 624410 | Child care services | 223,511 | 240,445 | 255,470 | 271,062 | 287,053 | 297,679 | 292,538 |
| 711110 | Theater companies and dinner theaters | 48,386 | 44,044 | 38,278 | 39,837 | 40,461 | 38,762 | 37,580 |
| 711120 | Dance companies | 5,794 | 5,835 | 6,065 | 6,437 | 6,748 | 6,640 | 6,974 |
| 711130 | Musical groups and artists | 27,374 | 28,707 | 29,147 | 30,229 | 29,167 | 28,241 | 27,291 |
| 711190 | Other performing arts companies | 406 | 398 | 395 | 355 | 325 | 319 | 412 |
| 711310 | Promoters of performing arts, sports, and similar events with facilities | 14,216 | 13,775 | 13,719 | 14,076 | 14,099 | 14,289 | 15,442 |
| 711320 | Promoters of performing arts, sports, and similar events without facilities | 2,950 | 3,590 | 4,535 | 5,914 | 7,284 | 8,770 | 7,559 |
| 712110 | Museums | 54,370 | 56,872 | 60,041 | 62,820 | 65,620 | 65,806 | 65,585 |
| 712120 | Historical sites | 9,947 | 10,374 | 10,802 | 11,466 | 11,658 | 11,628 | 11,859 |
| 712130 | Zoos and botancial gardens | 19,000 | 20,084 | 21,794 | 22,619 | 22,888 | 22,679 | 22,804 |
| 712190 | Nature parks and other similar institutions | 3,454 | 3,419 | 3,539 | 3,917 | 4,140 | 4,336 | 4,477 |

| NAICS | Industry | | | | | | |
|---|---|---|---|---|---|---|---|
| 713910 | Golf courses and country clubs | 99,710 | 104,501 | 107,468 | 112,362 | 114,112 | 116,614 | 120,427 |
| 713940 | Fitness and recreational sports centers | 85,242 | 92,136 | 99,469 | 106,758 | 113,596 | 118,901 | 126,149 |
| 713990 | All other amusement and recreation industries | 17,950 | 19,506 | 20,228 | 21,183 | 22,022 | 23,313 | 25,118 |
| 813110 | Religious organizations | 130,366 | 135,897 | 145,352 | 151,810 | 159,212 | 166,785 | 172,669 |
| 813211 | Grantmaking foundations | 33,614 | 35,399 | 37,747 | 39,540 | 42,080 | 44,396 | 41,453 |
| 813212 | Voluntary health organizations | 33,467 | 33,207 | 33,734 | 35,061 | 37,795 | 37,295 | 37,833 |
| 813219 | Other grantmaking and giving services | 40,695 | 38,526 | 40,060 | 41,903 | 43,687 | 43,508 | 42,527 |
| 813311 | Human rights organizations | 35,615 | 37,811 | 40,621 | 40,486 | 41,956 | 43,282 | 43,600 |
| 813312 | Environment, conservation, and wildlife organizations | 22,876 | 23,856 | 25,393 | 26,727 | 27,991 | 30,235 | 33,123 |
| 813319 | Other social advocacy organizations | 66,441 | 69,103 | 73,210 | 78,308 | 83,914 | 85,063 | 83,602 |
| 813410 | Civic and social organizations | 382,585 | 379,212 | 387,132 | 401,243 | 411,679 | 419,690 | 416,569 |
| 813910 | Business associations | 115,265 | 117,490 | 119,619 | 121,378 | 121,232 | 119,146 | 118,583 |
| 813920 | Professional organizations | 60,395 | 63,178 | 65,881 | 68,051 | 69,707 | 72,333 | 71,708 |
| 813930 | Labor unions and similar labor organizations | 142,447 | 141,582 | 141,659 | 143,340 | 142,221 | 141,300 | 139,149 |
| 813940 | Political organizations | 5,404 | 7,713 | 5,859 | 8,191 | 5,866 | 9,395 | 6,196 |
| 813990 | Other similar organizations (except business, professional, labor, and political organizations) | 82,941 | 84,218 | 83,601 | 84,926 | 85,646 | 86,143 | 87,481 |

*Sources*: Authors' estimates based on private employment from the U.S. Department of Labor, Bureau of Labor Statistics, Quarterly Census of Employment and Wages (1990–2011). Tax-exempt share of employment from the U.S. Census Bureau, Economic Census (1997, 2002, and 2007).
*Notes*: Industries are listed as classified by the North American Industry Classification System (NAICS). Industries 541710 (physical, engineering, and biological research services) and 541720 (research and development in the social sciences and humanities) are also included in the Economic Census, but the authors believe these data are flawed.

**Table 2.17.**   Nonprofit Employment Covered by Unemployment Insurance for Six-Digit Industries with Tax Status Identified in the Economic Census, 2004–10 (millions)

| NAICS code | Industry | 2004 | 2005 | 2006 | 2007 | 2008 | 2009 | 2010 |
|---|---|---|---|---|---|---|---|---|
| 541110 | Offices of lawyers | 25,755 | 25,828 | 25,842 | 25,972 | 26,007 | 25,280 | 24,991 |
| 611110 | Elementary and secondary schools | 570,964 | 590,152 | 607,855 | 631,710 | 655,568 | 665,890 | 663,513 |
| 611210 | Junior colleges | 7,681 | 7,604 | 7,037 | 6,140 | 6,197 | 6,681 | 7,404 |
| 611310 | Colleges, universities, and professional schools | 904,399 | 914,968 | 934,536 | 956,634 | 980,277 | 1,007,926 | 1,019,282 |
| 611410 | Business and secretarial schools | 1,454 | 1,417 | 1,298 | 1,171 | 1,226 | 1,391 | 1,489 |
| 611420 | Computer training | 917 | 958 | 938 | 958 | 934 | 875 | 860 |
| 611430 | Professional and management development training | 10,028 | 10,249 | 10,473 | 10,861 | 11,306 | 11,020 | 11,098 |
| 611511 | Cosmetology and barber schools | 536 | 438 | 337 | 229 | 239 | 253 | 276 |
| 611512 | Flight training | 629 | 759 | 857 | 1,031 | 1,072 | 1,049 | 1,147 |
| 611513 | Apprenticeship training | 9,775 | 9,800 | 9,816 | 10,774 | 11,367 | 10,841 | 10,569 |
| 611519 | Other technical and trade schools | 10,757 | 10,861 | 10,538 | 10,584 | 11,097 | 11,614 | 12,642 |
| 611610 | Fine arts schools | 17,230 | 17,201 | 17,060 | 16,978 | 17,690 | 17,756 | 18,128 |
| 611620 | Sports and recreation instruction | 10,305 | 10,590 | 10,762 | 10,886 | 11,346 | 11,351 | 11,720 |
| 611630 | Language schools | 5,432 | 5,301 | 5,527 | 5,924 | 6,786 | 6,725 | 7,077 |
| 611691 | Exam preparation and tutoring | 11,348 | 12,555 | 13,629 | 15,220 | 16,605 | 16,780 | 17,802 |
| 611692 | Automobile driving schools | 1,061 | 919 | 809 | 684 | 688 | 689 | 697 |
| 611699 | All other miscellaneous schools and instruction | 15,687 | 16,166 | 16,228 | 16,151 | 16,690 | 16,951 | 17,725 |
| 611710 | Educational support services | 30,322 | 33,136 | 34,605 | 35,233 | 38,709 | 40,812 | 43,091 |
| 621410 | Family planning centers | 16,165 | 14,963 | 15,610 | 15,252 | 15,648 | 15,652 | 15,654 |
| 621420 | Outpatient mental health and substance abuse centers | 121,242 | 125,961 | 127,018 | 129,498 | 134,261 | 135,230 | 138,439 |

|  |  | | | | | | |
|---|---|---|---|---|---|---|---|
| 621491 | HMO medical centers | 55,890 | 57,436 | 60,112 | 59,459 | 58,821 | 59,390 | 87,658 |
| 621492 | Kidney dialysis center | 8,884 | 8,946 | 9,105 | 9,252 | 10,047 | 10,280 | 10,729 |
| 621493 | Freestanding ambulatory surgical and emergency centers | 10,923 | 11,684 | 12,848 | 13,554 | 14,338 | 15,062 | 15,705 |
| 621498 | All other outpatient care centers | 53,244 | 60,518 | 63,410 | 66,160 | 68,969 | 71,500 | 76,121 |
| 621610 | Home health care services | 203,930 | 207,070 | 208,956 | 209,660 | 219,487 | 235,457 | 248,087 |
| 621910 | Ambulance services | 31,372 | 32,299 | 32,933 | 33,899 | 35,107 | 36,571 | 37,736 |
| 621991 | Blood and organ banks | 43,777 | 44,389 | 45,634 | 48,508 | 52,338 | 55,360 | 52,697 |
| 621999 | All other miscellaneous ambulatory health care services | 3,458 | 3,746 | 4,152 | 4,545 | 4,604 | 4,473 | 4,749 |
| 622110 | General medical and surgical hospitals | 3,549,433 | 3,585,339 | 3,628,419 | 3,696,036 | 3,783,237 | 3,823,029 | 3,819,401 |
| 622210 | Psychiatric and substance abuse hospitals | 42,700 | 40,380 | 38,930 | 36,499 | 37,622 | 38,149 | 38,432 |
| 622310 | Specialty (except psychiatric and substance abuse) hospitals | 88,753 | 91,098 | 94,420 | 99,952 | 107,370 | 111,627 | 117,781 |
| 623110 | Nursing care facilities | 402,611 | 397,903 | 393,721 | 393,934 | 399,134 | 405,263 | 408,528 |
| 623210 | Residential mental retardation facilities | 233,375 | 236,063 | 241,437 | 248,822 | 256,793 | 263,980 | 267,350 |
| 623220 | Residential mental health and substance abuse facilities | 111,170 | 112,530 | 116,006 | 121,443 | 126,392 | 128,646 | 130,284 |
| 623311 | Continuing care retirement communities | 177,492 | 184,703 | 189,562 | 191,056 | 200,673 | 215,778 | 225,378 |
| 623312 | Homes for the elderly | 62,772 | 63,644 | 64,518 | 66,439 | 68,363 | 69,991 | 71,287 |
| 623990 | Other residential care facilities | 140,025 | 139,617 | 138,311 | 138,957 | 141,471 | 138,568 | 134,860 |
| 624110 | Child and youth services | 136,342 | 136,890 | 140,700 | 148,378 | 151,382 | 151,043 | 152,687 |
| 624120 | Services for the elderly and persons with disabilities | 269,838 | 281,242 | 287,291 | 289,038 | 315,875 | 340,830 | 364,491 |

(continued)

**Table 2.17.** Nonprofit Employment Covered by Unemployment Insurance for Six-Digit Industries with Tax Status Identified in the Economic Census, 2004–10 (millions) *(continued)*

| NAICS code | Industry | 2004 | 2005 | 2006 | 2007 | 2008 | 2009 | 2010 |
|---|---|---|---|---|---|---|---|---|
| 624190 | Other individual and family services | 270,550 | 276,626 | 283,076 | 299,224 | 306,528 | 313,684 | 319,983 |
| 624210 | Community food services | 26,905 | 25,906 | 25,035 | 25,924 | 26,503 | 26,312 | 27,463 |
| 624221 | Temporary shelters | 51,609 | 52,690 | 53,454 | 53,630 | 54,768 | 54,803 | 56,303 |
| 624229 | Other community housing services | 20,643 | 21,451 | 22,424 | 23,069 | 24,050 | 25,348 | 27,110 |
| 624230 | Emergency and other relief services | 27,218 | 25,945 | 25,756 | 25,442 | 25,689 | 25,163 | 25,704 |
| 624310 | Vocational rehabilitation services | 276,315 | 275,866 | 277,678 | 280,014 | 284,247 | 289,879 | 292,969 |
| 624410 | Child care services | 287,497 | 288,540 | 290,389 | 292,036 | 298,227 | 293,767 | 293,240 |
| 711110 | Theater companies and dinner theaters | 35,460 | 33,711 | 33,651 | 32,876 | 33,687 | 31,951 | 31,615 |
| 711120 | Dance companies | 7,696 | 7,328 | 7,537 | 7,809 | 8,295 | 8,101 | 8,103 |
| 711130 | Musical groups and artists | 27,166 | 26,882 | 26,697 | 26,977 | 26,443 | 24,422 | 23,688 |
| 711190 | Other performing arts companies | 428 | 442 | 502 | 602 | 651 | 646 | 671 |
| 711310 | Promotors of performing arts, sports, and similar events with facilities | 16,891 | 17,568 | 18,973 | 20,467 | 21,297 | 22,003 | 22,215 |
| 711320 | Promoters of performing arts, sports, and similar events without facilities | 6,950 | 6,371 | 5,596 | 5,004 | 4,936 | 4,899 | 5,114 |
| 712110 | Museums | 65,488 | 66,513 | 67,853 | 70,253 | 72,570 | 69,739 | 68,704 |
| 712120 | Historical sites | 12,414 | 12,191 | 12,233 | 12,743 | 12,999 | 12,442 | 13,459 |
| 712130 | Zoos and botancial gardens | 23,766 | 24,536 | 25,610 | 26,963 | 27,856 | 27,301 | 28,129 |

| NAICS | Organization | | | | | | |
|---|---|---|---|---|---|---|---|
| 712190 | Nature parks and other similar institutions | 4,434 | 4,339 | 4,186 | 4,711 | 4,981 | 4,998 | 5,076 |
| 713910 | Golf courses and country clubs | 125,358 | 127,651 | 129,312 | 132,390 | 135,272 | 130,598 | 128,822 |
| 713940 | Fitness and recreational sports centers | 135,006 | 142,252 | 151,036 | 159,467 | 160,326 | 158,743 | 155,771 |
| 713990 | All other amusement and recreation industries | 27,109 | 28,660 | 30,874 | 33,054 | 33,024 | 32,193 | 32,964 |
| 813110 | Religious organizations | 175,119 | 177,104 | 179,417 | 183,678 | 186,379 | 184,929 | 181,449 |
| 813211 | Grantmaking foundations | 40,329 | 41,778 | 42,739 | 45,477 | 48,537 | 49,625 | 51,212 |
| 813212 | Voluntary health organizations | 36,516 | 36,834 | 37,123 | 39,126 | 39,776 | 39,358 | 37,912 |
| 813219 | Other grantmaking and giving services | 40,741 | 39,884 | 39,402 | 38,667 | 38,638 | 37,362 | 35,543 |
| 813311 | Human rights organizations | 43,991 | 42,879 | 44,747 | 45,900 | 48,226 | 49,049 | 48,496 |
| 813312 | Environment, conservation, and wildlife organizations | 35,585 | 37,354 | 39,014 | 44,064 | 48,307 | 49,024 | 50,302 |
| 813319 | Other social advocacy organizations | 84,219 | 85,072 | 84,250 | 85,755 | 89,969 | 90,294 | 92,772 |
| 813410 | Civic and social organizations | 412,083 | 414,028 | 415,336 | 417,069 | 418,135 | 395,833 | 391,003 |
| 813910 | Business associations | 117,688 | 118,662 | 120,446 | 122,141 | 123,324 | 119,320 | 115,423 |
| 813920 | Professional organizations | 71,123 | 70,571 | 71,198 | 73,364 | 75,269 | 75,092 | 74,244 |
| 813930 | Labor unions and similar labor organizations | 136,507 | 133,036 | 132,629 | 131,386 | 133,216 | 127,989 | 122,270 |
| 813940 | Political organizations | 11,775 | 6,223 | 10,544 | 7,808 | 12,507 | 7,474 | 11,102 |
| 813990 | Other similar organizations (except business, professional, labor, and political organizations) | 91,479 | 92,938 | 95,560 | 99,138 | 102,441 | 102,212 | 101,951 |

Sources: Authors' estimates based on private employment from the U.S. Department of Labor, Bureau of Labor Statistics, Quarterly Census of Employment and Wages (1990–2011). Tax-exempt share of employment from the U.S. Census Bureau, Economic Census (1997, 2002, and 2007).
Notes: Industries are listed as classified by the North American Industry Classification System (NAICS). Industries 541710 (physical, engineering, and biological research services) and 541720 (research and development in the social sciences and humanities) are also included in the Economic Census, but the authors believe these data are flawed.

**Table 2.18.** Estimated Nonprofit Wages with Calculation for Nonprofits Serving Business, 1990–2010 ($ billions)

|  | Nonprofit physical, engineering, and biological research services[a] | Nonprofit physical, engineering, and biological research services × 10%[b] | Business associations[c] | Nonprofits serving business[b] | NPISH[d] | Total estimated NPISH |
|---|---|---|---|---|---|---|
| 1990 | 5.8 | 0.6 | 3.0 | 3.6 | 193.0 | 196.6 |
| 1991 | 6.0 | 0.6 | 3.2 | 3.8 | 208.3 | 212.1 |
| 1992 | 6.1 | 0.6 | 3.4 | 4.0 | 225.5 | 229.5 |
| 1993 | 6.4 | 0.6 | 3.5 | 4.1 | 236.9 | 241.0 |
| 1994 | 6.6 | 0.7 | 3.7 | 4.4 | 248.3 | 252.7 |
| 1995 | 7.0 | 0.7 | 3.9 | 4.6 | 264.8 | 269.4 |
| 1996 | 7.1 | 0.7 | 4.1 | 4.8 | 278.2 | 283.0 |
| 1997 | 7.8 | 0.8 | 4.3 | 5.1 | 294.4 | 299.5 |
| 1998 | 7.8 | 0.8 | 6.1 | 6.9 | 311.3 | 318.2 |
| 1999 | 7.2 | 0.7 | 6.4 | 7.1 | 329.3 | 336.4 |
| 2000 | 7.6 | 0.8 | 6.7 | 7.5 | 351.7 | 359.2 |
| 2001 | 6.5 | 0.7 | 7.0 | 7.6 | 374.4 | 382.0 |
| 2002 | 5.4 | 0.5 | 7.4 | 7.9 | 400.0 | 407.9 |
| 2003 | 6.0 | 0.6 | 7.7 | 8.3 | 421.3 | 429.6 |
| 2004 | 6.6 | 0.7 | 8.2 | 8.8 | 441.9 | 450.7 |
| 2005 | 7.7 | 0.8 | 8.5 | 9.3 | 458.4 | 467.7 |
| 2006 | 8.5 | 0.9 | 9.1 | 9.9 | 485.9 | 495.8 |
| 2007 | 9.3 | 0.9 | 9.5 | 10.4 | 514.3 | 524.7 |
| 2008 | 10.0 | 1.0 | 10.0 | 11.0 | 543.8 | 554.8 |
| 2009 | 8.0 | 0.8 | 9.9 | 10.7 | 562.9 | 573.6 |
| 2010 | 8.8 | 0.9 | 9.9 | 10.8 | 576.9 | 587.7 |

*Sources:*
a. Authors' estimates based on private wages from U.S. Department of Labor, Bureau of Labor Statistics, Quarterly Census of Employment and Wages (1990–2011), and U.S. Census Bureau, Economic Census (1997, 2002, and 2007).
b. Authors' estimates. Total estimated NPISH is the sum of data in the nonprofits serving business and NPISH columns.
c. Authors' estimates based on private wages from U.S. Department of Labor, Bureau of Labor Statistics, Quarterly Census of Employment and Wages (1990–2011).
d. U.S. Department of Commerce, Bureau of Economic Analysis, National Income and Product Accounts, table 1.13 (2011).
NPISH = nonprofit institutions serving households

**Table 2.19.** National Taxonomy of Exempt Entities Core Codes Comprising NAICS Industries Whose Reported Wages Were Aggregated from Internal Revenue Service Data

**NAICS 11: Agriculture, forestry, fishing, and hunting**
K20. Agricultural programs
K25. Farmland preservation
K26. Animal husbandry
K99. Food, agriculture, and nutrition n.e.c.

**NAICS 22: Utilities**
W80. Public utilities

**NAICS 48, 49: Transportation and warehousing**
W40. Public transportation systems

**NAICS 51: Information**
A27. Community celebrations
A30. Media and communications
A31. Film and video
A32. Television
A33. Printing and publishing
A34. Radio
B70. Libraries
W50. Telecommunications
X80. Religious media and communications
X81. Religious film and video
X82. Religious television
X83. Religious printing and publishing
X84. Religious radio

**NAICS 52: Finance and insurance**
E80. Health (general and financing)
W60. Financial institutions
W61. Credit unions
Y20. Insurance providers
Y22. Local benevolent life insurance associations, mutual irrigation and telephone companies, and like organizations
Y23. Mutual insurance companies and associations
Y30. Pension and retirement funds
Y33. Teachers' retirement fund associations
Y34. Employee-funded pension trusts
Y35. Multiemployer pension plans

**NAICS 53: Real estate and rental and leasing**
S47. Real estate associations

**NAICS 54: Professional, scientific, and technical services**
I20. Crime prevention
I21. Youth violence prevention
I30. Correctional facilities
I40. Rehabilitation services for offenders
I43. Inmate support
I44. Prison alternatives

*(continued)*

**Table 2.19.** National Taxonomy of Exempt Entities Core Codes Comprising NAICS Industries Whose Reported Wages Were Aggregated from Internal Revenue Service Data *(continued)*

I50. Administration of justice
I60. Law enforcement
I80. Legal services
I83. Public interest law
I99. Crime and legal related n.e.c.
A02. Management and technical assistance
B02. Management and technical assistance
C02. Management and technical assistance
D02. Management and technical assistance
E02. Management and technical assistance
F02. Management and technical assistance
G02. Management and technical assistance
H02. Management and technical assistance
I02. Management and technical assistance
J02. Management and technical assistance
K02. Management and technical assistance
L02. Management and technical assistance
M02. Management and technical assistance
N02. Management and technical assistance
O02. Management and technical assistance
P02. Management and technical assistance
Q02. Management and technical assistance
R02. Management and technical assistance
S02. Management and technical assistance
T02. Management and technical assistance
U02. Management and technical assistance
V02. Management and technical assistance
W02. Management and technical assistance
X02. Management and technical assistance
Y02. Management and technical assistance
S43. Small business development
S50. Nonprofit management
H20. Birth defects and genetic diseases research
H25. Down syndrome research
H30. Cancer research
H32. Breast cancer research
H40. Diseases of specific organs research
H41. Eye diseases, blindness, and vision impairments research
H42. Ear and throat diseases research
H43. Heart and circulatory system diseases and disorders research
H44. Kidney diseases research
H45. Lung diseases research
H48. Brain disorders research
H50. Nerve, muscle, and bone diseases research
H51. Arthritis research

*(continued)*

**Table 2.19.** National Taxonomy of Exempt Entities Core Codes Comprising NAICS Industries Whose Reported Wages Were Aggregated from Internal Revenue Service Data *(continued)*

H54. Epilepsy research
H60. Allergy-related diseases research
H61. Asthma research
H70. Digestive diseases and disorders research
H80. Specifically named diseases research
H81. AIDS research
H83. Alzheimer's disease research
H84. Autism research
H90. Medical disciplines research
H92. Biomedicine and bioengineering research
H94. Geriatrics research
H96. Neurology and neuroscience research
H98. Pediatrics research
H99. Medical research n.e.c.
H9b. Surgical specialties research
U20. General science
U21. Marine science and oceanography
U30. Physical and earth sciences
U31. Astronomy
U33. Chemistry and chemical engineering
U34. Mathematics
U36. Geology
U40. Engineering and technology
U41. Computer science
U42. Engineering
U50. Biological and life sciences
U99. Science and technology n.e.c.
A05. Research institutes and public policy analysis
B05. Research institutes and public policy analysis
C05. Research institutes and public policy analysis
D05. Research institutes and public policy analysis
E05. Research institutes and public policy analysis
F05. Research institutes and public policy analysis
G05. Research institutes and public policy analysis
H05. Research institutes and public policy analysis
I05. Research institutes and public policy analysis
J05. Research institutes and public policy analysis
K05. Research institutes and public policy analysis
L05. Research institutes and public policy analysis
M05. Research institutes and public policy analysis
N05. Research institutes and public policy analysis
O05. Research institutes and public policy analysis
P05. Research institutes and public policy analysis
Q05. Research institutes and public policy analysis
R05. Research institutes and public policy analysis

*(continued)*

**Table 2.19.** National Taxonomy of Exempt Entities Core Codes Comprising NAICS Industries Whose Reported Wages Were Aggregated from Internal Revenue Service Data *(continued)*

S05. Research institutes and public policy analysis
T05. Research institutes and public policy analysis
U05. Research institutes and public policy analysis
V05. Research institutes and public policy analysis
W05. Research institutes and public policy analysis
X05. Research institutes and public policy analysis
Y05. Research institutes and public policy analysis
A24. Folk arts
Q35. International democracy and civil society development
Q50. International affairs, foreign policy, and globalization
Q51. International economic and trade policy
V20. Social science
V21. Anthropology and sociology
V22. Economics
V23. Behavioral science
V24. Political science
V25. Population studies
V26. Law and jurisprudence
V30. Interdisciplinary research
V31. Black studies
V32. Women's studies
V33. Ethnic studies
V34. Urban studies
V35. International studies
V36. Gerontology
V37. Labor studies
V99. Social science n.e.c.
D40. Veterinary services
A40. Visual arts

**NAICS 56: Administrative and support and waste management and remediation services**

C20. Pollution abatement & control
J20. Employment preparation and procurement
J99. Employment n.e.c.

**NAICS 72: Accommodation and food services**

L40. Temporary housing
N20. Camps

*Source:* Urban Institute, National Center for Charitable Statistics, NCCS NTEE/NAICS/SIC Crosswalk (2004).
NAICS = North American Industry Classification System
n.e.c. = not elsewhere classified

# 3

# Trends in Private Giving and Volunteering

The nonprofit sector is distinguished from the business and government sectors by the substantial role that donations of time and money play in its financing. Without such donations many nonprofits would cease to exist. This chapter paints a portrait of giving and volunteering in the United States. It provides statistics from various sources on giving from individuals, foundations, and corporations. It also examines who is volunteering at nonprofits, where they are volunteering, and the economic value of volunteer time.

## Summary

- Private giving reached an estimated $290.89 billion in 2010. While this figure is up from 2009, it is still below the pre-recession high of $310.57 billion in 2007. In fact, when looked at in constant dollars, private giving fell by 11 percent from 2007 to 2010.

- Giving by individuals or households accounted for 72.8 percent of private giving in 2010 with an estimated $211.77 billion. Not surprisingly, individual giving dropped during the recession—by 11.6 percent in 2008 and 3.3 percent in 2009 (in constant dollars).

- In 2009, people who itemized contributions on their income tax forms accounted for 77 percent of total individual or household contributions. Over the past 10 years, itemizers have accounted for approximately 80 percent of individual or household contributions.

- In constant dollars, itemizers' charitable deductions dropped 14 percent from 2007 to 2008 and by another 8 percent from 2008 to 2009.

- Grants from foundations account for the second-largest proportion of private giving, contributing $41.0 billion to charities in 2009 ($45.8 billion if you include gifts from corporate foundations).

- Foundation assets plummeted 17 percent from 2007 to 2008. In 2008, however, foundation giving reached an all-time high of $46.8 billion, fueled by increased giving from the Bill and Melinda Gates Foundation.
- While corporate giving dropped around 13 percent from 2007 to 2008, corporate gifts began rising steadily in 2008. By 2010, corporate giving surpassed pre-recession levels.
- Volunteers spent 14.9 billion hours volunteering in 2010, the equivalent of 8.8 million full-time employees. Assuming that these employees would have earned the average private nonfarm hourly wage ($19.07), volunteers' time contributed $283.8 billion to the nonprofit sector in 2010, almost as much as all donations.

## Private Giving

According to *Giving USA*, private giving (comprising giving by living individuals and households, personal bequests, gifts from foundations, and gifts from corporations) reached an estimated $290.89 billion in 2010. While this figure is up from 2009, it is still below the pre-recession high of $310.6 billion in 2007. In fact, in constant dollars, private giving declined by 11 percent from 2007 through 2010.

Figure 3.1 displays private giving as a percentage of national income. While this percentage has declined since 2005, when it reached a high of 2.61 percent, 2010 marked

**Figure 3.1.** Private Giving Compared with National Income, 1970–2010 (percent)

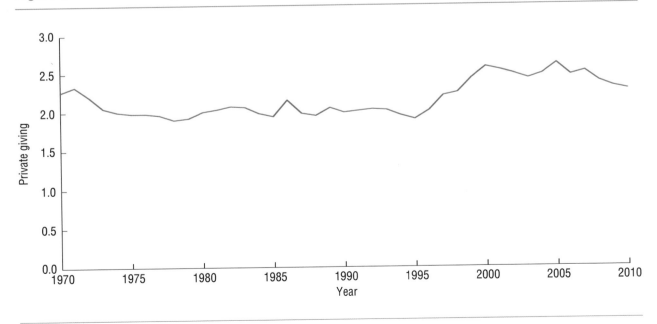

*Sources:* Authors' calculations based on private giving from Giving USA Foundation, *Giving USA* (2011) and national income from U.S. Department of Commerce, Bureau of Economic Analysis, National Income and Product Accounts, table 1.13 (2011).

the lowest percentage of giving as a share of national income in the past 10 years—2.27 percent.

Private contributions as a percentage of nonprofit expenditures or outlays[1] (consumption expenditures, transfer payments, and savings) have also been on a downward trend after peaking in 2000 at 33.6 percent. While the numbers did trend upward from 2003 to 2005, 2010 marked the lowest percentage seen in over 10 years at 23.8 percent (table 3.1). This number, however, overestimates private philanthropy to the nonprofit sector because the BEA definition of nonprofits excludes organizations that serve business, which generally receive fewer donations from individuals. When calculated using IRS data from the Form 990, private contributions account for 13.3 percent of total expenses in 2010 (see chapter 5 for more details). Figure 3.2 shows private contributions as a percentage of nonprofit outlays, or expenditures, for the past 18 years.

Figure 3.3 shows the distribution of private contributions by recipient type. Once again, religious organizations received the greatest proportion of private giving—34.6 percent in 2010. While religious organizations continued to receive the lion's share of private giving, the percentage of giving going to these organizations began to decline after its peak of 53.3 percent in 1985. Educational organizations received the second-largest percentage of private giving in 2010 with 14.3 percent of all private contributions. The proportion of gifts going to foundations increased from 8.3 percent in 2005 to 11.3 percent in 2010 (see table 3.2).

Up to this point, this chapter has discussed private contributions overall. The next four sections look at each component of private giving: by living individuals, personal bequests, foundations, and corporations.

## Giving by Living Individuals

Individuals gave an estimated $211.77 billion to charities in 2010. Not surprisingly, individual giving dropped in both 2008 and 2009; down 11.6 percent from 2007 to 2008 and down 3.3 percent from 2008 to 2009 (in constant dollars). While still not up to pre-recession levels, individual giving did increase by an estimated 1.1 percent in 2010 (see figure 3.4, table 3.3).

Giving by living individuals accounted for 72.8 percent of all private giving in 2010. The proportion of giving from individuals began trending downward after 1979, when gifts from individuals accounted for about 85 percent of total giving. During recessionary times, the proportion of giving from individuals has dropped; during economic expansions, the proportion of gifts from individuals has risen. In 2008, the proportion

---

1. The Bureau of Economic Analysis, which produces the National Income and Product Accounts (NIPA), uses the term *outlays* to discuss expenditures. Outlays include the sum of personal consumption expenditures (expenses to obtain goods and services), personal interest payments (interest payments required to obtain goods and services), and personal current transfer payments (donations, fines, and fees paid to federal, state, and local governments as well as payments to the rest of the world). Outlays reported by the BEA differ from the expenses nonprofit organizations report on their Forms 990. Therefore, expenses discussed in chapter 1 are not comparable to outlays discussed in this chapter. Additional information on BEA data is available at http://www.bea.gov.

**Table 3.1.** Private Contributions to Nonprofit Organizations by National Income and Nonprofit Outlays, 1970–2010 (current dollars)

| Year | $ Billions | | | Private Giving as a % of | |
|---|---|---|---|---|---|
| | Private giving | National income | Nonprofit outlays | National income | Nonprofit outlays |
| 1970 | 21.04 | 929.5 | — | 2.26 | — |
| 1971 | 23.44 | 1,005.6 | — | 2.33 | — |
| 1972 | 24.44 | 1,110.3 | — | 2.20 | — |
| 1973 | 25.59 | 1,246.1 | — | 2.05 | — |
| 1974 | 26.88 | 1,341.5 | — | 2.00 | — |
| 1975 | 28.56 | 1,444.0 | — | 1.98 | — |
| 1976 | 31.85 | 1,609.8 | — | 1.98 | — |
| 1977 | 35.21 | 1,797.4 | — | 1.96 | — |
| 1978 | 38.57 | 2,027.9 | — | 1.90 | — |
| 1979 | 43.11 | 2,248.3 | — | 1.92 | — |
| 1980 | 48.63 | 2,433.0 | — | 2.00 | — |
| 1981 | 55.28 | 2,729.8 | — | 2.03 | — |
| 1982 | 59.11 | 2,851.4 | — | 2.07 | — |
| 1983 | 63.21 | 3,070.9 | — | 2.06 | — |
| 1984 | 68.58 | 3,461.3 | — | 1.98 | — |
| 1985 | 71.69 | 3,696.3 | — | 1.94 | — |
| 1986 | 83.25 | 3,871.5 | — | 2.15 | — |
| 1987 | 82.20 | 4,150.0 | — | 1.98 | — |
| 1988 | 88.04 | 4,522.3 | — | 1.95 | — |
| 1989 | 98.30 | 4,800.5 | — | 2.05 | — |
| 1990 | 100.52 | 5,059.5 | — | 1.99 | — |
| 1991 | 104.92 | 5,217.9 | — | 2.01 | — |
| 1992 | 111.79 | 5,517.1 | 424.0 | 2.03 | 26.4 |
| 1993 | 116.86 | 5,784.7 | 449.5 | 2.02 | 26.0 |
| 1994 | 120.29 | 6,181.3 | 473.3 | 1.95 | 25.4 |
| 1995 | 123.68 | 6,522.3 | 492.1 | 1.90 | 25.1 |
| 1996 | 139.10 | 6,931.7 | 522.3 | 2.01 | 26.6 |
| 1997 | 162.99 | 7,406.0 | 546.0 | 2.20 | 29.9 |
| 1998 | 176.80 | 7,875.6 | 594.2 | 2.24 | 29.8 |
| 1999 | 202.74 | 8,358.0 | 634.1 | 2.43 | 32.0 |

*(continued)*

**Table 3.1.** Private Contributions to Nonprofit Organizations by National Income and Nonprofit Outlays, 1970–2010 (current dollars) *(continued)*

| Year | $ Billions | | | Private Giving as a % of | |
|------|----------------|-----------------|------------------|-----------------|-------------------|
|      | Private giving | National income | Nonprofit outlays | National income | Nonprofit outlays |
| 2000 | 229.71 | 8,938.9 | 683.7 | 2.57 | 33.6 |
| 2001 | 232.04 | 9,185.2 | 746.7 | 2.53 | 31.1 |
| 2002 | 233.11 | 9,408.5 | 811.6 | 2.48 | 28.7 |
| 2003 | 238.06 | 9,840.2 | 851.5 | 2.42 | 28.0 |
| 2004 | 261.20 | 10,534.0 | 897.4 | 2.48 | 29.1 |
| 2005 | 294.44 | 11,273.8 | 951.0 | 2.61 | 31.0 |
| 2006 | 296.21 | 12,031.2 | 1,015.3 | 2.46 | 29.2 |
| 2007 | 310.57 | 12,396.4 | 1,075.9 | 2.51 | 28.9 |
| 2008 | 299.81 | 12,609.1 | 1,139.5 | 2.38 | 26.3 |
| 2009 | 280.30 | 12,147.6 | 1,175.6 | 2.31 | 23.8 |
| 2010 | 290.89 | 12,840.1 | 1,223.6 | 2.27 | 23.8 |

*Sources:* Private giving from Giving USA Foundation, *Giving USA* (2011); national income from the U.S. Department of Commerce, Bureau of Economic Analysis, National Income and Product Accounts, table 1.13 (2011); nonprofit outlays from National Income and Product Accounts, table 2.9 (2011).
*Notes:* Outlays include grants and allocations, specific assistance to individuals, and benefits paid to members made by nonprofit institutions, along with grants and allocations made by private foundations that directly support households. They also include legal services, labor unions, professional association expenses, and club and fraternal housing. Expenditures are net of unrelated sales, secondary sales, and sales to other sectors.
— = no data available

of private giving (which includes giving by individuals, foundations, and corporations) attributed to individuals declined to 71.3 percent of total giving, the lowest proportion on record.

Per capita contributions also fell during the recession. As displayed in figure 3.5, the per capita contribution (inflation adjusted) dropped 15.5 percent from 2007 to 2010. Giving as a percentage of personal income dropped from 2 percent to 1.7 percent over this same period (see table 3.4).

In general, contributions per capita increased between 1970 and 2010. After adjusting for inflation, contributions per capita increased 55 percent over the period. During the late 1990s, per capita contributions grew steadily, increasing 53 percent between 1995 and 2000 alone. While the gifts per capita have increased in dollars, giving as a percentage of income has remained steady at about 2 percent over the past 40 years.

Figure 3.6 displays individual giving by recipient organization for 2007—the latest year of data available from the panel study conducted by the Center on Philanthropy

**Figure 3.2.** Private Contributions in Constant 2010 Dollars and as a Percentage of Nonprofit Outlays, 1992–2010

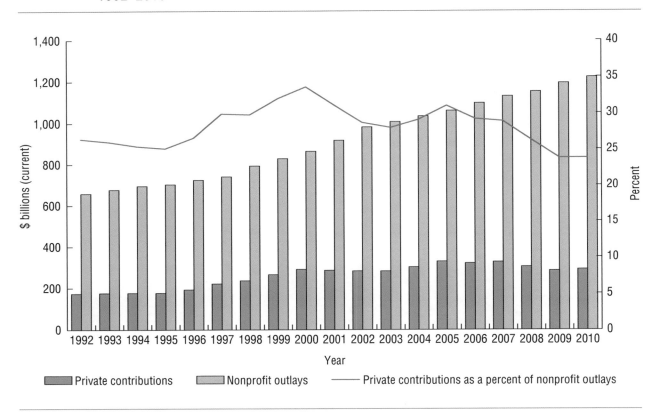

*Sources:* Authors' calculations based on private giving from Giving USA Foundation, *Giving USA* (2011) and nonprofit outlays from U.S. Department of Commerce, Bureau of Economic Analysis, National Income and Product Accounts, table 2.9 (2011).

**Figure 3.3.** Estimated Distribution of Private Contributions by Recipient Type, 2010 (percent)

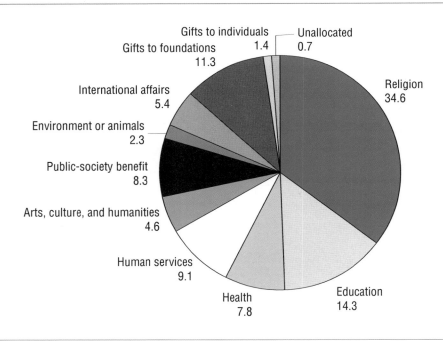

*Source:* Giving USA Foundation, *Giving USA* (2011).
*Note:* Percentages do not sum to 100 because of rounding.

**Table 3.2.** Distribution of Private Contributions by Type of Nonprofit, 1970–2010

| Year | Total contributions ($ billions) | Percent | | | | | | | | | | |
|---|---|---|---|---|---|---|---|---|---|---|---|---|
| | | Religion | Education | Health | Human services | Arts, culture, and humanities | Public-society benefit | Environment and animals | International affairs | Gifts to foundations | Gifts to individuals | Unallocated |
| 1970 | 21.04 | 44.4 | 12.4 | 11.4 | 13.9 | 3.1 | 2.2 | — | — | — | — | 12.6 |
| 1971 | 23.44 | 43.0 | 11.7 | 16.7 | 12.8 | 4.3 | 2.9 | — | — | — | — | 14.1 |
| 1972 | 24.44 | 41.3 | 12.2 | 11.5 | 12.9 | 4.5 | 3.4 | — | — | — | — | 14.2 |
| 1973 | 25.59 | 41.1 | 13.0 | 12.1 | 12.0 | 4.9 | 2.4 | — | — | — | — | 14.4 |
| 1974 | 26.88 | 44.0 | 12.6 | 13.1 | 14.5 | 5.4 | 3.3 | — | — | — | — | 7.0 |
| 1975 | 28.56 | 44.9 | 11.2 | 12.8 | 13.7 | 5.2 | 4.3 | — | — | — | — | 7.9 |
| 1976 | 31.85 | 44.5 | 11.3 | 11.7 | 12.7 | 4.8 | 4.6 | — | — | — | — | 10.3 |
| 1977 | 35.21 | 48.2 | 11.0 | 11.2 | 11.6 | 5.2 | 3.7 | — | — | — | — | 9.0 |
| 1978 | 38.57 | 47.6 | 11.2 | 10.6 | 10.9 | 4.8 | 3.9 | — | — | 4.2 | — | 6.7 |
| 1979 | 43.11 | 46.8 | 10.9 | 9.9 | 10.0 | 4.6 | 4.2 | — | — | 5.1 | — | 8.4 |
| 1980 | 48.63 | 45.7 | 10.4 | 9.2 | 9.2 | 4.4 | 4.7 | — | — | 4.1 | — | 12.4 |
| 1981 | 55.28 | 45.3 | 10.7 | 8.4 | 8.3 | 4.1 | 3.9 | — | — | 4.3 | — | 15.0 |
| 1982 | 59.11 | 47.5 | 10.4 | 8.2 | 8.1 | 4.6 | 4.1 | — | — | 6.8 | — | 10.4 |
| 1983 | 63.21 | 50.4 | 10.6 | 7.8 | 7.8 | 3.9 | 3.9 | — | — | 4.3 | — | 11.4 |
| 1984 | 68.58 | 51.8 | 10.6 | 7.8 | 7.3 | 3.7 | 4.2 | — | — | 4.9 | — | 9.6 |
| 1985 | 71.69 | 53.3 | 11.2 | 7.9 | 7.2 | 3.8 | 4.5 | — | — | 6.6 | — | 5.5 |
| 1986 | 83.25 | 50.1 | 11.3 | 7.2 | 6.4 | 3.6 | 4.5 | — | — | 6.0 | — | 11.0 |
| 1987 | 82.20 | 52.9 | 11.9 | 7.4 | 6.6 | 3.8 | 5.2 | 1.3 | 1.0 | 6.3 | — | 3.5 |
| 1988 | 88.04 | 51.3 | 11.5 | 7.1 | 6.4 | 3.8 | 5.8 | 1.3 | 1.0 | 4.5 | — | 7.4 |
| 1989 | 98.30 | 48.6 | 11.3 | 6.6 | 6.4 | 3.8 | 7.1 | 1.4 | 1.7 | 4.5 | — | 8.6 |

(continued)

**Table 3.2.** Distribution of Private Contributions by Type of Nonprofit, 1970–2010 *(continued)*

| Year | Total contributions ($ billions) | Religion | Education | Health | Human services | Arts, culture, and humanities | Public-society benefit | Environment and animals | International affairs | Gifts to foundations | Gifts to individuals | Unallocated |
|---|---|---|---|---|---|---|---|---|---|---|---|---|
| 1990 | 100.52 | 49.5 | 11.6 | 7.3 | 6.4 | 4.0 | 7.3 | 1.5 | 2.2 | 3.8 | — | 6.2 |
| 1991 | 104.92 | 47.7 | 11.8 | 7.4 | 7.1 | 4.1 | 7.9 | 1.6 | 2.0 | 4.3 | — | 6.2 |
| 1992 | 111.79 | 45.6 | 11.6 | 7.6 | 7.5 | 4.0 | 7.6 | 1.5 | 2.1 | 4.5 | — | 7.9 |
| 1993 | 116.86 | 45.3 | 12.2 | 7.5 | 7.5 | 4.2 | 7.4 | 1.7 | 1.9 | 5.4 | — | 7.1 |
| 1994 | 120.29 | 46.9 | 11.7 | 7.6 | 7.4 | 3.9 | 8.3 | 1.7 | 2.3 | 5.3 | — | 4.9 |
| 1995 | 123.68 | 47.0 | 12.6 | 11.3 | 7.9 | 4.6 | 9.1 | 1.9 | 2.4 | 6.8 | — | -3.5 |
| 1996 | 139.10 | 44.5 | 13.3 | 10.2 | 7.5 | 4.6 | 8.1 | 1.9 | 2.6 | 9.1 | — | -1.7 |
| 1997 | 162.99 | 39.7 | 12.5 | 7.8 | 7.7 | 4.5 | 7.9 | 1.9 | 2.6 | 8.6 | — | 6.8 |
| 1998 | 176.80 | 38.6 | 13.5 | 7.5 | 8.8 | 5.6 | 7.9 | 2.0 | 2.9 | 11.3 | — | 2.0 |
| 1999 | 202.74 | 35.1 | 13.4 | 7.5 | 8.8 | 4.6 | 6.4 | 2.1 | 3.2 | 14.2 | — | 4.6 |
| 2000 | 229.71 | 33.5 | 12.9 | 7.2 | 8.7 | 4.6 | 6.7 | 2.1 | 3.1 | 10.8 | — | 10.5 |
| 2001 | 232.04 | 34.4 | 14.1 | 7.9 | 9.4 | 4.9 | 7.1 | 2.3 | 3.6 | 11.1 | — | 5.3 |
| 2002 | 233.11 | 35.6 | 12.9 | 7.6 | 10.5 | 4.6 | 7.7 | 2.3 | 3.7 | 8.2 | — | 6.9 |
| 2003 | 238.06 | 35.5 | 12.5 | 8.6 | 9.9 | 4.5 | 6.9 | 2.3 | 4.1 | 9.1 | — | 6.5 |
| 2004 | 261.20 | 33.7 | 12.9 | 7.7 | 9.3 | 4.5 | 7.2 | 2.1 | 4.4 | 7.8 | 0.7 | 9.7 |
| 2005 | 294.44 | 31.6 | 12.7 | 7.6 | 8.9 | 4.0 | 7.2 | 2.0 | 5.2 | 8.3 | 1.1 | 11.5 |
| 2006 | 296.21 | 32.9 | 13.8 | 7.4 | 9.2 | 4.3 | 7.2 | 2.1 | 3.8 | 9.1 | 1.3 | 8.8 |
| 2007 | 310.57 | 32.4 | 13.9 | 7.5 | 9.5 | 4.4 | 7.3 | 2.2 | 4.3 | 12.1 | 1.1 | 5.3 |
| 2008 | 299.81 | 33.8 | 14.0 | 7.2 | 8.6 | 4.3 | 8.0 | 2.2 | 4.4 | 10.2 | 1.2 | 6.0 |
| 2009 | 280.30 | 35.6 | 14.1 | 8.0 | 9.4 | 4.5 | 8.1 | 2.4 | 4.9 | 11.6 | 1.5 | -0.2 |
| 2010 | 290.89 | 34.6 | 14.3 | 7.8 | 9.1 | 4.6 | 8.3 | 2.3 | 5.4 | 11.3 | 1.4 | 0.7 |

Percent

*Source:* Giving USA Foundation, *Giving USA* (2011).
*Note:* Percentages may not sum to 100 because of rounding.
— = no data available

**Figure 3.4.** Private Giving by Living Individuals, 1970–2010 (constant 2010 dollars)

*Source:* Giving USA Foundation, *Giving USA* (2011).

at Indiana University. According to this study, religious organizations continue to be the major recipients of donated dollars. Forty-three percent of households report giving to religious organizations, followed by 30.9 percent giving to charities to help the needy.

In addition to the giving estimates based on survey data reported above, the IRS Statistics of Income (SOI) Division provides data on individual giving from individuals who itemized their annual 1040 tax return. To get a better picture of individual giving, this section examines SOI data on the deductions taken by personal income tax filers who itemize their tax return. In addition to the total contributions and average contributions of itemizers, it presents data on high-income earners and cash versus noncash donations by itemizers.

Table 3.5 displays individual giving broken out by whether or not the givers itemized deductions on their personal income tax returns. Nonitemizers' contributions are estimated by subtracting itemizers' contributions from the total individual giving found in table 3.3. (Contributions by those who do not file tax returns are not included in the table 3.5 estimates.)

In 2009, itemizers accounted for 77 percent of total individual contributions. Over the past 10 years, itemizer contributions have accounted for approximately 80 percent

**Table 3.3.** Total Private Contributions by Source, 1970–2010 (billions of dollars)

| | Total Private Giving | | | Gifts by Living Individuals | | | Personal Bequests | | | Gifts by Foundations | | | Gifts by Corporations | | |
|---|---|---|---|---|---|---|---|---|---|---|---|---|---|---|---|
| | $ | $ 2010 | % | $ | $ 2010 | % | $ | $ 2010 | % | $ | $ 2010 | % | $ | $ 2010 | % |
| 1970 | 21.04 | 118.21 | 100.0 | 16.19 | 90.96 | 77.0 | 2.13 | 11.97 | 10.0 | 1.90 | 10.67 | 9.0 | 0.82 | 4.61 | 3.8 |
| 1971 | 23.44 | 126.02 | 100.0 | 17.64 | 94.84 | 75.1 | 3.00 | 16.13 | 12.8 | 2.00 | 10.48 | 8.5 | 0.85 | 4.57 | 3.8 |
| 1972 | 24.44 | 127.30 | 100.0 | 19.37 | 100.89 | 79.4 | 2.10 | 10.94 | 8.6 | 2.00 | 10.42 | 8.2 | 0.97 | 5.05 | 4.1 |
| 1973 | 25.59 | 125.44 | 100.0 | 20.53 | 100.64 | 80.1 | 2.00 | 9.80 | 7.8 | 2.00 | 9.80 | 7.8 | 1.06 | 5.20 | 4.3 |
| 1974 | 26.88 | 118.95 | 100.0 | 21.60 | 95.58 | 80.4 | 2.07 | 9.16 | 7.8 | 2.10 | 9.34 | 7.8 | 1.10 | 4.87 | 4.1 |
| 1975 | 28.56 | 115.63 | 100.0 | 23.53 | 95.26 | 82.3 | 2.23 | 9.03 | 7.7 | 1.70 | 6.68 | 6.0 | 1.15 | 4.66 | 4.2 |
| 1976 | 31.85 | 122.03 | 100.0 | 26.32 | 100.84 | 82.6 | 2.30 | 8.81 | 7.2 | 1.90 | 7.28 | 6.0 | 1.33 | 5.10 | 4.1 |
| 1977 | 35.21 | 126.65 | 100.0 | 29.55 | 106.29 | 84.1 | 2.12 | 7.63 | 6.0 | 2.00 | 7.19 | 5.7 | 1.54 | 5.54 | 4.3 |
| 1978 | 38.57 | 129.01 | 100.0 | 32.10 | 107.36 | 83.2 | 2.60 | 8.70 | 6.7 | 2.17 | 7.26 | 5.7 | 1.70 | 5.69 | 4.4 |
| 1979 | 43.11 | 129.47 | 100.0 | 36.59 | 109.88 | 84.9 | 2.23 | 6.70 | 5.1 | 2.24 | 6.73 | 5.1 | 2.05 | 6.16 | 4.9 |
| 1980 | 48.63 | 128.65 | 100.0 | 40.71 | 107.70 | 83.7 | 2.86 | 7.57 | 6.0 | 2.81 | 7.43 | 5.8 | 2.25 | 5.95 | 4.7 |
| 1981 | 55.28 | 132.57 | 100.0 | 45.99 | 110.29 | 83.2 | 3.58 | 8.59 | 6.5 | 3.17 | 7.36 | 5.6 | 2.64 | 6.33 | 4.7 |
| 1982 | 59.11 | 133.43 | 100.0 | 47.63 | 107.52 | 80.5 | 5.21 | 11.76 | 8.8 | 3.16 | 7.13 | 5.4 | 3.11 | 7.02 | 5.2 |
| 1983 | 63.21 | 138.32 | 100.0 | 52.06 | 113.92 | 82.4 | 3.88 | 8.49 | 6.2 | 3.60 | 7.88 | 5.7 | 3.67 | 8.03 | 5.9 |
| 1984 | 68.58 | 143.77 | 100.0 | 56.46 | 118.36 | 82.4 | 4.04 | 8.47 | 5.8 | 3.95 | 8.28 | 5.8 | 4.13 | 8.66 | 6.0 |
| 1985 | 71.69 | 148.12 | 100.0 | 57.39 | 118.57 | 80.1 | 4.77 | 9.86 | 6.7 | 4.90 | 10.12 | 6.8 | 4.63 | 9.57 | 6.4 |
| 1986 | 83.25 | 165.51 | 100.0 | 67.09 | 133.38 | 80.6 | 5.70 | 11.33 | 6.8 | 5.43 | 10.80 | 6.5 | 5.03 | 10.00 | 6.0 |
| 1987 | 82.20 | 157.78 | 100.0 | 64.53 | 123.86 | 78.5 | 6.58 | 12.63 | 8.0 | 5.88 | 11.29 | 7.2 | 5.21 | 10.00 | 6.3 |
| 1988 | 88.04 | 162.14 | 100.0 | 69.98 | 128.88 | 79.5 | 6.57 | 12.10 | 7.5 | 6.15 | 11.33 | 7.0 | 5.34 | 9.83 | 6.0 |

| 1989 | 98.30 | 172.76 | 100.0 | 79.45 | 139.63 | 80.9 | 6.84 | 12.02 | 6.9 | 6.55 | 11.51 | 6.7 | 5.46 | 9.60 | 5.6 |
|------|-------|--------|-------|-------|--------|------|------|-------|-----|------|-------|-----|------|------|-----|
| 1990 | 100.52 | 167.54 | 100.0 | 81.04 | 135.07 | 80.6 | 6.79 | 11.32 | 6.8 | 7.23 | 12.05 | 7.2 | 5.46 | 9.10 | 5.5 |
| 1991 | 104.92 | 167.87 | 100.0 | 84.27 | 134.83 | 80.3 | 7.68 | 12.29 | 7.3 | 7.72 | 12.35 | 7.3 | 5.25 | 8.40 | 5.1 |
| 1992 | 111.79 | 173.86 | 100.0 | 87.70 | 136.39 | 78.5 | 9.54 | 14.84 | 8.5 | 8.64 | 13.44 | 7.7 | 5.91 | 9.19 | 5.3 |
| 1993 | 116.86 | 176.25 | 100.0 | 92.00 | 138.76 | 78.7 | 8.86 | 13.36 | 7.6 | 9.53 | 14.37 | 8.1 | 6.47 | 9.76 | 5.6 |
| 1994 | 120.29 | 176.90 | 100.0 | 92.52 | 136.06 | 76.9 | 11.13 | 16.37 | 9.2 | 9.66 | 14.21 | 8.1 | 6.98 | 10.26 | 5.8 |
| 1995 | 123.68 | 176.94 | 100.0 | 95.36 | 136.42 | 77.1 | 10.41 | 14.89 | 8.4 | 10.56 | 15.11 | 8.6 | 7.35 | 10.52 | 6.0 |
| 1996 | 139.10 | 193.20 | 100.0 | 107.56 | 149.39 | 77.4 | 12.03 | 16.71 | 8.6 | 12.00 | 16.67 | 8.6 | 7.51 | 10.43 | 5.4 |
| 1997 | 162.99 | 221.45 | 100.0 | 124.20 | 168.75 | 76.2 | 16.25 | 22.08 | 10.0 | 13.92 | 18.91 | 8.5 | 8.62 | 11.71 | 5.3 |
| 1998 | 176.80 | 236.66 | 100.0 | 138.35 | 184.96 | 78.3 | 12.98 | 17.35 | 7.4 | 17.01 | 22.74 | 9.6 | 8.46 | 11.31 | 4.8 |
| 1999 | 202.74 | 265.38 | 100.0 | 154.63 | 202.40 | 76.3 | 17.37 | 22.74 | 8.6 | 20.51 | 26.85 | 10.1 | 10.23 | 13.39 | 5.0 |
| 2000 | 229.71 | 290.76 | 100.0 | 174.51 | 220.90 | 76.0 | 19.88 | 25.16 | 8.7 | 24.58 | 31.11 | 10.7 | 10.74 | 13.59 | 4.7 |
| 2001 | 232.04 | 285.76 | 100.0 | 173.36 | 213.50 | 74.7 | 19.80 | 24.38 | 8.5 | 27.22 | 33.52 | 11.7 | 11.66 | 14.36 | 5.0 |
| 2002 | 233.11 | 282.55 | 100.0 | 174.44 | 211.44 | 74.8 | 20.90 | 25.33 | 9.0 | 26.98 | 32.70 | 11.6 | 10.79 | 13.08 | 4.6 |
| 2003 | 238.06 | 282.06 | 100.0 | 181.97 | 215.60 | 76.4 | 18.19 | 21.55 | 7.6 | 26.84 | 31.80 | 11.3 | 11.06 | 13.10 | 4.6 |
| 2004 | 261.20 | 301.27 | 100.0 | 202.97 | 234.11 | 77.7 | 18.46 | 21.29 | 7.1 | 28.41 | 32.77 | 10.9 | 11.36 | 13.10 | 4.3 |
| 2005 | 294.44 | 327.16 | 100.0 | 221.99 | 246.66 | 75.4 | 23.45 | 26.06 | 8.0 | 32.41 | 36.01 | 11.0 | 16.59 | 18.43 | 5.6 |
| 2006 | 296.21 | 320.23 | 100.0 | 224.76 | 242.98 | 75.9 | 21.65 | 23.41 | 7.3 | 34.91 | 37.74 | 11.8 | 14.89 | 16.10 | 5.0 |
| 2007 | 310.57 | 326.57 | 100.0 | 233.11 | 245.12 | 75.1 | 23.22 | 24.42 | 7.5 | 40.00 | 42.06 | 12.9 | 14.24 | 14.97 | 4.6 |
| 2008 | 299.81 | 303.76 | 100.0 | 213.86 | 216.68 | 71.3 | 31.33 | 31.74 | 10.4 | 42.21 | 42.77 | 14.1 | 12.41 | 12.57 | 4.1 |
| 2009 | 280.30 | 284.85 | 100.0 | 206.16 | 209.51 | 73.5 | 19.22 | 19.53 | 6.9 | 41.09 | 41.76 | 14.7 | 13.83 | 14.05 | 4.9 |
| 2010 | 290.89 | 290.89 | 100.0 | 211.77 | 211.77 | 72.8 | 22.83 | 22.83 | 7.8 | 41.00 | 41.00 | 14.1 | 15.29 | 15.29 | 5.3 |

*Source:* Giving USA Foundation, *Giving USA* (2011).
*Note:* Inflation adjustments were calculated using actual dollar values and then rounded.

**Figure 3.5.** Per Capita Individual Charitable Contributions, 1970–2010

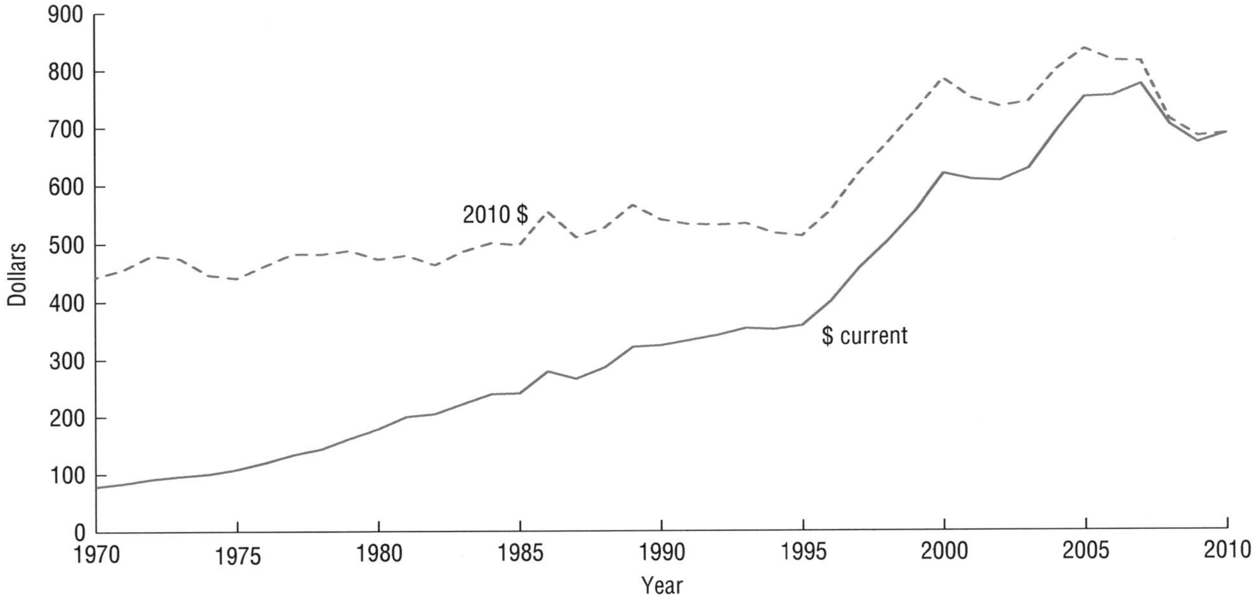

*Sources:* Private and individual giving from Giving USA Foundation, *Giving USA* (2011); population from Chairman of the Council of Economic Advisers, *Economic Report of the President*, table B-34 (2011); personal income from U.S. Department of Commerce, Bureau of Economic Analysis, National Income and Product Accounts, table 2.1 (2011).

of individual contributions. The average itemizer's charitable gift was about 7 times larger than nonitemizers' contributions in 2009. This is slightly down from earlier years when contributions were 8 to 9 times larger. In fact, until 2007, itemizers typically gave twice the percentage of income of nonitemizers. This ratio has been falling slightly, and was closer to 1.5 times more in 2009.

From 2000 to 2010, the number of itemizers claiming charitable deductions has dropped slightly. Approximately 88 percent of itemizers claimed a charitable deduction in 1999 compared with 82 percent in 2009. From 2005 to 2009, the general trend in total charitable contributions on itemized tax returns was downward. In constant dollars, charitable deductions dropped 14 percent from 2007 to 2008 and another 8 percent from 2008 to 2009. The average charitable deduction taken by itemizers also declined from $4,874 in 2007 to $4,388 in 2008 and $4,243 in 2009 (see table 3.6).

Table 3.7 displays charitable contributions for itemizers with adjusted gross incomes of $1 million or more. Itemizers at this income level that claim charitable deductions accounted for less than 1 percent of all itemized returns with charitable deductions and 18 percent of total charitable contributions reported. In 2009, these high-income earners reported total contributions of nearly $29.2 million. This accounts for about 4 percent of the total adjusted gross income of high-income itemizers. Between 2008 and 2009, adjusted gross income declined 32.3 percent and the amount of contributions

**Table 3.4.** Per Capita Contributions and Individual Contributions as a Percentage of National Income, 1970–2010

| Year | Private Giving | | Population (midyear, millions) | Per Capita Individual Giving | | Total personal income ($ billions) | Individual giving as a % of income |
|---|---|---|---|---|---|---|---|
| | Total | By individuals | | $ | $ 2010 | | |
| 1970 | 21.04 | 16.19 | 205.1 | 79.0 | 443.5 | 838.6 | 1.9 |
| 1971 | 23.44 | 17.64 | 207.7 | 84.7 | 456.6 | 903.1 | 1.9 |
| 1972 | 24.44 | 19.37 | 209.9 | 92.4 | 480.7 | 992.6 | 2.0 |
| 1973 | 25.59 | 20.53 | 211.9 | 96.7 | 474.9 | 1,110.5 | 1.8 |
| 1974 | 26.88 | 21.60 | 213.9 | 101.0 | 446.8 | 1,222.7 | 1.8 |
| 1975 | 28.56 | 23.53 | 216.0 | 108.8 | 441.0 | 1,334.9 | 1.8 |
| 1976 | 31.85 | 26.32 | 218.0 | 120.6 | 462.6 | 1,474.7 | 1.8 |
| 1977 | 35.21 | 29.55 | 220.2 | 134.4 | 482.7 | 1,632.5 | 1.8 |
| 1978 | 38.57 | 32.10 | 222.6 | 144.2 | 482.3 | 1,836.7 | 1.7 |
| 1979 | 43.11 | 36.59 | 225.1 | 162.6 | 488.1 | 2,059.5 | 1.8 |
| 1980 | 48.63 | 40.71 | 227.7 | 178.7 | 473.0 | 2,301.5 | 1.8 |
| 1981 | 55.28 | 45.99 | 230.0 | 200.0 | 479.5 | 2,582.3 | 1.8 |
| 1982 | 59.11 | 47.63 | 232.2 | 205.0 | 463.0 | 2,766.8 | 1.7 |
| 1983 | 63.21 | 52.06 | 234.3 | 222.4 | 486.2 | 2,952.2 | 1.8 |
| 1984 | 68.58 | 56.46 | 236.3 | 239.1 | 500.9 | 3,268.9 | 1.7 |
| 1985 | 71.69 | 57.39 | 238.5 | 240.7 | 497.1 | 3,496.7 | 1.6 |
| 1986 | 83.25 | 67.09 | 240.7 | 278.8 | 554.1 | 3,696.0 | 1.8 |
| 1987 | 82.20 | 64.53 | 242.8 | 265.7 | 510.1 | 3,924.4 | 1.6 |
| 1988 | 88.04 | 69.98 | 245.0 | 285.7 | 526.0 | 4,231.2 | 1.7 |
| 1989 | 98.30 | 79.45 | 247.3 | 321.5 | 564.6 | 4,557.5 | 1.7 |
| 1990 | 100.52 | 81.04 | 250.1 | 323.9 | 540.1 | 4,846.7 | 1.7 |
| 1991 | 104.92 | 84.27 | 253.5 | 332.5 | 531.9 | 5,031.5 | 1.7 |
| 1992 | 111.79 | 87.70 | 256.9 | 341.4 | 530.9 | 5,347.3 | 1.6 |
| 1993 | 116.86 | 92.00 | 260.3 | 353.4 | 533.1 | 5,568.1 | 1.7 |
| 1994 | 120.29 | 92.52 | 263.4 | 351.2 | 516.6 | 5,874.8 | 1.6 |
| 1995 | 123.68 | 95.36 | 266.6 | 357.8 | 511.7 | 6,200.9 | 1.5 |
| 1996 | 139.10 | 107.56 | 269.7 | 399.0 | 553.9 | 6,591.6 | 1.6 |
| 1997 | 162.99 | 124.20 | 272.9 | 455.1 | 618.4 | 7,000.7 | 1.8 |
| 1998 | 176.80 | 138.35 | 276.1 | 501.3 | 669.9 | 7,525.4 | 1.8 |

*(continued)*

**Table 3.4.** Per Capita Contributions and Individual Contributions as a Percentage of National Income, 1970–2010 *(continued)*

| Year | Private Giving | | Population (midyear, millions) | Per Capita Individual Giving | | Total personal income ($ billions) | Individual giving as a % of income |
|------|-------|---------------|------|------|--------|---------|------|
| | Total | By individuals | | $ | $ 2010 | | |
| 1999 | 202.74 | 154.63 | 279.3 | 553.5 | 724.7 | 7,910.8 | 2.0 |
| 2000 | 229.71 | 174.51 | 282.4 | 617.9 | 782.2 | 8,559.4 | 2.0 |
| 2001 | 232.04 | 173.36 | 285.3 | 607.6 | 748.3 | 8,883.3 | 2.0 |
| 2002 | 233.11 | 174.44 | 288.1 | 605.5 | 733.9 | 9,060.1 | 1.9 |
| 2003 | 238.06 | 181.97 | 290.8 | 625.7 | 741.4 | 9,378.1 | 1.9 |
| 2004 | 261.20 | 202.97 | 293.5 | 691.6 | 797.7 | 9,937.2 | 2.0 |
| 2005 | 294.44 | 221.99 | 296.2 | 749.5 | 832.8 | 10,485.9 | 2.1 |
| 2006 | 296.21 | 224.76 | 299.0 | 751.7 | 812.7 | 11,268.1 | 2.0 |
| 2007 | 310.57 | 233.11 | 302.0 | 771.9 | 811.6 | 11,912.3 | 2.0 |
| 2008 | 299.81 | 213.86 | 304.8 | 701.6 | 710.9 | 12,460.2 | 1.7 |
| 2009 | 280.30 | 206.16 | 307.4 | 670.6 | 681.5 | 11,930.2 | 1.7 |
| 2010 | 290.89 | 211.77 | 308.7 | 685.9 | 685.9 | 12,373.5 | 1.7 |

*Sources:* Private and individual giving from Giving USA Foundation, *Giving USA* (2011); population from Chairman of the Council of Economic Advisers, *Economic Report of the President,* table B-34 (2011); personal income from U.S. Department of Commerce, Bureau of Economic Analysis, National Income and Product Accounts, table 2.1 (2011).
*Note:* Inflation adjustments were calculated using actual dollar values and then rounded.

**Figure 3.6.** Household Charitable Gifts by Recipient Organization, 2007 (percent)

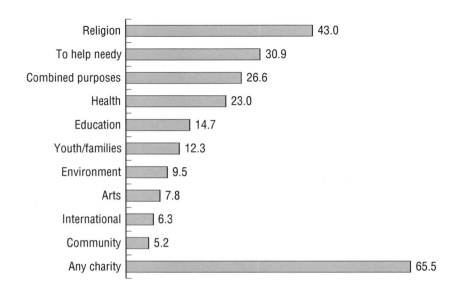

| | |
|------|------|
| Religion | 43.0 |
| To help needy | 30.9 |
| Combined purposes | 26.6 |
| Health | 23.0 |
| Education | 14.7 |
| Youth/families | 12.3 |
| Environment | 9.5 |
| Arts | 7.8 |
| International | 6.3 |
| Community | 5.2 |
| Any charity | 65.5 |

*Source:* Center on Philanthropy, Center on Philanthropy Panel Study (2007).

**Table 3.5.** Estimates of Individual Charitable Contributions by Tax-Itemization Status, 1985–2009 (current dollars)

| | Returns | Adjusted gross income ($ millions) | Adjusted gross income per return | Charitable contributions ($ millions) | Average charitable contributions | As a % of adjusted gross income |
|---|---|---|---|---|---|---|
| **1985** | | | | | | |
| All | 101,660,287 | 2,305,952 | 22,683 | 57,390 | 565 | 2.49 |
| Itemizer | 39,848,184 | 1,582,587 | 39,715 | 47,963 | 1,204 | 3.03 |
| Nonitemizer | 61,812,103 | 723,365 | 11,703 | 9,427 | 153 | 1.30 |
| **1986** | | | | | | |
| All | 103,045,170 | 2,481,681 | 24,083 | 67,090 | 651 | 2.70 |
| Itemizer | 40,667,008 | 1,725,714 | 42,435 | 53,816 | 1,323 | 3.12 |
| Nonitemizer | 62,378,162 | 755,967 | 12,119 | 13,274 | 213 | 1.76 |
| **1987** | | | | | | |
| All | 106,996,270 | 2,772,824 | 25,915 | 64,530 | 603 | 2.33 |
| Itemizer | 35,627,790 | 1,799,048 | 50,496 | 49,624 | 1,393 | 2.76 |
| Nonitemizer | 71,368,480 | 973,776 | 13,644 | 14,906 | 209 | 1.53 |
| **1988** | | | | | | |
| All | 109,708,280 | 3,083,020 | 28,102 | 69,980 | 638 | 2.27 |
| Itemizer | 31,902,985 | 1,887,494 | 59,164 | 50,949 | 1,597 | 2.70 |
| Nonitemizer | 77,805,295 | 1,195,526 | 15,366 | 19,031 | 245 | 1.59 |
| **1989** | | | | | | |
| All | 112,135,673 | 3,256,359 | 29,039 | 79,450 | 709 | 2.44 |
| Itemizer | 31,972,317 | 1,971,222 | 61,654 | 55,459 | 1,735 | 2.81 |
| Nonitemizer | 80,163,356 | 1,285,137 | 16,031 | 23,991 | 299 | 1.87 |
| **1990** | | | | | | |
| All | 113,717,136 | 3,405,428 | 29,946 | 81,040 | 713 | 2.38 |
| Itemizer | 32,174,938 | 2,046,651 | 63,610 | 57,243 | 1,779 | 2.80 |
| Nonitemizer | 81,542,198 | 1,358,777 | 16,663 | 23,797 | 292 | 1.75 |
| **1991** | | | | | | |
| All | 114,730,124 | 3,464,524 | 30,197 | 84,270 | 735 | 2.43 |
| Itemizer | 32,489,919 | 2,056,805 | 63,306 | 60,574 | 1,864 | 2.95 |
| Nonitemizer | 82,240,205 | 1,407,719 | 17,117 | 23,696 | 288 | 1.68 |

*(continued)*

**Table 3.5.** Estimates of Individual Charitable Contributions by Tax-Itemization Status, 1985–2009 (current dollars) *(continued)*

| | Returns | Adjusted gross income ($ millions) | Adjusted gross income per return | Charitable contributions ($ millions) | Average charitable contributions | As a % of adjusted gross income |
|---|---|---|---|---|---|---|
| **1992** | | | | | | |
| All | 113,604,503 | 3,629,129 | 31,945 | 87,700 | 772 | 2.42 |
| Itemizer | 32,540,614 | 2,183,969 | 67,115 | 63,843 | 1,962 | 2.92 |
| Nonitemizer | 81,063,889 | 1,445,160 | 17,827 | 23,857 | 294 | 1.65 |
| **1993** | | | | | | |
| All | 114,601,819 | 3,723,340 | 32,489 | 92,000 | 803 | 2.47 |
| Itemizer | 32,821,464 | 2,241,087 | 68,281 | 68,354 | 2,083 | 3.05 |
| Nonitemizer | 81,780,355 | 1,482,253 | 18,125 | 23,646 | 289 | 1.60 |
| **1994** | | | | | | |
| All | 115,943,131 | 3,907,518 | 33,702 | 92,520 | 798 | 2.37 |
| Itemizer | 33,017,754 | 2,342,834 | 70,957 | 70,545 | 2,137 | 3.01 |
| Nonitemizer | 82,925,377 | 1,564,684 | 18,869 | 21,975 | 265 | 1.40 |
| **1995** | | | | | | |
| All | 118,218,327 | 4,189,354 | 35,437 | 95,360 | 807 | 2.28 |
| Itemizer | 34,007,717 | 2,542,781 | 74,771 | 74,992 | 2,205 | 2.95 |
| Nonitemizer | 84,210,610 | 1,646,573 | 19,553 | 20,368 | 242 | 1.24 |
| **1996** | | | | | | |
| All | 120,351,208 | 4,535,974 | 37,689 | 107,560 | 894 | 2.37 |
| Itemizer | 35,414,589 | 2,812,927 | 79,428 | 86,159 | 2,433 | 3.06 |
| Nonitemizer | 84,936,619 | 1,723,048 | 20,286 | 21,401 | 252 | 1.24 |
| **1997** | | | | | | |
| All | 122,421,991 | 4,969,950 | 40,597 | 124,200 | 1,015 | 2.50 |
| Itemizer | 36,624,595 | 3,130,184 | 85,467 | 99,192 | 2,708 | 3.17 |
| Nonitemizer | 85,797,396 | 1,839,766 | 21,443 | 25,008 | 291 | 1.36 |
| **1998** | | | | | | |
| All | 124,770,662 | 5,415,973 | 43,407 | 138,350 | 1,109 | 2.55 |
| Itemizer | 38,186,186 | 3,466,035 | 90,767 | 109,240 | 2,861 | 3.15 |
| Nonitemizer | 86,584,476 | 1,949,938 | 22,521 | 29,110 | 336 | 1.49 |

*(continued)*

**Table 3.5.** Estimates of Individual Charitable Contributions by Tax-Itemization Status, 1985–2009 (current dollars) *(continued)*

| | Returns | Adjusted gross income ($ millions) | Adjusted gross income per return | Charitable contributions ($ millions) | Average charitable contributions | As a % of adjusted gross income |
|---|---|---|---|---|---|---|
| **1999** | | | | | | |
| All | 127,075,145 | 5,855,468 | 46,079 | 154,630 | 1,217 | 2.64 |
| Itemizer | 40,244,305 | 3,853,151 | 95,744 | 125,799 | 3,126 | 3.26 |
| Nonitemizer | 86,830,840 | 2,002,317 | 23,060 | 28,831 | 332 | 1.44 |
| **2000** | | | | | | |
| All | 129,373,500 | 6,365,377 | 49,202 | 174,510 | 1,349 | 2.74 |
| Itemizer | 42,534,320 | 4,294,262 | 100,960 | 140,682 | 3,307 | 3.28 |
| Nonitemizer | 86,839,180 | 2,071,115 | 23,850 | 33,828 | 389 | 1.63 |
| **2001** | | | | | | |
| All | 130,255,237 | 6,170,604 | 47,373 | 173,360 | 1,324 | 2.79 |
| Itemizer | 44,562,308 | 4,164,470 | 93,453 | 139,241 | 3,125 | 3.34 |
| Nonitemizer | 85,692,929 | 2,006,134 | 23,411 | 34,119 | 398 | 1.70 |
| **2002** | | | | | | |
| All | 130,076,443 | 6,033,586 | 46,385 | 174,440 | 1,329 | 2.87 |
| Itemizer | 45,647,551 | 4,080,678 | 89,395 | 140,571 | 3,079 | 3.44 |
| Nonitemizer | 84,428,892 | 1,952,907 | 23,131 | 33,869 | 401 | 1.73 |
| **2003** | | | | | | |
| All | 130,423,626 | 6,207,109 | 47,592 | 181,970 | 1,382 | 2.90 |
| Itemizer | 43,949,591 | 4,103,653 | 93,372 | 145,702 | 3,315 | 3.55 |
| Nonitemizer | 86,474,035 | 2,103,455 | 24,325 | 36,268 | 419 | 1.72 |
| **2004** | | | | | | |
| All | 132,226,042 | 6,788,805 | 51,342 | 202,970 | 1,519 | 2.96 |
| Itemizer | 46,335,237 | 4,643,404 | 100,213 | 165,564 | 3,573 | 3.57 |
| Nonitemizer | 85,890,805 | 2,145,402 | 24,978 | 37,406 | 436 | 1.74 |
| **2005** | | | | | | |
| All | 134,372,678 | 7,422,496 | 55,238 | 221,990 | 1,589 | 2.99 |
| Itemizer | 47,755,427 | 5,185,666 | 108,588 | 183,391 | 3,840 | 3.54 |
| Nonitemizer | 86,617,251 | 2,236,830 | 25,824 | 38,599 | 446 | 1.73 |

*(continued)*

**Table 3.5.** Estimates of Individual Charitable Contributions by Tax-Itemization Status, 1985–2009 (current dollars) *(continued)*

| | Returns | Adjusted gross income ($ millions) | Adjusted gross income per return | Charitable contributions ($ millions) | Average charitable contributions | As a % of adjusted gross income |
|---|---|---|---|---|---|---|
| **2006** | | | | | | |
| All | 138,394,754 | 8,030,843 | 58,029 | 224,760 | 1,624 | 2.80 |
| Itemizer | 49,123,555 | 5,703,411 | 116,103 | 186,647 | 3,800 | 3.27 |
| Nonitemizer | 89,271,199 | 2,327,432 | 26,071 | 38,113 | 427 | 1.64 |
| **2007** | | | | | | |
| All | 142,978,806 | 8,687,719 | 60,762 | 233,110 | 1,630 | 2.68 |
| Itemizer | 50,544,470 | 6,187,836 | 122,424 | 193,604 | 3,830 | 3.13 |
| Nonitemizer | 92,434,336 | 2,499,883 | 27,045 | 39,506 | 427 | 1.58 |
| **2008** | | | | | | |
| All | 142,450,569 | 8,262,860 | 58,005 | 213,860 | 1,501 | 2.59 |
| Itemizer | 48,167,223 | 5,731,767 | 118,997 | 172,936 | 3,590 | 3.02 |
| Nonitemizer | 94,283,346 | 2,531,093 | 26,846 | 40,924 | 434 | 1.62 |
| **2009** | | | | | | |
| All | 140,494,127 | 7,626,431 | 54,283 | 206,160 | 1,467 | 2.70 |
| Itemizer | 45,695,736 | 5,098,314 | 111,571 | 158,017 | 3,458 | 3.10 |
| Nonitemizer | 94,798,391 | 2,528,116 | 26,668 | 48,143 | 508 | 1.90 |

*Sources:* U.S. Department of the Treasury, Internal Revenue Service, Statistics of Income, table 1.2 (1985–2009) and table 2.1 (1985–2009); Giving USA Foundation, *Giving USA* (2011).
*Notes:* Statistics of Income data are based on a sample of individual tax returns. Nonitemizer giving is the difference between individual giving from table 3.3 and itemizer giving.

dropped almost $10 million, a 25 percent decline in itemized donations. The average charitable contribution, in constant dollars, for these donors peaked in 1997 at $188,465. Since then, however, tax data show a generally downward trend. Since 2000, the average charitable contribution has declined by a third from $185,609 in 2000 to $126,700 in 2009 (in constant dollars).

Gifts to charities can be either cash contributions or noncash contributions such as vehicles or investments. While cash contributions have always accounted for most itemizer deductions, the proportion of cash contributions had been trending generally downward since peaking in 1987 at 88 percent. However, cash contributions are starting to rise again. In 2009, 82 percent of itemizer contributions were in cash. This is the highest proportion of cash contributions in the past 10 years (see figure 3.7, table 3.8). For itemizers with $1 million or more in adjusted gross income, cash

**Table 3.6.** Average Charitable Deduction of All Itemizers and Itemizers with Charitable Deductions, 1985–2009

| Year | Returns — All itemized returns | Returns — With charitable contributions | Total Charitable Deductions — Current $, millions | Total Charitable Deductions — Constant $2009, millions | Avg Charitable Contribution — All Itemized Returns — Current $ | Avg Charitable Contribution — All Itemized Returns — Constant $2009 | Avg Charitable Contribution — With Charitable Deductions — Current $ | Avg Charitable Contribution — With Charitable Deductions — Constant $2009 |
|---|---|---|---|---|---|---|---|---|
| 1985 | 39,848,184 | 36,228,636 | 47,963 | 95,544 | 1,204 | 2,398 | 1,324 | 2,637 |
| 1986 | 40,667,008 | 36,857,590 | 53,816 | 105,315 | 1,323 | 2,590 | 1,460 | 2,857 |
| 1987 | 35,627,790 | 32,229,545 | 49,624 | 93,630 | 1,393 | 2,628 | 1,540 | 2,905 |
| 1988 | 31,902,985 | 29,110,570 | 50,949 | 92,466 | 1,597 | 2,898 | 1,750 | 3,176 |
| 1989 | 31,972,317 | 29,132,485 | 55,459 | 95,950 | 1,735 | 3,001 | 1,904 | 3,294 |
| 1990 | 32,174,938 | 29,230,264 | 57,243 | 93,995 | 1,779 | 2,921 | 1,958 | 3,216 |
| 1991 | 32,489,919 | 29,551,348 | 60,574 | 95,392 | 1,864 | 2,936 | 2,050 | 3,228 |
| 1992 | 32,540,614 | 29,603,407 | 63,843 | 97,619 | 1,962 | 3,000 | 2,157 | 3,298 |
| 1993 | 32,821,464 | 29,799,001 | 68,354 | 101,415 | 2,083 | 3,090 | 2,294 | 3,403 |
| 1994 | 33,017,754 | 29,848,727 | 70,545 | 102,091 | 2,137 | 3,092 | 2,363 | 3,420 |
| 1995 | 34,007,717 | 30,540,637 | 74,992 | 105,623 | 2,205 | 3,106 | 2,455 | 3,458 |
| 1996 | 35,414,589 | 31,591,983 | 86,159 | 117,865 | 2,433 | 3,328 | 2,727 | 3,731 |
| 1997 | 36,624,595 | 32,612,634 | 99,192 | 132,610 | 2,708 | 3,621 | 3,042 | 4,066 |
| 1998 | 38,186,186 | 33,835,992 | 109,240 | 143,737 | 2,861 | 3,764 | 3,229 | 4,248 |
| 1999 | 40,244,305 | 35,523,471 | 125,799 | 161,903 | 3,126 | 4,023 | 3,541 | 4,558 |
| 2000 | 42,534,320 | 37,524,825 | 140,682 | 175,196 | 3,307 | 4,119 | 3,749 | 4,669 |
| 2001 | 44,562,308 | 39,386,782 | 139,241 | 168,777 | 3,125 | 3,787 | 3,535 | 4,285 |
| 2002 | 45,647,551 | 40,399,695 | 140,571 | 167,546 | 3,079 | 3,670 | 3,480 | 4,147 |
| 2003 | 43,949,591 | 38,626,902 | 145,702 | 169,816 | 3,315 | 3,864 | 3,772 | 4,396 |
| 2004 | 46,335,237 | 40,623,426 | 165,564 | 187,927 | 3,573 | 4,056 | 4,076 | 4,626 |
| 2005 | 47,755,427 | 41,381,465 | 183,391 | 201,529 | 3,840 | 4,220 | 4,432 | 4,870 |
| 2006 | 49,123,555 | 41,437,749 | 186,647 | 198,560 | 3,800 | 4,042 | 4,504 | 4,792 |
| 2007 | 50,544,470 | 41,119,033 | 193,604 | 200,418 | 3,830 | 3,965 | 4,708 | 4,874 |
| 2008 | 48,167,223 | 39,250,369 | 172,936 | 172,247 | 3,590 | 3,576 | 4,406 | 4,388 |
| 2009 | 45,695,736 | 37,243,302 | 158,017 | 158,017 | 3,458 | 3,458 | 4,243 | 4,243 |

*Sources:* U.S. Department of the Treasury, Internal Revenue Service, Statistics of Income, Individual Complete Report (Publication 1304), table 2.1 (1985–2009); constant dollar values are authors' calculations using the Consumer Price Index for Urban Consumers, all items, U.S. City Average, from the Bureau of Labor Statistics and using the 2009 figure as the baseline for comparison (i.e., rebased to 2009 = 100).

**Table 3.7.** Charitable Contributions of Itemizers with Adjusted Gross Income of $1 Million or More, 1993–2009

| Year | Returns filed | Returns with charitable deductions | % of returns with contribution deductions | % of all returns filed with contribution deductions | $ Thousands (current) | |
|------|------|------|------|------|------|------|
| | | | | | AGI | Total contributions |
| 1993 | 62,392 | 60,904 | 97.6 | 0.20 | 163,049,402 | 7,050,906 |
| 1994 | 64,814 | 63,323 | 97.7 | 0.21 | 172,014,314 | 7,872,412 |
| 1995 | 80,362 | 78,447 | 97.6 | 0.26 | 214,365,387 | 8,845,408 |
| 1996 | 102,129 | 99,728 | 97.6 | 0.32 | 296,349,836 | 13,648,238 |
| 1997 | 132,072 | 128,684 | 97.4 | 0.39 | 397,475,502 | 18,618,418 |
| 1998 | 155,879 | 151,683 | 97.3 | 0.45 | 496,505,525 | 21,141,556 |
| 1999 | 186,729 | 181,701 | 97.3 | 0.51 | 610,730,186 | 27,245,122 |
| 2000 | 218,949 | 212,157 | 96.9 | 0.57 | 770,956,226 | 32,633,045 |
| 2001 | 178,520 | 173,957 | 97.4 | 0.44 | 547,369,318 | 24,932,570 |
| 2002 | 155,055 | 151,300 | 97.6 | 0.37 | 447,482,537 | 20,811,652 |
| 2003 | 165,399 | 161,136 | 97.4 | 0.42 | 503,009,522 | 24,196,568 |
| 2004 | 219,411 | 214,027 | 97.5 | 0.53 | 718,083,999 | 34,123,211 |
| 2005 | 278,701 | 271,010 | 97.2 | 0.65 | 970,597,258 | 45,412,078 |
| 2006 | 338,761 | 326,164 | 96.3 | 0.79 | 1,177,100,230 | 48,977,919 |
| 2007 | 375,567 | 361,317 | 96.2 | 0.88 | 1,363,116,669 | 55,491,266 |
| 2008 | 310,829 | 298,432 | 96.0 | 0.76 | 1,051,670,613 | 39,133,378 |
| 2009 | 230,323 | 220,455 | 95.7 | 0.59 | 711,598,278 | 29,181,815 |

*Sources:* U.S. Department of the Treasury, Internal Revenue Service, Statistics of Income, Individual Complete Report (Publication 1304), table 2.1 (1993–2009); constant dollar values are authors' calculations using the Consumer Price Index for Urban Consumers, all items, U.S. City Average, from the Bureau of Labor Statistics and using the 2009 figure as the baseline for comparison (i.e., rebased to 2009 = 100).
*Note:* Cash and noncash contributions may not sum to total contributions because the values are derived from Form 8283, which is filed by itemizers that report more than $500 of noncash contributions.
AGI = adjusted gross income

contributions accounted for 67 percent of reported donations in 2009, the highest value on record. This is a shift from 2007, when 51 percent of contributions were cash gifts (table 3.7).

The shift from noncash to cash contributions may result partly from the recession. Investments, including stocks, mutual funds, real estate, and other assets, account for a large proportion of noncash donations. The market value of these types of gifts likely declined during the recession, so some donors were more reluctant to use these assets for charitable donations or simply had fewer assets to donate.

| Average Contributions | | Contributions as a % of AGI | Cash Contributions | | Noncash Contributions | |
|---|---|---|---|---|---|---|
| Current $ | Constant $2009 | | $ thousands | % | $ thousands | % |
| 113,010 | 167,671 | 4.3 | 3,907,828 | 54.5 | 3,265,085 | 45.5 |
| 121,462 | 175,777 | 4.6 | 3,882,070 | 48.7 | 4,092,446 | 51.3 |
| 110,070 | 155,028 | 4.1 | 4,667,770 | 59.6 | 3,168,163 | 40.4 |
| 133,637 | 182,814 | 4.6 | 5,808,136 | 43.7 | 7,479,736 | 56.3 |
| 140,972 | 188,465 | 4.7 | 7,365,764 | 38.8 | 11,641,343 | 61.2 |
| 135,628 | 178,458 | 4.3 | 9,299,041 | 45.3 | 11,238,947 | 54.7 |
| 145,907 | 187,782 | 4.5 | 10,208,251 | 38.9 | 16,021,218 | 61.1 |
| 149,044 | 185,609 | 4.2 | 12,384,192 | 32.9 | 25,304,866 | 67.1 |
| 139,663 | 169,288 | 4.6 | 11,772,323 | 43.0 | 15,576,513 | 57.0 |
| 134,221 | 159,977 | 4.7 | 11,159,827 | 53.1 | 9,843,792 | 46.9 |
| 146,292 | 170,503 | 4.8 | 12,169,102 | 49.8 | 12,255,944 | 50.2 |
| 155,522 | 176,529 | 4.8 | 17,231,783 | 50.4 | 16,958,795 | 49.6 |
| 162,942 | 179,057 | 4.5 | 25,960,921 | 54.6 | 21,547,363 | 45.4 |
| 144,580 | 153,808 | 4.2 | 27,269,896 | 49.8 | 27,451,809 | 50.2 |
| 147,753 | 152,954 | 4.1 | 30,864,409 | 51.1 | 29,552,084 | 48.9 |
| 125,900 | 125,398 | 3.7 | 28,273,674 | 63.8 | 16,013,777 | 36.2 |
| 126,700 | 126,700 | 4.1 | 21,610,432 | 66.9 | 10,677,556 | 33.1 |

Another factor in the decline of noncash contributions is the American Jobs Creation Act of 2004, which changed how deductions in vehicle donations, boats, and planes were valued. Under the new rules, if the charity sold the motor vehicle, the taxpayer could claim only the gross proceeds from the sale. Previously, the taxpayer could claim the fair-market value of the car, boat, or plane. The amount of vehicle donations reported dropped 75 percent from 2003 to 2008.

IRS Form 8283 details the types, amounts, and recipients of noncash contributions from itemizers that donated more than $500 in noncash property. Donated property

**Figure 3.7.** Cash versus Noncash Charitable Contributions, 1985–2009 (percent)

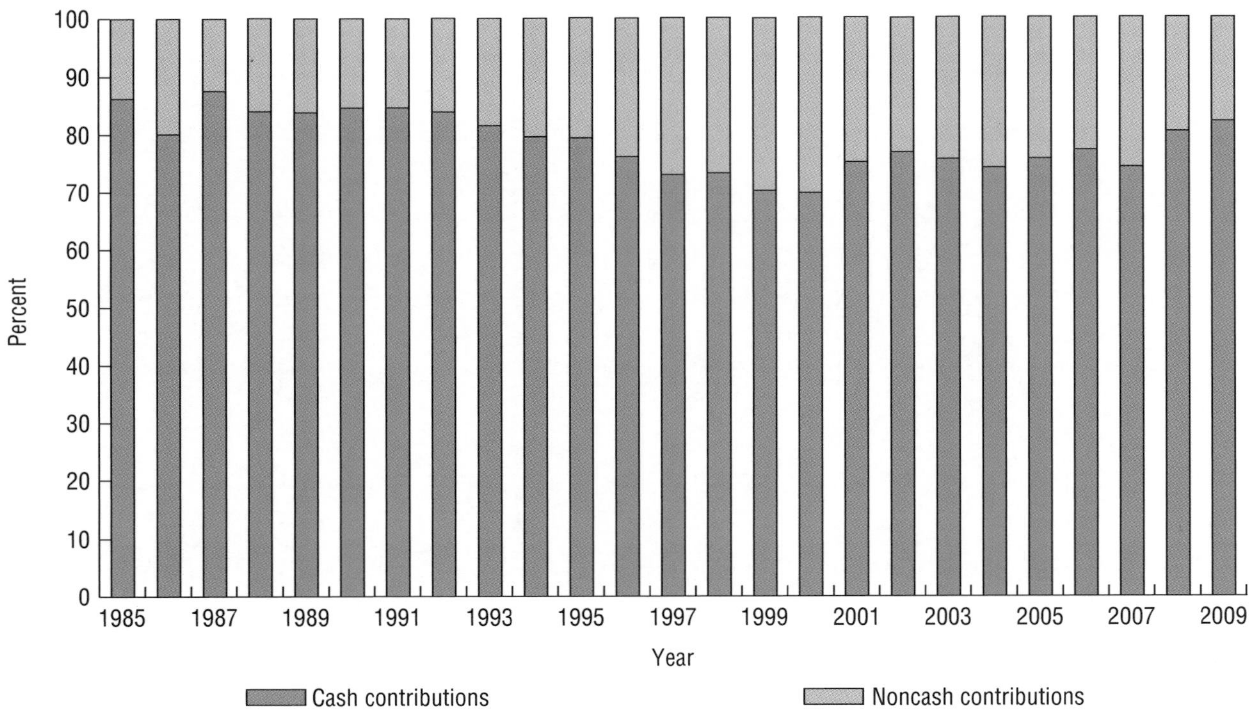

Cash contributions          Noncash contributions

*Source:* U.S. Department of the Treasury, Internal Revenue Service, Statistics of Income, Individual Complete Report (Publication 1304), table 2.1 (1985–2009).

includes clothing, motor vehicles, real estate, and corporate stock, mutual funds, and other investments. Table 3.9 shows the composition of noncash gifts. In 2008, $34.6 billion in noncash contributions was reported on Form 8283. Investments such as corporate stocks, mutual funds, and other investments account for the largest proportion of noncash contributions, about 43 percent. Donations of investments dropped 45 percent between 2007 and 2008. Clothing donations account for the second-largest type of noncash gift at 23 percent. Earners with adjusted gross income of $1 million or more contribute one-third of all noncash donations (see table 3.7).

## Giving by Bequests

Many individuals leave stocks, bonds, or other property such as land or artwork to charitable organizations in their wills or trusts. This form of donation is known as a bequest. The proportion of private giving accounted for by personal bequests spiked in 2008 at 10.4 percent—up 3 percentage points from 2007 (see table 3.3). After 2008, personal bequests as a percentage of private giving returned to pre-recession levels of between 7 and 8 percent.

**Table 3.8.** Distribution of Itemizers' Cash and Noncash Charitable Contributions, 1985–2009

| Year | Total Charitable Contributions | | Cash Contributions | | Noncash Contributions | |
|---|---|---|---|---|---|---|
| | $ thousands | % | $ thousands | % | $ thousands | % |
| 1985 | 47,962,848 | 100.0 | 41,371,619 | 86.3 | 6,591,229 | 13.7 |
| 1986 | 53,815,978 | 100.0 | 43,168,816 | 80.2 | 10,647,169 | 19.8 |
| 1987 | 49,623,906 | 100.0 | 43,448,099 | 87.6 | 6,175,807 | 12.4 |
| 1988 | 50,949,273 | 100.0 | 42,834,342 | 84.1 | 6,711,616 | 13.2 |
| 1989 | 55,459,205 | 100.0 | 46,553,194 | 83.9 | 7,550,914 | 13.6 |
| 1990 | 57,242,767 | 100.0 | 48,485,664 | 84.7 | 7,494,016 | 13.1 |
| 1991 | 60,573,565 | 100.0 | 51,277,927 | 84.7 | 9,681,786 | 16.0 |
| 1992 | 63,843,281 | 100.0 | 53,647,612 | 84.0 | 9,632,779 | 15.1 |
| 1993 | 68,354,293 | 100.0 | 55,784,521 | 81.6 | 12,278,893 | 18.0 |
| 1994 | 70,544,542 | 100.0 | 56,229,759 | 79.7 | 14,739,299 | 20.9 |
| 1995 | 74,991,519 | 100.0 | 59,589,837 | 79.5 | 13,521,937 | 18.0 |
| 1996 | 86,159,305 | 100.0 | 65,658,168 | 76.2 | 21,298,819 | 24.7 |
| 1997 | 99,191,962 | 100.0 | 72,425,402 | 73.0 | 27,961,174 | 28.2 |
| 1998 | 109,240,078 | 100.0 | 80,114,372 | 73.3 | 29,255,985 | 26.8 |
| 1999 | 125,798,548 | 100.0 | 88,276,422 | 70.2 | 38,286,580 | 30.4 |
| 2000 | 140,681,631 | 100.0 | 98,247,539 | 69.8 | 47,256,104 | 33.6 |
| 2001 | 139,241,476 | 100.0 | 104,747,173 | 75.2 | 37,997,546 | 27.3 |
| 2002 | 140,571,365 | 100.0 | 108,130,267 | 76.9 | 34,293,125 | 24.4 |
| 2003 | 145,702,137 | 100.0 | 110,336,696 | 75.7 | 38,041,067 | 26.1 |
| 2004 | 165,564,388 | 100.0 | 122,874,926 | 74.2 | 43,373,209 | 26.2 |
| 2005 | 183,390,686 | 100.0 | 139,054,112 | 75.8 | 48,056,520 | 26.2 |
| 2006 | 186,646,644 | 100.0 | 144,223,015 | 77.3 | 52,631,443 | 28.2 |
| 2007 | 193,603,968 | 100.0 | 143,826,766 | 74.3 | 58,747,438 | 30.3 |
| 2008 | 172,936,002 | 100.0 | 139,159,654 | 80.5 | 40,421,411 | 23.4 |
| 2009 | 158,016,526 | 100.0 | 129,946,302 | 82.2 | 31,816,050 | 20.1 |

*Source:* U.S. Department of the Treasury, Internal Revenue Service (IRS), Statistics of Income, Individual Complete Report (Publication 1304), table 2.1 (1985–2009).
*Note:* Due to treatment of tax-year carryovers by the IRS, the sum of cash and noncash contributions may not equal total contributions.

**Table 3.9.** Individual Noncash Charitable Contributions, All Itemized Returns with Donations Reported on Form 8283, by Donation Type, 2003–08

| Year | All Donation Types | | Corporate Stock, Mutual Funds, and Other Investments | | Real Estate and Easements | | Food | |
|---|---|---|---|---|---|---|---|---|
| | $ thousands | % | $ thousands | % | $ thousands | % | $ thousands | % |
| 2003 | 36,902,794 | 100.0 | 15,396,932 | 41.7 | 7,386,425 | 20.0 | 79,364 | 0.2 |
| 2004 | 37,189,160 | 100.0 | 16,551,693 | 44.5 | 4,561,737 | 12.3 | 104,409 | 0.3 |
| 2005 | 41,070,632 | 100.0 | 18,583,331 | 45.2 | 6,222,394 | 15.2 | 105,870 | 0.3 |
| 2006 | 46,841,245 | 100.0 | 26,075,272 | 55.7 | 5,357,813 | 11.4 | 96,294 | 0.2 |
| 2007 | 52,827,286 | 100.0 | 27,094,040 | 51.3 | 8,120,833 | 15.4 | 98,698 | 0.2 |
| 2008 | 34,597,290 | 100.0 | 14,865,203 | 43.0 | 3,561,485 | 10.3 | 116,550 | 0.3 |

*Source:* Internal Revenue Source, Statistics of Income Division, SOI Bulletin, Publication 1136 (2007–11).
*Note:* All figures reported are the amount carried to Schedule A from Form 8283.

The number of estate returns filed has decreased 68 percent in the past 10 years—a drastic decline. Given this, it is no surprise that the number of bequests recorded by the IRS has also declined—from 18,652 in 2001 to 6,242 in 2009. The sharp decline in estate returns is primarily due to changes in the estate tax. The Economic Growth and Tax Relief Reconciliation Act of 2001 incrementally increased estate tax exemption levels while simultaneously decreasing the highest marginal tax rates for estates. Bequests accounted for an estimated $16 billion of private giving in 2009. In constant dollars, this amount is the lowest since 1998. In 2008, however, the value of bequests given was at its highest since 1987—$28 billion (figure 3.8, table 3.10). As reported by the Foundation Center, the largest bequests in 2008 were made by Leona Helmsley, who left an estimated $5.2 billion to a charitable trust, and medical inventor James Sorenson, who left the Sorenson Legacy Foundation an estimated $4.5 billion (Foundation Center 2009).

Given the nature of charitable bequests, which are most likely to be from the nation's wealthiest people, their number and dollar value vary each year. There is no way to predict the number of bequests that will occur each year because it depends upon the number of donors' deaths. Changes in the economy and changes in estate tax law are factors in the dollar value of bequests.

## Giving by Foundations

Giving by foundations accounts for the second-largest proportion of private giving, contributing $45.8 billion to charities in 2009. Table 3.11 displays the overall picture of foundations in the United States since 1975. The data on foundations in this section are

| Clothing | | Household Items | | Other | | Cars and Other Vehicles | |
|---|---|---|---|---|---|---|---|
| $ thousands | % | $ thousands | % | $ thousands | % | $ thousands | % |
| 5,836,108 | 15.8 | 3,228,065 | 8.7 | 2,627,407 | 7.1 | 2,348,492 | 6.4 |
| 6,331,348 | 17.0 | 3,464,077 | 9.3 | 3,549,202 | 9.5 | 2,626,695 | 7.1 |
| 7,080,266 | 17.2 | 3,858,494 | 9.4 | 4,609,961 | 11.2 | 610,317 | 1.5 |
| 6,297,085 | 13.4 | 3,821,313 | 8.2 | 4,632,831 | 9.9 | 560,637 | 1.2 |
| 7,717,286 | 14.6 | 3,920,893 | 7.4 | 5,180,910 | 9.8 | 694,627 | 1.3 |
| 7,939,810 | 22.9 | 3,131,977 | 9.1 | 4,409,069 | 12.7 | 573,197 | 1.7 |

**Figure 3.8.** Number and Value of Charitable Bequests by Year Filed, 1987–2009 (current 2010 dollars)

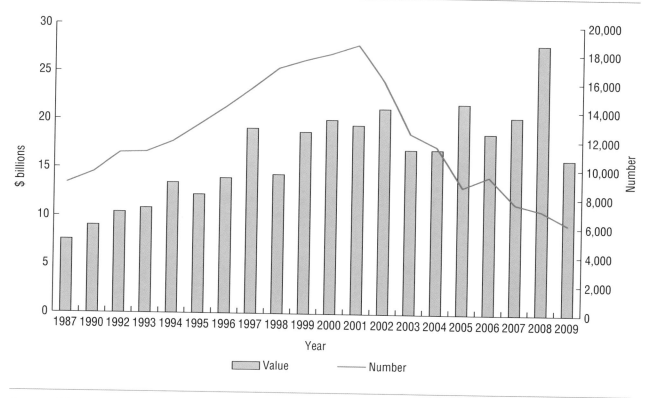

Sources: U.S. Department of the Treasury, Internal Revenue Service, Statistics of Income, Estate Tax Returns (1987, 1990, 1992–2009); constant dollar values are authors' calculations using the Consumer Price Index (2011).

**Table 3.10.** Estate Tax Returns and Charitable Bequests, Selected Years, 1987–2009

| Year | Returns | Gross Estate | | Number of bequests | % of total returns | Value of Bequests | | % of gross estate |
|---|---|---|---|---|---|---|---|---|
| | | $ billions | $ 2009, billions | | | $ billions | $ 2009, billions | |
| 1987 | 45,113 | 66.6 | 125.7 | 8,967 | 19.9 | 4.0 | 7.5 | 6.0 |
| 1990 | 50,367 | 87.1 | 143.0 | 9,709 | 19.3 | 5.5 | 9.0 | 6.3 |
| 1992 | 59,176 | 98.9 | 151.2 | 11,053 | 18.7 | 6.8 | 10.4 | 6.9 |
| 1993 | 60,211 | 103.7 | 153.9 | 11,119 | 18.5 | 7.3 | 10.8 | 7.0 |
| 1994 | 68,595 | 117.0 | 169.3 | 11,869 | 17.3 | 9.3 | 13.5 | 7.9 |
| 1995 | 69,755 | 117.7 | 165.8 | 13,039 | 18.7 | 8.7 | 12.3 | 7.4 |
| 1996 | 79,321 | 137.4 | 188.0 | 14,233 | 17.9 | 10.2 | 14.0 | 7.4 |
| 1997 | 90,006 | 162.3 | 217.0 | 15,575 | 17.3 | 14.3 | 19.1 | 8.8 |
| 1998 | 97,856 | 173.8 | 228.7 | 16,982 | 17.4 | 10.9 | 14.3 | 6.2 |
| 1999 | 103,979 | 196.4 | 252.8 | 17,554 | 16.9 | 14.6 | 18.8 | 7.4 |
| 2000 | 108,322 | 217.4 | 270.7 | 18,011 | 16.6 | 16.1 | 20.0 | 7.4 |
| 2001 | 106,885 | 214.8 | 260.4 | 18,652 | 17.5 | 16.1 | 19.5 | 7.5 |
| 2002 | 98,356 | 211.2 | 251.7 | 16,104 | 16.4 | 17.8 | 21.2 | 8.4 |
| 2003 | 66,042 | 194.5 | 226.7 | 12,492 | 18.9 | 14.6 | 17.0 | 7.5 |
| 2004 | 62,718 | 192.6 | 218.6 | 11,599 | 18.5 | 15.0 | 17.0 | 7.8 |
| 2005 | 45,070 | 184.7 | 203.0 | 8,785 | 19.5 | 19.8 | 21.8 | 10.7 |
| 2006 | 49,050 | 211.5 | 225.0 | 9,522 | 19.4 | 17.6 | 18.7 | 8.3 |
| 2007 | 38,000 | 203.0 | 210.1 | 7,666 | 20.2 | 19.7 | 20.4 | 9.7 |
| 2008 | 38,354 | 228.3 | 227.4 | 7,199 | 18.8 | 28.1 | 28.0 | 12.3 |
| 2009 | 33,515 | 194.6 | 194.6 | 6,242 | 18.6 | 16.0 | 16.0 | 8.2 |

*Source:* U.S. Department of the Treasury, Internal Revenue Service, Statistics of Income, Estate Tax Returns (1987, 1990, 1992–2009).

drawn from the Foundation Center and are based on a sample of all U.S. independent, corporate, community, and grantmaking operating foundations. When comparing the Foundation Center data to *Giving USA,* be aware that *Giving USA* classifies gifts from corporate foundations under giving by corporations, while the Foundation Center reports them as gifts from foundations.

According to the Foundation Center, there were 76,545 U.S. grantmaking foundations in 2009—a 52 percent increase over the past 10 years. In 2007, foundation assets hit an all-time high at $682.2 billion. However, assets dropped by 17 percent in 2008, by far the largest decline in the past 35 years. Although foundation assets were down,

**Table 3.11.** Grants Made, Gifts Received, and Assets Held by Foundations, 1975–2009

| Year | Number of grantmaking foundations | Grants Made | | Gifts Received | | Assets | |
|---|---|---|---|---|---|---|---|
| | | $ billions | % of 1978[a] | $ billions | % of 1978[a] | $ billions | % of 1978[a] |
| 1975 | 21,877 | 1.9 | 76.1 | — | — | 30.1 | 100.0 |
| 1976 | 21,447 | 2.2 | 87.5 | — | — | 34.8 | 115.5 |
| 1977 | 22,152 | 2.4 | 92.2 | — | — | 35.4 | 117.4 |
| 1978 | 22,484 | 2.6 | 100.0 | 1.6 | 100.0 | 37.3 | 100.0 |
| 1979 | 22,535 | 2.9 | 111.8 | 2.2 | 137.3 | 41.6 | 111.6 |
| 1980 | 22,088 | 3.4 | 134.5 | 2.0 | 123.0 | 48.2 | 129.2 |
| 1981 | 21,967 | 3.8 | 148.6 | 2.4 | 148.4 | 47.6 | 127.6 |
| 1982 | 23,770 | 4.5 | 176.1 | 4.0 | 248.4 | 58.7 | 157.4 |
| 1983 | 24,261 | 4.5 | 175.7 | 2.7 | 168.3 | 67.9 | 182.1 |
| 1984 | 24,859 | 5.0 | 197.6 | 3.4 | 208.7 | 74.1 | 198.7 |
| 1985 | 25,639 | 6.0 | 236.5 | 5.2 | 321.7 | 102.1 | 273.8 |
| 1986 | — | — | — | — | — | — | — |
| 1987 | 27,661 | 6.7 | 261.2 | 5.0 | 308.1 | 115.4 | 309.7 |
| 1988 | 30,338 | 7.4 | 291.0 | 5.2 | 320.5 | 122.1 | 327.6 |
| 1989 | 31,990 | 7.9 | 310.2 | 5.5 | 342.9 | 137.5 | 369.0 |
| 1990 | 32,401 | 8.7 | 340.4 | 5.0 | 308.7 | 142.5 | 382.3 |
| 1991 | 33,356 | 9.2 | 361.2 | 5.5 | 339.8 | 162.9 | 437.1 |
| 1992 | 35,765 | 10.2 | 400.4 | 6.2 | 383.9 | 176.8 | 474.4 |
| 1993 | 37,571 | 11.1 | 435.7 | 7.8 | 482.0 | 189.2 | 507.7 |
| 1994 | 38,807 | 11.3 | 442.7 | 8.1 | 501.9 | 195.8 | 525.3 |
| 1995 | 40,140 | 12.3 | 480.8 | 10.3 | 637.3 | 226.7 | 608.4 |
| 1996 | 41,588 | 13.8 | 542.7 | 16.0 | 995.0 | 267.6 | 718.0 |
| 1997 | 44,146 | 16.0 | 627.1 | 15.8 | 983.2 | 329.9 | 885.2 |
| 1998 | 46,832 | 19.5 | 763.1 | 22.6 | 1,401.9 | 385.1 | 1,033.1 |
| 1999 | 50,201 | 23.3 | 914.5 | 32.1 | 1,992.5 | 448.6 | 1,203.7 |
| 2000 | 56,582 | 27.6 | 1,080.8 | 27.6 | 1,714.9 | 486.1 | 1,304.2 |
| 2001 | 61,810 | 30.5 | 1,196.1 | 28.7 | 1,783.2 | 467.3 | 1,253.9 |
| 2002 | 64,843 | 30.4 | 1,193.3 | 22.2 | 1,376.4 | 435.2 | 1,167.7 |
| 2003 | 66,398 | 30.3 | 1,188.6 | 24.9 | 1,544.1 | 476.7 | 1,279.1 |
| 2004 | 67,736 | 31.8 | 1,248.6 | 24.0 | 1,490.1 | 510.5 | 1,369.7 |
| 2005 | 71,095 | 36.4 | 1,427.5 | 31.5 | 1,954.7 | 550.6 | 1,477.2 |
| 2006 | 72,477 | 39.0 | 1,529.4 | 36.6 | 2,271.4 | 614.7 | 1,649.2 |
| 2007 | 75,187 | 44.4 | 1,740.8 | 46.8 | 2,909.3 | 682.2 | 1,830.5 |
| 2008 | 75,595 | 46.8 | 1,834.5 | 39.6 | 2,456.5 | 565.0 | 1,515.8 |
| 2009 | 76,545 | 45.8 | 1,795.3 | 40.9 | 2,537.9 | 590.2 | 1,583.6 |

*Source:* Foundation Center, "Research Studies: National Trends" (2011).
*Notes:* Grants made include grants, scholarships, employee-matching gifts, and other amounts separated as "grants and contributions paid during the year" on Form 990-PF. Asset figures represent the market value of assets.
a. Dollar value from the previous column compared with the 1978 value (i.e., rebased to 1978 = 100).
— = data not available

**Figure 3.9.** Foundations Assets and Grants Made by Year, 1999–2009 (billions of dollars)

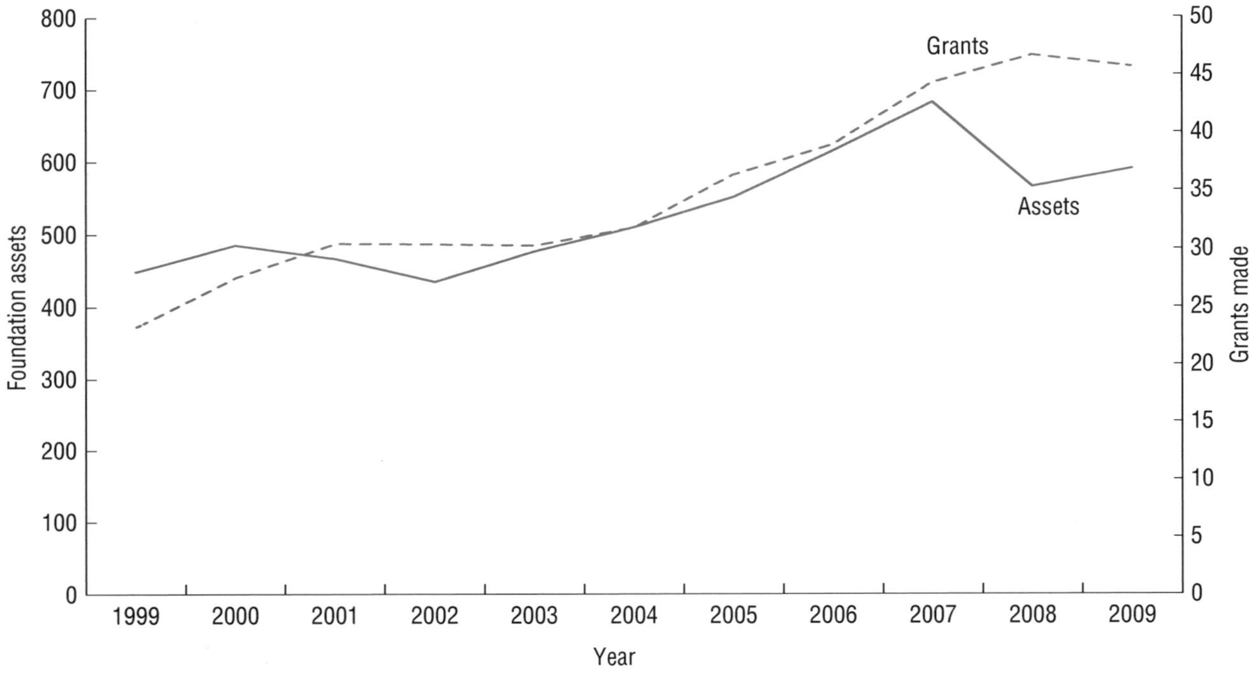

*Source:* Foundation Center, "Research Studies: National Trends" (2011).

foundation giving accounted for a greater proportion of private giving during both 2008 and 2009 than it had in previous years. From 2008 to 2010, foundation giving hovered around 14 percent of private giving—up just over 1 percent from 2007. Foundation giving increased by 96 percent from 1999 to 2010. While foundation assets plummeted in 2008, foundation giving reached an all-time high of $46.8 billion (figure 3.9). The record was fueled by increased giving from the Bill and Melinda Gates Foundation, which awarded over $2 billion in grants in 2007, a 28.7 percent increase from their 2006 grants awarded.

Foundations continue to receive contributions and bequests from donors and estates. In 2009, these gifts to foundations totaled $40.9 billion. Gifts received by foundations between 1999 and 2009 increased 27 percent.

One important trend in foundation grantmaking is the increase in the number, assets, and grantmaking of family foundations. The Foundation Center reports that 63 percent of dollars given by independent foundations come from family foundations, and that one-third of family foundations have been established since 2000. The Foundation Center defines family foundations as those grantmaking independent foundations with measurable donor or donor-family involvement. These include foundations with "family" or "families" in their name, a living donor whose surname matches the foundation name, or at least two trustee surnames that match a living or

**Figure 3.10.** Distribution of Foundations by Number, Assets, and Grants, 2009 (percent)

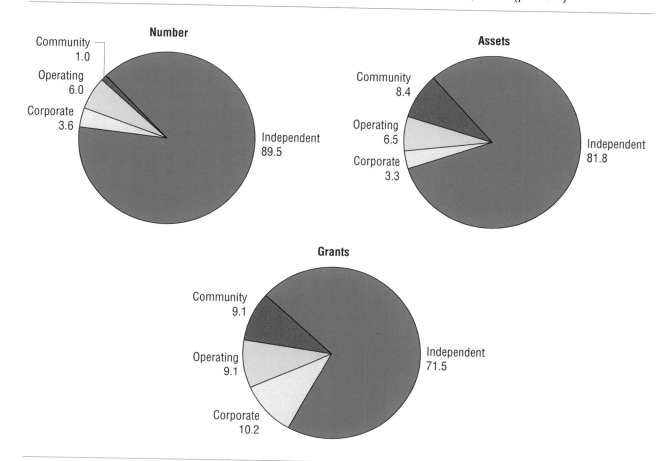

*Source:* Foundation Center, "Research Studies: National Trends" (2011).
*Notes:* The data are based on all grants of $10,000 or more awarded by a sample of 1,384 larger foundations. These grants totaled $22.1 billion and represented nearly half of total grant dollars awarded by all U.S. independent, corporate, community, and grantmaking operating foundations. Numbers may not total 100 because of rounding.

deceased donor's name, along with any independent foundations that self-identify as family foundations on annual Foundation Center surveys.

In 2009, independent foundations accounted for about 90 percent of all foundations, followed by operating foundations (6 percent), corporate foundations (3.6 percent), and community foundations (1 percent). Independent foundations also hold the majority of foundation assets (81.8 percent) and give the greatest proportion of grants (71.5 percent). Community foundations, while representing just 1 percent of foundations, gave over 9 percent of foundation grant dollars (figure 3.10, table 3.12).

Figure 3.11 displays the proportion of both the number of grants and value of grants by type of recipient organization. Human service organizations received over a quarter of all grants in terms of numbers in 2009. However, these organizations received only 13 percent of the amount of grants given by foundations. Health and

**Table 3.12.** Number of Foundations, Grants Made, Gifts Received, and Assets by Type of Foundation, 2000–09

| | Foundations | | Grants Made | | Gifts Received | | Assets | |
|---|---|---|---|---|---|---|---|---|
| | Number | % | $ millions | % | $ millions | % | $ millions | % |
| **2000** | | | | | | | | |
| Independent | 50,532 | 89.3 | 21,346 | 77.4 | 19,156 | 69.4 | 408,749 | 84.1 |
| Corporate | 2,018 | 3.6 | 2,985 | 10.8 | 2,902 | 10.5 | 15,899 | 3.3 |
| Operating | 3,472 | 6.1 | 1,066 | 3.9 | 1,727 | 6.3 | 30,973 | 6.4 |
| Community | 560 | 1.0 | 2,166 | 7.9 | 3,829 | 13.9 | 30,464 | 6.3 |
| Total | 56,582 | 100.0 | 27,563 | 100.0 | 27,614 | 100.0 | 486,085 | 100.0 |
| **2001** | | | | | | | | |
| Independent | 55,120 | 89.2 | 23,705 | 77.7 | 20,539 | 71.5 | 403,526 | 84.6 |
| Corporate | 2,170 | 3.5 | 3,284 | 10.8 | 3,040 | 10.6 | 15,578 | 3.3 |
| Operating | 3,918 | 6.3 | 1,110 | 3.6 | 1,950 | 6.8 | 27,384 | 5.7 |
| Community | 602 | 1.0 | 2,403 | 7.9 | 3,185 | 11.1 | 30,301 | 6.4 |
| Total | 61,810 | 100.0 | 30,502 | 100.0 | 28,714 | 100.0 | 467,336 | 100.0 |
| **2002** | | | | | | | | |
| Independent | 57,834 | 89.2 | 23,254 | 76.4 | 13,952 | 62.9 | 364,143 | 83.7 |
| Corporate | 2,362 | 3.6 | 3,457 | 11.4 | 3,002 | 13.5 | 14,428 | 3.3 |
| Operating | 3,986 | 6.1 | 1,195 | 3.9 | 2,035 | 9.2 | 26,847 | 6.2 |
| Community | 661 | 1.0 | 2,526 | 8.3 | 3,175 | 14.3 | 29,772 | 6.8 |
| Total | 64,843 | 100.0 | 30,432 | 100.0 | 22,163 | 100.0 | 435,190 | 100.0 |
| **2003** | | | | | | | | |
| Independent | 58,991 | 88.8 | 22,568 | 74.5 | 15,846 | 63.7 | 399,138 | 83.7 |
| Corporate | 2,549 | 3.8 | 3,466 | 11.4 | 3,234 | 13.0 | 15,447 | 3.2 |
| Operating | 4,159 | 6.3 | 1,744 | 5.8 | 2,302 | 9.3 | 27,975 | 5.9 |
| Community | 699 | 1.1 | 2,532 | 8.4 | 3,476 | 14.0 | 34,153 | 7.2 |
| Total | 66,398 | 100.0 | 30,309 | 100.0 | 24,858 | 100.0 | 476,713 | 100.0 |
| **2004** | | | | | | | | |
| Independent | 60,031 | 88.6 | 23,334 | 73.3 | 13,655 | 56.9 | 425,103 | 83.3 |
| Corporate | 2,596 | 3.8 | 3,430 | 10.8 | 3,667 | 15.3 | 16,645 | 3.3 |
| Operating | 4,409 | 6.5 | 2,164 | 6.8 | 2,808 | 11.7 | 29,951 | 5.9 |
| Community | 700 | 1.0 | 2,916 | 9.2 | 3,859 | 16.1 | 38,782 | 7.6 |
| Total | 67,736 | 100.0 | 31,844 | 100.0 | 23,989 | 100.0 | 510,481 | 100.0 |

*(continued)*

**Table 3.12.** Number of Foundations, Grants Made, Gifts Received, and Assets by Type of Foundation, 2000–09 *(continued)*

| | Foundations | | Grants Made | | Gifts Received | | Assets | |
|---|---|---|---|---|---|---|---|---|
| | Number | % | $ millions | % | $ millions | % | $ millions | % |
| **2005** | | | | | | | | |
| Independent | 63,059 | 88.7 | 25,199 | 69.2 | 17,366 | 55.2 | 455,570 | 82.7 |
| Corporate | 2,607 | 3.7 | 3,996 | 11.0 | 4,008 | 12.7 | 17,795 | 3.2 |
| Operating | 4,722 | 6.6 | 3,990 | 11.0 | 4,505 | 14.3 | 32,603 | 5.9 |
| Community | 707 | 1.0 | 3,217 | 8.8 | 5,587 | 17.8 | 44,583 | 8.1 |
| Total | 71,095 | 100.0 | 36,403 | 100.0 | 31,465 | 100.0 | 550,552 | 100.0 |
| **2006** | | | | | | | | |
| Independent | 64,405 | 88.9 | 27,457 | 70.4 | 21,591 | 59.0 | 509,077 | 82.8 |
| Corporate | 2,548 | 3.5 | 4,098 | 10.5 | 4,374 | 12.0 | 19,703 | 3.2 |
| Operating | 4,807 | 6.6 | 3,853 | 9.9 | 4,571 | 12.5 | 35,906 | 5.8 |
| Community | 717 | 1.0 | 3,596 | 9.2 | 6,033 | 16.5 | 49,942 | 8.1 |
| Total | 72,477 | 100.0 | 39,004 | 100.0 | 36,569 | 100.0 | 614,656 | 100.0 |
| **2007** | | | | | | | | |
| Independent | 67,034 | 89.2 | 32,220 | 72.6 | 31,279 | 66.8 | 564,216 | 82.7 |
| Corporate | 2,498 | 3.3 | 4,397 | 9.9 | 4,418 | 9.4 | 21,924 | 3.2 |
| Operating | 4,938 | 6.6 | 3,429 | 7.7 | 4,915 | 10.5 | 39,403 | 5.8 |
| Community | 717 | 1.0 | 4,348 | 9.8 | 6,232 | 13.3 | 56,680 | 8.3 |
| Total | 75,187 | 100.0 | 44,394 | 100.0 | 46,844 | 100.0 | 682,222 | 100.0 |
| **2008** | | | | | | | | |
| Independent | 67,379 | 89.1 | 33,819 | 72.3 | 24,068 | 60.8 | 456,025 | 80.7 |
| Corporate | 2,745 | 3.6 | 4,570 | 9.8 | 4,615 | 11.7 | 20,335 | 3.6 |
| Operating | 4,762 | 6.3 | 3,900 | 8.3 | 5,250 | 13.3 | 38,968 | 6.9 |
| Community | 709 | 0.9 | 4,492 | 9.6 | 5,620 | 14.2 | 49,623 | 8.8 |
| Total | 75,595 | 100.0 | 46,781 | 100.0 | 39,554 | 100.0 | 564,951 | 100.0 |
| **2009** | | | | | | | | |
| Independent | 68,508 | 89.5 | 32,753 | 71.5 | 27,054 | 66.2 | 482,954 | 81.8 |
| Corporate | 2,733 | 3.6 | 4,691 | 10.2 | 3,966 | 9.7 | 19,299 | 3.3 |
| Operating | 4,567 | 6.0 | 4,161 | 9.1 | 5,027 | 12.3 | 38,444 | 6.5 |
| Community | 737 | 1.0 | 4,174 | 9.1 | 4,814 | 11.8 | 49,491 | 8.4 |
| Total | 76,545 | 100.0 | 45,778 | 100.0 | 40,862 | 100.0 | 590,188 | 100.0 |

*Source:* Foundation Center, "Research Studies: National Trends" (2011).
*Notes:* Grants made include grants, scholarships, and employee-matching gifts. They do not include program-related investments (such as loans, loan guarantees, equity investments, and other investments made by foundations to organizations to forward their charitable purposes), set-asides, or program expenses. Asset figures represent the market value of assets. Percentages may not sum to 100 because of rounding.

**Figure 3.11.** Number and Value of Grants Given by Organization Type, 2009 (percent)

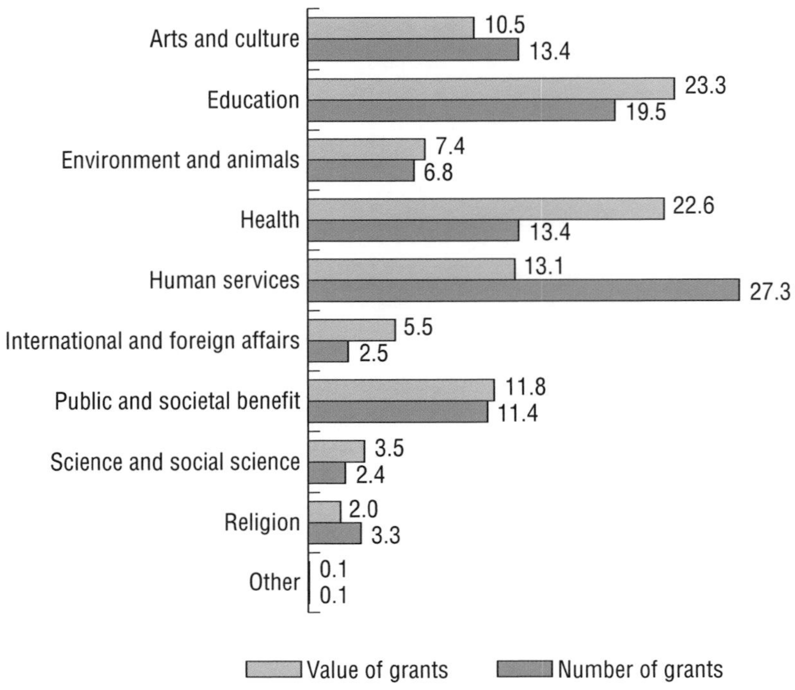

| Organization Type | Value of grants | Number of grants |
|---|---|---|
| Arts and culture | 10.5 | 13.4 |
| Education | 23.3 | 19.5 |
| Environment and animals | 7.4 | 6.8 |
| Health | 22.6 | 13.4 |
| Human services | 13.1 | 27.3 |
| International and foreign affairs | 5.5 | 2.5 |
| Public and societal benefit | 11.8 | 11.4 |
| Science and social science | 3.5 | 2.4 |
| Religion | 2.0 | 3.3 |
| Other | 0.1 | 0.1 |

*Source:* Foundation Center, "Research Studies: Foundation Giving Trends" (2011).
*Notes:* The data are based on all grants of $10,000 or more awarded by a sample of 1,384 larger foundations. These grants totaled $22.1 billion and represented nearly half of total grant dollars awarded by all U.S.independent, corporate, community, and grantmaking operating foundations. Subtotals may not add to total because of rounding. "Other" includes civil rights and social action, community improvement and development, philanthropy and voluntarism, and public affairs.

education organizations combined received almost half the total grant dollars given (table 3.13).

## Giving by Corporations

Giving by corporations is the final component of private giving. Corporate contributions can be made directly by the corporation or through a corporate foundation. According to *Giving USA*, corporate giving, which includes both types of giving mentioned above, reached an estimated $15.3 billion in 2010. This represents just over 5 percent of private giving. While corporate giving dropped around 13 percent from 2007 to 2008 (current dollars), it has risen steadily since 2008 and has nearly returned to pre-recession levels (figure 3.12).

**Table 3.13.** Number and Value of Grants Made by Foundations by Organization Type, 2001–09

| | Number of Grants | | Value of Grants | | |
|---|---|---|---|---|---|
| | Number | % | $ thousands | % | Average value ($) |
| **2001** | | | | | |
| Arts and culture | 18,412 | 14.7 | 2,047,972 | 12.2 | 111,230 |
| Education | 25,629 | 20.5 | 4,492,540 | 26.8 | 175,291 |
| Environment and animals | 7,587 | 6.1 | 1,043,896 | 6.2 | 137,590 |
| Health | 15,550 | 12.5 | 3,434,967 | 20.5 | 220,898 |
| Human services | 30,933 | 24.8 | 2,312,124 | 13.8 | 74,746 |
| International and foreign affairs | 3,014 | 2.4 | 398,816 | 2.4 | 132,321 |
| Public and societal benefit | 15,368 | 12.3 | 1,826,594 | 10.9 | 118,857 |
| Science and social science | 4,521 | 3.6 | 837,652 | 5.0 | 185,280 |
| Religion | 3,729 | 3.0 | 351,396 | 2.1 | 94,233 |
| Other | 101 | 0.1 | 17,348 | 0.1 | 171,762 |
| Total | 124,844 | 100.0 | 16,763,304 | 100.0 | 134,274 |
| **2002** | | | | | |
| Arts and culture | 18,674 | 14.6 | 1,945,785 | 12.2 | 104,198 |
| Education | 26,490 | 20.7 | 4,209,352 | 26.4 | 158,903 |
| Environment and animals | 7,830 | 6.1 | 943,136 | 5.9 | 120,452 |
| Health | 15,188 | 11.9 | 2,920,053 | 18.3 | 192,261 |
| Human services | 33,250 | 26.0 | 2,349,813 | 14.8 | 70,671 |
| International and foreign affairs | 3,025 | 2.4 | 413,422 | 2.6 | 136,668 |
| Public and societal benefit | 15,480 | 12.1 | 1,821,082 | 11.4 | 117,641 |
| Science and social science | 3,767 | 2.9 | 877,904 | 5.5 | 233,051 |
| Religion | 3,912 | 3.1 | 429,336 | 2.7 | 109,748 |
| Other | 112 | 0.1 | 15,012 | 0.1 | 134,036 |
| Total | 127,728 | 100.0 | 15,924,895 | 100.0 | 124,678 |
| **2003** | | | | | |
| Arts and culture | 17,881 | 14.8 | 1,790,269 | 12.5 | 100,121 |
| Education | 24,531 | 20.3 | 3,505,713 | 24.5 | 142,910 |
| Environment and animals | 7,393 | 6.1 | 892,321 | 6.2 | 120,698 |
| Health | 14,604 | 12.1 | 2,798,070 | 19.5 | 191,596 |
| Human services | 30,960 | 25.6 | 2,232,212 | 15.6 | 72,100 |

*(continued)*

**Table 3.13.** Number and Value of Grants Made by Foundations by Organization Type, 2001–09 *(continued)*

| | Number of Grants | | Value of Grants | | |
|---|---|---|---|---|---|
| | Number | % | $ thousands | % | Average value ($) |
| International and foreign affairs | 2,562 | 2.1 | 360,802 | 2.5 | 140,828 |
| Public and societal benefit | 15,674 | 13.0 | 1,825,760 | 12.7 | 116,483 |
| Science and social science | 3,512 | 2.9 | 565,594 | 3.9 | 161,046 |
| Religion | 3,498 | 2.9 | 340,003 | 2.4 | 97,199 |
| Other | 106 | 0.1 | 12,647 | 0.1 | 119,311 |
| Total | 120,721 | 100.0 | 14,323,389 | 100.0 | 118,649 |
| **2004** | | | | | |
| Arts and culture | 18,516 | 14.6 | 1,979,541 | 12.8 | 106,910 |
| Education | 25,689 | 20.3 | 3,625,448 | 23.4 | 141,128 |
| Environment and animals | 7,374 | 5.8 | 813,320 | 5.3 | 110,296 |
| Health | 16,208 | 12.8 | 3,447,203 | 22.3 | 212,685 |
| Human services | 32,294 | 25.5 | 2,146,396 | 13.9 | 66,464 |
| International and foreign affairs | 2,796 | 2.2 | 419,965 | 2.7 | 150,202 |
| Public and societal benefit | 16,097 | 12.7 | 2,004,661 | 13.0 | 124,536 |
| Science and social science | 3,521 | 2.8 | 669,690 | 4.3 | 190,199 |
| Religion | 3,907 | 3.1 | 362,044 | 2.3 | 92,665 |
| Other | 95 | 0.1 | 9,329 | 0.1 | 98,200 |
| Total | 126,497 | 100.0 | 15,477,595 | 100.0 | 122,355 |
| **2005** | | | | | |
| Arts and culture | 18,698 | 14.3 | 2,054,627 | 13.9 | 109,885 |
| Education | 26,114 | 19.9 | 3,936,636 | 26.6 | 150,748 |
| Environment and animals | 8,195 | 6.3 | 1,040,153 | 7.0 | 126,925 |
| Health | 17,138 | 13.1 | 3,417,483 | 23.1 | 199,410 |
| Human services | 34,085 | 26.0 | 2,425,458 | 16.4 | 71,159 |
| International and foreign affairs | 3,430 | 2.6 | 591,214 | 4.0 | 172,366 |
| Public and societal benefit | 15,785 | 12.1 | 183,368 | 1.2 | 11,617 |
| Science and social science | 3,402 | 2.6 | 709,075 | 4.8 | 208,429 |
| Religion | 4,011 | 3.1 | 408,826 | 2.8 | 101,926 |
| Other | 103 | 0.1 | 10,918 | 0.1 | 106,000 |
| Total | 130,961 | 100.0 | 14,777,758 | 100.0 | 112,841 |

*(continued)*

**Table 3.13.** Number and Value of Grants Made by Foundations by Organization Type, 2001–09 *(continued)*

| | Number of Grants | | Value of Grants | | |
| --- | --- | --- | --- | --- | --- |
| | Number | % | $ thousands | % | Average value ($) |
| **2006** | | | | | |
| Arts and culture | 20,095 | 14.3 | 2,329,708 | 12.2 | 115,935 |
| Education | 28,521 | 20.3 | 4,306,090 | 22.5 | 150,980 |
| Environment and animals | 8,633 | 6.1 | 1,145,100 | 6.0 | 132,642 |
| Health | 18,260 | 13.0 | 4,394,462 | 23.0 | 240,661 |
| Human services | 36,047 | 25.7 | 2,645,895 | 13.8 | 73,401 |
| International and foreign affairs | 3,763 | 2.7 | 1,019,739 | 5.3 | 270,991 |
| Public and societal benefit | 16,807 | 12.0 | 2,042,490 | 10.7 | 121,526 |
| Science and social science | 3,750 | 2.7 | 809,683 | 4.2 | 215,915 |
| Religion | 4,486 | 3.2 | 412,955 | 2.2 | 92,054 |
| Other | 122 | 0.1 | 16,912 | 0.1 | 138,623 |
| Total | 140,484 | 100.0 | 19,123,034 | 100.0 | 136,123 |
| **2007** | | | | | |
| Arts and culture | 21,527 | 14.3 | 2,293,719 | 10.6 | 106,551 |
| Education | 30,099 | 20.0 | 4,944,387 | 22.8 | 164,271 |
| Environment and animals | 9,884 | 6.6 | 1,471,804 | 6.8 | 148,908 |
| Health | 19,690 | 13.1 | 4,910,707 | 22.7 | 249,401 |
| Human services | 39,051 | 26.0 | 3,232,565 | 14.9 | 82,778 |
| International and foreign affairs | 3,566 | 2.4 | 975,900 | 4.5 | 273,668 |
| Public and societal benefit | 17,158 | 11.4 | 2,358,153 | 10.9 | 137,438 |
| Science and social science | 4,090 | 2.7 | 931,155 | 4.3 | 227,666 |
| Religion | 5,210 | 3.5 | 452,925 | 2.1 | 86,934 |
| Other | 117 | 0.1 | 78,593 | 0.4 | 671,735 |
| Total | 150,392 | 100.0 | 21,649,908 | 100.0 | 143,957 |
| **2008** | | | | | |
| Arts and culture | 22,902 | 13.9 | 3,155,895 | 12.5 | 137,800 |
| Education | 32,106 | 19.5 | 5,500,632 | 21.8 | 171,327 |
| Environment and animals | 10,785 | 6.6 | 2,173,101 | 8.6 | 201,493 |
| Health | 22,165 | 13.5 | 5,778,632 | 22.9 | 260,710 |
| Human services | 43,393 | 26.4 | 3,149,049 | 12.5 | 72,570 |

*(continued)*

**Table 3.13.** Number and Value of Grants Made by Foundations by Organization Type, 2001–09 *(continued)*

| | Number of Grants | | Value of Grants | | |
| --- | --- | --- | --- | --- | --- |
| | Number | % | $ thousands | % | Average value ($) |
| International and foreign affairs | 4,422 | 2.7 | 1,449,507 | 5.7 | 327,794 |
| Public and societal benefit | 18,329 | 11.2 | 2,514,533 | 10.0 | 137,189 |
| Science and social science | 4,315 | 2.6 | 961,350 | 3.8 | 222,793 |
| Religion | 5,811 | 3.5 | 567,518 | 2.2 | 97,663 |
| Other | 124 | 0.1 | 15,641 | 0.1 | 126,137 |
| Total | 164,352 | 100.0 | 25,265,858 | 100.0 | 153,730 |
| 2009 | | | | | |
| Arts and culture | 20,685 | 13.4 | 2,332,162 | 10.5 | 112,747 |
| Education | 30,108 | 19.5 | 5,149,553 | 23.3 | 171,036 |
| Environment and animals | 10,452 | 6.8 | 1,648,717 | 7.4 | 157,742 |
| Health | 20,702 | 13.4 | 5,004,410 | 22.6 | 241,736 |
| Human services | 42,289 | 27.3 | 2,909,215 | 13.1 | 68,794 |
| International and foreign affairs | 3,934 | 2.5 | 1,224,952 | 5.5 | 311,376 |
| Public and societal benefit | 17,603 | 11.4 | 2,612,555 | 11.8 | 148,415 |
| Science and social science | 3,628 | 2.3 | 788,153 | 3.6 | 217,242 |
| Religion | 5,158 | 3.3 | 451,745 | 2.0 | 87,581 |
| Other | 105 | 0.1 | 16,095 | 0.1 | 153,286 |
| Total | 154,664 | 100.0 | 22,137,557 | 100.0 | 143,133 |

*Source:* Foundation Center, "Research Studies: Foundation Giving Trends" (2011).
*Notes:* Major categories are defined by the National Taxonomy of Exempt Entities. The data are based on all grants of $10,000 or more awarded by a sample of 1,384 larger foundations. These grants totaled $22.1 billion and represented nearly half of total grant dollars awarded by all U.S. independent, corporate, community, and grantmaking operating foundations. Subtotals may not add to total because of rounding. "Other" includes civil rights and social action, community improvement and development, philanthropy and voluntarism, and public affairs.

# Volunteering

Volunteering is just as important as gifts of cash or goods for many nonprofit organizations. Many charities rely on volunteers to help further their mission. Whether volunteers are stuffing envelopes, serving food, serving on governing boards, or organizing a public relations campaign, they are a vital component of the nonprofit sector. Using data

**Figure 3.12.** Corporate Giving, 2000–10 (constant 2010 dollars)

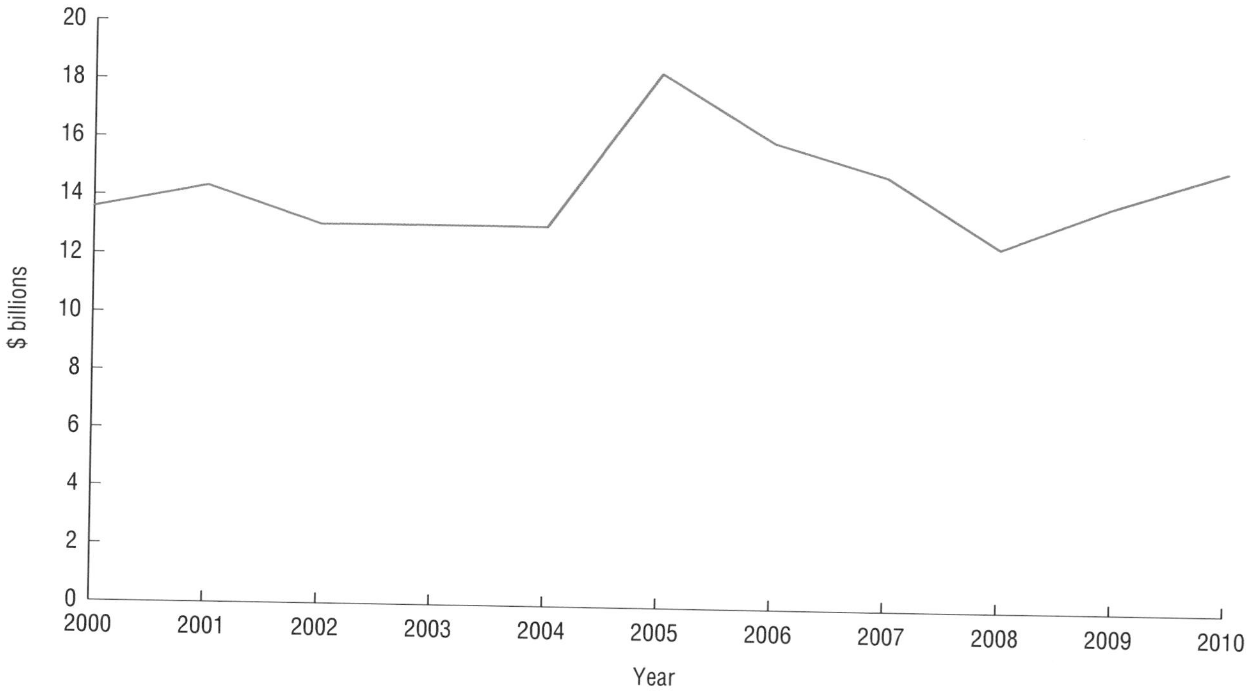

Source: Giving USA Foundation, *Giving USA* (2011).

collected from the Current Population Survey (CPS) and the American Time Use Survey (ATUS), this section estimates the number of people volunteering, who is volunteering, where they are volunteering, how volunteers spend their time, the amount of hours volunteered, and the economic value of volunteers to the sector.

Table 3.14 provides key indicators from the two major government surveys that collect data on volunteering, the Current Population Survey and the American Time Use Survey. These data can be used to calculate the economic value of volunteering. While the CPS asks questions on volunteering throughout the year, the ATUS asks in greater detail how people spent the past 24 hours. Therefore, the survey shows volunteer activity on an average day.

According to the CPS, 26.3 percent of the civilian population age 16 and older volunteered in 2010. This translates to 62.8 million volunteers. When asked how many hours they volunteered in that year, volunteers' median response was 52 hours. The rate and amount of time volunteered in 2010 are similar to the numbers reported from 2006 onward.

According to the ATUS, 6.8 percent of the adult population volunteered on an average day in 2010. This translates into 16.6 million volunteers a day. These people spent 2.46 hours, on average, volunteering in day.

**Table 3.14. Number, Hours, and Dollar Value of Volunteers, 2005–10**

|  | 2005 | 2006 | 2007 | 2008 | 2009 | 2010 |
|---|---|---|---|---|---|---|
| **Per year** | | | | | | |
| Percent of population volunteering | 28.8 | 26.7 | 26.2 | 26.4 | 26.8 | 26.3 |
| Number of volunteers | 65.4 million | 61.2 million | 60.8 million | 61.8 million | 63.4 million | 62.8 million |
| Hours volunteered | 13.5 billion | 12.9 billion | 15.5 billion | 14.4 billion | 14.9 billion | 14.9 billion |
| Average hours per volunteer | 204 | 207 | 251 | 229 | 232 | 234 |
| Median hours per volunteer | 50 | 52 | 52 | 52 | 50 | 52 |
| **Per average day** | | | | | | |
| Percent of population volunteering | 7.1 | 6.5 | 7.0 | 6.8 | 7.1 | 6.8 |
| Number of volunteers | 16.5 million | 15.2 million | 16.6 million | 16.2 million | 17.1 million | 16.6 million |
| Hours per day per volunteer | 2.25 | 2.31 | 2.56 | 2.43 | 2.39 | 2.46 |
| **Value of volunteers** | | | | | | |
| Population age 15 and over | 230.4 million | 233.1 million | 236.1 million | 238.7 million | 239.9 million | 241.9 million |
| Full-time-equivalent employees | 7.9 million | 7.6 million | 9.1 million | 8.4 million | 8.8 million | 8.8 million |
| Assigned hourly wages for volunteers | $16.13 | $16.76 | $17.43 | $18.08 | $18.63 | $19.07 |
| Assigned value of volunteer time | $217.9 billion | $215.6 billion | $270.2 billion | $270.2 billion | $277.7 billion | $283.8 billion |

*Source:* Authors' calculations based on per year figures from U.S. Department of Labor, Bureau of Labor Statistics, Current Population Survey, Volunteer Supplement (2005–10); per average day figures from U.S. Department of Labor, Bureau of Labor Statistics, American Time Use Survey (2005–10); and hourly wages from U.S. Department of Labor, Bureau of Labor Statistics, Current Employment Statistics (2011).

Extrapolating these average day figures to a year, volunteers spent an estimated 14.9 billion hours volunteering in 2010. Assuming a full-time employee works 1,700 hours a year, those volunteer hours were the equivalent of 8.8 million full-time employees. Further assuming that those employees would have earned the average private nonfarm hourly wage, volunteers' time contributed $283.8 billion in 2010.

The CPS asks various demographic questions that allow researchers to see who is volunteering. The 2010 data show no major changes in the demographics of volunteers. In general, women are more likely to volunteer than men. The peak ages for volunteering are between 35 and 54 years old. Whites volunteer at higher rates than other racial/ ethnic groups. College graduates volunteer at higher rates that those with less schooling. Part-time employees continue to be more likely to volunteer than those with any other employment status. Married people are more likely to volunteer than single people or people with another marital status (table 3.15).

**Table 3.15.** Volunteers by Demographic Group, 2002–10 (percent)

| | 2002 | 2003 | 2004 | 2005 | 2006 | 2007 | 2008 | 2009 | 2010 |
|---|---|---|---|---|---|---|---|---|---|
| Total | 27.4 | 28.8 | 28.8 | 28.8 | 26.7 | 26.2 | 26.4 | 26.8 | 26.3 |
| Gender | | | | | | | | | |
| Male | 23.6 | 25.1 | 25.0 | 25.0 | 23.0 | 22.9 | 23.2 | 23.3 | 23.2 |
| Female | 31.0 | 32.2 | 32.4 | 32.4 | 30.1 | 29.3 | 29.4 | 30.1 | 29.3 |
| Race/Ethnicity | | | | | | | | | |
| White | 29.2 | 30.6 | 30.5 | 30.4 | 28.3 | 27.9 | 27.9 | 28.3 | 27.8 |
| Black or African American | 19.1 | 20.0 | 20.8 | 22.1 | 19.2 | 18.2 | 19.1 | 20.2 | 19.4 |
| Asian | — | 18.7 | 19.3 | 20.7 | 18.5 | 17.7 | 18.7 | 19.0 | 19.6 |
| Hispanic or Latino | 15.5 | 15.7 | 14.5 | 15.4 | 13.9 | 13.5 | 14.4 | 14.0 | 14.7 |
| Age | | | | | | | | | |
| 16 and older | 27.4 | 28.8 | 28.8 | 28.8 | 26.7 | 26.2 | 26.4 | 26.8 | 26.3 |
| 16–24 | 21.9 | 24.1 | 24.2 | 24.4 | 21.7 | 20.8 | 21.9 | 22.0 | 21.9 |
| 25–34 | 24.8 | 26.5 | 25.8 | 25.3 | 23.1 | 22.6 | 22.8 | 23.5 | 22.3 |
| 35–44 | 34.1 | 34.7 | 34.2 | 34.5 | 31.2 | 30.5 | 31.3 | 31.5 | 32.2 |
| 45–54 | 31.3 | 32.7 | 32.8 | 32.7 | 31.2 | 30.1 | 29.9 | 30.8 | 30.3 |
| 55–64 | 27.5 | 29.2 | 30.1 | 30.2 | 27.9 | 28.4 | 28.1 | 28.3 | 27.2 |
| 65 and older | 22.7 | 23.7 | 24.6 | 24.8 | 23.8 | 23.8 | 23.5 | 23.9 | 23.6 |
| Education | | | | | | | | | |
| Less than high school diploma | 10.1 | 9.9 | 9.6 | 10.0 | 9.3 | 9.0 | 9.4 | 8.6 | 8.8 |
| High school graduate, no college | 21.2 | 21.7 | 21.6 | 21.2 | 19.2 | 18.6 | 18.1 | 18.8 | 17.9 |

*(continued)*

**Table 3.15.** Volunteers by Demographic Group, 2002–10 (percent) *(continued)*

|  | 2002 | 2003 | 2004 | 2005 | 2006 | 2007 | 2008 | 2009 | 2010 |
|---|---|---|---|---|---|---|---|---|---|
| Less than a bachelor's degree | 32.8 | 34.1 | 34.2 | 33.7 | 30.9 | 30.7 | 30.0 | 30.5 | 29.2 |
| College graduate | 43.3 | 45.6 | 45.7 | 45.8 | 43.3 | 41.8 | 42.2 | 42.8 | 42.3 |
| Employment |  |  |  |  |  |  |  |  |  |
| Civilian labor force | 29.3 | 30.9 | 30.9 | 31.1 | 28.5 | 28.1 | 28.5 | 29.0 | 28.7 |
| Employed | 29.5 | 31.2 | 31.2 | 31.3 | 28.7 | 28.3 | 28.9 | 29.7 | 29.2 |
| Full time | 28.3 | 29.6 | 29.6 | 29.8 | 27.3 | 26.9 | 27.8 | 28.7 | 28.2 |
| Part time | 35.4 | 38.4 | 38.5 | 38.2 | 35.5 | 35.4 | 34.2 | 33.7 | 33.2 |
| Unemployed | 25.1 | 26.7 | 25.6 | 26.4 | 23.8 | 23.2 | 22.3 | 22.9 | 23.8 |
| Not in the labor force | 23.7 | 24.6 | 24.7 | 24.4 | 23.1 | 22.3 | 22.2 | 22.6 | 22.0 |
| Marital status |  |  |  |  |  |  |  |  |  |
| Single, never married | 21.2 | 22.8 | 23.2 | 23.0 | 20.3 | 19.2 | 20.4 | 20.6 | 20.3 |
| Married, spouse present | 32.7 | 34.0 | 33.9 | 34.1 | 32.2 | 31.9 | 31.6 | 32.3 | 32.0 |
| Other marital status | 22.1 | 22.5 | 22.9 | 23.1 | 21.3 | 20.9 | 20.9 | 21.5 | 20.9 |

*Source:* U.S. Department of Labor, Bureau of Labor Statistics, Current Population Survey, Volunteer Supplement (2002–10).
— = data not available

Both the CPS and the ATUS ask where people volunteer and what types of things they are doing. Because the CPS asks questions about time spent volunteering throughout the year, the survey asks people to choose the organizations where they spent the most hours volunteering. As displayed in figure 3.13, 34 percent of volunteers volunteered at a religious organization in 2010. Another 27 percent report volunteering at an educational or youth service organization, followed by 14 percent of volunteers spending time at a social or community service organization (table 3.16).

While the CPS asks where volunteers are spending their time, the ATUS asks about the types of activities volunteers are performing. Measured as the average amount of time across all volunteers, the single largest use of volunteers in 2010 was for social service and care. Social service and care includes preparing food and cleaning up, collecting and delivering clothing or other goods, providing direct care or services, teaching, leading, counseling, and mentoring. Administration and support is the second-largest activity reported among volunteers and includes fundraising, office work, computer use, making phone calls, writing, editing, and reading (see figure 3.14, table 3.17).

When the percentage of volunteers who performed each activity is considered instead of the average time, travel emerges as the most common activity. While the majority of individuals that volunteered spent some time traveling, time spent traveling is less than in many other categories (see figure 3.15, table 3.18).

**Figure 3.13.** Volunteers by Main Type of Organization, 2010 (percent)

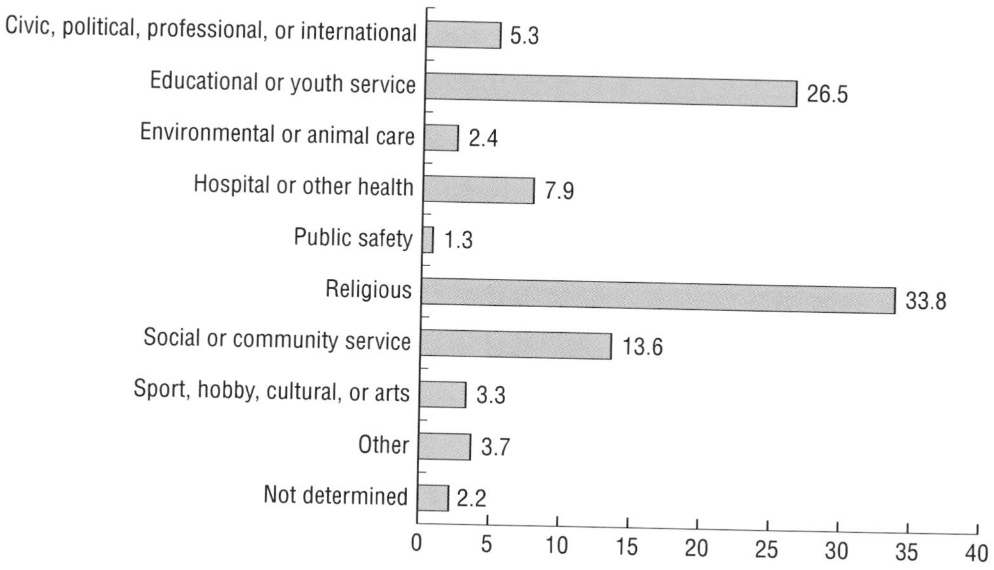

| | |
|---|---|
| Civic, political, professional, or international | 5.3 |
| Educational or youth service | 26.5 |
| Environmental or animal care | 2.4 |
| Hospital or other health | 7.9 |
| Public safety | 1.3 |
| Religious | 33.8 |
| Social or community service | 13.6 |
| Sport, hobby, cultural, or arts | 3.3 |
| Other | 3.7 |
| Not determined | 2.2 |

*Source:* U.S. Department of Labor, Bureau of Labor Statistics, Current Population Survey, Volunteer Supplement (2010).

**Table 3.16.** Primary Recipient of Volunteer Time by Type of Organization, 2002–10 (percent)

| Main type of organization | 2002 | 2003 | 2004 | 2005 | 2006 | 2007 | 2008 | 2009 | 2010 |
|---|---|---|---|---|---|---|---|---|---|
| All | 27.4 | 28.8 | 28.8 | 28.8 | 26.7 | 26.2 | 26.4 | 26.8 | 26.3 |
| Civic, political, professional, or international | 6.1 | 6.4 | 7.0 | 6.4 | 6.1 | 5.1 | 5.5 | 5.5 | 5.3 |
| Educational or youth service | 27.2 | 27.4 | 27.0 | 26.2 | 26.4 | 26.2 | 26.0 | 26.1 | 26.5 |
| Environmental or animal care | 1.6 | 1.7 | 1.7 | 1.8 | 1.6 | 1.9 | 2.0 | 2.2 | 2.4 |
| Hospital or other health | 8.6 | 8.2 | 7.5 | 7.7 | 8.1 | 7.8 | 8.2 | 8.5 | 7.9 |
| Public safety | 1.4 | 1.2 | 1.5 | 1.3 | 1.3 | 1.3 | 1.3 | 1.2 | 1.3 |
| Religious | 33.9 | 34.6 | 34.4 | 34.8 | 35.0 | 35.6 | 35.1 | 34.0 | 33.8 |
| Social or community service | 12.1 | 11.8 | 12.4 | 13.4 | 12.7 | 13.1 | 13.5 | 13.9 | 13.6 |
| Sport, hobby, cultural, or arts | 4.0 | 4.1 | 3.6 | 3.3 | 3.7 | 3.5 | 3.3 | 3.4 | 3.3 |
| Other | 3.5 | 3.1 | 3.3 | 3.5 | 3.4 | 3.7 | 3.3 | 3.4 | 3.7 |
| Not determined | 1.5 | 1.5 | 1.6 | 1.7 | 1.5 | 1.7 | 1.9 | 1.9 | 2.2 |

*Source:* U.S. Department of Labor, Bureau of Labor Statistics, Current Population Survey, Volunteer Supplement (2002–10).

**Figure 3.14.** Distribution of Average Volunteer Time by Activity, 2010 (percent)

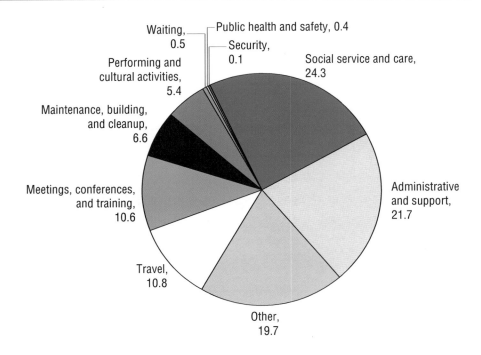

*Source:* Authors' calculations based on U.S. Department of Labor, Bureau of Labor Statistics, American Time Use Survey (2010).

**Table 3.17.** Distribution of Average Annual Volunteer Time by Activity, 2003–10 (percent)

|  | 2003 | 2004 | 2005 | 2006 | 2007 | 2008 | 2009 | 2010 |
|---|---|---|---|---|---|---|---|---|
| Administrative and support | 28.0 | 24.8 | 24.4 | 20.6 | 16.8 | 22.4 | 26.3 | 21.7 |
| Social service and care | 21.1 | 22.7 | 20.2 | 17.8 | 22.3 | 21.8 | 21.8 | 24.3 |
| Maintenance, building, and clean-up | 6.1 | 6.0 | 3.7 | 5.7 | 5.1 | 7.2 | 4.3 | 6.6 |
| Performing and cultural activities | 5.9 | 4.3 | 9.1 | 6.9 | 5.9 | 5.7 | 4.8 | 5.4 |
| Meetings, conferences, and training | 11.2 | 11.1 | 11.1 | 10.6 | 11.7 | 8.5 | 11.1 | 10.6 |
| Public health and safety | 1.3 | 2.4 | 1.1 | 0.9 | 0.4 | 2.0 | 0.7 | 0.4 |
| Waiting | — | 0.0 | 0.1 | 0.3 | 0.1 | 0.1 | 0.2 | 0.5 |
| Security | — | — | — | — | 0.0 | 0.0 | 0.0 | 0.1 |
| Other | 15.3 | 17.0 | 17.9 | 22.9 | 25.0 | 21.4 | 19.1 | 19.7 |
| Travel | 11.1 | 11.6 | 12.3 | 14.2 | 12.8 | 10.8 | 11.7 | 10.8 |
| Total | 100.0 | 100.0 | 100.0 | 100.0 | 100.0 | 100.0 | 100.0 | 100.0 |

*Source:* Authors' calculations based on U.S. Department of Labor, Bureau of Labor Statistics, American Time Use Survey (2003–10).
*Notes:* Waiting was not a separate category in 2003, so wait time was distributed across the other categories. Security was not a separate category until 2007, so time spent on security procedures related to the volunteer activity was distributed across the other categories.
— = no data available

**Figure 3.15.** Volunteers Who Performed Each Activity, 2010 (percent)

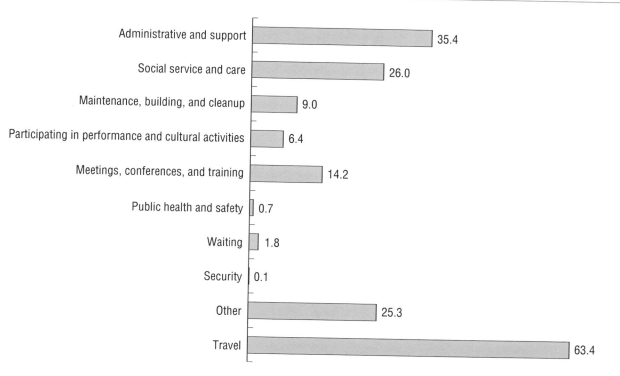

*Source:* Authors' calculations based on U.S. Department of Labor, Bureau of Labor Statistics, American Time Use Survey (2010).

**Table 3.18.** Volunteers Who Performed Each Activity, 2003–10 (percent)

|  | 2003 | 2004 | 2005 | 2006 | 2007 | 2008 | 2009 | 2010 |
|---|---|---|---|---|---|---|---|---|
| Administrative and support | 43.6 | 44.1 | 40.4 | 37.3 | 34.2 | 37.3 | 41.4 | 35.4 |
| Social service and care | 25.6 | 28.1 | 27.5 | 23.8 | 25.7 | 26.3 | 28.3 | 26.0 |
| Maintenance, building, and clean-up | 7.5 | 8.5 | 5.5 | 6.7 | 8.6 | 7.7 | 7.8 | 9.0 |
| Performing and cultural activities | 7.2 | 5.5 | 9.7 | 8.9 | 6.5 | 6.4 | 6.1 | 6.4 |
| Meetings, conferences, and training | 13.2 | 12.5 | 11.9 | 13.1 | 14.5 | 11.6 | 13.6 | 14.2 |
| Public health and safety | 1.8 | 2.3 | 1.6 | 1.3 | 0.9 | 2.5 | 1.4 | 0.7 |
| Waiting | — | 0.3 | 0.5 | 2.0 | 0.3 | 0.6 | 1.1 | 1.8 |
| Security | — | — | — | — | 0.2 | 0.3 | 0.3 | 0.1 |
| Other | 21.3 | 20.2 | 20.7 | 25.3 | 30.1 | 25.6 | 21.6 | 25.3 |
| Travel | 63.6 | 65.0 | 60.9 | 65.7 | 67.2 | 63.1 | 62.4 | 63.4 |

*Source:* Authors' calculations based on U.S. Department of Labor, Bureau of Labor Statistics, American Time Use Survey (2003–10).
*Notes:* Multiple responses were allowed. Waiting was not a separate category in 2003, so wait time was distributed across the other categories. Security was not a separate category until 2007, so time spent on security procedures related to the volunteer activity was distributed across the other categories.
— = no data available

# Conclusion

This chapter discussed trends in private giving and volunteering. In 2010, private giving reached $290.89 billion, which was below the pre-recession high of $310.57 billion in 2007 but up slightly from 2009. Individuals accounted for nearly three-quarters of private giving, followed by foundations, bequests, and corporations. Organizations also benefited from time individuals spent assisting nonprofits through volunteer work. Volunteer time contributed $283.8 billion to the nonprofit sector in 2010, almost as much as private giving. Individual donations of both time and money are vital to the livelihood of the nonprofit sector in the United States.

# Sources

The Bill and Melinda Gates Foundation. 2007. "Annual Report." http://www.gatesfoundation.org/nr/public/media/annualreports/annualreport07/assets/GatesFoundationAnnualReport2007.pdf (accessed May 17, 2012).

Center on Philanthropy at Indiana University. 2007. "Center on Philanthropy Panel Study." http://www.philanthropy.iupui.edu/cop-panel-study (accessed August 6, 2012).

Centre for Time Use Research. 2006. "American Heritage Time Use Study (AHTUS)." http://www.timeuse.org/ahtus/ (accessed May 17, 2012).

Chairman of the Council of Economic Advisers. 2011. *Economic Report of the President.* Washington, DC: U.S. Government Printing Office.

Foundation Center. 2011. "Research Studies: National Trends." http://foundationcenter.org/gainknowledge/research/nationaltrends.html (accessed May 16, 2012).

Giving USA Foundation. 2011. *Giving USA 2011: The Annual Report on Philanthropy for the Year 2010.* Glenview, IL: Giving USA Foundation.

U.S. Department of Commerce, Bureau of Economic Analysis. 2011. "National Income and Product Accounts Tables." http://www.bea.gov/iTable/iTable.cfm?ReqID=9&step=1 (accessed May 17, 2012).

U.S. Department of Labor, Bureau of Labor Statistics. 2005–10. "American Time Use Survey." http://www.bls.gov/tus/home.htm (accessed May 17, 2012).

———. 2005–10. "Current Population Survey." http://www.bls.gov/cps/home.htm (accessed May 17, 2012).

———. 2011. "Employment, Hours, and Earnings from the Current Employment Statistics Survey (National)." http://www.bls.gov/ces/home.htm (accessed May 17, 2012).

———. 2012. "Consumer Price Index." http://www.bls.gov/cpi/home.htm (accessed May 17, 2012).

U.S. Department of the Treasury, Internal Revenue Service. 1985–2009. "SOI Tax Stats—Individual Income Tax Returns Publication 1304 (Complete Report)." http://www.irs.gov/taxstats/indtaxstats/article/0,,id=134951,00.html (accessed May 17, 2012).

———. 1987, 1990, 1992–2009. "SOI Tax Stats—Estate Tax Returns." http://www.irs.gov/taxstats/indtaxstats/article/0,,id=96442,00.html (accessed May 17, 2012).

———. 2007–11. "Individual Noncash Contributions." http://www.irs.gov/taxstats/indtaxstats/article/0,,id=134951,00.html (accessed May 17, 2012).

APPENDIX

# Technical Notes

The following paragraphs explain the methodology for calculating volunteer values in tables 3.14, 3.17, and 3.18.

Per day values in table 3.14 are based on author calculations and do not match published numbers from the American Time Use Survey because ATUS includes travel time only in major categories and not in subcategories, thus excluding travel time associated with volunteering. Table 3.14 includes all time in the 2010 ATUS activity codes 15xxxx (volunteering) and 1815xx (travel associated with volunteering) and the analogous codes for 2005–10. Participation rates are calculated by summing the weights (*TUFINLWGT*) for all respondents with any time in the above categories and dividing by the sum of the weights of all respondents. The number of volunteers is calculated by summing the weights for all respondents with volunteer time and dividing by 365. Hours per day per volunteer result from a two-step process: Average minutes across the whole population are calculated by multiplying each respondent's minutes in the above categories by that respondent's weight, summing those products, and dividing by the sum of the weights of all respondents. This is converted to hours per day by dividing by 60, and to hours per day per volunteer by dividing by the volunteer participation rate calculated above. These are standard calculations, documented in ATUS codebooks.

The per year calculations in the bottom of table 3.14 are also author calculations. Population is calculated by dividing the sum of *TUFINLWGT* by 365. Total annual volunteer hours is calculated by multiplying population times the percent of population volunteering on an average day times 365, times the average hours volunteered per day per volunteer. Full-time-equivalent employment is calculated by dividing total annual volunteer hours per year by 1,700 working hours per full-time employee per year. Total assigned value of volunteer time is total annual volunteer hours times the average private nonfarm hourly wage.

The calculation of average annual hours per volunteer requires making an assumption about 15-year-olds' annual volunteer participation rates. Total volunteer hours a year are available from the ATUS only. The number of volunteers a year is available only from the volunteer supplement to the U.S. Census Current Population Survey. One cannot be simply divided by the other because, although both are based on the CPS sample, ATUS includes those age 15 and older, while the CPS volunteer supplement includes only those age 16 and older. If you use the number of volunteers from the CPS volunteer supplement, you overestimate average hours per volunteer, because 15-year-olds are included in total volunteer hours but not total volunteers. If you try to apply the percentage of population volunteering from the CPS volunteer supplement to the ATUS total population, you underestimate average hours per volunteer because young people volunteer at a lower rate than average, so we would be overestimating the number of volunteers. Researchers can identify the number of volunteers among 15-year-olds in ATUS, but only for an average day, not for the year.

Thus, the basic approach is to estimate the number of 15-year-old volunteers, add it to the CPS volunteer supplement total, and then divide that into total volunteer hours for the year. To calculate the implied 16-and-over population in the CPS, divide the number of volunteers by the volunteer participation rate. The 15-and-over population is already calculated from the ATUS above. Subtracting the first from the second yields the number of 15-year-olds. The number of 15-year-old volunteers per year is estimated by multiplying the number of 15-year-olds by the annual volunteering rate of 16-to-24-year-olds from the CPS volunteer supplement. The number of 15-year-old volunteers is added to the number of volunteers 16 and older from the CPS volunteer supplement, resulting in total annual volunteers 15 and older. Finally, total annual volunteer hours is divided by the annual number of volunteers 15 and older, resulting in average annual hours per volunteer 15 and older.

Table 3.17 is also based on author calculations using the ATUS. The categories shown correspond to the activity codes given above—15xxxx and 1815xx—summed to the four-digit level. For each category shown, each respondent's time was multiplied by that respondent's weight (*TUFINLWGT*) and the results summed. The sum was divided by the sum of weights of all volunteers, even those who did not perform that particular activity on the diary day. The result is the average minutes per day per volunteer for each activity. Converted to hours, these totals would sum to the average hours volunteered per volunteer per day in table 3.14.

Table 3.18 is also based on author calculations using the ATUS. Participation rates for each activity are calculated by summing *TUFINLWGT* of respondents who reported any time in that activity and dividing by the sum of the weights of all volunteers.

# 4

# Financial Trends

I n this chapter, we seek to understand the nonprofit sector's revenue and expenses by examining revenue sources, types of expenditures, and how these have changed over time. We pay special attention to the period from 2007 to 2010 for effects of the recession. As in chapter 1, the primary source of data is the Bureau of Economic Analysis's National Income and Product Accounts. The analysis, therefore, is limited to nonprofit institutions serving households (NPISH). Since this chapter focuses on trends, all figures have been adjusted for inflation and are shown in 2010 dollars.

## Summary

- NPISH revenue was $1.16 trillion in 2010, a 28 percent growth since 2000, when adjusting for inflation. Revenue growth slowed slightly in 2008 but picked back up in 2009 and 2010.
- Sales receipts or fee-for-service revenue accounted for 72 percent of nonprofit revenues; transfer receipts[1] accounted for 23 percent; and asset income, such as interest, dividends, or rental income, accounted for another 4 percent.
- After the recession began in December 2007, asset income was the hardest hit revenue source—declining 13 percent in 2008, over 5 percent in 2009, and over 7 percent in 2010. Sales receipts held steady in 2008. Receipts rebounded in 2009 and 2010, however, growing around 4 percent in both years.

---

1. The BEA defines transfer receipts as funds that NPISHs receive from private and public sources, such as donations and grants. The authors use the BEA's terminology in this chapter.

- NPISHs had $1.22 trillion in outlays or expenditures in 2010. Ninety-one percent of nonprofit funds were spent directly,[2] and the remaining 9 percent were given away.[3] NPISH does include grantmaking foundations in these figures.

- In 2010, NPISHs spent more than they generated in revenue. Outlays exceeded revenues by $65.5 billion.

- Nonprofits have had a surplus of funds two times in the past 10 years and have run deficits in eight years.

- More than half of NPISH consumption expenditures were in the health care field in 2010. Another 16 percent were in education, and 10 percent were in social services.

- In 2010, more than three-quarters of nonprofit transfer payments (77 percent) went to households in the United States. Twenty-three percent of payments went to help people internationally, and 0.6 percent went to pay excise taxes.

- International transfer payments as a proportion of overall transfer payments have nearly doubled since 2000, increasing from 13 percent in 2000 to 23 percent in 2010.

## Nonprofit Institutions Serving Households

The BEA's National Income and Product Accounts provide data on nonprofit institutions serving households. What is included in the BEA's definition of NPISH? Nonprofit organizations serving households such as social service organizations or museums would fall under the criteria. For a nonprofit to be included in the NPISH definition, it needs to provide services in one of the following five categories (Mead et al. 2003):

1. religious and welfare, which includes human services, grantmaking foundations, libraries, and some fraternal organizations;
2. recreation, such as athletic organizations or cultural activities;
3. education and research;
4. medical care; and
5. personal business, which includes labor unions, legal aid, and professional associations.

Nonprofit organizations that serve business, such as chambers of commerce, trade associations and homeowners associations, are excluded from the NPISH figures; they are included in the business sector. In addition, nonprofits that sell goods and services in the same way as for-profit organizations are excluded. These include tax-exempt cooperatives, credit unions, mutual financial institutions, and tax-exempt manufacturers like university presses. NPISH figures, therefore, do not encompass the entire nonprofit sector.

---

2. The BEA describes funds spent directly by NPISHs to obtain goods and provide services as consumption expenditures. The authors use the BEA's terminology in this chapter.

3. The BEA describes funds transferred from NPISHs to households as transfer payments. The authors use the BEA's terminology in this chapter.

# Trends in Revenues

In 2010, NPISH revenue was $1.16 trillion, an inflation-adjusted increase of 2.5 percent from 2009 (figure 4.1). From 2000 to 2010, revenue grew 28 percent after adjusting for inflation. Revenues declined in 2008 during the recession, down 1.2 percent from 2007. They picked back up in 2009 and 2010, however, growing at 3.5 and 2.5 percent, respectively.

Figure 4.2 displays the sources of revenue for NPISHs in 2010. Revenues are generated from three primary sources: sales receipts, asset income, and transfer payments (grants and donations). Sales receipts, or fees for services and goods, which include hospital payments, tuition payments, and entrance fees, account for the lion's share of nonprofit revenue—72 percent. Transfer payments, which consist of contributions from public and private sources, account for 23 percent, and asset income accounts for another 4 percent.

Nonprofit organizations providing health services such as hospitals, nursing care facilities, mental health centers, home health care services, and senior care account for the bulk of fee-for-service revenue, 74 percent in 2010 (table 4.1). Education, a distant second at 12 percent, collected $97.8 billion in tuition and other sales receipts in 2010. Growth in sales receipts between 2000 and 2010 was largest for social advocacy establishments, whose fee-for-service revenue grew 58 percent. Social advocacy establishments include human rights organizations, environment, conservations, wildlife, and

**Figure 4.1.** Revenue of Nonprofit Institutions Serving Households, 2000–10 (billions of 2010 dollars)

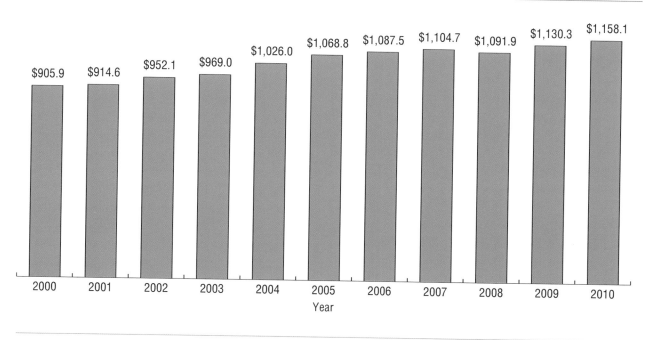

*Source:* U.S. Department of Commerce, Bureau of Economic Analysis, National Income and Product Accounts, table 2.9 (2011).
*Notes:* Estimates exclude nonprofit institutions serving business and government. Values are adjusted for inflation.

**Figure 4.2.** Sources of Revenue for Nonprofit Institutions Serving Households, 2010

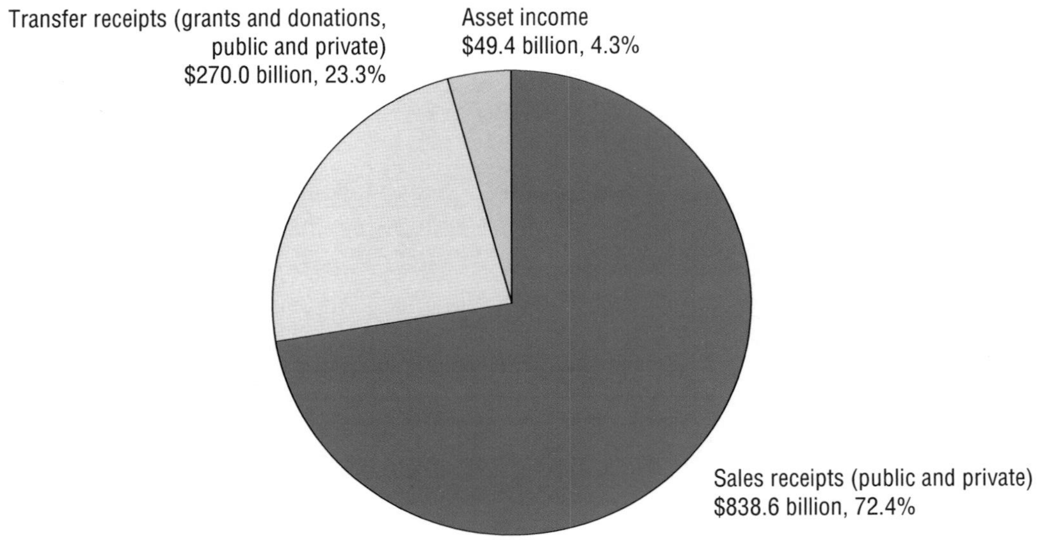

Transfer receipts (grants and donations, public and private)
$270.0 billion, 23.3%

Asset income
$49.4 billion, 4.3%

Sales receipts (public and private)
$838.6 billion, 72.4%

*Source:* U.S. Department of Commerce, Bureau of Economic Analysis, National Income and Product Accounts, table 2.9 (2011).
*Notes:* Estimates exclude nonprofit institutions serving business and government. Values are in 2010 dollars.

other social advocacy organizations. While growth was the largest for these organizations, they account for less than 1 percent of all sales receipts for the sector.

Figure 4.3 shows the value of total sales receipts, transfer receipts, and asset income since 2000. Sales receipts had the greatest growth, increasing 42 percent from 2000 to 2010, while transfer receipts grew 7 percent. Asset income declined 21 percent between 2000 and 2010.

Examining the revenue growth following the recession, asset income was hit the hardest. It declined 13 percent in 2008, over 5 percent in 2009, and over 7 percent in 2010. Sales receipts also showed a slight decline in 2008, with a decrease of 0.2 percent (down from a nearly 3 percent growth rate the previous year). Growth in sales receipts, however, rebounded in 2009 and 2010, increasing around 5 percent in the first year and 3 percent in the second. Interestingly, transfer receipts began decreasing in 2006, going from $274.6 billion in 2005 to $263.7 billion in 2008, falling 4 percent over the three years before the recession. Transfer receipts began increasing in 2009 and continued to increase in 2010.

As displayed in figure 4.4, the composition of nonprofit revenue has changed only slightly since 2000. Sales receipts, which accounted for 65 percent of revenue in 2000, accounted for 72 percent in 2010. Over the same period, transfer receipts dropped from 28 percent of revenue to 23 percent of revenue, and asset income dropped from 7 percent to 4 percent.

The next few paragraphs focus more specifically on the components of transfer receipts and asset income. While the BEA breaks out transfer receipts into public and private sources, a similar breakout is not provided for sales receipts.

**Table 4.1.** Revenue of Nonprofit Institutions Serving Households, 2000–10 (billions of 2010 dollars)

| | 2000 | 2001 | 2002 | 2003 | 2004 | 2005 | 2006 | 2007 | 2008 | 2009 | 2010 |
|---|---|---|---|---|---|---|---|---|---|---|---|
| Sales receipts (public and private)[a] | 590.9 | 617.8 | 660.2 | 681.1 | 713.6 | 739.8 | 751.9 | 773.5 | 771.6 | 811.0 | 838.6 |
| Health | 420.0 | 438.3 | 476.2 | 491.0 | 517.6 | 538.7 | 547.1 | 563.7 | 562.4 | 595.2 | 616.9 |
| Education | 68.6 | 72.0 | 72.2 | 74.9 | 77.7 | 80.5 | 83.0 | 85.8 | 88.0 | 93.5 | 97.8 |
| Social services | 44.1 | 49.7 | 54.7 | 56.5 | 58.2 | 59.3 | 59.4 | 60.8 | 60.3 | 61.7 | 63.5 |
| Professional advocacy | 27.0 | 26.6 | 26.3 | 26.9 | 27.1 | 27.2 | 27.9 | 28.4 | 28.2 | 28.7 | 28.3 |
| Recreation | 14.6 | 14.9 | 14.8 | 15.2 | 16.0 | 17.4 | 17.6 | 17.4 | 16.3 | 15.6 | 15.3 |
| Civic and social organizations | 7.5 | 7.4 | 7.4 | 7.9 | 8.1 | 7.6 | 7.5 | 7.4 | 7.0 | 6.9 | 7.0 |
| Religious organizations | 6.2 | 6.2 | 5.9 | 5.9 | 6.1 | 6.0 | 6.1 | 6.3 | 6.1 | 5.9 | 6.1 |
| Social advocacy establishments | 2.0 | 2.0 | 2.1 | 2.3 | 2.3 | 2.3 | 2.7 | 2.9 | 3.0 | 3.0 | 3.2 |
| Foundations and grantmaking/giving establishments | 0.9 | 0.7 | 0.5 | 0.5 | 0.6 | 0.6 | 0.6 | 0.7 | 0.6 | 0.6 | 0.6 |
| Transfer receipts | 252.6 | 244.3 | 246.3 | 243.7 | 264.8 | 274.6 | 272.2 | 266.4 | 263.7 | 266.0 | 270.0 |
| From households[b] | 222.9 | 211.3 | 214.3 | 212.0 | 232.8 | 238.3 | 239.6 | 234.7 | 233.1 | 233.3 | 234.5 |
| From government | 15.6 | 17.2 | 18.8 | 19.7 | 20.1 | 19.4 | 19.0 | 18.4 | 19.0 | 20.2 | 21.8 |
| From business (net) | 14.2 | 15.6 | 13.2 | 12.1 | 11.8 | 16.7 | 13.6 | 13.3 | 11.5 | 12.5 | 13.7 |
| Asset income | 62.4 | 52.3 | 45.7 | 44.3 | 47.7 | 54.5 | 63.4 | 64.9 | 56.4 | 53.4 | 49.5 |
| Interest income | 45.2 | 35.5 | 28.2 | 24.4 | 25.9 | 29.6 | 34.8 | 34.9 | 33.0 | 32.3 | 31.2 |
| Dividend income | 12.7 | 11.9 | 12.4 | 15.4 | 17.4 | 20.9 | 24.4 | 25.1 | 18.0 | 14.6 | 11.7 |
| Rental income | 4.6 | 4.9 | 5.1 | 4.5 | 4.4 | 4.0 | 4.1 | 4.8 | 5.4 | 6.4 | 6.6 |
| Total | 905.9 | 914.6 | 952.1 | 969.0 | 1,026.0 | 1,068.8 | 1,087.5 | 1,104.7 | 1,091.9 | 1,130.3 | 1,158.1 |

*Source:* U.S. Department of Commerce, Bureau of Economic Analysis, National Income and Product Accounts, table 2.9 (2011).
*Notes:* Estimates exclude nonprofit institutions serving business and government. Values are adjusted for inflation. Revenues have been revised from the 2008 *Almanac.*
a. Sales receipts exclude unrelated sales, secondary sales, and sales to business, government, and the rest of the world; sales receipts include membership dues and fees.
b. Transfer receipts from households include individual contributions and bequests from households.

**Figure 4.3.** Revenue of Nonprofit Institutions Serving Households by Source, 2000–10 (billions of 2010 dollars)

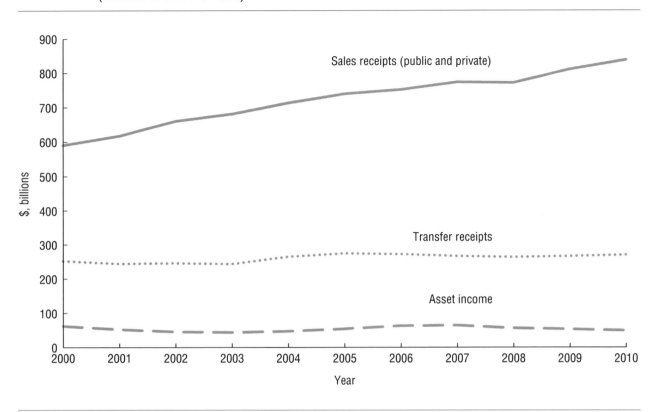

*Source:* U.S. Department of Commerce, Bureau of Economic Analysis, National Income and Product Accounts, table 2.9 (2011).
*Notes:* Estimates exclude nonprofit institutions serving business and government. Values are adjusted for inflation.

**Figure 4.4.** Types of Revenue for Nonprofit Institutions Serving Households, 2000–10 (percent)

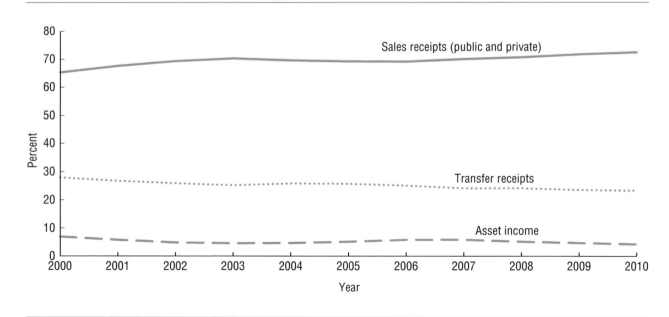

*Source:* U.S. Department of Commerce, Bureau of Economic Analysis, National Income and Product Accounts, table 2.9 (2011).
*Note:* Estimates exclude nonprofit institutions serving business and government.

**Figure 4.5.** Transfer Receipts for Nonprofit Institutions Serving Households by Source, 2000–10 (billions of 2010 dollars)

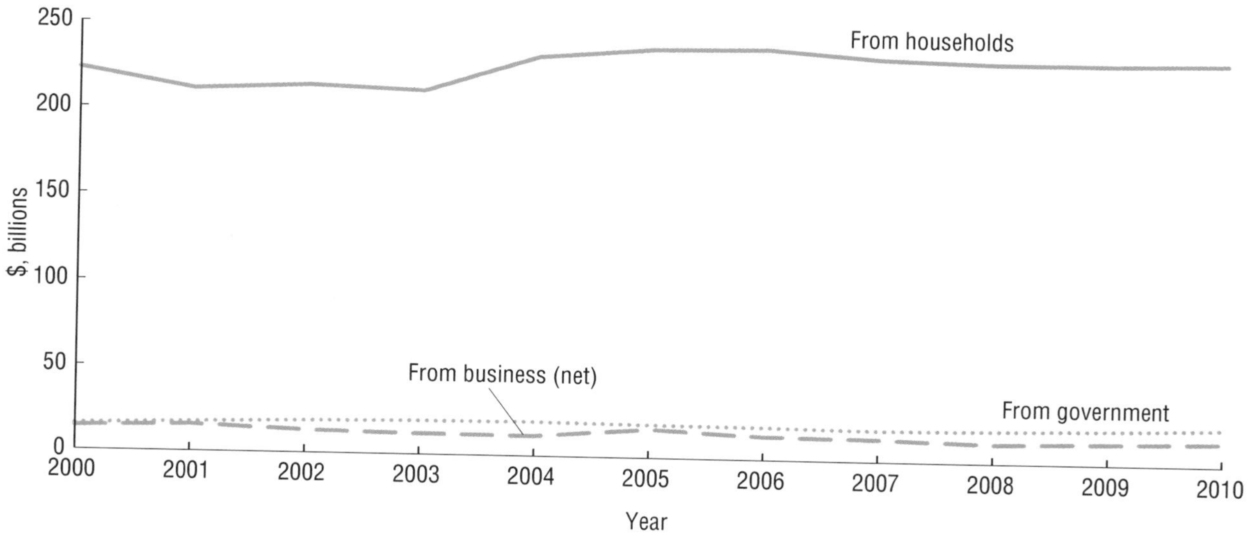

Source: U.S. Department of Commerce, Bureau of Economic Analysis, National Income and Product Accounts, table 2.9 (2011).
Notes: Estimates exclude nonprofit institutions serving business and government. Values are adjusted for inflation.

In 2010, transfer receipts contributed $270 billion to overall nonprofit revenue. Contributions from households accounted for 87 percent of all transfer receipts, government accounted for 8 percent, and business accounted for 5 percent. Figure 4.5 displays the trend in transfer receipts by funding source. Transfer receipts from government saw the largest growth from 2000 to 2010, with a 40 percent growth rate, followed by transfer receipts from households (5 percent). Transfer receipts from business declined 3 percent. From 2007 to 2008, contributions from government saw slight growth with an increase from $18.4 billion in 2007 to $19.0 billion in 2008, a growth of 3 percent. Contributions from households and business, though, saw declines. Transfer receipts from households declined about 1 percent and contributions from business declined 13 percent during this same period.

Figure 4.6 displays the shares of transfer receipts by source from 2000 to 2010. The percentage of transfer receipts by households remained remarkably steady over the 10 years, hovering between 86 and 88 percent. Government contributions increased slightly from 6 percent in 2000 to 8 percent in 2010. The proportion of transfer receipts attributed to business contributions has decreased slightly since 2005, dropping by about 1 percentage point.

Asset income accounted for $49.5 billion in 2010. As displayed in figure 4.7, interest income accounts for 63 percent of this income, followed by dividend income at 24 percent and rental income at 13 percent. Figure 4.8 shows how interest income, dividend income, and rental income have changed since 2000. Not surprisingly, both

**Figure 4.6.** Transfer Receipts for Nonprofit Institutions Serving Households by Source, 2000–10 (percent)

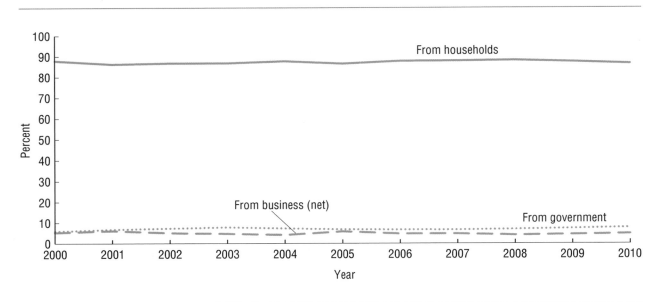

*Source:* U.S. Department of Commerce, Bureau of Economic Analysis, National Income and Product Accounts, table 2.9 (2011).
*Note:* Estimates exclude nonprofit institutions serving business and government.

**Figure 4.7.** Asset Income for Nonprofit Institutions Serving Households by Source, 2010 (percent)

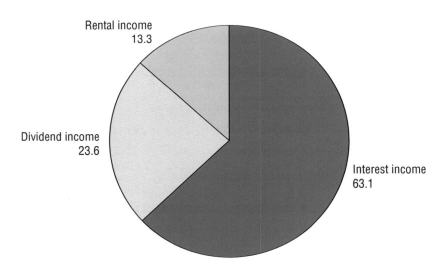

*Source:* U.S. Department of Commerce, Bureau of Economic Analysis, National Income and Product Accounts, table 2.9 (2011).
*Note:* Estimates exclude nonprofit institutions serving business and government.

**Figure 4.8.** Asset Income for Nonprofit Institutions Serving Households by Source, 2000–10 (billions of 2010 dollars)

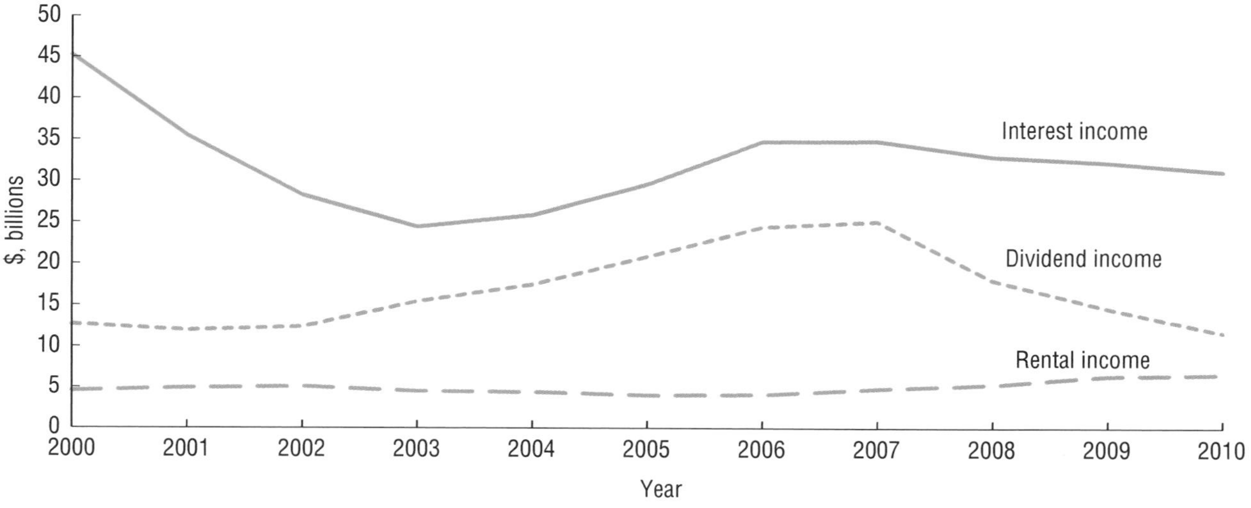

*Source:* U.S. Department of Commerce, Bureau of Economic Analysis, National Income and Product Accounts, table 2.9 (2011).
*Notes:* Estimates exclude nonprofit institutions serving business and government. Values are adjusted for inflation.

dividend and interest income have been declining since 2007. Dividend income from stocks, mutual funds, and other investments plummeted 53 percent between 2007 and 2010 during the recession. Interest income, which includes interest earned from savings accounts, certificates of deposits, or other temporary cash investments, declined 11 percent from 2007 to 2010. Rental income, however, has been on the rise, increasing 45 percent since 2000 and 38 percent between 2007 and 2010. The three components of asset income—dividends, interest, and rental income—are not growing as fast as nonprofit sector income. This suggests that the nonprofit sector may be undercapitalized.

# Trends in Outlays

Now that we know where nonprofit funds come from, we turn our attention to how these funds are spent. In 2010, NPISHs had $1.22 trillion in outlays. Figure 4.9 displays how funds were spent. Ninety-one percent of nonprofit funds were spent directly to obtain goods and provide services, and the remaining 9 percent were distributed to the government, domestic households, or internationally. Comparing total NPISH revenue and outlays, outlays exceeded revenues by $65.5 billion, or 6 percent. This indicates that nonprofit organizations either used reserves to fund their activities or were running deficits.

Figure 4.10 and table 4.2 show nonprofit outlays from 2000 to 2010. Between 2007 and 2008 consumption expenditures saw the slowest growth rate, 2 percent, during

**Figure 4.9.** Uses of Funds by Nonprofit Institutions Serving Households, 2010 (percent)

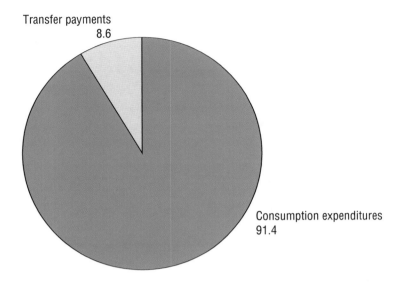

*Source:* U.S. Department of Commerce, Bureau of Economic Analysis, National Income and Product Accounts, table 2.9 (2011).
*Note:* Estimates exclude nonprofit institutions serving business and government.

**Figure 4.10.** Outlays from Nonprofit Institutions Serving Households by Use, 2000–10 (billions of 2010 dollars)

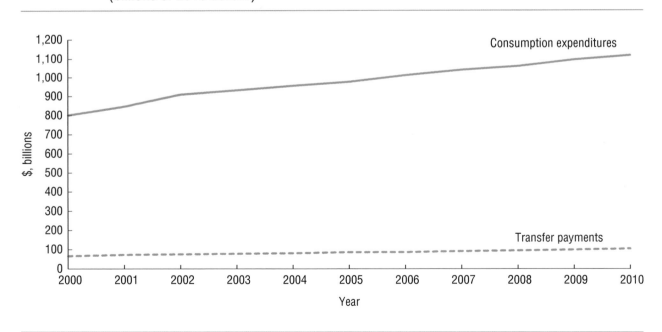

*Source:* U.S. Department of Commerce, Bureau of Economic Analysis, National Income and Product Accounts, table 2.9 (2011).
*Notes:* Estimates exclude nonprofit institutions serving business and government. Values are adjusted for inflation.

**Table 4.2.** Outlays from Nonprofit Institutions Serving Households, 2000–10 (billions of 2010 dollars)

| | 2000 | 2001 | 2002 | 2003 | 2004 | 2005 | 2006 | 2007 | 2008 | 2009 | 2010 |
|---|---|---|---|---|---|---|---|---|---|---|---|
| Consumption expenditures[a] | 800.3 | 847.1 | 908.7 | 931.4 | 955.3 | 976.2 | 1,011.5 | 1,040.5 | 1,059.9 | 1,095.9 | 1,118.9 |
| Health | 433.5 | 454.3 | 489.0 | 506.2 | 520.8 | 538.4 | 554.6 | 567.0 | 574.7 | 608.1 | 620.1 |
| Education | 118.8 | 126.8 | 133.8 | 137.2 | 140.4 | 143.7 | 151.5 | 161.5 | 164.9 | 172.3 | 178.8 |
| Social services | 82.8 | 93.0 | 100.0 | 103.0 | 101.5 | 102.9 | 103.6 | 105.2 | 107.1 | 111.0 | 112.0 |
| Professional advocacy | 67.9 | 71.5 | 74.8 | 74.4 | 77.1 | 77.7 | 78.1 | 81.3 | 77.6 | 76.0 | 78.0 |
| Recreation | 29.3 | 30.9 | 32.1 | 33.5 | 34.5 | 35.8 | 37.5 | 39.1 | 40.1 | 39.6 | 39.0 |
| Civic and social organizations | 32.7 | 30.3 | 34.2 | 31.4 | 35.7 | 31.7 | 36.2 | 33.4 | 39.6 | 33.4 | 37.4 |
| Religious organizations | 17.1 | 20.6 | 21.9 | 21.6 | 21.8 | 22.4 | 25.3 | 27.1 | 29.2 | 28.0 | 26.4 |
| Social advocacy establishments | 8.6 | 9.4 | 11.4 | 12.3 | 12.1 | 12.5 | 13.7 | 15.1 | 16.3 | 16.8 | 16.9 |
| Foundations and grantmaking/giving establishments | 9.9 | 10.5 | 11.3 | 11.7 | 11.4 | 10.9 | 10.8 | 10.6 | 10.6 | 10.7 | 10.4 |
| Transfer payments | 65.5 | 72.3 | 75.0 | 77.7 | 80.6 | 85.6 | 86.6 | 91.0 | 94.2 | 99.0 | 104.7 |
| To households[b] | 55.8 | 63.0 | 65.7 | 67.8 | 71.0 | 73.9 | 75.3 | 76.5 | 75.6 | 78.2 | 80.1 |
| To the rest of the world (net) | 8.7 | 8.9 | 9.1 | 9.6 | 9.0 | 10.9 | 10.5 | 13.7 | 18.1 | 20.2 | 23.9 |
| To government[c] | 0.8 | 0.4 | 0.2 | 0.4 | 0.6 | 0.7 | 0.9 | 0.9 | 0.6 | 0.6 | 0.6 |
| Total NPISH outlays | 865.8 | 919.4 | 983.7 | 1,009.1 | 1,035.9 | 1,061.8 | 1,098.2 | 1,131.5 | 1,154.1 | 1,194.9 | 1,223.6 |

*Source:* U.S. Department of Commerce, Bureau of Economic Analysis, National Income and Product Accounts, table 2.9 (2011).

*Notes:* Estimates exclude nonprofit institutions serving business and government. Values are adjusted for inflation. Outlays have been revised from the 2008 *Almanac.*

NPISH = nonprofit institutions serving households

a. Consumption expenditures are net of unrelated sales, secondary sales, and sales to business, government, and the rest of the world; excludes own-account investment (construction and software).

b. Payments to households include benefits paid to members, specific assistance to individuals, and grants and allocations.

c. Payments to government consist of excise taxes paid by nonprofit institutions serving households.

**Figure 4.11.** Outlays from Nonprofit Institutions Serving Households by Use, 2000–10 (percent)

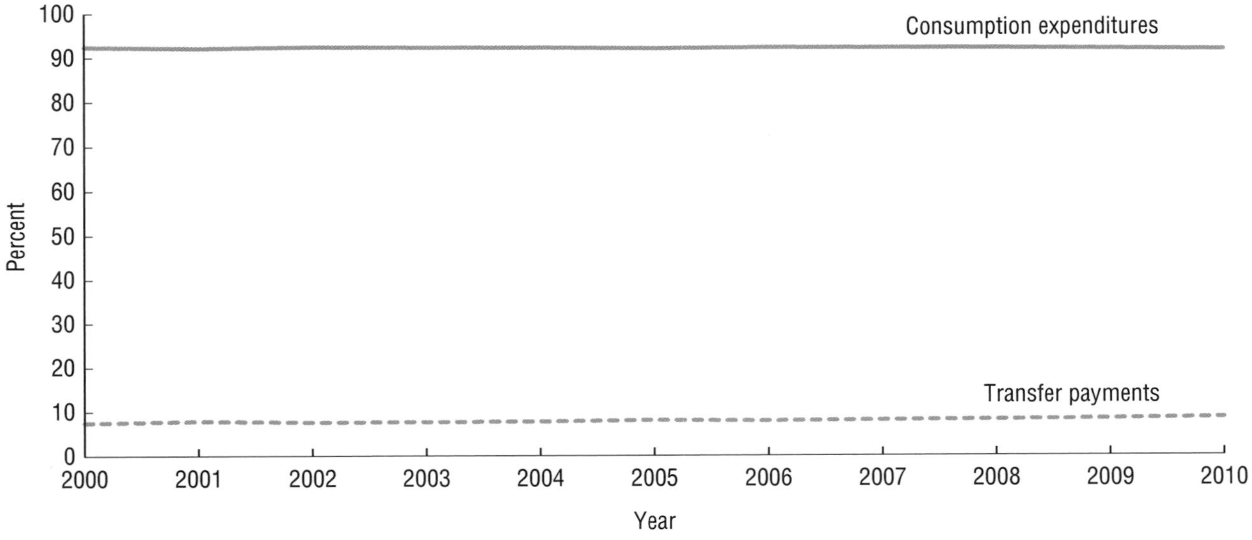

*Source:* U.S. Department of Commerce, Bureau of Economic Analysis, National Income and Product Accounts, table 2.9 (2011).
*Note:* Estimates exclude nonprofit institutions serving business and government.

the decade. Expenditures grew by 3 percent and 2 percent, respectively, in 2009 and 2010. Transfer payments continued to grow at a steady pace throughout the recession, from $91 billion in 2007 to $104.7 billion in 2010, an increase of 15 percent. Table 4.2 also provides data on nonprofit outlays and breaks out consumption expenditures by type of NPISH. While health NPISHs expend the largest dollar amount, social advocacy establishments, religious organizations, and social services had the largest increase in expenses between 2000 and 2010, after adjusting for inflation.

Figure 4.11 shows the proportion of each type of outlay from 2000 to 2010. Over the years, consumption expenditures have accounted for the largest proportion of outlays, hovering around 90 percent. The share of transfer payments has been rising slightly over the decade but still accounts for less than 10 percent of expenditures.

Diving deeper into consumption expenditures and transfer payments, figure 4.12 shows consumption expenditures by type of organization, or subsector, in 2010. (The industries included in each subsector are listed in table 4.5.) More than half of NPISH expenditures were in the health care field. Another 16 percent were in education, and 10 percent were in social services. As displayed in table 4.3, the proportion going to each subsector has remained fairly consistent since 2000—usually staying within 1 to 2 percentage points.

Table 4.4 displays the amount of money spent by type of organization, or subsector, since 2000. Nonprofits in the health subsector have the highest expenditures, which reached $620.1 billion in 2010. Education follows with $178.8 billion. Expenditures of civic and social organizations are the smallest, spending $10.4 billion in 2010.

**Figure 4.12.** Consumption Expenditures for Nonprofit Institutions Serving Households by Subsector, 2010 (percent)

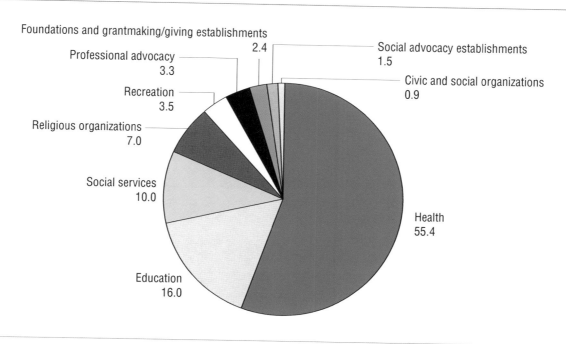

Foundations and grantmaking/giving establishments 2.4

Professional advocacy 3.3

Recreation 3.5

Religious organizations 7.0

Social services 10.0

Education 16.0

Social advocacy establishments 1.5

Civic and social organizations 0.9

Health 55.4

*Source:* U.S. Department of Commerce, Bureau of Economic Analysis, National Income and Product Accounts, table 2.9 (2011).
*Note:* Estimates exclude nonprofit institutions serving business and government.

Expenditures of social advocacy establishments have nearly doubled in the past 10 years, after adjusting for inflation. Over the same period, expenditures also saw tremendous growth in foundations and grantmaking, and education organizations, increasing 54 and 51 percent, respectively. Growth was slowest in the civic and social organization subsector, with expenditures increasing only 5 percent.

Transfer payments from nonprofits can go to U.S. households, to government, or outside the United States. As displayed in figure 4.13, over three-quarters of transfer payments (77 percent) go to households in the United States. This includes benefits paid to members, specific assistance to individuals, and grants and allocations. Twenty-three percent of payments go to help people internationally, such as assistance provided by relief organizations. Finally, the BEA treats the excise taxes paid by grantmaking foundations as transfer payments to government. These taxes account for less than 1 percent of total transfer payments.

Figure 4.14 shows the dollar trend of transfer payments by type from 2000 to 2010. International transfer payments saw the greatest growth over the decade, nearly tripling in size (174 percent growth). Transfer payments to households grew 43 percent over the same period. These payments saw the greatest increase in 2001, when they grew by 13 percent. Transfer payments to government actually declined by 21 percent over the 10 years.

**Table 4.3.** Consumption Expenditures for Nonprofit Institutions Serving Households by Subsector, 2000–10 (percent)

| | 2000 | 2001 | 2002 | 2003 | 2004 | 2005 | 2006 | 2007 | 2008 | 2009 | 2010 |
|---|---|---|---|---|---|---|---|---|---|---|---|
| Health | 54.2 | 53.6 | 53.8 | 54.3 | 54.5 | 55.2 | 54.8 | 54.5 | 54.2 | 55.5 | 55.4 |
| Education | 14.8 | 15.0 | 14.7 | 14.7 | 14.7 | 14.7 | 15.0 | 15.5 | 15.6 | 15.7 | 16.0 |
| Social services | 10.3 | 11.0 | 11.0 | 11.1 | 10.6 | 10.5 | 10.2 | 10.1 | 10.1 | 10.1 | 10.0 |
| Religious organizations | 8.5 | 8.4 | 8.2 | 8.0 | 8.1 | 8.0 | 7.7 | 7.8 | 7.3 | 6.9 | 7.0 |
| Recreation | 3.7 | 3.6 | 3.5 | 3.6 | 3.6 | 3.7 | 3.7 | 3.8 | 3.8 | 3.6 | 3.5 |
| Professional advocacy | 4.1 | 3.6 | 3.8 | 3.4 | 3.7 | 3.2 | 3.6 | 3.2 | 3.7 | 3.1 | 3.3 |
| Foundations and grantmaking/giving establishments | 2.1 | 2.4 | 2.4 | 2.3 | 2.3 | 2.3 | 2.5 | 2.6 | 2.8 | 2.6 | 2.4 |
| Social advocacy establishments | 1.1 | 1.1 | 1.3 | 1.3 | 1.3 | 1.3 | 1.4 | 1.5 | 1.5 | 1.5 | 1.5 |
| Civic and social organizations | 1.2 | 1.2 | 1.2 | 1.3 | 1.2 | 1.1 | 1.1 | 1.0 | 1.0 | 1.0 | 0.9 |
| Total NPISH consumption expenditures | 100.0 | 100.0 | 100.0 | 100.0 | 100.0 | 100.0 | 100.0 | 100.0 | 100.0 | 100.0 | 100.0 |

*Source:* U.S. Department of Commerce, Bureau of Economic Analysis, National Income and Product Accounts, table 2.9 (2011).
*Note:* Estimates exclude nonprofit institutions serving business and government.

**Table 4.4.** Consumption Expenditures for Nonprofit Institutions Serving Households by Subsector, 2000–10 (billions of 2010 dollars)

| | 2000 | 2001 | 2002 | 2003 | 2004 | 2005 | 2006 | 2007 | 2008 | 2009 | 2010 |
|---|---|---|---|---|---|---|---|---|---|---|---|
| Health | 433.5 | 454.3 | 489.0 | 506.2 | 520.8 | 538.4 | 554.6 | 567.0 | 574.7 | 608.1 | 620.1 |
| Education | 118.8 | 126.8 | 133.8 | 137.2 | 140.4 | 143.7 | 151.5 | 161.5 | 164.9 | 172.3 | 178.8 |
| Social services | 82.8 | 93.0 | 100.0 | 103.0 | 101.5 | 102.9 | 103.6 | 105.2 | 107.1 | 111.0 | 112.0 |
| Religious organizations | 67.9 | 71.5 | 74.8 | 74.4 | 77.1 | 77.7 | 78.1 | 81.3 | 77.6 | 76.0 | 78.0 |
| Recreation | 29.3 | 30.9 | 32.1 | 33.5 | 34.5 | 35.8 | 37.5 | 39.1 | 40.1 | 39.6 | 39.0 |
| Professional advocacy | 32.7 | 30.3 | 34.2 | 31.4 | 35.7 | 31.7 | 36.2 | 33.4 | 39.6 | 33.4 | 37.4 |
| Foundations and grantmaking/giving establishments | 17.1 | 20.6 | 21.9 | 21.6 | 21.8 | 22.4 | 25.3 | 27.1 | 29.2 | 28.0 | 26.4 |
| Social advocacy establishments | 8.6 | 9.4 | 11.4 | 12.3 | 12.1 | 12.5 | 13.7 | 15.1 | 16.3 | 16.8 | 16.9 |
| Civic and social organizations | 9.9 | 10.5 | 11.3 | 11.7 | 11.4 | 10.9 | 10.8 | 10.6 | 10.6 | 10.7 | 10.4 |
| Total NPISH consumption expenditures | 800.3 | 847.1 | 908.7 | 931.4 | 955.3 | 976.2 | 1,011.5 | 1,040.5 | 1,059.9 | 1,095.9 | 1,118.9 |

*Source*: U.S. Department of Commerce, Bureau of Economic Analysis, National Income and Product Accounts, table 2.9 (2011).
*Notes*: Estimates exclude nonprofit institutions serving business and government. Values are adjusted for inflation.

**Table 4.5.** NAICS Industries Included in Bureau of Economic Analysis Consumption Categories, 2010

**Health**

| | |
|---|---|
| 621410 | Family planning centers |
| 621420 | Outpatient mental health |
| 621491 | HMO medical centers |
| 621492 | Kidney dialysis centers |
| 621493 | Freestanding ambulatory surgical and emergency centers |
| 621498 | All other outpatient care centers |
| 621610 | Home health care services |
| 621910 | Ambulance services |
| 621999 | All other miscellaneous ambulatory services |
| 622119 | General medical and surgical hospitals |
| 622219 | Psychiatric and substance abuse hospitals |
| 622319 | Specialty hospitals, excluding psychiatric and substance abuse |
| 623110 | Nursing care facilities |
| 623210 | Residential mental retardation facilities |
| 623311 | Continuing care retirement communities |

**Education**

| | |
|---|---|
| 541710 | Research and development in life sciences, physical sciences, and engineering |
| 541720 | Research and development in social sciences and humanities |
| 611110 | Elementary and secondary education services |
| 611210 | Private higher education services |
| 611310 | Colleges, universities, professional schools, and junior colleges |
| 611400 | Professional/management, business/secretarial, and computer schools |
| 611500 | Apprenticeship, flight, cosmetology, and other training schools |
| 611600 | Art/drama/music, language, exam preparation, auto driving, and all other misc. schools, and incidental and support services |
| 611710 | Educational support services |
| 624410 | Child day care services |

**Social services**

| | |
|---|---|
| 623220 | Residential mental health and substance abuse facilities |
| 623312 | Homes for the elderly |
| 623900 | Other residential care facilities |
| 624110 | Child and youth services |
| 624120 | Services for the elderly and persons with disabilities |
| 624190 | Other individual and family services |

**Table 4.5.** NAICS Industries Included in Bureau of Economic Analysis Consumption Categories, 2010 *(continued)*

| | |
|---|---|
| 624210 | Community food services |
| 624221 | Temporary shelters |
| 624229 | Other community housing services |
| 624230 | Emergency and other relief services |
| 624300 | Vocational rehabilitation services |
| 624400 | Child day care services |

**Religious organizations**

| | |
|---|---|
| 813110 | Religious organizations |

**Foundations and grantmaking and giving establishments**

| | |
|---|---|
| 813211 | Grantmaking foundations |
| 813212 | Voluntary health organizations, grantmaking and giving |
| 813219 | Other grantmaking and giving services |

**Social advocacy establishments**

| | |
|---|---|
| 813311 | Human rights organizations |
| 813312 | Environment, conservation, and wildlife organizations |
| 813319 | Social advocacy organizations |

**Civic and social organizations**

| | |
|---|---|
| 813400 | Civic and social organizations |

**Professional advocacy**

| | |
|---|---|
| 541110 | Legal aid societies and similar legal services |
| 813920 | Professional associations |
| 813930 | Labor organizations |
| 813940 | Political organizations |
| 813990 | All other similar organizations, excl. condos and homeowners association services to households |

*Source:* Private communication from analysts at the Bureau of Economic Analysis, October 2011.
NAICS = North American Industry Classification System

As displayed in figure 4.15, while the dollar amount of transfer payments to households in the United States has been on the rise, the share of transfer payments going to households has been declining since 2006. This reduction likely stems from the huge growth in transfer payments going outside the United States. International transfer payments as a proportion of transfer payments have nearly doubled since 2000, increasing from 13 percent in 2000 to 23 percent in 2010. The percentage of transfers going to the government was 1.2 percent in 2000 but by 2010, that percentage had declined by half to 0.6 percent.

**Figure 4.13.** Transfer Payments from Nonprofit Institutions Serving Households by Recipient, 2010 (percent)

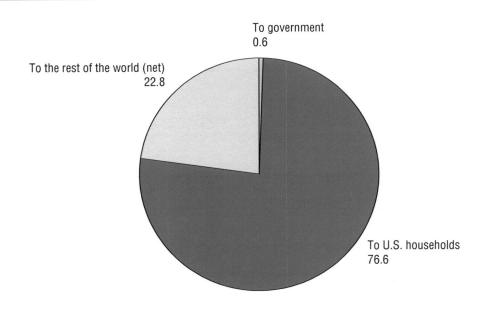

*Source:* U.S. Department of Commerce, Bureau of Economic Analysis, National Income and Product Accounts, table 2.9 (2011).
*Note:* Estimates exclude nonprofit institutions serving business and government.

**Figure 4.14.** Transfer Payments from Nonprofit Institutions Serving Households by Recipient, 2000–10 (billions of 2010 dollars)

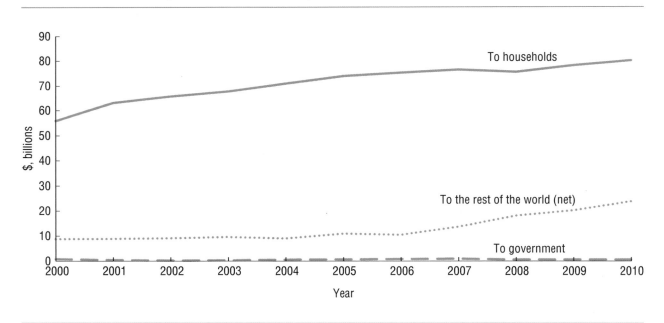

*Source:* U.S. Department of Commerce, Bureau of Economic Analysis, National Income and Product Accounts, table 2.9 (2011).
*Notes:* Estimates exclude nonprofit institutions serving business and government. Values are adjusted for inflation.

**Figure 4.15.** Transfer Payments from Nonprofit Institutions Serving Households by Recipient, 2000–10 (percent)

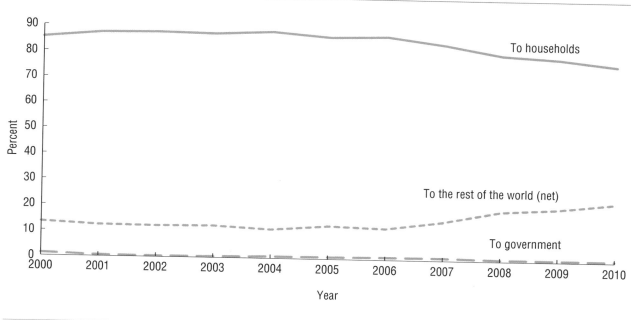

*Source:* U.S. Department of Commerce, Bureau of Economic Analysis, National Income and Product Accounts, table 2.9 (2011).
*Note:* Estimates exclude nonprofit institutions serving business and government.

Table 4.6 shows a trend for savings. The BEA defines saving as total revenue minus consumption expenditures and transfer payments. As displayed, saving by nonprofits has been declining steadily since 2005—from an adjusted inflation surplus of $7.0 billion in 2005 to a deficit of $65.5 billion in 2010. In fact, nonprofits have had surplus funds in only two of the past 10 years. This indicates that many nonprofit organizations are spending more money than they are able to generate, highlighting a major financial problem for the sector. Those that are able to sustain operations may be drawing down reserves or taking out lines of credit.

**Table 4.6.** Savings from Nonprofit Institutions Serving Households, 2000–10 (billons of 2010 dollars)

|         | 2000  | 2001  | 2002  | 2003    | 2004    | 2005    | 2006    | 2007    | 2008    | 2009    | 2010    |
|---------|-------|-------|-------|---------|---------|---------|---------|---------|---------|---------|---------|
| Revenue | 905.9 | 914.6 | 952.1 | 969.0   | 1,026.0 | 1,068.8 | 1,087.5 | 1,104.7 | 1,091.9 | 1,130.3 | 1,158.1 |
| Outlays | 865.8 | 919.4 | 983.7 | 1,009.1 | 1,035.9 | 1,061.8 | 1,098.2 | 1,131.5 | 1,154.1 | 1,194.9 | 1,223.6 |
| Savings | 40.1  | −4.9  | −31.6 | −40.2   | −9.8    | 7.0     | −10.6   | −26.8   | −62.2   | −64.5   | −65.5   |

*Source:* U.S. Department of Commerce, Bureau of Economic Analysis, National Income and Product Accounts, table 2.9 (2011).
*Notes:* Estimates in this table exclude nonprofit institutions serving business and government. Figures are adjusted for inflation. The difference between revenues and outlays was calculated before rounding. Revenues and outlays have been revised from the 2008 *Almanac.*

## Conclusion

Analysis of nonprofit revenues and outlays shows that both have increased for the past decade. However, in eight of the last 10 years, the nonprofit sector has spent more money than it earned. The gap between revenues and outlays was accentuated by the start of the recession, with nonprofits experiencing a shortage of over $60 billion between revenues and outlays for each year since 2008. Nonprofits may be drawing down savings or taking out lines of credit to sustain their operations. The data further suggest a major financial problem for the sector.

## Sources

Mead, Charles Ian, Clinton P. McCully, and Marshall B. Reinsdorf. 2003. "Income and Outlays of Households and of Nonprofit Institutions Serving Households." *Survey of Current Business* 83(4): 13–17.

U.S. Department of Commerce, Bureau of Economic Analysis. 2011a. "National Income and Product Accounts Tables." http://www.bea.gov/iTable/iTable.cfm?ReqID=9&step=1 (Accessed May 17, 2012).

———. 2011b. Private communication from analysts at the Bureau of Economic Analysis, October.

# 5

# The Size, Scope, and Finances of Public Charities

This chapter examines the size, scope, and financial conditions of public charities, those organizations exempt from taxation under section 501(c)(3) of the Internal Revenue Code. We first provide an overview of the nonprofit sector and then discuss public charities in detail, including a look at these organizations by subsector and state.

## Summary

- In 2010, nearly 1.6 million nonprofits were registered with the IRS. Of these, about 1 million were registered as 501(c)(3) public charities.
- The 366,086 reporting public charities spent $1.45 trillion and had $2.71 trillion in assets in 2010.
- Public charities with $10 million or more in expenses, while only accounting for 4 percent of total public charities, account for more than 85 percent of expenses. Conversely, organizations with less than $500,000 in expenses account for nearly 75 percent of all public charities but less than 3 percent of expenses.
- Sixty-three percent of public charities were founded in the past 20 years.
- Human services public charities, which include organizations that provide job training, legal aid, housing and disaster assistance, youth development, and food distribution programs, among others, account for one-third of public charities. Education, with just under one-fifth of organizations, is the second-largest subsector.
- Fees for services and goods from private sources and government account for 74 percent of public charity revenue. If hospitals and higher education institutions are excluded, the proportion of revenue from fees for services and goods drops from 74 percent to 56 percent.
- The number of reporting public charities grew from 249,859 in 2000 to 366,086 in 2010, an increase of 47 percent.

- Over this same 10-year period, revenue of reporting public charities grew by 81 percent (an inflation-adjusted 43 percent), public support grew by 79 percent (an inflation-adjusted 41 percent), expenses grew by 94 percent (an inflation-adjusted 53 percent), and assets grew by 81 percent (an inflation-adjusted 43 percent).
- The number of reporting public charities per state ranged from 1,077 in Wyoming to 42,479 in California. Highly populated states like California, New York, and Texas have the most charities, while less-populated states like Wyoming and North Dakota have fewer.
- Less-populated states have more reporting public charities per capita than the more populated states. Vermont, Montana, Alaska, Maine, and Wyoming have the highest nonprofit density per person.

## Overview of the Nonprofit Sector

Approximately 1.6 million nonprofit organizations were registered with the IRS in 2010, a 24 percent increase over the past 10 years. This figure includes an eclectic group of organizations ranging from hospitals and social service organizations to advocacy groups and chambers of commerce. It excludes organizations that are not required to register with the Internal Revenue Service, such as nonprofits with less than $5,000 in annual revenue or religious congregations (although many congregations choose to register), and organizations that had their tax-exempt status revoked for failing to file a financial return for three consecutive years. See the "Reporting Public Charities" section and tables 5.2 and 5.3 for more information on changes to filing requirements for nonprofit organizations.

The Internal Revenue Code defines more than 30 different categories of tax-exempt organizations. The largest group—501(c)(3) public charities—accounts for 63 percent of all nonprofit organizations and holds most of the sector's revenue and assets, nearly three-quarters and three-fifths, respectively. Other categories of nonprofit organizations include social welfare organizations (501(c)(4)), labor and agricultural associations (501(c)(5)), business leagues (501(c)(6)), and fraternal beneficiary societies (501(c)(8)); see table 1.1 for a complete listing.

Approximately 40 percent of nonprofit organizations registered with the IRS were required to file a Form 990 (Form 990, Form 990-EZ, or Form 990-PF) in 2010. Private foundations, regardless of size, were required to file, as were other organizations that collected more than $50,000 in gross receipts. We refer to these 618,062 entities as **reporting nonprofits.** Reporting nonprofits accounted for approximately $2.06 trillion in revenue, $1.94 trillion in expenses, and $4.49 trillion in assets.

As displayed in table 5.1, while the overall number of nonprofits registered with the IRS grew 24 percent from 2000 to 2010, the number of reporting nonprofits grew 39 percent. Most growth in the sector occurred between 2000 and 2005. When only 501(c)(3) public charities registered with the IRS are considered, we see a 42 percent increase—more than 18 percentage points greater than the growth rate for all registered nonprofits over the decade. Public charities increased from just over half of all nonprofits in 2000 to about 63 percent of nonprofits by 2010.

**Table 5.1.** Size and Financial Scope of the Nonprofit Sector, 2000–10

| | 2000 | 2005 | 2010 | % change, 2000–10 | % change, 2000–10 (inflation adjusted) |
|---|---|---|---|---|---|
| All registered nonprofits | 1.26 million | 1.41 million | 1.56 million | 23.6 | — |
| Reporting nonprofits | 444,161 | 552,569 | 618,062 | 39.2 | — |
|   Revenues ($) | 1.15 trillion | 1.63 trillion | 2.06 trillion | 78.3 | 40.8 |
|   Expenses ($) | 1.01 trillion | 1.48 trillion | 1.94 trillion | 91.8 | 51.5 |
|   Assets ($) | 2.57 trillion | 3.50 trillion | 4.49 trillion | 74.8 | 38.1 |
| Public charities, 501(c)(3) | 688,600 | 847,954 | 979,901 | 42.3 | — |
| Reporting public charities | 249,859 | 313,164 | 366,086 | 46.5 | — |
|   Revenues ($) | 837 billion | 1.17 trillion | 1.51 trillion | 80.9 | 42.9 |
|   Expenses ($) | 750 billion | 1.08 trillion | 1.45 trillion | 94.0 | 53.2 |
|   Assets ($) | 1.50 trillion | 2.07 trillion | 2.71 trillion | 80.6 | 42.6 |

*Sources:* Urban Institute, National Center for Charitable Statistics, Core Files (Public Charities, 2000, 2005, and 2010); and Internal Revenue Service Business Master Files, Exempt Organizations (2000–11).
*Notes:* Reporting public charities include only organizations that both reported (filed IRS Forms 990) and were required to do so (had more than $25,000 in gross receipts in 2000 and 2005 or $50,000 or more in gross receipts in 2010). Organizations that had their tax-exempt status revoked for failing to file financial returns for three consecutive years have been removed from the 2010 nonprofit total. Foreign organizations, government-associated organizations, and organizations without state identifiers have also been excluded. All amounts are in current dollars and are not adjusted for inflation.
— = not applicable

While we are reporting on finances in the midst of a recession, nonprofit revenue and assets grew at respectable rates over the past 10 years: 41 and 38 percent, respectively, after adjusting for inflation. This compares to a 16 percent inflation-adjusted growth rate of the U.S. gross domestic product over the same period. Note, however, that revenue growth slowed in the second five-year period and that expenses outpaced revenue, with expenses growing 92 percent (52 percent after adjusting for inflation) in the decade. A similar pattern is evident for public charities. These trends, however, should not mask the cutbacks and hardships that nonprofit organizations, especially small ones, have experienced these past few years.

## Reporting Public Charities

The remainder of this chapter focuses on reporting public charities. These are 501(c)(3) organizations that have charitable purposes (i.e., includes assisting the poor and underprivileged; advancing religion, education, health, science, art, or culture; protecting the environment; or other purposes beneficial to the community), rely primarily on support from the general public or government, and are required to file Form 990 or Form 990-EZ with the IRS. Table 5.2 outlines the registration and filing requirements for all 501(c)(3) nonprofits.

**Table 5.2.** Registration and Filing Requirements for 501(c)(3) Organizations, 2010

|  | One-time registration for tax exemption | Annual reporting to IRS on Form 990 |
|---|---|---|
| **Nonreligious public charities** | | |
| Less than $5,000 in annual gross receipts | Optional | Required |
| $5,000–$49,999 in annual gross receipts | Required | Required |
| $50,000 or more in annual gross receipts | Required | Required |
| **Religious public charities** | | |
| Congregations, religious primary and secondary schools, denominations and integrated auxiliaries | Optional | Optional |
| Religiously affiliated hospitals, universities, human services organizations, and others | Required to follow nonreligious public charity regulations | Required to follow nonreligious public charity regulations |
| Private foundations | Required regardless of size | Required regardless of size |

*Source:* Internal Revenue Service, http://www.irs.gov.

Congregations, most religious primary and secondary schools, and other religious organizations are not required to apply for tax-exempt status with the IRS, so most do not register. Financial figures in this chapter include religious organizations that nonetheless filed Forms 990 or Forms 990-EZ.

The Pension Protection Act of 2006 mandated that nonprofits with less than $25,000 in annual gross receipts file a Form 990-N, also known as the e-Postcard.[1] It also called for automatic revocation of tax-exempt status for nonprofits that failed to file returns for three consecutive years. These smaller organizations previously had no reporting responsibilities to the IRS, but they are now required to file with the IRS annually. As an alternative to the Form 990-N, these smaller organizations can opt to complete the Form 990 or Form 990-EZ to satisfy their filing requirement.

In addition, the IRS redesigned the Form 990 for organizations starting with tax year 2008. Given the extent of the changes on the form, the IRS adjusted the filing thresholds to allow organizations additional time to collect the information needed to complete the redesigned form. Table 5.3 lists the filing thresholds for tax years 2007 through 2010.

## Reporting Public Charities by Size and Age

In 2010, public charities reported $1.51 trillion in revenue, $1.45 trillion in expenses, and $2.71 trillion in total assets. These figures are dominated by the largest organizations, primarily hospitals and higher education organizations. Three-quarters of public charities

---

1. The threshold for filing increased to $50,000 starting in tax year 2010.

**Table 5.3.** IRS Filing Requirements for Tax-Exempt Organizations, Tax Years 2007–10

|  | Form to file |
|---|---|
| **2007 tax year (filed in 2008 or 2009)** | |
| Gross receipts normally ≤ $25,000 | 990-N or 990-EZ or 990 |
| Gross receipts < $100,000 and total assets < $250,000 | 990-EZ or 990 |
| Gross receipts ≥ $100,000 or total assets ≥ $250,000 | 990 |
| Private foundation | 990-PF |
| **2008 tax year (filed in 2009 or 2010)** | |
| Gross receipts normally ≤ $25,000 | 990-N or 990-EZ or 990 |
| Gross receipts < $1 million, and total assets < $2.5 million | 990-EZ or 990 |
| Gross receipts ≥ $1 million or total assets ≥ $2.5 million | 990 |
| Private foundation | 990-PF |
| **2009 tax year (filed in 2010 or 2011)** | |
| Gross receipts normally ≤ $25,000 | 990-N or 990-EZ or 990 |
| Gross receipts < $500,000 and total assets < $1.25 million | 990-EZ or 990 |
| Gross receipts ≥ $500,000 or total assets ≥ $1.25 million | 990 |
| Private foundation | 990-PF |
| **2010 tax year and later (filed in 2011 and later)** | |
| Gross receipts normally ≤ $50,000 | 990-N or 990-EZ or 990 |
| Gross receipts < $200,000 and total assets < $500,000 | 990-EZ or 990 |
| Gross receipts ≥ $200,000 or total assets ≥ $500,000 | 990 |
| Private foundation | 990-PF |

*Source:* Internal Revenue Service, http://www.irs.gov.

report less than $500,000 in total expenses (figure 5.1). In 2010, 45 percent of organizations reported less than $100,000 in expenses, and another 29 percent of organizations reported between $100,000 and $499,999 in expenses. Less than 18 percent of public charities report expenses greater than $1 million. These larger organizations, however, account for the vast majority of total expenditures. Organizations with $10 million or more in expenses account for just 4 percent of all nonprofits but more than 85 percent of total expenses. Conversely, organizations reporting under $500,000 in total expenses account for approximately 75 percent of all charities but just over 2 percent of total expenditures.

Not surprisingly, larger organizations tend to be older. Fifty-six percent of organizations with $10 million or more in total expenses report a founding date before 1980. Over two-thirds of organizations with less than $500,000 in total expenses report a founding date after 1989 (table 5.4).

**Figure 5.1.** Number and Expenses of Reporting Public Charities, 2010

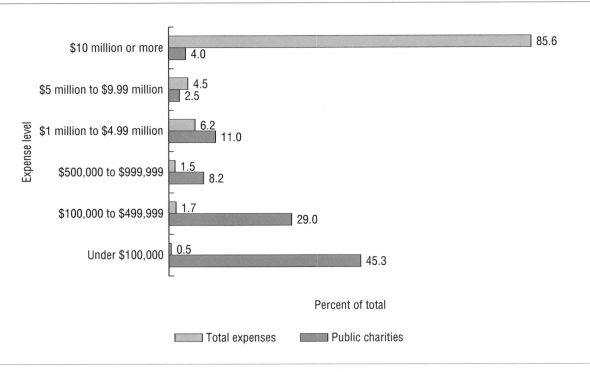

*Source:* Urban Institute, National Center for Charitable Statistics, Core Files (Public Charities, 2010).

**Table 5.4.** Reporting Public Charities by Founding Date, 2010 (percent)

| Total expenses | Before 1950 | 1950–59 | 1960–69 | 1970–79 | 1980–89 | 1990–99 | 2000–10 | Unknown | Total |
|---|---|---|---|---|---|---|---|---|---|
| Under $100,000 | 2.0 | 1.6 | 5.1 | 7.3 | 12.4 | 23.1 | 48.0 | 0.7 | 100.0 |
| $100,000 to $499,999 | 1.9 | 1.9 | 4.3 | 9.0 | 16.2 | 27.5 | 38.7 | 0.5 | 100.0 |
| $500,000 to $999,999 | 3.1 | 2.8 | 5.6 | 12.9 | 20.3 | 27.5 | 27.5 | 0.4 | 100.0 |
| $1 million to $4.99 million | 5.5 | 3.9 | 7.7 | 16.2 | 20.5 | 24.4 | 21.4 | 0.4 | 100.0 |
| $5 million to $9.99 million | 9.6 | 5.8 | 11.7 | 17.9 | 19.0 | 20.0 | 15.5 | 0.5 | 100.0 |
| $10 million or more | 20.9 | 8.3 | 11.7 | 15.1 | 16.0 | 15.8 | 11.8 | 0.4 | 100.0 |
| All public charities | 3.4 | 2.4 | 5.6 | 9.8 | 15.4 | 24.5 | 38.6 | 0.5 | 100.0 |

*Source:* Urban Institute, National Center for Charitable Statistics, Core Files (Public Charities, 2010).
*Note:* The founding date is the year in which the organization officially received tax-exempt status from the IRS. It may not be the year in which the organization was founded.

**Table 5.5.** Reporting Public Charities by Subsector, 2010

| Subsector | Operating public charities | % | Supporting public charities | % | Total public charities | % |
|---|---|---|---|---|---|---|
| Arts, culture, and humanities | 36,914 | 11.8 | 2,622 | 5.0 | 39,536 | 10.8 |
| Education | 50,644 | 16.1 | 16,125 | 30.9 | 66,769 | 18.2 |
| Environment and animals | 15,166 | 4.8 | 1,217 | 2.3 | 16,383 | 4.5 |
| Health | 36,132 | 11.5 | 7,996 | 15.3 | 44,128 | 12.1 |
| Human services | 116,277 | 37.0 | 8,083 | 15.5 | 124,360 | 34.0 |
| International and foreign affairs | 6,905 | 2.2 | 628 | 1.2 | 7,533 | 2.1 |
| Other public and social benefit | 30,047 | 9.6 | 13,828 | 26.5 | 43,875 | 12.0 |
| Religion-related | 21,765 | 6.9 | 1,737 | 3.3 | 23,502 | 6.4 |
| Total | 313,850 | 100.0 | 52,236 | 100.0 | 366,086 | 100.0 |

*Source:* Urban Institute, National Center for Charitable Statistics, Core Files (Public Charities, 2010).

## Reporting Public Charities by Subsector

One-third of all public charities are human services providers, which include organizations that provide job training, legal aid, housing, youth development services, disaster assistance, food distribution, and other similar programs (table 5.5). Education organizations account for the second-largest proportion of public charities, 18 percent. This category includes both higher education as well as preschools, parent-teacher organizations, and alumni associations. Health organizations such as hospitals, blood banks, medical research, and mental health centers account for the third-highest share at 12 percent.

Table 5.5 also distinguishes operating public charities from supporting charities. Supporting public charities primarily distribute funds to operating public charities. Such charities can support a particular operating public charity or a group of public charities. In 2010, supporting organizations accounted for 14 percent of all public charities. The education subsector reported the largest number of supporting organizations. Education support organizations include school booster clubs, college fundraising organizations, and public education funds that raise money to help public school districts. Other supporting organizations include community foundations and federating giving programs, such as United Way organizations.

## Finances of Reporting Public Charities

In 2010, public charities reported total revenue of $1.51 trillion. The single largest source of funding for the nonprofit sector is fee-for-service revenue from private sources, which includes tuition payments, hospital patient revenues (excluding

**Figure 5.2.** Revenue Sources for Reporting Public Charities, 2010 (percent)

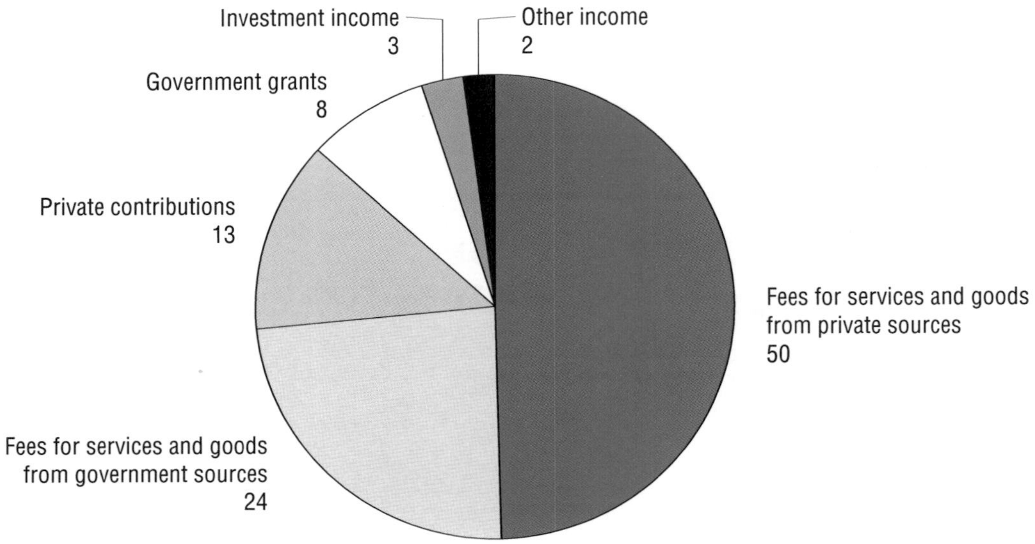

*Sources:* NCCS calculations of IRS Statistics of Income Division Exempt Organizations Sample (2007); Urban Institute, National Center for Charitable Statistics, Core Files (Public Charities, 2010); American Hospital Association (AHA) 2010 survey; and the National Health Accounts, produced by CMS.

Medicare and Medicaid), and ticket sales. Fee-for-service revenue from private sources accounted for 50 percent of total nonprofit revenue in 2010. Fees from government sources, such as Medicare and Medicaid payments and government contracts, accounted for another 24 percent of revenue. Private contributions, including individual contributions and grants from foundations and corporations, accounted for 13 percent, and government grants accounted for another 8 percent of total revenue. Funding from government, both fees for services and government grants, accounted for nearly a third of all nonprofit revenue (32 percent). Other income, which includes dues and assessments, rental income, and income from special events accounted for 2 percent of revenue (figure 5.2). In 2010, investment income began to recover from stock market losses associated with the recession and accounted for 3 percent of nonprofit revenue.[2]

The distribution of sources of revenue changes significantly if hospitals and higher education institutions are excluded. The combined proportion of revenue from fees for services and goods from government and private sources drops from 74 to 55 percent. Public support, or private contributions and government grants, accounts for 39 percent for these organizations, compared with only 21 percent when hospital and higher education institutions are included (figure 5.3).

Table 5.6 shows a detailed view of public charities' revenue, expenses, and assets. Revenue generated from contributions, fees for services, investment income, and gov-

---

2. Because of changes made to the investment portion of the redesigned Form 990, investment income may be missing amounts reported on Part 8, line 4, income from investment of tax-exempt bonds.

**Figure 5.3.** Revenue Sources for Reporting Public Charities, Excluding Hospitals and Higher Education, 2010 (percent)

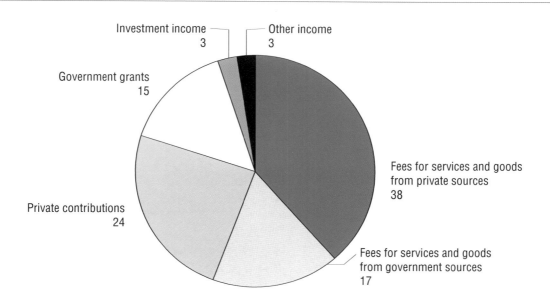

*Sources:* NCCS calculations of IRS Statistics of Income Division Exempt Organizations Sample (2007); Urban Institute, National Center for Charitable Statistics, Core Files (Public Charities, 2010); American Hospital Association (AHA) 2010 survey; and the National Health Accounts, produced by CMS.

ernment grants are included. Expenses are broken down into wages, benefits, fees, interest, and more. Public charities reported $1.51 trillion in revenue, $1.45 trillion in expenses, and $2.71 trillion in assets in 2010.

Revenue, expenses, and assets are further broken down by supporting public charities and operating public charities. There are distinct differences in the distribution of revenue and expenses between operating and supporting public charities. Supporting organizations rely more heavily on contributions (38 percent vs. 20 percent) and less on fees for services (52 percent vs. 77 percent).

Of the nearly $1.45 trillion in expenses reported by public charities in 2010, 91 percent was used for operating expenses such as wages, supplies, and fees. Expenses for paid personnel, which includes salaries, wages, benefits, and payroll tax, accounted for 43 percent of total expenses. "Other expenses" was the second-largest category at 23 percent. While the IRS Form 990 provides over 25 separate expense breakdowns designed to cover most expenses nonprofits incur, more than 80 percent of organizations reported "other" expenses in 2010. Often the expenses listed in the other category can be allocated to an existing line item. Common types of expenses reported as "other" include consulting and insurance.

Operating expenses also vary between operating and supporting organizations. Operating organizations spend more on salaries and benefits than supporting organizations (45 percent vs. 30 percent) and less on grants (6 percent vs. 25 percent).

**Table 5.6.** Revenue and Expenses for Reporting Public Charities, 2010

| | All Organizations | | Operating Organizations | | Supporting Organizations | |
|---|---|---|---|---|---|---|
| | $ millions | % | $ millions | % | $ millions | % |
| Public support | 327,816 | 22 | 262,065 | 20 | 65,751 | 38 |
|   Private contributions | 202,020 | 13 | 149,000 | 11 | 53,020 | 31 |
|     Direct contributions | 181,290 | 12 | 134,880 | 10 | 46,410 | 27 |
|     Indirect contributions | 20,730 | 1 | 14,121 | 1 | 6,609 | 4 |
|   Government grants | 125,796 | 8 | 113,065 | 8 | 12,731 | 7 |
| Fees for services | 1,118,363 | 74 | 1,028,418 | 77 | 89,945 | 52 |
|   Fees from government sources | 357,156 | 24 | 328,659 | 24 | 28,497 | 17 |
|   Fees from private sources | 755,605 | 50 | 695,315 | 52 | 60,290 | 35 |
|   Net income from sale of inventory | 5,602 | 0 | 4,444 | 0 | 1,158 | 1 |
| Investment income | 42,229 | 3 | 29,877 | 2 | 12,352 | 7 |
|   Dividends, interest, and other similar amounts | 26,279 | 2 | 17,603 | 1 | 8,676 | 5 |
|   Net gain on sale of assets or securities | 13,095 | 1 | 9,959 | 1 | 3,136 | 2 |
|   Other investment income | 2,855 | 0 | 2,315 | 0 | 540 | 0 |
| Other income | 25,744 | 2 | 21,315 | 2 | 4,429 | 3 |
|   Net income from special events | 2,968 | 0 | 2,402 | 0 | 566 | 0 |
|   Other revenue | 22,776 | 2 | 18,913 | 1 | 3,863 | 2 |
| **Total revenue** | **1,514,153** | **100** | **1,341,676** | **100** | **172,477** | **100** |
| Paid personnel | 625,596 | 43 | 576,455 | 45 | 49,141 | 30 |
|   Wages and salaries | 499,369 | 34 | 459,829 | 36 | 39,540 | 24 |
|     Compensation of officers | 26,397 | 2 | 22,165 | 2 | 4,232 | 3 |
|     Other wages and salaries | 472,971 | 33 | 437,663 | 34 | 35,308 | 21 |
|   Fringe benefits and payroll taxes | 126,228 | 9 | 116,627 | 9 | 9,601 | 6 |
|     Pension plan contributions | 22,646 | 2 | 20,824 | 2 | 1,822 | 1 |
|     Other employee benefits | 68,357 | 5 | 63,064 | 5 | 5,293 | 3 |
|     Payroll taxes | 35,225 | 2 | 32,739 | 3 | 2,486 | 2 |
| Supplies | 108,573 | 7 | 102,286 | 8 | 6,287 | 4 |
| Communications (printing, phone, etc.) | 42,465 | 3 | 36,090 | 3 | 6,375 | 4 |
| Professional fees | 99,080 | 7 | 88,886 | 7 | 10,194 | 6 |
| Occupancy | 43,524 | 3 | 39,916 | 3 | 3,608 | 2 |
| Interest | 22,051 | 2 | 19,240 | 1 | 2,811 | 2 |

*(continued)*

**Table 5.6.** Revenue and Expenses for Reporting Public Charities, 2010 *(continued)*

|  | All Organizations | | Operating Organizations | | Supporting Organizations | |
|---|---|---|---|---|---|---|
|  | $ millions | % | $ millions | % | $ millions | % |
| Depreciation and depletion | 59,278 | 4 | 54,353 | 4 | 4,925 | 3 |
| Other | 327,624 | 23 | 288,242 | 22 | 39,382 | 24 |
| Total current operating expenses | 1,328,191 | 91 | 1,205,467 | 93 | 122,724 | 75 |
| Grants and benefits | 121,042 | 8 | 80,017 | 6 | 41,025 | 25 |
|   Grants and allocations | 73,203 | 5 | 36,493 | 3 | 36,710 | 22 |
|   Specific assistance to individuals | 35,832 | 2 | 33,767 | 3 | 2,065 | 1 |
|   Benefits paid to members | 12,007 | 1 | 9,757 | 1 | 2,250 | 1 |
| Payments to affiliates | 5,521 | 0 | 4,786 | 0 | 735 | 0 |
| **Total expenses** | **1,454,753** | **100** | **1,290,269** | **100** | **164,484** | **100** |
| Net income (revenue-expenses) | 59,400 | | 51,407 | | 7,993 | |
| **Total assets** | **2,708,905** | | **2,125,027** | | **583,878** | |
| Total liabilities | 1,110,849 | | 925,148 | | 185,701 | |
| **Net assets (assets-liabilities)** | **1,598,057** | | **1,199,880** | | **398,177** | |

*Sources:* Urban Institute, National Center for Charitable Statistics, Core Files (Public Charities, 2005–10) and Core Supplement Files (2005); and Internal Revenue Service, Statistics of Income Sample Files (Public Charities, 2005–08).

*Notes:* Authors' calculations are based on Internal Revenue Service Forms 990 and 990-EZ, classified according to the National Taxonomy of Exempt Entities–Core Codes, and adjusted by the National Center for Charitable Statistics based on available data. See the methodology section at the end of the chapter for more information on how the estimates were created. Reporting public charities include only organizations that both reported (filed Forms 990) and were required to do so. The following were excluded: foreign organizations, government-associated organizations, organizations without state identifiers, and other organizations at the authors' discretion. Organizations not required to report include religious congregations and organizations with less than $50,000 in gross receipts. The table includes separate analyses for operating public charities and supporting organizations to clarify the distribution of funds and to avoid double-counting the financial information for supporting organizations. Dollar amounts may not sum to totals because of rounding. Percentages for revenue items and net income are expressed as percentages of total revenue. Program service revenue figures may include sizable income via government contracts, which the data source is unable to differentiate from funds raised via the public (i.e., fees for services). Percentages for current operating expense items are expressed as percentages of total current operating expenses. Percentages for other expense items, assets, and liabilities are expressed as percentages of total expenses.

## Growth in the Number of Reporting Public Charities, 2000–10

The number of reporting public charities grew 47 percent from 2000 to 2010, increasing by 116,227 organizations. Growth among individual subsectors varied greatly over this period. Health organizations saw the smallest growth at 22 percent, while the number of environment and animal organizations increased 83 percent (table 5.7).

The three smallest subsectors—environment and animals, international, and religion-related—exhibited the greatest growth in number of organizations over the 10 years.

**Table 5.7.** Change in the Number of Reporting Public Charities by Subsector, 2000, 2005, and 2010

| Subsector | Reporting Public Charities | | | Total % Change | Average Annual % Change | | |
|---|---|---|---|---|---|---|---|
| | 2000 | 2005 | 2010 | 2000–10 | 2000–10 | 2000–05 | 2005–10 |
| Arts, culture, and humanities | 27,302 | 34,514 | 39,536 | 44.8 | 3.8 | 4.8 | 2.8 |
| Education | 42,591 | 56,121 | 66,769 | 56.8 | 4.6 | 5.7 | 3.5 |
| Environment and animals | 8,976 | 12,754 | 16,383 | 82.5 | 6.2 | 7.3 | 5.1 |
| Health | 36,057 | 40,638 | 44,128 | 22.4 | 2.0 | 2.4 | 1.7 |
| Human services | 86,068 | 106,248 | 124,360 | 44.5 | 3.7 | 4.3 | 3.2 |
| International and foreign affairs | 4,345 | 5,726 | 7,533 | 73.4 | 5.7 | 5.7 | 5.6 |
| Public and societal benefit | 30,521 | 38,379 | 43,875 | 43.8 | 3.7 | 4.7 | 2.7 |
| Religion-related | 13,999 | 18,784 | 23,502 | 67.9 | 5.3 | 6.1 | 4.6 |
| All public charities | 249,859 | 313,164 | 366,086 | 46.5 | 3.9 | 4.6 | 3.2 |

*Sources:* Urban Institute, National Center for Charitable Statistics, Core Files (Public Charities, 2000, 2005, and 2010).

Environment and animals grew 83 percent, for an average annual increase of 6.2 percent; international and foreign affairs grew 73 percent, for an average annual increase of 5.7 percent; and religion-related organizations grew 68 percent, for an average annual increase of 5.3 percent.

Human services, the largest subsector, grew 45 percent from 2000 to 2010. Within human services, growth was smallest for residential and custodial care organizations and employment and job-related organizations, which grew only 7 and 12 percent, respectively. Growth was greatest among public safety and disaster preparedness organizations, which nearly doubled in size. Recreation and sports organizations, such as amateur sports leagues, Special Olympics, fairs, and playgrounds, grew 88 percent (table 5.8).

The health subsector showed the least growth in number of public charities from 2000 to 2010—22 percent. Disease-specific organizations contributed to most of the increase in the number of organizations, with a 68 percent increase. The number of nursing service organizations declined almost 6 percent.

## Growth in Revenue of Reporting Public Charities

Total revenue grew from about $837 billion in 2000 to about $1.51 trillion in 2010, an increase of nearly 81 percent, for an average annual growth of roughly 6.1 percent (table 5.9). This represents a 43 percent inflation-adjusted increase over the past 10 years.

Growth varied widely across subsectors. Arts, culture, and humanities organizations had the smallest growth in resources at just 26 percent (−0.7 percent after adjusting for inflation). Within this group, performing arts organizations grew approximately

**Table 5.8.** Change in the Number of Reporting Public Charities by Detailed Subsector, 2000, 2005, and 2010

| Subsector | Reporting Public Charities | | | Total % Change | Average Annual % Change | | |
|---|---|---|---|---|---|---|---|
| | 2000 | 2005 | 2010 | 2000–10 | 2000–10 | 2000–05 | 2005–10 |
| **All public charities** | **249,859** | **313,164** | **366,086** | **46.5** | **3.9** | **4.6** | **3.2** |
| Arts, culture, and humanities | 27,302 | 34,514 | 39,536 | 44.8 | 3.8 | 4.8 | 2.8 |
| Performing arts organizations | 9,307 | 12,040 | 13,865 | 49.0 | 4.1 | 5.3 | 2.9 |
| Historical societies and related | 4,230 | 5,240 | 5,934 | 40.3 | 3.4 | 4.4 | 2.5 |
| Museums and museum activities | 2,881 | 3,511 | 3,965 | 37.6 | 3.2 | 4.0 | 2.5 |
| Other arts, culture, and humanities | 10,884 | 13,723 | 15,772 | 44.9 | 3.8 | 4.7 | 2.8 |
| Education | 42,591 | 56,121 | 66,769 | 56.8 | 4.6 | 5.7 | 3.5 |
| Higher education institutions | 1,773 | 1,871 | 2,129 | 20.1 | 1.8 | 1.1 | 2.6 |
| Student services and organizations | 5,172 | 6,652 | 7,823 | 51.3 | 4.2 | 5.2 | 3.3 |
| Elementary and secondary education | 9,440 | 11,737 | 13,499 | 43.0 | 3.6 | 4.5 | 2.8 |
| Other education | 26,206 | 35,861 | 43,318 | 65.3 | 5.2 | 6.5 | 3.9 |
| Environment and animals | 8,976 | 12,754 | 16,383 | 82.5 | 6.2 | 7.3 | 5.1 |
| Environment | 5,204 | 7,009 | 8,351 | 60.5 | 4.8 | 6.1 | 3.6 |
| Animal-related | 3,772 | 5,745 | 8,032 | 112.9 | 7.9 | 8.8 | 6.9 |
| Health | 36,057 | 40,638 | 44,128 | 22.4 | 2.0 | 2.4 | 1.7 |
| Nursing services | 2,863 | 2,833 | 2,699 | −5.7 | −0.6 | −0.2 | −1.0 |
| Hospitals and primary treatment facilities | 3,917 | 3,954 | 4,084 | 4.3 | 0.4 | 0.2 | 0.6 |
| Treatment facilities—outpatient | 2,904 | 3,207 | 3,484 | 20.0 | 1.8 | 2.0 | 1.7 |
| Mental health | 7,807 | 8,833 | 9,275 | 18.8 | 1.7 | 2.5 | 1.0 |
| Disease-specific–general | 5,503 | 7,314 | 9,215 | 67.5 | 5.3 | 5.9 | 4.7 |
| Medical research | 1,822 | 2,079 | 2,206 | 21.1 | 1.9 | 2.7 | 1.2 |
| Other health | 11,241 | 12,418 | 13,165 | 17.1 | 1.6 | 2.0 | 1.2 |

*(continued)*

**Table 5.8.** Change in the Number of Reporting Public Charities by Detailed Subsector, 2000, 2005, and 2010 *(continued)*

| Subsector | Reporting Public Charities | | | Total % Change | Average Annual % Change | | |
|---|---|---|---|---|---|---|---|
| | 2000 | 2005 | 2010 | 2000–10 | 2000–10 | 2000–05 | 2005–10 |
| Human services | 86,068 | 106,248 | 124,360 | 44.5 | 3.7 | 4.3 | 3.2 |
| Crime and legal-related | 4,640 | 5,559 | 6,307 | 35.9 | 3.1 | 3.7 | 2.6 |
| Employment and job-related | 3,809 | 4,103 | 4,264 | 11.9 | 1.1 | 1.5 | 0.8 |
| Food, agriculture, and nutrition | 2,425 | 3,013 | 3,912 | 61.3 | 4.9 | 4.4 | 5.4 |
| Housing and shelter | 13,400 | 16,144 | 17,673 | 31.9 | 2.8 | 3.8 | 1.8 |
| Public safety and disaster preparedness | 3,507 | 5,234 | 6,835 | 94.9 | 6.9 | 8.3 | 5.5 |
| Recreation and sports | 17,226 | 24,190 | 32,315 | 87.6 | 6.5 | 7.0 | 6.0 |
| Youth development | 6,376 | 7,569 | 8,629 | 35.3 | 3.1 | 3.5 | 2.7 |
| Children and youth services | 6,534 | 7,474 | 7,467 | 14.3 | 1.3 | 2.7 | 0.0 |
| Family services | 3,842 | 4,475 | 4,860 | 26.5 | 2.4 | 3.1 | 1.7 |
| Residential and custodial care | 5,557 | 5,917 | 5,921 | 6.6 | 0.6 | 1.3 | 0.0 |
| Services promoting independence | 8,264 | 9,435 | 10,360 | 25.4 | 2.3 | 2.7 | 1.9 |
| Other human services | 10,488 | 13,135 | 15,817 | 50.8 | 4.2 | 4.6 | 3.8 |
| International and foreign affairs | 4,345 | 5,726 | 7,533 | 73.4 | 5.7 | 5.7 | 5.6 |
| Public and societal benefit | 30,521 | 38,379 | 43,875 | 43.8 | 3.7 | 4.7 | 2.7 |
| Civil rights and advocacy | 1,692 | 2,086 | 2,311 | 36.6 | 3.2 | 4.3 | 2.1 |
| Community improvement | 11,515 | 14,777 | 17,516 | 52.1 | 4.3 | 5.1 | 3.5 |
| Philanthropy and voluntarism | 11,972 | 14,735 | 15,432 | 28.9 | 2.6 | 4.2 | 0.9 |
| Science and technology | 1,697 | 1,970 | 2,263 | 33.4 | 2.9 | 3.0 | 2.8 |
| Social science | 670 | 801 | 896 | 33.7 | 2.9 | 3.6 | 2.3 |
| Other public and societal benefit | 2,975 | 4,010 | 5,457 | 83.4 | 6.3 | 6.2 | 6.4 |
| Religion-related | 13,999 | 18,784 | 23,502 | 67.9 | 5.3 | 6.1 | 4.6 |

*Sources:* Urban Institute, National Center for Charitable Statistics, Core Files (Public Charities, 2000, 2005, and 2010).

**Table 5.9.** Change in Total Revenue for Reporting Public Charities by Subsector, 2000, 2005, and 2010

| Subsector | $ Millions | | | Total % Change | Average Annual % Change | | |
|---|---|---|---|---|---|---|---|
| | 2000 | 2005 | 2010 | 2000–10 | 2000–10 | 2000–05 | 2005–10 |
| Arts, culture, and humanities | 23,323 | 26,159 | 29,338 | 25.8 | 2.3 | 2.3 | 2.3 |
| Education | 163,881 | 208,405 | 248,038 | 51.4 | 4.2 | 4.9 | 3.5 |
| Environment and animals | 8,201 | 10,687 | 13,721 | 67.3 | 5.3 | 5.4 | 5.1 |
| Health | 459,461 | 673,822 | 907,749 | 97.6 | 7.0 | 8.0 | 6.1 |
| Human services | 110,889 | 152,326 | 196,396 | 77.1 | 5.9 | 6.6 | 5.2 |
| International and foreign affairs | 13,035 | 25,336 | 31,441 | 141.2 | 9.2 | 14.2 | 4.4 |
| Public and societal benefit | 50,678 | 66,598 | 74,444 | 46.9 | 3.9 | 5.6 | 2.3 |
| Religion-related | 7,384 | 10,129 | 13,026 | 76.4 | 5.8 | 6.5 | 5.2 |
| All public charities | 836,852 | 1,173,461 | 1,514,153 | 80.9 | 6.1 | 7.0 | 5.2 |

*Sources:* Urban Institute, National Center for Charitable Statistics, Core Files (Public Charities, 2000, 2005, and 2010).
*Note:* Figures are shown in current dollars and are not adjusted for inflation.

35 percent (about 7 percent after adjusting for inflation), while museums and museum activity grew by only 4 percent, down 18 percent after adjusting for inflation (table 5.10). Public and societal benefit organizations experienced the second-slowest revenue growth over the 10 years, with revenue growing by 47 percent (16 percent after adjusting for inflation). Within this subsector, philanthropy and voluntarism organizations had the slowest growth in total revenue from 2000 to 2010, growing 24 percent (–2 percent after adjusting for inflation). International and foreign affairs organizations had the greatest revenue growth at 141 percent (90 percent after adjusting for inflation). Health, which accounts for over half the sector's revenue, had the second-highest revenue growth at 98 percent (56 percent after adjusting for inflation). The revenue of health organizations is growing more quickly than the number of organizations (98 percent versus 22 percent). Human services organizations, the largest subsector by number of organizations, experienced the third-largest growth rate—from $110.9 billion in 2000 to $196.4 billion in 2010—a 77 percent increase (40 percent after adjusting for inflation).

While we cannot tell from these data the full impact of the recession, it is evident in the last two columns of table 5.9 that most of the revenue growth occurred between 2000 and 2005. The average annual change dropped from 7.0 percent for the years 2000 to 2005 to 5.2 percent for 2005 to 2010. Almost every subsector, except arts, culture, and humanities, witnessed a similar drop. International and foreign affairs organizations saw the largest decline in growth, dropping from an average annual percentage change of 14.2 percent for 2000 to 2005 to 4.4 percent for 2005 to 2010.

**Table 5.10.** Change in Total Revenue for Reporting Public Charities by Detailed Subsector, 2000, 2005, and 2010

| Subsector | $ Millions | | | Total % Change | Average Annual % Change | | |
|---|---|---|---|---|---|---|---|
| | 2000 | 2005 | 2010 | 2000–10 | 2000–10 | 2000–05 | 2005–10 |
| **All public charities** | **836,852** | **1,173,461** | **1,514,153** | **80.9** | **6.1** | **7.0** | **5.2** |
| Arts, culture, and humanities | 23,323 | 26,159 | 29,338 | 25.8 | 2.3 | 2.3 | 2.3 |
| Performing arts organizations | 6,750 | 7,985 | 9,142 | 35.4 | 3.1 | 3.4 | 2.7 |
| Historical societies and related | 1,813 | 1,992 | 2,256 | 24.5 | 2.2 | 1.9 | 2.5 |
| Museums and museum activities | 6,192 | 6,530 | 6,458 | 4.3 | 0.4 | 1.1 | -0.2 |
| Other arts, culture, and humanities | 8,568 | 9,653 | 11,482 | 34.0 | 3.0 | 2.4 | 3.5 |
| Education | 163,881 | 208,405 | 248,038 | 51.4 | 4.2 | 4.9 | 3.5 |
| Higher education institutions | 110,266 | 136,979 | 159,324 | 44.5 | 3.7 | 4.4 | 3.1 |
| Student services and organizations | 4,146 | 5,169 | 5,577 | 34.5 | 3.0 | 4.5 | 1.5 |
| Elementary and secondary education | 20,932 | 29,254 | 39,684 | 89.6 | 6.6 | 6.9 | 6.3 |
| Other education | 28,537 | 37,004 | 43,452 | 52.3 | 4.3 | 5.3 | 3.3 |
| Environment and animals | 8,201 | 10,687 | 13,721 | 67.3 | 5.3 | 5.4 | 5.1 |
| Environment | 4,825 | 6,151 | 7,775 | 61.1 | 4.9 | 5.0 | 4.8 |
| Animal-related | 3,376 | 4,535 | 5,946 | 76.1 | 5.8 | 6.1 | 5.6 |
| Health | 459,461 | 673,822 | 907,749 | 97.6 | 7.0 | 8.0 | 6.1 |
| Nursing services | 18,536 | 24,204 | 28,323 | 52.8 | 4.3 | 5.5 | 3.2 |
| Hospitals and primary treatment facilities | 331,403 | 494,682 | 659,878 | 99.1 | 7.1 | 8.3 | 5.9 |
| Treatment facilities—outpatient | 50,605 | 72,916 | 111,730 | 120.8 | 8.2 | 7.6 | 8.9 |
| Mental health | 17,776 | 24,091 | 29,037 | 63.3 | 5.0 | 6.3 | 3.8 |
| Disease-specific–general | 8,412 | 11,560 | 14,666 | 74.3 | 5.7 | 6.6 | 4.9 |
| Medical research | 6,726 | 8,883 | 9,476 | 40.9 | 3.5 | 5.7 | 1.3 |
| Other health | 26,001 | 37,486 | 54,639 | 110.1 | 7.7 | 7.6 | 7.8 |

| | | | | | | | |
|---|---|---|---|---|---|---|---|
| Human services | 110,889 | 152,326 | 196,396 | 77.1 | 5.9 | 6.6 | 5.2 |
| Crime and legal-related | 4,374 | 5,703 | 7,228 | 65.3 | 5.2 | 5.5 | 4.9 |
| Employment and job-related | 8,115 | 11,149 | 14,903 | 83.7 | 6.3 | 6.6 | 6.0 |
| Food, agriculture, and nutrition | 3,635 | 5,218 | 8,904 | 145.0 | 9.4 | 7.5 | 11.3 |
| Housing and shelter | 10,228 | 15,767 | 21,398 | 109.2 | 7.7 | 9.0 | 6.3 |
| Public safety and disaster preparedness | 880 | 1,559 | 2,323 | 164.1 | 10.2 | 12.1 | 8.3 |
| Recreation and sports | 6,769 | 9,049 | 12,461 | 84.1 | 6.3 | 6.0 | 6.6 |
| Youth development | 4,938 | 6,202 | 6,968 | 41.1 | 3.5 | 4.7 | 2.4 |
| Children and youth services | 8,316 | 10,986 | 12,807 | 54.0 | 4.4 | 5.7 | 3.1 |
| Family services | 4,470 | 5,656 | 6,603 | 47.7 | 4.0 | 4.8 | 3.1 |
| Residential and custodial care | 20,095 | 28,107 | 34,865 | 73.5 | 5.7 | 6.9 | 4.4 |
| Services promoting independence | 16,547 | 23,126 | 30,775 | 86.0 | 6.4 | 6.9 | 5.9 |
| Other human services | 22,523 | 29,805 | 37,160 | 65.0 | 5.1 | 5.8 | 4.5 |
| International and foreign affairs | 13,035 | 25,336 | 31,441 | 141.2 | 9.2 | 14.2 | 4.4 |
| Public and societal benefit | 50,678 | 66,598 | 74,444 | 46.9 | 3.9 | 5.6 | 2.3 |
| Civil rights and advocacy | 1,323 | 1,782 | 2,247 | 69.8 | 5.4 | 6.1 | 4.7 |
| Community improvement | 11,473 | 13,228 | 17,202 | 49.9 | 4.1 | 2.9 | 5.4 |
| Philanthropy and voluntarism | 21,430 | 25,567 | 26,542 | 23.9 | 2.2 | 3.6 | 0.8 |
| Science and technology | 7,963 | 14,244 | 14,094 | 77.0 | 5.9 | 12.3 | −0.2 |
| Social science | 1,247 | 1,672 | 2,396 | 92.2 | 6.8 | 6.0 | 7.5 |
| Other public and societal benefit | 7,242 | 10,105 | 11,964 | 65.2 | 5.1 | 6.9 | 3.4 |
| Religion-related | 7,384 | 10,129 | 13,026 | 76.4 | 5.8 | 6.5 | 5.2 |

Sources: Urban Institute, National Center for Charitable Statistics, Core Files (Public Charities, 2000, 2005, and 2010).
Note: Figures are shown in current dollars and are not adjusted for inflation.

**Table 5.11.** Change in Public Support for Reporting Public Charities by Subsector, 2000, 2005, and 2010

| Subsector | $ Millions | | | Total % Change | Average Annual % Change | | |
|---|---|---|---|---|---|---|---|
| | 2000 | 2005 | 2010 | 2000–10 | 2000–10 | 2000–05 | 2005–10 |
| Arts, culture, and humanities | 12,059 | 14,304 | 16,527 | 37.1 | 3.2 | 3.5 | 2.9 |
| Education | 44,036 | 59,326 | 71,186 | 61.7 | 4.9 | 6.1 | 3.7 |
| Environment and animals | 4,708 | 6,460 | 8,610 | 82.9 | 6.2 | 6.5 | 5.9 |
| Health | 34,104 | 46,750 | 66,200 | 94.1 | 6.9 | 6.5 | 7.2 |
| Human services | 46,734 | 61,631 | 85,089 | 82.1 | 6.2 | 5.7 | 6.7 |
| International and foreign affairs | 10,787 | 22,366 | 27,558 | 155.5 | 9.8 | 15.7 | 4.3 |
| Public and societal benefit | 26,435 | 38,038 | 44,353 | 67.8 | 5.3 | 7.5 | 3.1 |
| Religion-related | 4,526 | 6,355 | 8,293 | 83.2 | 6.2 | 7.0 | 5.5 |
| All public charities | 183,389 | 255,229 | 327,816 | 78.8 | 6.0 | 6.8 | 5.1 |

*Sources:* Urban Institute, National Center for Charitable Statistics, Core Files (Public Charities, 2000, 2005, and 2010).
*Note:* Figures are shown in current dollars and are not adjusted for inflation.

## Growth in Public Support for Reporting Public Charities

Table 5.11 displays the growth in public support for reporting public charities from 2000 to 2010. A major component of revenue for many public charities, public support consists of private contributions from individuals, foundations, corporations, and other public charities as well as government grants. It does not include government contracts, Medicare or Medicaid funding, or program service revenue.

Public support grew from $183.4 billion in 2000 to $327.8 billion in 2010. This represents a 79 percent increase (41 percent after adjusting for inflation). Arts, culture, and humanities organizations experienced the least growth over the 10 years at 37 percent (8 percent after adjusting for inflation).

International and foreign affairs organizations saw the largest increase in public support: 156 percent (102 percent after adjusting for inflation). Health organizations followed with a 94 percent increase (53 percent after adjusting for inflation).

Human services organizations, which receive a quarter of all public support in the sector, saw an 82 percent increase in public support—growing from $46.7 billion in 2000 to $85.1 billion in 2010. This is a 44 percent increase after adjusting for inflation. Within the human services subsector, public safety and disaster preparedness had the largest increase in public support: 267 percent, or 190 percent after adjusting for inflation (table 5.12). Food, agriculture, and nutrition and housing and shelter also more than doubled in contributions from 2000 to 2010. Overall, public support grew more robustly in the first period than in the second.

**Table 5.12.** Change in Public Support for Reporting Public Charities by Detailed Subsector, 2000, 2005, and 2010

| Subsector | $ Millions | | | Total % Change | Average Annual % Change | | |
|---|---|---|---|---|---|---|---|
| | 2000 | 2005 | 2010 | 2000–10 | 2000–10 | 2000–05 | 2005–10 |
| **All public charities** | **183,389** | **255,229** | **327,816** | **78.8** | **6.0** | **6.8** | **5.1** |
| Arts, culture, and humanities | 12,059 | 14,304 | 16,527 | 37.1 | 3.2 | 3.5 | 2.9 |
| Performing arts organizations | 2,913 | 3,539 | 4,157 | 42.7 | 3.6 | 4.0 | 3.3 |
| Historical societies and related | 967 | 1,198 | 1,452 | 50.2 | 4.1 | 4.4 | 3.9 |
| Museums and museum activities | 3,445 | 3,982 | 4,106 | 19.2 | 1.8 | 2.9 | 0.6 |
| Other arts, culture, and humanities | 4,734 | 5,585 | 6,812 | 43.9 | 3.7 | 3.4 | 4.1 |
| Education | 44,036 | 59,326 | 71,186 | 61.7 | 4.9 | 6.1 | 3.7 |
| Higher education institutions | 23,594 | 29,300 | 30,837 | 30.7 | 2.7 | 4.4 | 1.0 |
| Student services and organizations | 1,461 | 1,848 | 2,255 | 54.4 | 4.4 | 4.8 | 4.1 |
| Elementary and secondary education | 5,733 | 8,664 | 13,365 | 133.1 | 8.8 | 8.6 | 9.1 |
| Other education | 13,249 | 19,513 | 24,730 | 86.6 | 6.4 | 8.1 | 4.9 |
| Environment and animals | 4,708 | 6,460 | 8,610 | 82.9 | 6.2 | 6.5 | 5.9 |
| Environment | 2,881 | 3,821 | 5,031 | 74.6 | 5.7 | 5.8 | 5.7 |
| Animal-related | 1,827 | 2,638 | 3,579 | 95.9 | 7.0 | 7.6 | 6.3 |
| Health | 34,104 | 46,750 | 66,200 | 94.1 | 6.9 | 6.5 | 7.2 |
| Nursing services | 1,074 | 1,167 | 1,158 | 7.9 | 0.8 | 1.7 | -0.2 |
| Hospitals and primary treatment facilities | 8,513 | 12,361 | 18,915 | 122.2 | 8.3 | 7.7 | 8.9 |
| Treatment facilities–outpatient | 2,875 | 4,321 | 6,396 | 122.5 | 8.3 | 8.5 | 8.2 |
| Mental health | 6,903 | 8,368 | 10,519 | 52.4 | 4.3 | 3.9 | 4.7 |
| Disease-specific–general | 5,015 | 6,892 | 8,418 | 67.9 | 5.3 | 6.6 | 4.1 |
| Medical research | 3,248 | 4,535 | 6,934 | 113.5 | 7.9 | 6.9 | 8.9 |
| Other health | 6,477 | 9,106 | 13,859 | 114.0 | 7.9 | 7.0 | 8.8 |

(continued)

**Table 5.12.** Change in Public Support for Reporting Public Charities by Detailed Subsector, 2000, 2005, and 2010 *(continued)*

| Subsector | $ Millions | | | Total % Change | Average Annual % Change | | |
|---|---|---|---|---|---|---|---|
| | 2000 | 2005 | 2010 | 2000–10 | 2000–10 | 2000–05 | 2005–10 |
| Human services | 46,734 | 61,631 | 85,089 | 82.1 | 6.2 | 5.7 | 6.7 |
| Crime and legal-related | 2,926 | 3,794 | 5,168 | 76.7 | 5.9 | 5.3 | 6.4 |
| Employment and job-related | 3,342 | 4,463 | 6,420 | 92.1 | 6.7 | 6.0 | 7.5 |
| Food, agriculture, and nutrition | 3,073 | 4,405 | 7,817 | 154.3 | 9.8 | 7.5 | 12.2 |
| Housing and shelter | 3,579 | 4,784 | 8,008 | 123.7 | 8.4 | 6.0 | 10.9 |
| Public safety and disaster preparedness | 381 | 878 | 1,399 | 267.2 | 13.9 | 18.2 | 9.8 |
| Recreation and sports | 1,957 | 2,483 | 3,798 | 94.1 | 6.9 | 4.9 | 8.9 |
| Youth development | 2,562 | 3,488 | 4,114 | 60.6 | 4.8 | 6.4 | 3.4 |
| Children and youth services | 3,961 | 5,049 | 6,743 | 70.2 | 5.5 | 5.0 | 6.0 |
| Family services | 2,308 | 2,877 | 3,616 | 56.6 | 4.6 | 4.5 | 4.7 |
| Residential and custodial care | 3,004 | 3,336 | 4,046 | 34.7 | 3.0 | 2.1 | 3.9 |
| Services promoting independence | 7,958 | 10,625 | 13,237 | 66.3 | 5.2 | 6.0 | 4.5 |
| Other human services | 11,682 | 15,449 | 20,723 | 77.4 | 5.9 | 5.7 | 6.0 |
| International and foreign affairs | 10,787 | 22,366 | 27,558 | 155.5 | 9.8 | 15.7 | 4.3 |
| Public and societal benefit | 26,435 | 38,038 | 44,353 | 67.8 | 5.3 | 7.5 | 3.1 |
| Civil rights and advocacy | 1,054 | 1,442 | 1,791 | 69.8 | 5.4 | 6.5 | 4.4 |
| Community improvement | 5,565 | 7,458 | 10,583 | 90.2 | 6.6 | 6.0 | 7.2 |
| Philanthropy and voluntarism | 15,140 | 18,777 | 21,495 | 42.0 | 3.6 | 4.4 | 2.7 |
| Science and technology | 2,573 | 6,690 | 5,433 | 111.2 | 7.8 | 21.1 | −4.1 |
| Social science | 708 | 1,107 | 1,672 | 136.3 | 9.0 | 9.4 | 8.6 |
| Other public and societal benefit | 1,395 | 2,563 | 3,379 | 142.2 | 9.3 | 12.9 | 5.7 |
| Religion-related | 4,526 | 6,355 | 8,293 | 83.2 | 6.2 | 7.0 | 5.5 |

*Sources*: Urban Institute, National Center for Charitable Statistics, Core Files (Public Charities, 2000, 2005, and 2010).
*Note*: Figures are shown in current dollars and are not adjusted for inflation.

**Table 5.13.** Change in Total Expenses for Reporting Public Charities by Subsector, 2000, 2005, and 2010

| Subsector | $ Millions | | | Total % Change | Average Annual % Change | | |
|---|---|---|---|---|---|---|---|
| | 2000 | 2005 | 2010 | 2000–10 | 2000–10 | 2000–05 | 2005–10 |
| Arts, culture, and humanities | 18,000 | 22,820 | 27,838 | 54.7 | 4.5 | 4.9 | 4.1 |
| Education | 121,397 | 174,286 | 241,616 | 99.0 | 7.1 | 7.5 | 6.8 |
| Environment and animals | 6,481 | 9,130 | 12,858 | 98.4 | 7.1 | 7.1 | 7.1 |
| Health | 444,552 | 639,541 | 869,873 | 95.7 | 6.9 | 7.5 | 6.3 |
| Human services | 103,665 | 145,411 | 189,940 | 83.2 | 6.2 | 7.0 | 5.5 |
| International and foreign affairs | 11,712 | 22,598 | 29,681 | 153.4 | 9.7 | 14.0 | 5.6 |
| Public and societal benefit | 37,658 | 55,198 | 70,791 | 88.0 | 6.5 | 7.9 | 5.1 |
| Religion-related | 6,402 | 8,713 | 12,155 | 89.9 | 6.6 | 6.4 | 6.9 |
| All public charities | 749,869 | 1,077,696 | 1,454,753 | 94.0 | 6.9 | 7.5 | 6.2 |

*Sources:* Urban Institute, National Center for Charitable Statistics, Core Files (Public Charities, 2000, 2005, and 2010).
*Note:* Figures are shown in current dollars and are not adjusted for inflation.

## Growth in Expenses of Reporting Public Charities

Public charity expenses grew from $750 billion in 2000 to $1.45 trillion in 2010 (table 5.13). This is a 94 percent increase, or a 53 percent inflation-adjusted increase. The growth in expenses outpaced the growth in revenue over the period by 13 percent. In fact, expenses as a proportion of revenue for all public charities grew from 90 percent in 2000 to 96 percent in 2010. This is most likely due to changes in funding due to the recession that began in the late 2000s.

The change in total expenses for each subsector is shown in detail in table 5.14. International and foreign affairs organizations experienced the greatest growth in expenses, rising from $11.7 billion in 2000 to $29.7 billion in 2010—an increase of 153 percent or an inflation-adjusted 100 percent. This was the largest percentage increase among the subsectors, but the rate of growth was much higher in the first period than in the second. Education nonprofits had the second-highest growth in expenses with a 99 percent increase (57 percent after adjusting for inflation). Health organizations, which account for about 60 percent of total public charity expenses, saw average growth compared to other subsectors. Health expenses grew from $444.6 billion in 2000 to $869.9 billion in 2010, an increase of 96 percent (55 percent after adjusting for inflation).

## Growth in Assets of Reporting Public Charities

As displayed in table 5.15, total assets grew from roughly $1.5 trillion in 2000 to $2.7 trillion in 2010, a 81 percent increase (or 43 percent after adjusting for inflation). International and foreign affairs organizations and health organizations saw the greatest

**Table 5.14.** Change in Total Expenses for Reporting Public Charities by Detailed Subsector, 2000, 2005, and 2010

| Subsector | $ Millions | | | Total % Change | Average Annual % Change | | |
|---|---|---|---|---|---|---|---|
| | 2000 | 2005 | 2010 | 2000–10 | 2000–10 | 2000–05 | 2005–10 |
| **All public charities** | **749,869** | **1,077,696** | **1,454,753** | **94.0** | **6.9** | **7.5** | **6.2** |
| Arts, culture, and humanities | 18,000 | 22,820 | 27,838 | 54.7 | 4.5 | 4.9 | 4.1 |
| Performing arts organizations | 5,805 | 7,370 | 8,933 | 53.9 | 4.4 | 4.9 | 3.9 |
| Historical societies and related | 1,208 | 1,550 | 1,809 | 49.7 | 4.1 | 5.1 | 3.1 |
| Museums and museum activities | 3,918 | 5,100 | 6,123 | 56.3 | 4.6 | 5.4 | 3.7 |
| Other arts, culture, and humanities | 7,069 | 8,800 | 10,973 | 55.2 | 4.5 | 4.5 | 4.5 |
| Education | 121,397 | 174,286 | 241,616 | 99.0 | 7.1 | 7.5 | 6.8 |
| Higher education institutions | 81,244 | 115,526 | 155,712 | 91.7 | 6.7 | 7.3 | 6.2 |
| Student services and organizations | 2,976 | 4,212 | 5,018 | 68.6 | 5.4 | 7.2 | 3.6 |
| Elementary and secondary education | 16,374 | 26,125 | 38,206 | 133.3 | 8.8 | 9.8 | 7.9 |
| Other education | 20,803 | 28,423 | 42,681 | 105.2 | 7.5 | 6.4 | 8.5 |
| Environment and animals | 6,481 | 9,130 | 12,858 | 98.4 | 7.1 | 7.1 | 7.1 |
| Environment | 3,690 | 5,151 | 7,296 | 97.7 | 7.1 | 6.9 | 7.2 |
| Animal-related | 2,791 | 3,979 | 5,562 | 99.3 | 7.1 | 7.3 | 6.9 |
| Health | 444,552 | 639,541 | 869,873 | 95.7 | 6.9 | 7.5 | 6.3 |
| Nursing services | 18,332 | 23,729 | 27,617 | 50.7 | 4.2 | 5.3 | 3.1 |
| Hospitals and primary treatment facilities | 322,815 | 470,082 | 627,329 | 94.3 | 6.9 | 7.8 | 5.9 |
| Treatment facilities–outpatient | 51,507 | 71,936 | 111,749 | 117.0 | 8.1 | 6.9 | 9.2 |
| Mental health | 17,031 | 23,443 | 28,335 | 66.4 | 5.2 | 6.6 | 3.9 |
| Disease-specific–general | 7,798 | 10,855 | 14,107 | 80.9 | 6.1 | 6.8 | 5.4 |
| Medical research | 4,824 | 6,688 | 9,382 | 94.5 | 6.9 | 6.8 | 7.0 |
| Other health | 22,246 | 32,807 | 51,354 | 130.8 | 8.7 | 8.1 | 9.4 |

| | | | | | | | |
|---|---|---|---|---|---|---|---|
| Human services | 103,665 | 145,411 | 189,940 | 83.2 | 6.2 | 7.0 | 5.5 |
| Crime and legal-related | 4,139 | 5,455 | 7,078 | 71.0 | 5.5 | 5.7 | 5.3 |
| Employment and job-related | 7,766 | 10,775 | 14,394 | 85.4 | 6.4 | 6.8 | 6.0 |
| Food, agriculture, and nutrition | 3,473 | 5,009 | 8,554 | 146.3 | 9.4 | 7.6 | 11.3 |
| Housing and shelter | 9,343 | 14,940 | 20,386 | 118.2 | 8.1 | 9.8 | 6.4 |
| Public safety and disaster preparedness | 778 | 1,352 | 2,014 | 158.7 | 10.0 | 11.7 | 8.3 |
| Recreation and sports | 6,170 | 8,413 | 11,928 | 93.3 | 6.8 | 6.4 | 7.2 |
| Youth development | 4,185 | 5,510 | 6,698 | 60.0 | 4.8 | 5.7 | 4.0 |
| Children and youth services | 7,956 | 10,765 | 12,702 | 59.7 | 4.8 | 6.2 | 3.4 |
| Family services | 4,250 | 5,449 | 6,486 | 52.6 | 4.3 | 5.1 | 3.5 |
| Residential and custodial care | 18,877 | 27,144 | 33,933 | 79.8 | 6.0 | 7.5 | 4.6 |
| Services promoting independence | 15,881 | 22,432 | 29,581 | 86.3 | 6.4 | 7.2 | 5.7 |
| Other human services | 20,847 | 28,167 | 36,185 | 73.6 | 5.7 | 6.2 | 5.1 |
| International and foreign affairs | 11,712 | 22,598 | 29,681 | 153.4 | 9.7 | 14.0 | 5.6 |
| Public and societal benefit | 37,658 | 55,198 | 70,791 | 88.0 | 6.5 | 7.9 | 5.1 |
| Civil rights and advocacy | 1,169 | 1,662 | 2,217 | 89.7 | 6.6 | 7.3 | 5.9 |
| Community improvement | 8,670 | 11,400 | 16,464 | 89.9 | 6.6 | 5.6 | 7.6 |
| Philanthropy and voluntarism | 13,823 | 18,705 | 24,819 | 79.5 | 6.0 | 6.2 | 5.8 |
| Science and technology | 6,953 | 13,515 | 13,919 | 100.2 | 7.2 | 14.2 | 0.6 |
| Social science | 1,031 | 1,530 | 2,332 | 126.1 | 8.5 | 8.2 | 8.8 |
| Other public and societal benefit | 6,012 | 8,386 | 11,041 | 83.7 | 6.3 | 6.9 | 5.7 |
| Religion-related | 6,402 | 8,713 | 12,155 | 89.9 | 6.6 | 6.4 | 6.9 |

*Sources:* Urban Institute, National Center for Charitable Statistics, Core Files (Public Charities, 2000, 2005, and 2010).
*Note:* Figures are shown in current dollars and are not adjusted for inflation.

**Table 5.15.** Change in Total Assets for Reporting Public Charities by Subsector, 2000, 2005, and 2010

| Subsector | $ Millions | | | Total % Change | Average Annual % Change | | |
|---|---|---|---|---|---|---|---|
| | 2000 | 2005 | 2010 | 2000–10 | 2000–10 | 2000–05 | 2005–10 |
| Arts, culture, and humanities | 58,970 | 81,250 | 98,907 | 67.7 | 5.3 | 6.6 | 4.0 |
| Education | 464,292 | 663,895 | 806,409 | 73.7 | 5.7 | 7.4 | 4.0 |
| Environment and animals | 18,798 | 26,392 | 35,203 | 87.3 | 6.5 | 7.0 | 5.9 |
| Health | 606,906 | 825,505 | 1,141,809 | 88.1 | 6.5 | 6.3 | 6.7 |
| Human services | 164,511 | 225,681 | 297,279 | 80.7 | 6.1 | 6.5 | 5.7 |
| International and foreign affairs | 14,401 | 23,688 | 31,941 | 121.8 | 8.3 | 10.5 | 6.2 |
| Public and societal benefit | 156,039 | 197,129 | 268,149 | 71.8 | 5.6 | 4.8 | 6.3 |
| Religion-related | 16,245 | 22,282 | 29,207 | 79.8 | 6.0 | 6.5 | 5.6 |
| All public charities | 1,500,163 | 2,065,822 | 2,708,905 | 80.6 | 6.1 | 6.6 | 5.6 |

*Sources:* Urban Institute, National Center for Charitable Statistics, Core Files (Public Charities, 2000, 2005, and 2010).
*Note:* Figures are shown in current dollars and are not adjusted for inflation.

growth over the 10 years. International organizations saw an increase of 122 percent (75 percent after adjusting for inflation), and health organizations grew by 88 percent (49 percent after adjusting for inflation). Health organizations account for just over 40 percent of the sector's assets.

For six subsectors, assets averaged greater annual growth between 2000 and 2005 than between 2005 and 2010. Table 5.16 shows that growth of assets in health were fueled by hospitals and treatment facilities with an increase of 99 percent (57 percent after adjusting for inflation). Civil rights and advocacy organizations saw an increase of 109 percent in total assets for 2010 (65 percent after adjusting for inflation). The assets of health and public and societal benefit organizations grew more strongly in the second period.

Tables 5.17 and 5.18 display the growth in net assets, defined as total assets minus liabilities, between 2000 and 2010. Net assets grew from $1.0 trillion in 2000 to about $1.6 trillion in 2010—an increase of 60 percent (26 percent after adjusting for inflation). This is approximately 20 percentage points lower than the growth in total assets, indicating that liabilities grew faster than assets over the 10 years.

International and foreign affairs organizations exhibited the greatest increase in net assets. Net assets for these organizations increased from $11.5 billion in 2000 to $24.6 billion in 2010, an increase of 114 percent (an inflation-adjusted 69 percent). Environment and animal organizations also had a large increase in net assets, growing 88 percent (49 percent after adjusting for inflation).

**Table 5.16.** Change in Total Assets for Reporting Public Charities by Detailed Subsector, 2000, 2005, and 2010

| Subsector | $ Millions | | | Total % Change | Average Annual % Change | | |
|---|---|---|---|---|---|---|---|
| | 2000 | 2005 | 2010 | 2000–10 | 2000–10 | 2000–05 | 2005–10 |
| **All public charities** | **1,500,163** | **2,065,822** | **2,708,905** | **80.6** | **6.1** | **6.6** | **5.6** |
| Arts, culture, and humanities | 58,970 | 81,250 | 98,907 | 67.7 | 5.3 | 6.6 | 4.0 |
| Performing arts organizations | 11,609 | 16,725 | 20,719 | 78.5 | 6.0 | 7.6 | 4.4 |
| Historical societies and related | 6,252 | 8,299 | 10,793 | 72.6 | 5.6 | 5.8 | 5.4 |
| Museums and museum activities | 24,037 | 33,549 | 40,215 | 67.3 | 5.3 | 6.9 | 3.7 |
| Other arts, culture, and humanities | 17,072 | 22,677 | 27,180 | 59.2 | 4.8 | 5.8 | 3.7 |
| Education | 464,292 | 663,895 | 806,409 | 73.7 | 5.7 | 7.4 | 4.0 |
| Higher education institutions | 318,903 | 434,570 | 505,601 | 58.5 | 4.7 | 6.4 | 3.1 |
| Student services and organizations | 15,425 | 36,010 | 46,586 | 202.0 | 11.7 | 18.5 | 5.3 |
| Elementary and secondary education | 48,476 | 72,747 | 91,250 | 88.2 | 6.5 | 8.5 | 4.6 |
| Other education | 81,487 | 120,567 | 162,972 | 100.0 | 7.2 | 8.2 | 6.2 |
| Environment and animals | 18,798 | 26,392 | 35,203 | 87.3 | 6.5 | 7.0 | 5.9 |
| Environment | 11,030 | 15,917 | 21,845 | 98.0 | 7.1 | 7.6 | 6.5 |
| Animal-related | 7,768 | 10,475 | 13,358 | 72.0 | 5.6 | 6.2 | 5.0 |
| Health | 606,906 | 825,505 | 1,141,809 | 88.1 | 6.5 | 6.3 | 6.7 |
| Nursing services | 22,094 | 25,228 | 30,017 | 35.9 | 3.1 | 2.7 | 3.5 |
| Hospitals and primary treatment facilities | 436,885 | 617,251 | 870,155 | 99.2 | 7.1 | 7.2 | 7.1 |
| Treatment facilities–outpatient | 30,186 | 33,982 | 54,978 | 82.1 | 6.2 | 2.4 | 10.1 |
| Mental health | 13,648 | 18,793 | 23,075 | 69.1 | 5.4 | 6.6 | 4.2 |
| Disease-specific–general | 10,908 | 14,063 | 18,721 | 71.6 | 5.5 | 5.2 | 5.9 |
| Medical research | 27,508 | 32,203 | 34,035 | 23.7 | 2.2 | 3.2 | 1.1 |
| Other health | 65,677 | 83,985 | 110,828 | 68.7 | 5.4 | 5.0 | 5.7 |

*(continued)*

**Table 5.16.** Change in Total Assets for Reporting Public Charities by Detailed Subsector, 2000, 2005, and 2010 *(continued)*

| Subsector | $ Millions | | | Total % Change | Average Annual % Change | | |
|---|---|---|---|---|---|---|---|
| | 2000 | 2005 | 2010 | 2000–10 | 2000–10 | 2000–05 | 2005–10 |
| Human services | 164,511 | 225,681 | 297,279 | 80.7 | 6.1 | 6.5 | 5.7 |
| Crime and legal-related | 3,356 | 4,718 | 6,565 | 95.6 | 6.9 | 7.1 | 6.8 |
| Employment and job-related | 6,090 | 8,629 | 12,026 | 97.5 | 7.0 | 7.2 | 6.9 |
| Food, agriculture, and nutrition | 1,958 | 2,826 | 4,798 | 145.1 | 9.4 | 7.6 | 11.2 |
| Housing and shelter | 35,669 | 53,882 | 75,577 | 111.9 | 7.8 | 8.6 | 7.0 |
| Public safety and disaster preparedness | 2,163 | 3,593 | 5,503 | 154.4 | 9.8 | 10.7 | 8.9 |
| Recreation and sports | 8,911 | 12,482 | 17,093 | 91.8 | 6.7 | 7.0 | 6.5 |
| Youth development | 8,617 | 11,041 | 13,590 | 57.7 | 4.7 | 5.1 | 4.2 |
| Children and youth services | 5,676 | 7,192 | 8,946 | 57.6 | 4.7 | 4.8 | 4.5 |
| Family services | 3,768 | 4,867 | 6,190 | 64.3 | 5.1 | 5.3 | 4.9 |
| Residential and custodial care | 44,416 | 58,467 | 73,397 | 65.2 | 5.2 | 5.7 | 4.7 |
| Services promoting independence | 13,187 | 17,745 | 23,914 | 81.3 | 6.1 | 6.1 | 6.1 |
| Other human services | 30,701 | 40,239 | 49,681 | 61.8 | 4.9 | 5.6 | 4.3 |
| International and foreign affairs | 14,401 | 23,688 | 31,941 | 121.8 | 8.3 | 10.5 | 6.2 |
| Public and societal benefit | 156,039 | 197,129 | 268,149 | 71.8 | 5.6 | 4.8 | 6.3 |
| Civil rights and advocacy | 1,359 | 2,001 | 2,842 | 109.2 | 7.7 | 8.0 | 7.3 |
| Community improvement | 42,639 | 39,409 | 64,447 | 51.1 | 4.2 | –1.6 | 10.3 |
| Philanthropy and voluntarism | 69,912 | 96,516 | 130,012 | 86.0 | 6.4 | 6.7 | 6.1 |
| Science and technology | 12,389 | 15,900 | 19,065 | 53.9 | 4.4 | 5.1 | 3.7 |
| Social science | 2,199 | 3,101 | 4,178 | 90.0 | 6.6 | 7.1 | 6.1 |
| Other public and societal benefit | 27,541 | 40,202 | 47,605 | 72.8 | 5.6 | 7.9 | 3.4 |
| Religion-related | 16,245 | 22,282 | 29,207 | 79.8 | 6.0 | 6.5 | 5.6 |

*Sources:* Urban Institute, National Center for Charitable Statistics, Core Files (Public Charities, 2000, 2005, and 2010).
*Note:* Figures are shown in current dollars and are not adjusted for inflation.

**Table 5.17.** Change in Net Assets for Reporting Public Charities by Subsector, 2000, 2005, and 2010

| Subsector | $ Millions | | | Total % Change | Average Annual % Change | | |
|---|---|---|---|---|---|---|---|
| | 2000 | 2005 | 2010 | 2000–10 | 2000–10 | 2000–05 | 2005–10 |
| Arts, culture, and humanities | 51,061 | 66,541 | 79,092 | 54.9 | 4.5 | 5.4 | 3.5 |
| Education | 370,916 | 473,271 | 546,058 | 47.2 | 3.9 | 5.0 | 2.9 |
| Environment and animals | 15,584 | 21,837 | 29,322 | 88.2 | 6.5 | 7.0 | 6.1 |
| Health | 331,915 | 438,198 | 558,615 | 68.3 | 5.3 | 5.7 | 5.0 |
| Human services | 86,093 | 110,755 | 142,829 | 65.9 | 5.2 | 5.2 | 5.2 |
| International and foreign affairs | 11,503 | 18,941 | 24,635 | 114.2 | 7.9 | 10.5 | 5.4 |
| Public and societal benefit | 120,983 | 143,846 | 196,117 | 62.1 | 4.9 | 3.5 | 6.4 |
| Religion-related | 13,030 | 17,298 | 21,390 | 64.2 | 5.1 | 5.8 | 4.3 |
| All public charities | 1,001,084 | 1,290,687 | 1,598,057 | 59.6 | 4.8 | 5.2 | 4.4 |

*Sources:* Urban Institute, National Center for Charitable Statistics, Core Files (Public Charities, 2000, 2005, and 2010).
*Note:* Figures are shown in current dollars and are not adjusted for inflation.

# Reporting Public Charities by Major Subsector

We now explore reporting public charities by subsector in more detail. We begin by giving a financial snapshot for 2010 for each subsector. Then, we break the subsector into its component parts, or industries, and discuss the proportion of each subsector's resources belonging to each industry.

## Arts, Culture, and Humanities

Arts, culture, and humanities organizations accounted for nearly 11 percent of all reporting public charities, but only 2 percent of revenue and 2 percent of expenses, in 2010. Organizations such as museums, performing arts groups, folk life organizations, historical societies, and supporting organizations such as local arts agencies are included in this subsector. In 2010, arts, culture, and humanities nonprofits accounted for roughly 4 percent of public charity assets.

Arts, culture, and humanities groups reported $29.3 billion in revenue and $27.8 billion in total expenses in 2010 (table 5.19). Donations are the largest source of revenue for arts, culture, and humanities organizations. Contributions from individuals, foundations, corporations, and government grants accounted for 57 percent of arts, culture, and humanities revenue in 2010 (figure 5.4). This sector is the third most dependent on private contributions (45 percent) behind the international and foreign affairs and environment and animals sectors. About 36 percent of the total operating costs of arts, culture, and humanities organizations are spent on wages, salaries, and other personnel costs.

**Table 5.18.** Change in Net Assets for Reporting Public Charities by Detailed Subsector, 2000, 2005, and 2010

| Subsector | $ Millions | | | Total % Change | Average Annual % Change | | | |
|---|---|---|---|---|---|---|---|---|
| | 2000 | 2005 | 2010 | 2000–10 | 2000–10 | 2000–05 | 2005–10 | |
| **All public charities** | **1,001,084** | **1,290,687** | **1,598,057** | **59.6** | **4.8** | **5.2** | **4.4** | |
| Arts, culture, and humanities | 51,061 | 66,541 | 79,092 | 54.9 | 4.5 | 5.4 | 3.5 | |
| Performing arts organizations | 9,308 | 12,628 | 15,108 | 62.3 | 5.0 | 6.3 | 3.7 | |
| Historical societies and related | 5,681 | 7,305 | 9,502 | 67.3 | 5.3 | 5.2 | 5.4 | |
| Museums and museum activities | 21,607 | 28,671 | 33,663 | 55.8 | 4.5 | 5.8 | 3.3 | |
| Other arts, culture, and humanities | 14,465 | 17,937 | 20,819 | 43.9 | 3.7 | 4.4 | 3.0 | |
| Education | 370,916 | 473,271 | 546,058 | 47.2 | 3.9 | 5.0 | 2.9 | |
| Higher education institutions | 255,781 | 312,062 | 344,326 | 34.6 | 3.0 | 4.1 | 2.0 | |
| Student services and organizations | 8,019 | 11,201 | 13,470 | 68.0 | 5.3 | 6.9 | 3.8 | |
| Elementary and secondary education | 38,544 | 54,142 | 63,903 | 65.8 | 5.2 | 7.0 | 3.4 | |
| Other education | 68,572 | 95,866 | 124,360 | 81.4 | 6.1 | 6.9 | 5.3 | |
| Environment and animals | 15,584 | 21,837 | 29,322 | 88.2 | 6.5 | 7.0 | 6.1 | |
| Environment | 9,222 | 13,437 | 18,499 | 100.6 | 7.2 | 7.8 | 6.6 | |
| Animal-related | 6,362 | 8,400 | 10,824 | 70.1 | 5.5 | 5.7 | 5.2 | |
| Health | 331,915 | 438,198 | 558,615 | 68.3 | 5.3 | 5.7 | 5.0 | |
| Nursing services | 8,768 | 10,503 | 12,605 | 43.8 | 3.7 | 3.7 | 3.7 | |
| Hospitals and primary treatment facilities | 224,095 | 302,574 | 394,148 | 75.9 | 5.8 | 6.2 | 5.4 | |
| Treatment facilities—outpatient | 8,572 | 13,898 | 19,549 | 128.1 | 8.6 | 10.1 | 7.1 | |
| Mental health | 8,088 | 11,277 | 13,742 | 69.9 | 5.4 | 6.9 | 4.0 | |
| Disease-specific–general | 7,737 | 9,271 | 11,769 | 52.1 | 4.3 | 3.7 | 4.9 | |
| Medical research | 22,775 | 26,146 | 26,824 | 17.8 | 1.7 | 2.8 | 0.5 | |
| Other health | 51,880 | 64,528 | 79,977 | 54.2 | 4.4 | 4.5 | 4.4 | |

| | | | | | | |
|---|---|---|---|---|---|---|
| Human services | 86,093 | 110,755 | 142,829 | 65.9 | 5.2 | 5.2 | 5.2 |
| Crime and legal-related | 2,406 | 3,298 | 4,667 | 93.9 | 6.8 | 6.5 | 7.2 |
| Employment and job-related | 4,128 | 5,731 | 8,052 | 95.1 | 6.9 | 6.8 | 7.0 |
| Food, agriculture, and nutrition | 1,698 | 2,436 | 4,024 | 137.0 | 9.0 | 7.5 | 10.6 |
| Housing and shelter | 9,159 | 13,141 | 19,466 | 112.5 | 7.8 | 7.5 | 8.2 |
| Public safety and disaster preparedness | 1,729 | 2,837 | 4,287 | 148.0 | 9.5 | 10.4 | 8.6 |
| Recreation and sports | 6,624 | 9,521 | 12,528 | 89.1 | 6.6 | 7.5 | 5.6 |
| Youth development | 7,701 | 9,596 | 11,385 | 47.8 | 4.0 | 4.5 | 3.5 |
| Children and youth services | 3,931 | 4,844 | 6,004 | 52.7 | 4.3 | 4.3 | 4.4 |
| Family services | 2,809 | 3,544 | 4,365 | 55.4 | 4.5 | 4.8 | 4.3 |
| Residential and custodial care | 15,360 | 17,742 | 21,855 | 42.3 | 3.6 | 2.9 | 4.3 |
| Services promoting independence | 8,449 | 10,959 | 14,619 | 73.0 | 5.6 | 5.3 | 5.9 |
| Other human services | 22,097 | 27,106 | 31,577 | 42.9 | 3.6 | 4.2 | 3.1 |
| International and foreign affairs | 11,503 | 18,941 | 24,635 | 114.2 | 7.9 | 10.5 | 5.4 |
| Public and societal benefit | 120,983 | 143,846 | 196,117 | 62.1 | 4.9 | 3.5 | 6.4 |
| Civil rights and advocacy | 1,078 | 1,578 | 2,203 | 104.4 | 7.4 | 7.9 | 6.9 |
| Community improvement | 33,788 | 28,072 | 48,716 | 44.2 | 3.7 | -3.6 | 11.7 |
| Philanthropy and voluntarism | 62,961 | 85,670 | 115,308 | 83.1 | 6.2 | 6.4 | 6.1 |
| Science and technology | 9,082 | 11,071 | 12,699 | 39.8 | 3.4 | 4.0 | 2.8 |
| Social science | 1,779 | 2,171 | 2,928 | 64.6 | 5.1 | 4.1 | 6.2 |
| Other public and societal benefit | 12,294 | 15,284 | 14,263 | 16.0 | 1.5 | 4.5 | -1.4 |
| Religion-related | 13,030 | 17,298 | 21,390 | 64.2 | 5.1 | 5.8 | 4.3 |

Sources: Urban Institute, National Center for Charitable Statistics, Core Files (Public Charities, 2000, 2005, and 2010).
Note: Figures are not adjusted for inflation.

**Table 5.19.** Revenue and Expenses for Reporting Arts, Culture, and Humanities
Public Charities, 2010

| | All Organizations | |
| --- | --- | --- |
| | $ millions | % |
| Public support | 16,527 | 57 |
| Private contributions | 13,047 | 45 |
| Direct contributions | 12,605 | 43 |
| Indirect contributions | 442 | 2 |
| Government grants | 3,480 | 12 |
| Fees for services | 10,309 | 35 |
| Fees from government sources | 335 | 1 |
| Fees from private sources | 9,393 | 32 |
| Net income from sale of inventory | 581 | 2 |
| Investment income | 1,582 | 5 |
| Dividends, interest, and other similar amounts | 871 | 3 |
| Net gain on sale of assets or securities | 549 | 2 |
| Other investment income | 162 | 1 |
| Other income | 875 | 3 |
| Net income from special events | 242 | 1 |
| Other revenue | 632 | 2 |
| **Total revenue** | **29,293** | **100** |
| Paid personnel | 10,073 | 36 |
| Wages and salaries | 8,264 | 30 |
| Compensation of officers | 1,244 | 4 |
| Other wages and salaries | 7,020 | 25 |
| Fringe benefits and payroll taxes | 1,809 | 6 |
| Pension plan contributions | 320 | 1 |
| Other employee benefits | 838 | 3 |
| Payroll taxes | 651 | 2 |
| Supplies | 833 | 3 |
| Communications (printing, phone, etc.) | 1,617 | 6 |
| Professional fees | 1,739 | 6 |
| Occupancy | 1,252 | 4 |
| Interest | 370 | 1 |
| Depreciation and depletion | 1,654 | 6 |

*(continued)*

**Table 5.19.** Revenue and Expenses for Reporting Arts, Culture, and Humanities Public Charities, 2010 *(continued)*

|  | All Organizations | |
|---|---|---|
|  | $ millions | % |
| Other | 8,231 | 30 |
| Total current operating expenses | 25,769 | 93 |
| Grants and benefits | 1,833 | 7 |
|    Grants and allocations | 1,694 | 6 |
|    Specific assistance to individuals | 130 | 0 |
|    Benefits paid to members | 9 | 0 |
| Payments to affiliates | 237 | 1 |
| **Total expenses** | **27,839** | **100** |
| Net income (revenue-expenses) | 1,500 | |
| **Total assets** | **98,907** | |
| Total liabilities | 19,816 | |
| **Net assets (assets-liabilities)** | **79,092** | |

*Sources:* Urban Institute, National Center for Charitable Statistics, Core Files (Public Charities, 2005–10) and Core Supplement Files (2005); and Internal Revenue Service, Statistics of Income Sample Files (Public Charities, 2005–08).

*Notes:* Authors' calculations are based on Internal Revenue Service Forms 990 and 990-EZ, classified according to the National Taxonomy of Exempt Entities–Core Codes, and adjusted by the National Center for Charitable Statistics based on available data. See the methodology section at the end of the chapter for more information on how the estimates were created. Reporting public charities include only organizations that both reported (filed Forms 990) and were required to do so. The following were excluded: foreign organizations, government-associated organizations, organizations without state identifiers, and other organizations at the authors' discretion. Organizations not required to report include religious congregations and organizations with less than $50,000 in gross receipts. Subtotals may not sum to totals because of rounding.

The arts, culture, and humanities subsector had net income of $1.5 billion. Additionally, it held $98.9 billion in total assets and had net assets (assets minus liabilities) of $79.1 billion.

Figure 5.5 displays the number, assets, revenue, and expenses of major types of organizations within the arts, culture and humanities subsector. "Other" organizations, which include arts service organizations, arts education organizations, media and communications organizations, and arts councils and agencies, account for 40 percent of the subsector. These organizations also account for the highest proportion of revenue and expenses within the subsector, at 39 percent. Museums, while accounting for only 10 percent of organizations in the subsector, account for 41 percent of total assets, mainly land and buildings.

**Figure 5.4.** Revenue Sources for Reporting Arts, Culture, and Humanities Public Charities, 2010 (percent)

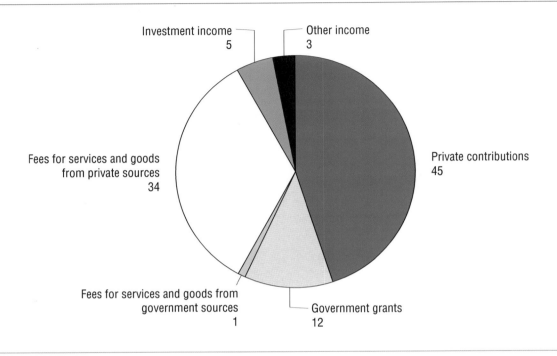

*Source:* Urban Institute, National Center for Charitable Statistics, Core Files (Public Charities, 2010).

## Education

The education subsector includes higher education institutions, student service organizations, elementary and secondary institutions, libraries, and parent-teacher groups. In 2010, these organizations accounted for 18 percent of public charities, 16 percent of total revenue, 17 percent of total expenses, and 30 percent of assets.

Education public charities reported $248.0 billion in revenue and $241.6 billion in expenses in 2010 (table 5.20). Figure 5.6 shows sources of income for the education subsector. Overall, fees for services, such as tuition, account for 64 percent of total revenue, making education the second most dependent sector, behind health, on fee revenue. Wages, salaries, and other personnel costs account for nearly half of education expenses, with other expenses accounting for another 15 percent.

Revenue exceeded expenses in the education subsector by $6.4 billion in 2010. These organizations reported $806.4 billion in total assets and had net assets (assets minus liabilities) of $546.1 billion.

The number, assets, revenue, and expenses of organizations within the education subsector are displayed in figure 5.7. The "other" category accounts for 65 percent of total organizations. This category includes special education programs, libraries, adult continuing education programs, and parent-teacher groups. Elementary and secondary education organizations account for another 20 percent of organizations. Higher edu-

**Figure 5.5.** Number, Assets, Revenue, and Expenses of Arts, Culture, and Humanities Public Charities, 2010 (percent of subsector)

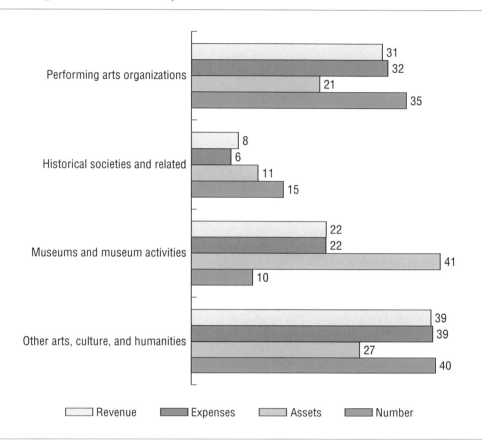

*Source:* Urban Institute, National Center for Charitable Statistics, Core Files (Public Charities, 2010).

cation organizations, while accounting for only 3 percent of total organizations within the subsector, account for 63 percent of assets and 64 percent of expenses and revenue.

Total assets for education organizations were $806.4 billion for 2010. Net assets among education organizations ranged from $13.5 billion for student services organizations to $344.3 billion for higher education organizations.

## Environment and Animals

Organizations focusing on environmental preservation, recycling, pollution abatement, animal protection, and wildlife preservation make up the environment and animals subsector. In 2010, environment and animal-related organizations accounted for 4 percent of public charities and 1 percent of revenue, expenses, and total assets of all public charities.

Environment and animal-related organizations reported $13.7 billion in revenue and $12.9 billion in expenses. Donations are a major source of revenue. Total contributions

**Table 5.20.** Revenue and Expenses for Reporting Education Public Charities, 2010

| | All Organizations | |
|---|---|---|
| | $ millions | % |
| Public support | 71,186 | 29 |
| Private contributions | 42,631 | 17 |
| Direct contributions | 38,208 | 15 |
| Indirect contributions | 4,423 | 2 |
| Government grants | 28,555 | 12 |
| Fees for services | 157,816 | 64 |
| Fees from government sources | 6,283 | 3 |
| Fees from private sources | 150,734 | 61 |
| Net income from sale of inventory | 799 | 0 |
| Investment income | 14,397 | 6 |
| Dividends, interest, and other similar amounts | 7,839 | 3 |
| Net gain on sale of assets or securities | 5,847 | 2 |
| Other investment income | 711 | 0 |
| Other income | 4,638 | 2 |
| Net income from special events | 773 | 0 |
| Other revenue | 3,865 | 2 |
| **Total revenue** | **248,037** | **100** |
| Paid personnel | 108,416 | 45 |
| Wages and salaries | 86,319 | 36 |
| Compensation of officers | 4,557 | 2 |
| Other wages and salaries | 81,762 | 34 |
| Fringe benefits and payroll taxes | 22,097 | 9 |
| Pension plan contributions | 4,842 | 2 |
| Other employee benefits | 11,542 | 5 |
| Payroll taxes | 5,713 | 2 |
| Supplies | 10,779 | 4 |
| Communications (printing, phone, etc.) | 8,043 | 3 |
| Professional fees | 12,075 | 5 |
| Occupancy | 9,747 | 4 |
| Interest | 5,289 | 2 |
| Depreciation and depletion | 10,923 | 5 |

*(continued)*

**Table 5.20.** Revenue and Expenses for Reporting Education Public Charities, 2010 *(continued)*

|  | All Organizations | |
| --- | --- | --- |
|  | $ millions | % |
| Other | 36,073 | 15 |
| Total current operating expenses | 201,345 | 83 |
| Grants and benefits | 39,794 | 16 |
| Grants and allocations | 15,705 | 6 |
| Specific assistance to individuals | 24,019 | 10 |
| Benefits paid to members | 70 | 0 |
| Payments to affiliates | 477 | 0 |
| **Total expenses** | **241,616** | **100** |
| Net income (revenue-expenses) | 6,421 | |
| **Total assets** | **806,409** | |
| Total liabilities | 260,351 | |
| **Net assets (assets-liabilities)** | **546,058** | |

*Sources:* Urban Institute, National Center for Charitable Statistics, Core Files (Public Charities, 2005–10) and Core Supplement Files (2005); and Internal Revenue Service, Statistics of Income Sample Files (Public Charities, 2005–08).
*Notes:* Authors' calculations are based on Internal Revenue Service Forms 990 and 990-EZ, classified according to the National Taxonomy of Exempt Entities–Core Codes, and adjusted by the National Center for Charitable Statistics based on available data. See the methodology section at the end of the chapter for more information on how the estimates were created. Reporting public charities include only organizations that both reported (filed Forms 990) and were required to do so. The following were excluded: foreign organizations, government-associated organizations, organizations without state identifiers, and other organizations at the authors' discretion. Organizations not required to report include religious congregations and organizations with less than $50,000 in gross receipts. Subtotals may not sum to totals because of rounding.

from individuals, foundations, corporations, and government grants accounted for 63 percent of environment and animal-related revenue in 2010 (figure 5.8). The environment and animals subsector is the second most dependent on private contributions (49 percent) behind international and foreign affairs.

As exhibited in table 5.21, wages, salaries, and other personnel costs account for 36 percent of expenses for environment and animal-related organizations. Another 31 percent is reported other expenses.

The environment and animals subsector had a surplus of revenue in 2010. This subsector reported net income of $862 million. Environment and animal-related organizations held $35.2 billion in assets and had net assets (assets minus liabilities) of $29.3 billion.

Figure 5.9 displays the number, assets, revenue, and expenses of organizations in the environment and animal subsector. Animal protection and welfare organizations

**Figure 5.6.** Revenue Sources for Reporting Education Public Charities, 2010 (percent)

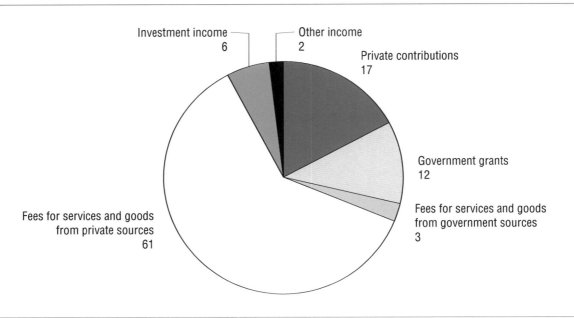

*Source:* Urban Institute, National Center for Charitable Statistics, Core Files (Public Charities, 2010).
*Note:* Totals may not sum to 100 because of rounding.

**Figure 5.7.** Number, Assets, Revenue, and Expenses of Education Public Charities, 2010 (percent of subsector)

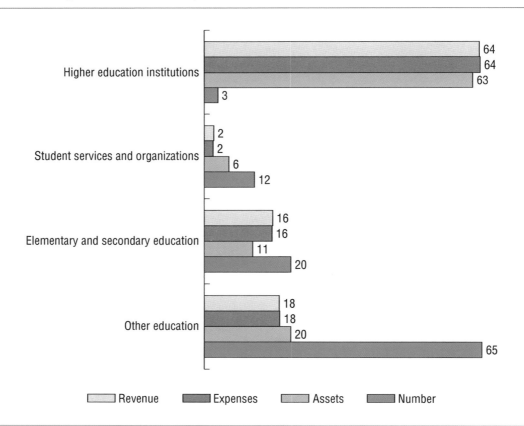

*Source:* Urban Institute, National Center for Charitable Statistics, Core Files (Public Charities, 2010).

**Figure 5.8.** Revenue Sources for Reporting Environment and Animals Public Charities, 2010 (percent)

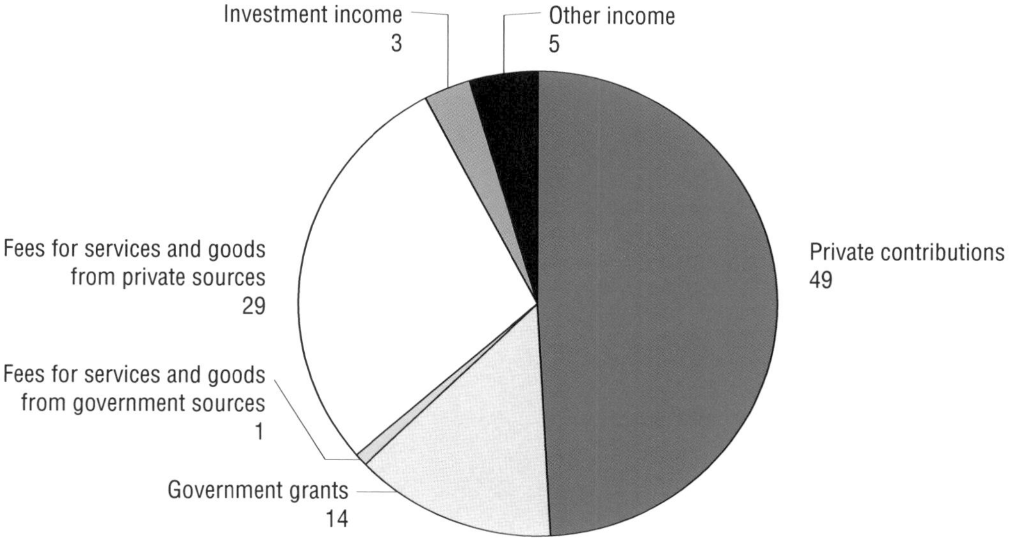

*Source:* Urban Institute, National Center for Charitable Statistics, Core Files (Public Charities, 2010).
*Note:* Totals may not sum to 100 because of rounding.

account for a third of organizations within the subsector followed by natural resources conservation and protection nonprofits (24 percent). Natural resources conservation and protection nonprofits account for the largest proportion of assets (35 percent), revenue (30 percent), and expenses (29 percent).

Environmental organizations reported $478.5 million in net income, and animal-related organizations reported $383.9 million in net income. Environmental organizations held $18.5 billion in net assets, and animal-related organizations held $10.8 billion in net assets.

## Health

The health subsector, which includes hospitals, nursing facilities, mental health organizations, and medical research organizations, accounts for 12 percent of all public charities, 60 percent of total revenue and expenses, and 42 percent of total assets.

In 2010, health nonprofits reported $907.7 billion in revenue and $869.9 billion in expenses (table 5.22), higher totals than all the other subsectors combined. About 89 percent of revenue in the health subsector comes from fees for goods and services, such as patient revenue (figure 5.10). The health subsector is the most reliant on fee-for-service revenue, which includes Medicare and Medicaid payments, and is the least reliant of all subsectors on donations, at 7 percent of total revenue. Private contributions accounted for 4 percent of revenue in 2010, and government grants accounted for 3 percent. Wages, salaries, and personnel costs account for 45 percent of expenses

**Table 5.21.** Revenue and Expenses for Reporting Environment and Animals Public
Charities, 2010

|  | All Organizations | |
| --- | --- | --- |
|  | $ millions | % |
| Public support | 8,611 | 63 |
|   Private contributions | 6,735 | 49 |
|     Direct contributions | 6,527 | 48 |
|     Indirect contributions | 208 | 2 |
|   Government grants | 1,876 | 14 |
| Fees for services | 4,262 | 31 |
|   Fees from government sources | 121 | 1 |
|   Fees from private sources | 3,919 | 29 |
|   Net income from sale of inventory | 222 | 2 |
| Investment income | 433 | 3 |
|   Dividends, interest, and other similar amounts | 291 | 2 |
|   Net gain on sale of assets or securities | 96 | 1 |
|   Other investment income | 46 | 0 |
| Other income | 415 | 3 |
|   Net income from special events | 171 | 1 |
|   Other revenue | 244 | 2 |
| **Total revenue** | **13,721** | **100** |
| Paid personnel | 4,592 | 36 |
|   Wages and salaries | 3,744 | 29 |
|     Compensation of officers | 530 | 4 |
|     Other wages and salaries | 3,214 | 25 |
|   Fringe benefits and payroll taxes | 848 | 7 |
|     Pension plan contributions | 120 | 1 |
|     Other employee benefits | 438 | 3 |
|     Payroll taxes | 290 | 2 |
| Supplies | 635 | 5 |
| Communications (printing, phone, etc.) | 763 | 6 |
| Professional fees | 937 | 7 |
| Occupancy | 401 | 3 |
| Interest | 89 | 1 |
| Depreciation and depletion | 467 | 4 |

*(continued)*

**Table 5.21.** Revenue and Expenses for Reporting Environment and Animals Public Charities, 2010 *(continued)*

|  | All Organizations | |
| --- | --- | --- |
|  | $ millions | % |
| Other | 3,984 | 31 |
| Total current operating expenses | 11,868 | 92 |
| Grants and benefits | 974 | 8 |
| Grants and allocations | 938 | 7 |
| Specific assistance to individuals | 29 | 0 |
| Benefits paid to members | 7 | 0 |
| Payments to affiliates | 16 | 0 |
| **Total expenses** | **12,858** | **100** |
| Net income (revenue-expenses) | 862 | |
| **Total assets** | **35,203** | |
| Total liabilities | 5,881 | |
| **Net assets (assets-liabilities)** | **29,322** | |

*Sources:* Urban Institute, National Center for Charitable Statistics, Core Files (Public Charities, 2005–10) and Core Supplement Files (2005); and Internal Revenue Service, Statistics of Income Sample Files (Public Charities, 2005–08).

*Notes:* Authors' calculations are based on Internal Revenue Service Forms 990 and 990-EZ, classified according to the National Taxonomy of Exempt Entities–Core Codes, and adjusted by the National Center for Charitable Statistics based on available data. See the methodology section at the end of the chapter for more information on how the estimates were created. Reporting public charities include only organizations that both reported (filed Forms 990) and were required to do so. The following were excluded: foreign organizations, government-associated organizations, organizations without state identifiers, and other organizations at the authors' discretion. Organizations not required to report include religious congregations and organizations with less than $50,000 in gross receipts. Subtotals may not sum to totals because of rounding.

in the health sector, followed by other expenses at 23 percent. The health subsector spends less on grants and benefits than any other subsector, just 3 percent in 2010.

The health subsector had net income of $37.9 billion. These organizations held over $1.1 trillion in total assets.

Figure 5.11 displays the number, assets, revenue, and expenses of public charities within the health subsector. Other health organizations, which include family planning organizations, blood banks, public health organizations, and patient and family support organizations, account for 30 percent of organizations within the health subsector. Disease-specific organizations (which include organizations like the March of Dimes and American Cancer Society) and mental health organizations each account for 21 percent of health organizations. Hospitals and primary treatment facilities, while

**Figure 5.9.** Number, Assets, Revenue, and Expenses of Environment and Animals Public Charities, 2010 (percent of subsector)

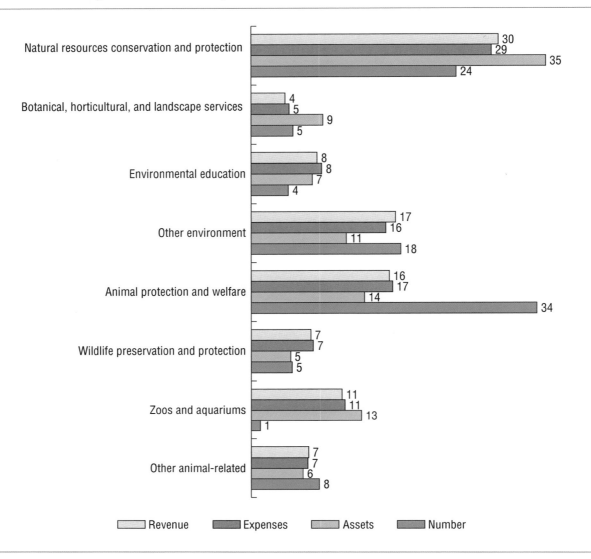

*Source:* Urban Institute, National Center for Charitable Statistics, Core Files (Public Charities, 2010).
*Notes:* Other environment organizations include pollution abatement and control, environmental beautification, and environmental supporting organizations. Other animal-related organizations include veterinary services, animal training, and animal-related supporting organizations.

accounting for only 9 percent of organizations, account for approximately three-quarters of assets, expenses, and revenue.

Outpatient treatment facilities report a negative net income for health organizations at −$19 million. Hospitals and primary treatment facilities have the highest net income by far, $32.5 billion.

Hospitals and primary treatment facilities have $394.1 billion in net assets—more than four times that of the "other" health organizations, which have the next-largest amount of net assets.

**Table 5.22.** Revenue and Expenses for Reporting Health Public Charities, 2010

| | All Organizations | |
| --- | --- | --- |
| | $ millions | % |
| Public support | 66,200 | 7 |
| Private contributions | 39,916 | 4 |
| Direct contributions | 31,073 | 3 |
| Indirect contributions | 8,843 | 1 |
| Government grants | 26,284 | 3 |
| Fees for services | 810,972 | 89 |
| Fees from government sources | 299,725 | 33 |
| Fees from private sources | 509,932 | 56 |
| Net income from sale of inventory | 1,315 | 0 |
| Investment income | 17,106 | 2 |
| Dividends, interest, and other similar amounts | 11,137 | 1 |
| Net gain on sale of assets or securities | 4,777 | 1 |
| Other investment income | 1,192 | 0 |
| Other income | 13,339 | 1 |
| Net income from special events | 407 | 0 |
| Other revenue | 13,064 | 1 |
| **Total revenue** | **907,749** | **100** |
| Paid personnel | 390,565 | 45 |
| Wages and salaries | 310,482 | 36 |
| Compensation of officers | 11,466 | 1 |
| Other wages and salaries | 299,016 | 34 |
| Fringe benefits and payroll taxes | 80,083 | 9 |
| Pension plan contributions | 14,513 | 2 |
| Other employee benefits | 44,111 | 5 |
| Payroll taxes | 21,459 | 2 |
| Supplies | 87,317 | 10 |
| Communications (printing, phone, etc.) | 20,175 | 2 |
| Professional fees | 71,098 | 8 |
| Occupancy | 20,180 | 2 |
| Interest | 11,135 | 1 |
| Depreciation and depletion | 36,700 | 4 |

*(continued)*

**Table 5.22.** Revenue and Expenses for Reporting Health Public Charities, 2010 *(continued)*

|  | All Organizations | |
| --- | ---: | ---: |
|  | $ millions | % |
| Other | 203,588 | 23 |
| Total current operating expenses | 840,758 | 97 |
| Grants and benefits | 25,369 | 3 |
|    Grants and allocations | 13,526 | 2 |
|    Specific assistance to individuals | 2,041 | 0 |
|    Benefits paid to members | 9,802 | 1 |
| Payments to affiliates | 3,746 | 0 |
| **Total expenses** | **869,873** | 100 |
| Net income (revenue-expenses) | 37,876 | |
| **Total assets** | **1,141,809** | |
| Total liabilities | 583,194 | |
| **Net assets (assets-liabilities)** | **558,615** | |

*Sources:* Urban Institute, National Center for Charitable Statistics, Core Files (Public Charities, 2005–10) and Core Supplement Files (2005); and Internal Revenue Service, Statistics of Income Sample Files (Public Charities, 2005–08).

*Notes:* Authors' calculations are based on Internal Revenue Service Forms 990 and 990-EZ, classified according to the National Taxonomy of Exempt Entities–Core Codes, and adjusted by the National Center for Charitable Statistics based on available data. See the methodology section at the end of the chapter for more information on how the estimates were created. Reporting public charities include only organizations that both reported (filed Forms 990) and were required to do so. The following were excluded: foreign organizations, government-associated organizations, organizations without state identifiers, and other organizations at the authors' discretion. Organizations not required to report include religious congregations and organizations with less than $50,000 in gross receipts. Subtotals may not sum to totals because of rounding.

## Human Services

The human services subsector, which accounts for about one-third of all reporting public charities, includes a broad array of organizations ranging from soup kitchens and youth development groups to farmland preservation alliances and amateur sporting clubs. In 2010, human services organizations accounted for 13 percent of total revenue and expenses and 11 percent of total assets.

The largest subsector by numbers, human services reported $196.4 billion in revenue and $189.9 billion in expenses in 2010 (table 5.23); each is roughly 13 percent of the total nonprofit sector. Figure 5.12 displays the sources of revenue for these organizations. Fees for services and goods account for 53 percent of revenue, making the human services sector the third most dependent on fees, behind health and education.

**Figure 5.10.** Revenue Sources for Reporting Health Public Charities, 2010 (percent)

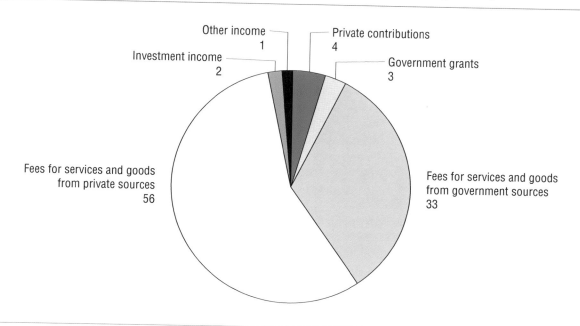

*Source:* Urban Institute, National Center for Charitable Statistics, Core Files (Public Charities, 2010).
*Note:* Totals may not sum to 100 because of rounding.

The number, assets, revenue, and expenses of reporting public charities in the human services subsector are displayed in figure 5.13. Recreation and sports organizations account for a quarter of human services organizations (the greatest number of reporting public charities in this subsector) but only a modest proportion of resources. Housing and shelter organizations follow with 14 percent of organizations. Youth development (7 percent), children and youth services (6 percent), and family services (4 percent) are smaller subsectors, but they include some of the most recognized human services organizations, such as Boy Scouts, Girl Scouts, Big Brothers and Big Sisters, Harlem Children's Zone, and Jewish Family and Children's services.

Housing and shelter as well as residential and custodial care organizations account for the highest proportions of assets, about 25 percent each. These groups of organizations are closely followed by "other" human services organizations (including multiservice, financial counseling, and transportation assistance), which account for 17 percent. Other human services (19 percent), residential and custodial care (18 percent), and services promoting independence (16 percent) account for over half the revenues and expenses in the human services subsector.

The human services subsector reported net income of $6.5 billion in 2010. These organizations held $297.3 billion in total assets and had net assets (assets minus liabilities) of $142.8 billion. Contributions from individuals, foundations, and corporations account for 20 percent of revenue for human services organizations in 2010. Grants from the government account for 23 percent of total revenue, making human services the subsector most reliant on government grants.

**Figure 5.11.** Number, Assets, Revenue, and Expenses of Health Public Charities, 2010 (percent of subsector)

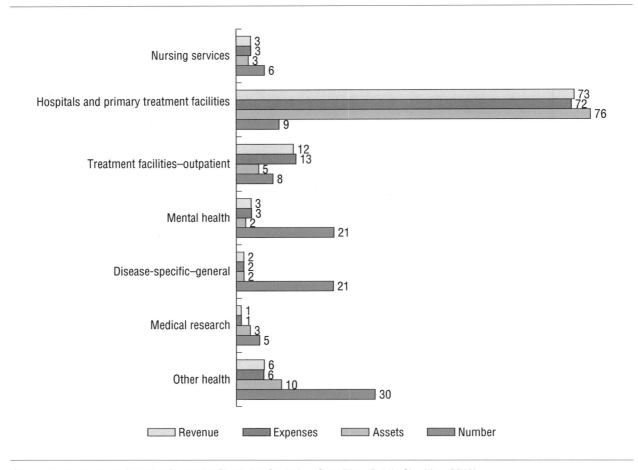

*Source:* Urban Institute, National Center for Charitable Statistics, Core Files (Public Charities, 2010).

Organizations promoting independence, which include senior centers, immigrant centers, and developmentally disabled centers, reported the highest net income in 2010, $1.2 billion. Within the human services subsector, net assets ranged from $4.0 billion for food, agricultural and nutrition organizations to $31.6 billion for other human services organizations.

## International and Foreign Affairs

International and foreign affairs organizations, which include international exchange programs, international development and relief services, international peace and security organization, and international human rights organizations, account for 2 percent of reporting public charities. In 2010, these organizations accounted for 2 percent of the nonprofit sector's revenue and expenses and 1 percent of total assets.

**Table 5.23.** Revenue and Expenses for Reporting Human Services Public Charities, 2010

| | All Organizations | |
|---|---|---|
| | $ millions | % |
| Public support | 85,089 | 43 |
|   Private contributions | 39,673 | 20 |
|     Direct contributions | 36,343 | 19 |
|     Indirect contributions | 3,330 | 2 |
|   Government grants | 45,416 | 23 |
| Fees for services | 103,789 | 53 |
|   Fees from government sources | 49,779 | 25 |
|   Fees from private sources | 51,914 | 26 |
|   Net income from sale of inventory | 2,096 | 1 |
| Investment income | 3,865 | 2 |
|   Dividends, interest, and other similar amounts | 2,140 | 1 |
|   Net gain on sale of assets or securities | 1,248 | 1 |
|   Other investment income | 477 | 0 |
| Other income | 3,653 | 2 |
|   Net income from special events | 1,039 | 1 |
|   Other revenue | 2,614 | 1 |
| **Total revenue** | **196,396** | **100** |
| Paid personnel | 83,298 | 44 |
|   Wages and salaries | 67,683 | 36 |
|     Compensation of officers | 5,251 | 3 |
|     Other wages and salaries | 62,432 | 33 |
|   Fringe benefits and payroll taxes | 15,616 | 8 |
|     Pension plan contributions | 1,668 | 1 |
|     Other employee benefits | 8,392 | 4 |
|     Payroll taxes | 5,556 | 3 |
| Supplies | 5,785 | 3 |
| Communications (printing, phone, etc.) | 6,087 | 3 |
| Professional fees | 7,108 | 4 |
| Occupancy | 9,011 | 5 |
| Interest | 3,827 | 2 |
| Depreciation and depletion | 7,379 | 4 |

*(continued)*

**Table 5.23.** Revenue and Expenses for Reporting Human Services Public Charities, 2010 *(continued)*

| | All Organizations | |
| --- | --- | --- |
| | $ millions | % |
| Other | 49,340 | 26 |
| Total current operating expenses | 171,835 | 90 |
| Grants and benefits | 17,737 | 9 |
|    Grants and allocations | 9,154 | 5 |
|       Specific assistance to individuals | 7,011 | 4 |
|       Benefits paid to members | 1,572 | 1 |
| Payments to affiliates | 368 | 0 |
| **Total expenses** | **189,940** | 100 |
| Net income (revenue-expenses) | 6,457 | |
| **Total assets** | **297,279** | |
| Total liabilities | 154,450 | |
| **Net assets (assets-liabilities)** | **142,829** | |

*Sources:* Urban Institute, National Center for Charitable Statistics, Core Files (Public Charities, 2005–10) and Core Supplement Files (2005); and Internal Revenue Service, Statistics of Income Sample Files (Public Charities, 2005–08). *Notes:* Authors' calculations are based on Internal Revenue Service Forms 990 and 990-EZ, classified according to the National Taxonomy of Exempt Entities–Core Codes, and adjusted by the National Center for Charitable Statistics based on available data. See the methodology section at the end of the chapter for more information on how the estimates were created. Reporting public charities include only organizations that both reported (filed Forms 990) and were required to do so. The following were excluded: foreign organizations, government-associated organizations, organizations without state identifiers, and other organizations at the authors' discretion. Organizations not required to report include religious congregations and organizations with less than $50,000 in gross receipts. Subtotals may not sum to totals because of rounding.

In 2010, international and foreign affairs organizations reported $31.4 billion in total revenue and $29.7 billion in expenses (table 5.24). Contributions from foundation, individuals, and corporations account for 69 percent of all revenue for international and foreign affairs organizations, a far higher share than that of any other subsector (figure 5.14). Government grants account for about 19 percent. Combined, roughly 88 percent of revenue for international and foreign affairs organizations comes from public support, making this subsector the most dependent on contributions.

As in the other subsectors, operating expenses for international and foreign affairs organizations are divided between other expenses (24 percent) and wages, salaries, and personnel costs (17 percent). Grants and allocations account for 38 percent of total expenses, making international and foreign affairs first among sectors providing grants to individuals and other organizations.

**Figure 5.12.** Revenue Sources for Reporting Human Services Public Charities, 2010 (percent)

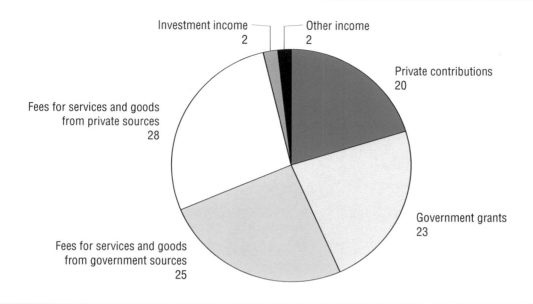

Investment income
2

Other income
2

Private contributions
20

Fees for services and goods
from private sources
28

Government grants
23

Fees for services and goods
from government sources
25

*Source:* Urban Institute, National Center for Charitable Statistics, Core Files (Public Charities, 2010).

The international and foreign affairs subsector reported net income of $1.8 billion. These organizations reported $31.9 billion in total assets and $24.6 billion in net assets.

## Other Public Charities

The 67,377 public charities classified as "other" include public and societal benefit organizations involved in civil rights and advocacy, community improvement, philanthropy and voluntarism, science and technology, telecommunications, veteran's affairs, insurance, cemeteries, and social science research organizations. Religion-related organizations are also included in this category. As a group, these organizations account for 18 percent of public charities, 11 percent of assets, and 6 percent of total revenue and expenses.

In 2010, these organizations reported $87.5 billion in revenue and $82.9 billion in expenses (table 5.25). The public charities in this category generate revenue from various sources. Private contributions account for 44 percent, followed by fees for goods and services at 32 percent and government grants at 16 percent (figure 5.15). Grants and allocations account for 25 percent of total expenses, making this the second largest group of organizations providing grants to individuals and other organizations.

Other public charity organizations reported a net income of $4.5 billion. These organizations reported $297.4 billion in total assets and had net assets of $217.5 billion.

Figure 5.16 displays the number, assets, revenue, and expenses of reporting public charities in this category. Religion-related organizations account for just over a

**Figure 5.13.** Number, Assets, Revenue, and Expenses of Human Services Public Charities, 2010 (percent of subsector)

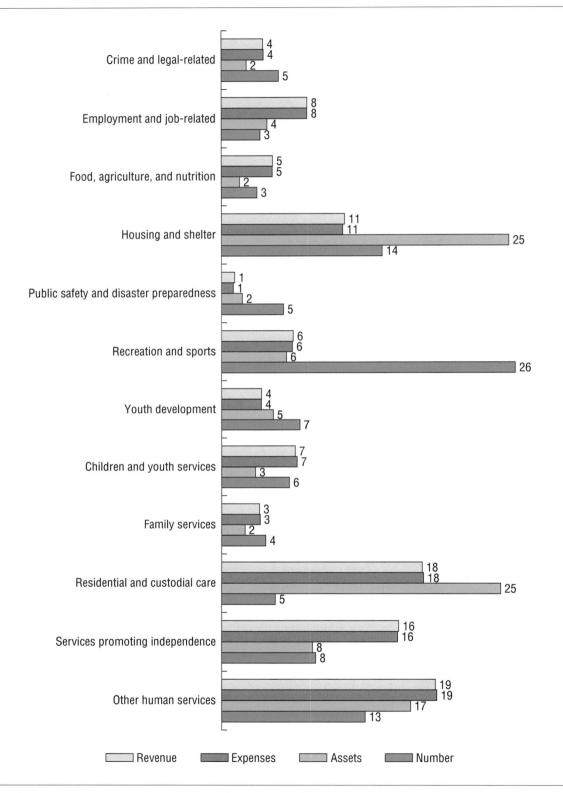

*Source:* Urban Institute, National Center for Charitable Statistics, Core Files (Public Charities, 2010).

**Table 5.24.** Revenue and Expenses for Reporting International and Foreign Affairs Public Charities, 2010

|  | All Organizations | |
|---|---|---|
|  | $ millions | % |
| Public support | 27,558 | 88 |
| Private contributions | 21,695 | 69 |
| Direct contributions | 20,270 | 64 |
| Indirect contributions | 1,425 | 5 |
| Government grants | 5,863 | 19 |
| Fees for services | 2,949 | 9 |
| Fees from government sources | 435 | 1 |
| Fees from private sources | 2,466 | 8 |
| Net income from sale of inventory | 48 | 0 |
| Investment income | 515 | 2 |
| Dividends, interest, and other similar amounts | 272 | 1 |
| Net gain on sale of assets or securities | 223 | 1 |
| Other investment income | 20 | 0 |
| Other income | 419 | 1 |
| Net income from special events | 16 | 0 |
| Other revenue | 403 | 1 |
| **Total revenue** | **31,441** | **100** |
| Paid personnel | 5,069 | 17 |
| Wages and salaries | 4,091 | 14 |
| Compensation of officers | 564 | 2 |
| Other wages and salaries | 3,527 | 12 |
| Fringe benefits and payroll taxes | 978 | 3 |
| Pension plan contributions | 170 | 1 |
| Other employee benefits | 579 | 2 |
| Payroll taxes | 229 | 1 |
| Supplies | 1,204 | 4 |
| Communications (printing, phone, etc.) | 1,525 | 5 |
| Professional fees | 1,475 | 5 |
| Occupancy | 564 | 2 |
| Interest | 95 | 0 |
| Depreciation and depletion | 221 | 1 |

*(continued)*

**Table 5.24.** Revenue and Expenses for Reporting International and Foreign Affairs Public Charities, 2010 *(continued)*

| | All Organizations | |
| --- | --- | --- |
| | $ millions | % |
| Other | 7,225 | 24 |
| Total current operating expenses | 17,378 | 59 |
| Grants and benefits | 12,245 | 41 |
|    Grants and allocations | 11,196 | 38 |
|    Specific assistance to individuals | 1,043 | 4 |
|    Benefits paid to members | 6 | 0 |
| Payments to affiliates | 57 | 0 |
| **Total expenses** | **29,680** | 100 |
| Net income (revenue-expenses) | 1,760 | |
| **Total assets** | **31,941** | |
| Total liabilities | 7,306 | |
| **Net assets (assets-liabilities)** | **24,635** | |

*Sources:* Urban Institute, National Center for Charitable Statistics, Core Files (Public Charities, 2005–10) and Core Supplement Files (2005); and Internal Revenue Service, Statistics of Income Sample Files (Public Charities, 2005–08).

*Notes:* Authors' calculations are based on Internal Revenue Service Forms 990 and 990-EZ, classified according to the National Taxonomy of Exempt Entities–Core Codes, and adjusted by the National Center for Charitable Statistics based on available data. See the methodology section at the end of the chapter for more information on how the estimates were created. Reporting public charities include only organizations that both reported (filed Forms 990) and were required to do so. The following were excluded: foreign organizations, government-associated organizations, organizations without state identifiers, and other organizations at the authors' discretion. Organizations not required to report include religious congregations and organizations with less than $50,000 in gross receipts. Subtotals may not sum to totals because of rounding.

third of organizations. Community improvement and philanthropy and voluntarism organizations each account for another quarter. Philanthropy and voluntarism organizations hold 44 percent of this group's assets and account for 30 percent of expenses and revenue.

In 2010, no organizations in this subsector ran a deficit. Philanthropy and voluntarism had the highest net income ($1.7 billion). Net assets for these organizations ranged from $2.2 billion for civil rights and advocacy groups to $115.3 billion for philanthropy and voluntarism organizations. Community foundations—place-based foundations that raise money from community members, hold assets, and make grants—are responsible for 39 percent of net assets and 25 percent of the grants and other assistance paid in this category.

**Figure 5.14.** Revenue Sources for Reporting International and Foreign Affairs Public Charities, 2010 (percent)

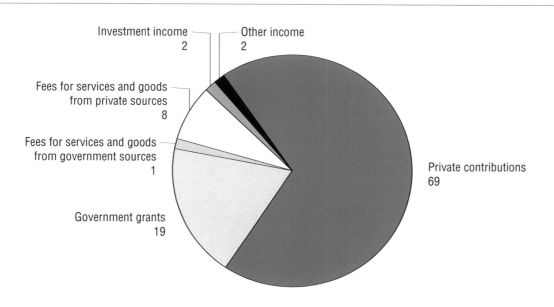

Investment income
2

Other income
2

Fees for services and goods from private sources
8

Fees for services and goods from government sources
1

Government grants
19

Private contributions
69

*Source:* Urban Institute, National Center for Charitable Statistics, Core Files (Public Charities, 2010).
*Note:* Totals may not sum to 100 because of rounding.

## Reporting Public Charities by State

The number of public charities by state ranged from 1,077 in Wyoming to 42,479 in California in 2010 (table 5.26). Not surprisingly, the number of reporting public charities in a state correlates directly with the state's population. Highly populated states like California, New York, and Texas have the most charities, while less-populated states like Wyoming and North Dakota have fewer.

Public charities in New York, California, Massachusetts, Pennsylvania, and Oregon reported the highest revenue and expenses in 2010. When states are ranked by total assets, four of the same states reappear in the top five. Texas replaces Oregon.

While these figures give some insight into the distribution of public charities nationwide, the density of public charities by state (as measured by the number of reporting public charities divided by the population) and the expenses, revenue, and assets per resident (as measured by the total expenses, revenue, or assets divided by the population) provide more meaningful information. The per capita rankings presented in the following paragraphs exclude the District of Columbia, as many nonprofits in the District have a national or international scope and may not directly benefit local residents.

The density of reporting public charities ranges from 6.1 organizations per 10,000 residents in Nevada to 28.6 organizations per 10,000 residents in Vermont. Less-populated states have more reporting public charities per person than more-populated

**Table 5.25.** Revenue and Expenses for Reporting Public Charities from
All Other Subsectors, 2010

| | All Organizations | |
|---|---|---|
| | $ millions | % |
| Public support | 52,647 | 60 |
| Private contributions | 38,324 | 44 |
| Direct contributions | 36,264 | 41 |
| Indirect contributions | 2,060 | 2 |
| Government grants | 14,323 | 16 |
| Fees for services | 28,265 | 32 |
| Fees from government sources | 4,472 | 5 |
| Fees from private sources | 23,253 | 27 |
| Net income from sale of inventory | 540 | 1 |
| Investment income | 4,331 | 5 |
| Dividends, interest, and other similar amounts | 3,728 | 4 |
| Net gain on sale of assets or securities | 356 | 0 |
| Other investment income | 247 | 0 |
| Other income | 2,227 | 3 |
| Net income from special events | 320 | 0 |
| Other revenue | 1,907 | 2 |
| **Total revenue** | **87,470** | **100** |
| Paid personnel | 23,584 | 28 |
| Wages and salaries | 18,786 | 23 |
| Compensation of officers | 2,786 | 3 |
| Other wages and salaries | 16,000 | 19 |
| Fringe benefits and payroll taxes | 4,796 | 6 |
| Pension plan contributions | 1,013 | 1 |
| Other employee benefits | 2,456 | 3 |
| Payroll taxes | 1,327 | 2 |
| Supplies | 2,020 | 2 |
| Communications (printing, phone, etc.) | 4,255 | 5 |
| Professional fees | 4,649 | 6 |
| Occupancy | 2,368 | 3 |
| Interest | 1,246 | 2 |

*(continued)*

**Table 5.25.** Revenue and Expenses for Reporting Public Charities from All Other Subsectors, 2010 *(continued)*

|  | All Organizations | |
| --- | --- | --- |
|  | $ millions | % |
| Depreciation and depletion | 1,934 | 2 |
| Other | 19,184 | 23 |
| Total current operating expenses | 59,240 | 71 |
| Grants and benefits | 23,087 | 28 |
|   Grants and allocations | 20,990 | 25 |
|   Specific assistance to individuals | 1,557 | 2 |
|   Benefits paid to members | 540 | 1 |
| Payments to affiliates | 619 | 1 |
| **Total expenses** | **82,946** | **100** |
| Net income (revenue-expenses) | 4,524 | |
| **Total assets** | **297,356** | |
| Total liabilities | 79,850 | |
| **Net assets (assets-liabilities)** | **217,506** | |

*Sources:* Urban Institute, National Center for Charitable Statistics, Core Files (Public Charities, 2005–10) and Core Supplement Files (2005); and Internal Revenue Service, Statistics of Income Sample Files (Public Charities, 2005–08).

*Notes:* Authors' calculations are based on Internal Revenue Service Forms 990 and 990-EZ, classified according to the National Taxonomy of Exempt Entities–Core Codes, and adjusted by the National Center for Charitable Statistics based on available data. See the methodology section at the end of the chapter for more information on how the estimates were created. Reporting public charities include only organizations that both reported (filed Forms 990) and were required to do so. The following were excluded: foreign organizations, government-associated organizations, organizations without state identifiers, and other organizations at the authors' discretion. Organizations not required to report include religious congregations and organizations with less than $50,000 in gross receipts. Subtotals may not sum to totals because of rounding.

states. Vermont, Montana, Alaska, Maine, and Wyoming are the top five states in nonprofit density.

Nonprofit expenses per resident in 2010 ranged from $948 in Nevada to $18,413 in Oregon. Oregon, Massachusetts, Rhode Island, New York, and Maine report the highest expenditures per resident. Oregon, Massachusetts, and New York are in the top five for both expenses per resident and total expenses per state.

Assets per resident for reporting public charities ranged from $1,943 in Nevada to $32,496 in Massachusetts. Massachusetts, Delaware, Connecticut, Oregon, and New Hampshire are the top five states in total assets per resident. Massachusetts is the only state ranked in the top five in both assets per resident and total assets per state.

**Figure 5.15.** Revenue Sources for Other Reporting Public Charities, 2010 (percent)

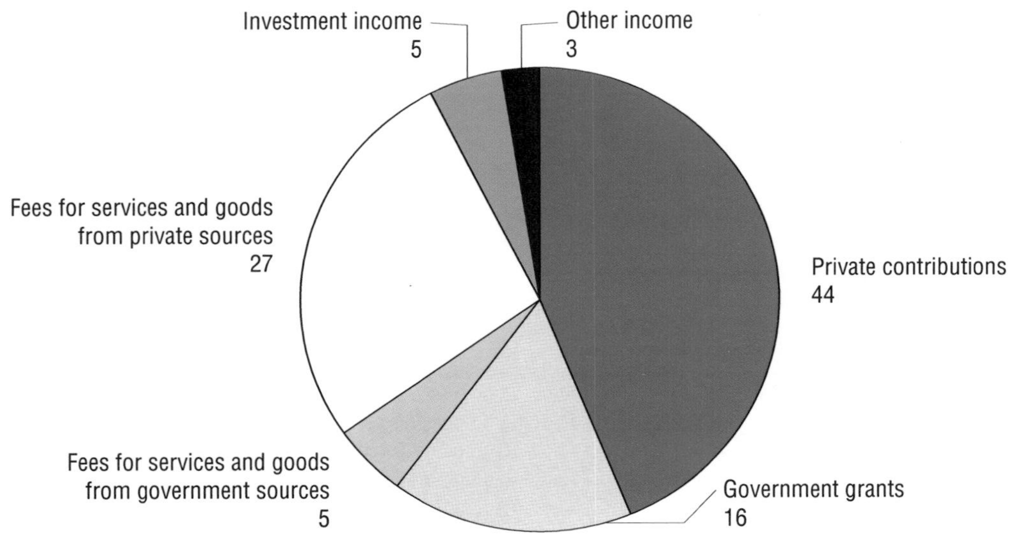

Investment income
5

Other income
3

Fees for services and goods
from private sources
27

Private contributions
44

Fees for services and goods
from government sources
5

Government grants
16

*Source:* Urban Institute, National Center for Charitable Statistics, Core Files (Public Charities, 2010).

## Trends in Reporting Public Charities by State

The number of reporting public charities nationwide grew from 249,859 in 2000 to 366,086 in 2010, an increase of 47 percent. Growth in public charities varied greatly among states, ranging from 18 percent in Rhode Island to 71 percent in Idaho and Nevada. Looking at growth across census regions, the South had the greatest growth at 54 percent, followed by the West at 52 percent. Within the West, the mountain states experienced growth of 58 percent (table 5.27).

Table 5.28 shows the top 10 states ranked by growth of public charities from 2000 to 2010. Eight of these states were also in the top 10 in population growth.

Total nonprofit revenue grew from $836.8 billion in 2000 to $1.5 trillion in 2010, an inflation-adjusted increase of 43 percent (table 5.29). Western states saw the greatest revenue increase over the period, growing 106 percent (63 percent after adjusting for inflation). Table 5.30 displays the top 10 states in public charity revenue growth. Arizona saw the greatest growth at 181 percent after adjusting for inflation. Idaho more than doubled its revenue over the 10 years, even after taking into account inflation. At the other end of the spectrum, Hawaii actually showed negative growth after adjusting for inflation.

As table 5.31 shows, total public support from individual donations, foundations, corporations, and government grants grew 79 percent (an inflation-adjusted 41 percent) from 2000 to 2010. The South showed the largest increase in public support over the period, increasing 95 percent (54 percent after adjusting for inflation). Table 5.32

**Figure 5.16.** Number, Assets, Revenue, and Expenses of Other Public Charities, 2010 (percent of subsector)

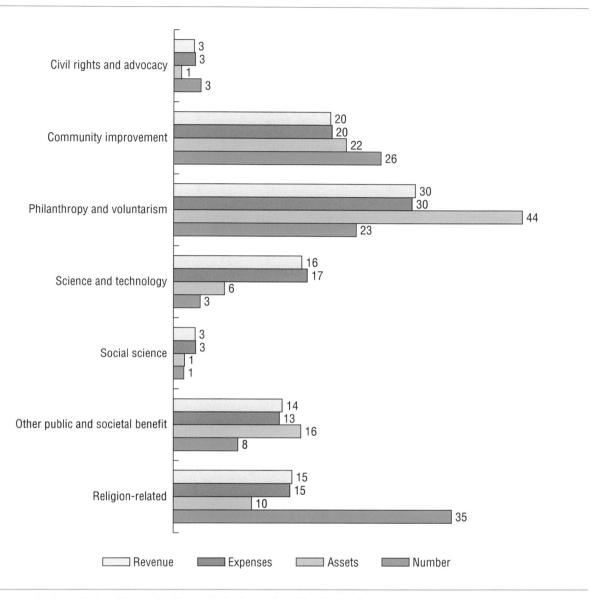

*Source:* Urban Institute, National Center for Charitable Statistics, Core Files (Public Charities, 2010).

shows the top 10 states by public support growth. Idaho reported the highest growth (86 percent after adjusting for inflation), followed by Arizona, Nevada, Louisiana, and Wyoming. Vermont showed the least growth among the states—26 percent (−0.3 percent after adjusting for inflation).

The expenses of public charities grew from $749.9 billion in 2000 to $1.45 trillion in 2010 (table 5.33), a 53 percent increase after adjusting for inflation. The Western region saw the largest increase in expenses over the 10 years, growing by

**Table 5.26. Number, Revenue, Expenses, and Assets of Reporting Public Charities by State, 2010**

| | | $ Millions | | | | Organizations per 10,000 residents | Expenses per resident | Assets per residents |
| --- | --- | --- | --- | --- | --- | --- | --- | --- |
| | Number | Revenue | Expenses | Assets | Population | | | |
| **United States** | **366,086** | **1,514,153** | **1,454,753** | **2,708,905** | **308,745,538** | **11.9** | **4,712** | **8,774** |
| Northeast | 80,356 | 427,427 | 415,687 | 806,978 | 55,317,240 | 14.5 | 7,515 | 14,588 |
| New England | 25,607 | 146,068 | 142,952 | 334,457 | 14,444,865 | 17.7 | 9,896 | 23,154 |
| Connecticut | 5,709 | 24,723 | 23,985 | 67,056 | 3,574,097 | 16.0 | 6,711 | 18,762 |
| Massachusetts | 11,462 | 90,273 | 88,737 | 212,770 | 6,547,629 | 17.5 | 13,553 | 32,496 |
| Maine | 2,600 | 9,628 | 9,277 | 13,496 | 1,328,361 | 19.6 | 6,984 | 10,160 |
| New Hampshire | 2,363 | 8,489 | 8,449 | 19,699 | 1,316,470 | 17.9 | 6,418 | 14,963 |
| Rhode Island | 1,683 | 9,071 | 8,745 | 14,995 | 1,052,567 | 16.0 | 8,308 | 14,246 |
| Vermont | 1,790 | 3,882 | 3,760 | 6,440 | 625,741 | 28.6 | 6,009 | 10,291 |
| Middle Atlantic | 54,749 | 281,359 | 272,735 | 472,521 | 40,872,375 | 13.4 | 6,673 | 11,561 |
| New Jersey | 10,735 | 37,954 | 37,173 | 69,335 | 8,791,894 | 12.2 | 4,228 | 7,886 |
| New York | 27,084 | 157,301 | 152,390 | 249,685 | 19,378,102 | 14.0 | 7,864 | 12,885 |
| Pennsylvania | 16,930 | 86,104 | 83,172 | 153,501 | 12,702,379 | 13.3 | 6,548 | 12,084 |
| Midwest | 83,196 | 350,689 | 333,511 | 616,358 | 66,927,001 | 12.4 | 4,983 | 9,209 |
| East North Central | 54,271 | 239,339 | 227,180 | 412,402 | 46,421,564 | 11.7 | 4,894 | 8,884 |
| Illinois | 13,974 | 66,047 | 62,801 | 121,227 | 12,830,632 | 10.9 | 4,895 | 9,448 |
| Indiana | 7,562 | 28,941 | 26,987 | 56,289 | 6,483,802 | 11.7 | 4,162 | 8,682 |
| Michigan | 10,342 | 43,646 | 41,706 | 66,937 | 9,883,640 | 10.5 | 4,220 | 6,772 |
| Ohio | 14,533 | 65,454 | 62,417 | 112,854 | 11,536,504 | 12.6 | 5,410 | 9,782 |
| Wisconsin | 7,860 | 35,252 | 33,268 | 55,095 | 5,686,986 | 13.8 | 5,850 | 9,688 |

| | | | | | | | |
|---|---|---|---|---|---|---|---|
| West North Central | 28,925 | 111,350 | 106,332 | 203,956 | 20,505,437 | 14.1 | 5,186 | 9,946 |
| Iowa | 4,480 | 11,888 | 11,278 | 27,021 | 3,046,355 | 14.7 | 3,702 | 8,870 |
| Kansas | 3,609 | 10,347 | 9,978 | 16,917 | 2,853,118 | 12.6 | 3,497 | 5,929 |
| Minnesota | 8,557 | 36,575 | 35,094 | 63,041 | 5,303,925 | 16.1 | 6,617 | 11,886 |
| Missouri | 7,018 | 33,478 | 31,991 | 64,688 | 5,988,927 | 11.7 | 5,342 | 10,801 |
| North Dakota | 1,174 | 4,271 | 4,067 | 5,383 | 672,591 | 17.5 | 6,047 | 8,003 |
| Nebraska | 2,723 | 9,388 | 8,855 | 18,116 | 1,826,341 | 14.9 | 4,848 | 9,919 |
| South Dakota | 1,364 | 5,402 | 5,069 | 8,790 | 814,180 | 16.8 | 6,226 | 10,796 |
| South | 117,091 | 416,764 | 398,891 | 802,711 | 114,555,744 | 10.2 | 3,482 | 7,007 |
| South Atlantic | 66,447 | 259,963 | 249,475 | 489,879 | 59,777,037 | 11.1 | 4,173 | 8,195 |
| District of Columbia | 4,127 | 29,160 | 26,898 | 43,701 | 601,723 | 68.6 | 44,702 | 72,627 |
| Delaware | 1,251 | 3,175 | 3,130 | 16,967 | 897,934 | 13.9 | 3,486 | 18,895 |
| Florida | 16,560 | 61,753 | 58,995 | 99,991 | 18,801,310 | 8.8 | 3,138 | 5,318 |
| Georgia | 9,014 | 34,922 | 33,946 | 67,599 | 9,687,653 | 9.3 | 3,504 | 6,978 |
| Maryland | 7,819 | 37,046 | 36,443 | 79,039 | 5,773,552 | 13.5 | 6,312 | 13,690 |
| North Carolina | 10,362 | 36,498 | 34,609 | 72,141 | 9,535,483 | 10.9 | 3,629 | 7,566 |
| South Carolina | 4,319 | 10,902 | 10,363 | 22,803 | 4,625,364 | 9.3 | 2,240 | 4,930 |
| Virginia | 10,836 | 39,202 | 37,893 | 77,948 | 8,001,024 | 13.5 | 4,736 | 9,742 |
| West Virginia | 2,159 | 7,305 | 7,198 | 9,689 | 1,852,994 | 11.7 | 3,885 | 5,229 |
| East South Central | 17,461 | 58,706 | 56,439 | 99,700 | 18,432,505 | 9.5 | 3,062 | 5,409 |
| Alabama | 4,383 | 9,191 | 8,950 | 16,377 | 4,779,736 | 9.2 | 1,872 | 3,426 |
| Kentucky | 4,286 | 18,864 | 18,284 | 25,112 | 4,339,367 | 9.9 | 4,214 | 5,787 |
| Mississippi | 2,286 | 6,110 | 5,757 | 10,571 | 2,967,297 | 7.7 | 1,940 | 3,563 |
| Tennessee | 6,506 | 24,542 | 23,448 | 47,640 | 6,346,105 | 10.3 | 3,695 | 7,507 |

*(continued)*

**Table 5.26.** Number, Revenue, Expenses, and Assets of Reporting Public Charities by State, 2010 *(continued)*

| | Number | $ Millions | | | Population | Organizations per 10,000 residents | Expenses per resident | Assets per residents |
|---|---|---|---|---|---|---|---|---|
| | | Revenue | Expenses | Assets | | | | |
| West South Central | 33,183 | 98,095 | 92,977 | 213,132 | 36,346,202 | 9.1 | 2,558 | 5,864 |
| Arkansas | 2,861 | 7,681 | 7,243 | 11,015 | 2,915,918 | 9.8 | 2,484 | 3,778 |
| Louisiana | 4,109 | 15,863 | 15,249 | 45,363 | 4,533,372 | 9.1 | 3,364 | 10,007 |
| Oklahoma | 3,923 | 9,186 | 8,599 | 22,690 | 3,751,351 | 10.5 | 2,292 | 6,048 |
| Texas | 22,290 | 65,365 | 61,887 | 134,063 | 25,145,561 | 8.9 | 2,461 | 5,331 |
| West | 85,443 | 319,273 | 306,664 | 482,857 | 71,945,553 | 11.9 | 4,262 | 6,711 |
| Mountain | 24,314 | 72,080 | 68,243 | 112,127 | 22,065,451 | 11.0 | 3,093 | 5,082 |
| Arizona | 5,484 | 30,836 | 29,648 | 37,109 | 6,392,017 | 8.6 | 4,638 | 5,806 |
| Colorado | 7,669 | 19,255 | 18,067 | 36,753 | 5,029,196 | 15.2 | 3,592 | 7,308 |
| Idaho | 1,656 | 3,337 | 3,188 | 5,196 | 1,567,582 | 10.6 | 2,034 | 3,314 |
| Montana | 2,111 | 3,859 | 3,642 | 6,856 | 989,415 | 21.3 | 3,681 | 6,929 |
| New Mexico | 2,590 | 4,630 | 4,379 | 8,936 | 2,059,179 | 12.6 | 2,127 | 4,340 |
| Nevada | 1,643 | 2,744 | 2,561 | 5,247 | 2,700,551 | 6.1 | 948 | 1,943 |
| Utah | 2,084 | 6,292 | 5,687 | 9,461 | 2,763,885 | 7.5 | 2,058 | 3,423 |
| Wyoming | 1,077 | 1,127 | 1,072 | 2,570 | 563,626 | 19.1 | 1,902 | 4,559 |
| Pacific | 61,129 | 247,193 | 238,421 | 370,730 | 49,880,102 | 12.3 | 4,780 | 7,432 |
| Alaska | 1,480 | 2,983 | 2,762 | 4,044 | 710,231 | 20.8 | 3,889 | 5,695 |
| California | 42,841 | 186,606 | 179,796 | 281,307 | 37,253,956 | 11.5 | 4,826 | 7,551 |
| Hawaii | 1,916 | 4,937 | 4,704 | 15,119 | 1,360,301 | 14.1 | 3,458 | 11,114 |
| Oregon | 6,174 | 21,526 | 21,003 | 25,629 | 3,831,074 | 16.1 | 5,482 | 6,690 |
| Washington | 9,078 | 31,141 | 30,155 | 44,631 | 6,724,540 | 13.5 | 4,484 | 6,637 |

*Sources:* Urban Institute, National Center for Charitable Statistics, Core Files (Public Charities, 2010); and U.S. Census Bureau, Statistical Abstract (2010).

**Table 5.27.** Change in the Number of Reporting Public Charities by State, 2000, 2005, and 2010

| | Number of Organizations | | | Total % Change | Average Annual % Change | | |
|---|---|---|---|---|---|---|---|
| | 2000 | 2005 | 2010 | 2000–10 | 2000–10 | 2000–05 | 2005–10 |
| **United States** | **249,856** | **313,164** | **366,086** | **46.5** | **3.9** | **4.6** | **3.2** |
| Northeast | 57,375 | 70,469 | 80,356 | 40.1 | 3.4 | 4.2 | 2.7 |
| New England | 18,693 | 22,875 | 25,607 | 37.0 | 3.2 | 4.1 | 2.3 |
| Connecticut | 4,216 | 5,033 | 5,709 | 35.4 | 3.1 | 3.6 | 2.6 |
| Massachusetts | 8,297 | 9,979 | 11,462 | 38.1 | 3.3 | 3.8 | 2.8 |
| Maine | 1,859 | 2,331 | 2,600 | 39.9 | 3.4 | 4.6 | 2.2 |
| New Hampshire | 1,606 | 2,004 | 2,363 | 47.1 | 3.9 | 4.5 | 3.4 |
| Rhode Island | 1,422 | 1,900 | 1,683 | 18.4 | 1.7 | 6.0 | −2.4 |
| Vermont | 1,293 | 1,628 | 1,790 | 38.4 | 3.3 | 4.7 | 1.9 |
| Middle Atlantic | 38,682 | 47,594 | 54,749 | 41.5 | 3.5 | 4.2 | 2.8 |
| New Jersey | 7,038 | 9,289 | 10,735 | 52.5 | 4.3 | 5.7 | 2.9 |
| New York | 19,184 | 23,444 | 27,084 | 41.2 | 3.5 | 4.1 | 2.9 |
| Pennsylvania | 12,460 | 14,861 | 16,930 | 35.9 | 3.1 | 3.6 | 2.6 |
| Midwest | 60,211 | 72,903 | 83,196 | 38.2 | 3.3 | 3.9 | 2.7 |
| East North Central | 39,607 | 47,889 | 54,271 | 37.0 | 3.2 | 3.9 | 2.5 |
| Illinois | 10,177 | 12,285 | 13,974 | 37.3 | 3.2 | 3.8 | 2.6 |
| Indiana | 5,428 | 6,615 | 7,562 | 39.3 | 3.4 | 4.0 | 2.7 |
| Michigan | 7,556 | 9,064 | 10,342 | 36.9 | 3.2 | 3.7 | 2.7 |
| Ohio | 10,981 | 12,993 | 14,533 | 32.3 | 2.8 | 3.4 | 2.3 |
| Wisconsin | 5,465 | 6,932 | 7,860 | 43.8 | 3.7 | 4.9 | 2.5 |
| West North Central | 20,604 | 25,014 | 28,925 | 40.4 | 3.5 | 4.0 | 2.9 |
| Iowa | 3,197 | 3,803 | 4,480 | 40.1 | 3.4 | 3.5 | 3.3 |
| Kansas | 2,637 | 3,198 | 3,609 | 36.9 | 3.2 | 3.9 | 2.4 |
| Minnesota | 5,988 | 7,400 | 8,557 | 42.9 | 3.6 | 4.3 | 2.9 |
| Missouri | 4,976 | 6,100 | 7,018 | 41.0 | 3.5 | 4.2 | 2.8 |
| North Dakota | 932 | 1,024 | 1,174 | 26.0 | 2.3 | 1.9 | 2.8 |
| Nebraska | 1,962 | 2,376 | 2,723 | 38.8 | 3.3 | 3.9 | 2.8 |
| South Dakota | 912 | 1,113 | 1,364 | 49.6 | 4.1 | 4.1 | 4.2 |

*(continued)*

**Table 5.27.** Change in the Number of Reporting Public Charities by State, 2000, 2005, and 2010 *(continued)*

| | Number of Organizations | | | Total % Change | Average Annual % Change | | |
|---|---|---|---|---|---|---|---|
| | 2000 | 2005 | 2010 | 2000–10 | 2000–10 | 2000–05 | 2005–10 |
| South | 76,056 | 97,763 | 117,091 | 54.0 | 4.4 | 5.1 | 3.7 |
| South Atlantic | 43,259 | 55,962 | 66,447 | 53.6 | 4.4 | 5.3 | 3.5 |
| District of Columbia | 3,282 | 3,834 | 4,127 | 25.7 | 2.3 | 3.2 | 1.5 |
| Delaware | 920 | 1,076 | 1,251 | 36.0 | 3.1 | 3.2 | 3.1 |
| Florida | 10,233 | 13,651 | 16,560 | 61.8 | 4.9 | 5.9 | 3.9 |
| Georgia | 5,342 | 7,214 | 9,014 | 68.7 | 5.4 | 6.2 | 4.6 |
| Maryland | 5,489 | 6,874 | 7,819 | 42.4 | 3.6 | 4.6 | 2.6 |
| North Carolina | 6,892 | 8,952 | 10,362 | 50.3 | 4.2 | 5.4 | 3.0 |
| South Carolina | 2,628 | 3,486 | 4,319 | 64.3 | 5.1 | 5.8 | 4.4 |
| Virginia | 6,853 | 8,924 | 10,836 | 58.1 | 4.7 | 5.4 | 4.0 |
| West Virginia | 1,620 | 1,951 | 2,159 | 33.3 | 2.9 | 3.8 | 2.0 |
| East South Central | 11,452 | 14,462 | 17,461 | 52.5 | 4.3 | 4.8 | 3.8 |
| Alabama | 2,832 | 3,622 | 4,383 | 54.8 | 4.5 | 5.0 | 3.9 |
| Kentucky | 2,927 | 3,642 | 4,286 | 46.4 | 3.9 | 4.5 | 3.3 |
| Mississippi | 1,499 | 1,907 | 2,286 | 52.5 | 4.3 | 4.9 | 3.7 |
| Tennessee | 4,194 | 5,291 | 6,506 | 55.1 | 4.5 | 4.8 | 4.2 |
| West South Central | 21,345 | 27,339 | 33,183 | 55.5 | 4.5 | 5.1 | 4.0 |
| Arkansas | 1,929 | 2,417 | 2,861 | 48.3 | 4.0 | 4.6 | 3.4 |
| Louisiana | 2,731 | 3,376 | 4,109 | 50.5 | 4.2 | 4.3 | 4.0 |
| Oklahoma | 2,717 | 3,318 | 3,923 | 44.4 | 3.7 | 4.1 | 3.4 |
| Texas | 13,968 | 18,228 | 22,290 | 59.6 | 4.8 | 5.5 | 4.1 |
| West | 56,214 | 72,029 | 85,443 | 52.0 | 4.3 | 5.1 | 3.5 |
| Mountain | 15,372 | 20,159 | 24,314 | 58.2 | 4.7 | 5.6 | 3.8 |
| Arizona | 3,411 | 4,583 | 5,484 | 60.8 | 4.9 | 6.1 | 3.7 |
| Colorado | 4,933 | 6,371 | 7,669 | 55.5 | 4.5 | 5.2 | 3.8 |
| Idaho | 967 | 1,332 | 1,656 | 71.3 | 5.5 | 6.6 | 4.5 |
| Montana | 1,371 | 1,756 | 2,111 | 54.0 | 4.4 | 5.1 | 3.8 |
| New Mexico | 1,811 | 2,190 | 2,590 | 43.0 | 3.6 | 3.9 | 3.4 |
| Nevada | 961 | 1,372 | 1,643 | 71.0 | 5.5 | 7.4 | 3.7 |
| Utah | 1,235 | 1,660 | 2,084 | 68.7 | 5.4 | 6.1 | 4.7 |
| Wyoming | 683 | 895 | 1,077 | 57.7 | 4.7 | 5.6 | 3.8 |

*(continued)*

**Table 5.27.** Change in the Number of Reporting Public Charities by State, 2000, 2005, and 2010 *(continued)*

|  | Number of Organizations | | | Total % Change | Average Annual % Change | | |
|---|---|---|---|---|---|---|---|
|  | 2000 | 2005 | 2010 | 2000–10 | 2000–10 | 2000–05 | 2005–10 |
| Pacific | 40,842 | 51,870 | 61,129 | 49.7 | 4.1 | 4.9 | 3.3 |
| Alaska | 1,023 | 1,292 | 1,480 | 44.7 | 3.8 | 4.8 | 2.8 |
| California | 28,589 | 36,067 | 42,481 | 48.6 | 4.0 | 4.8 | 3.3 |
| Hawaii | 1,231 | 1,567 | 1,916 | 55.6 | 4.5 | 4.9 | 4.1 |
| Oregon | 4,126 | 5,259 | 6,174 | 49.6 | 4.1 | 5.0 | 3.3 |
| Washington | 5,873 | 7,685 | 9,078 | 54.6 | 4.5 | 5.5 | 3.4 |

*Sources:* Urban Institute, National Center for Charitable Statistics, Core Files (Public Charities, 2000, 2005, and 2010).

**Table 5.28.** The 10 States with the Highest Growth in Number of Reporting Public Charities, 2000–10

| Rank | State | Reporting Public Charities | | % change in public charities, 2000–10 | % change in population, 2000–10 | Rank change in population, 2000–10 |
|---|---|---|---|---|---|---|
|  |  | 2000 | 2010 |  |  |  |
| 1 | Idaho | 967 | 1,656 | 71 | 21 | 4 |
| 2 | Nevada | 961 | 1,643 | 71 | 35 | 1 |
| 3 | Utah | 1,235 | 2,084 | 69 | 24 | 3 |
| 4 | Georgia | 5,342 | 9,014 | 69 | 18 | 7 |
| 5 | South Carolina | 2,628 | 4,319 | 64 | 15 | 10 |
| 6 | Florida | 10,233 | 16,560 | 62 | 18 | 8 |
| 7 | Arizona | 3,411 | 5,484 | 61 | 25 | 2 |
| 8 | Texas | 13,968 | 22,290 | 60 | 21 | 5 |
| 9 | Virginia | 6,853 | 10,836 | 58 | 13 | 16 |
| 10 | Wyoming | 683 | 1,077 | 58 | 14 | 12 |

*Sources:* Urban Institute, National Center for Charitable Statistics, Core Files (Public Charities, 2010); and U.S. Census Bureau, Statistical Abstract (2000, 2010).

**Table 5.29.  Change in Total Revenue for Reporting Public Charities by State, 2000, 2005, and 2010**

| | Total Revenue ($ millions) | | | Total % Change | Average Annual % Change | | |
|---|---|---|---|---|---|---|---|
| | 2000 | 2005 | 2010 | 2000–10 | 2000–10 | 2000–05 | 2005–10 |
| **United States** | **836,848** | **1,173,461** | **1,514,153** | **80.9** | **6.1** | **7.0** | **5.2** |
| Northeast | 255,826 | 336,091 | 427,427 | 67.1 | 5.3 | 5.6 | 4.9 |
| New England | 89,446 | 113,216 | 146,068 | 63.3 | 5.0 | 4.8 | 5.2 |
| Connecticut | 18,664 | 23,469 | 24,723 | 32.5 | 2.9 | 4.7 | 1.0 |
| Massachusetts | 52,991 | 65,121 | 90,273 | 70.4 | 5.5 | 4.2 | 6.7 |
| Maine | 4,983 | 7,573 | 9,628 | 93.2 | 6.8 | 8.7 | 4.9 |
| New Hampshire | 4,879 | 6,832 | 8,489 | 74.0 | 5.7 | 7.0 | 4.4 |
| Rhode Island | 5,491 | 7,378 | 9,071 | 65.2 | 5.1 | 6.1 | 4.2 |
| Vermont | 2,438 | 2,843 | 3,882 | 59.2 | 4.8 | 3.1 | 6.4 |
| Middle Atlantic | 166,380 | 222,874 | 281,359 | 69.1 | 5.4 | 6.0 | 4.8 |
| New Jersey | 25,696 | 31,830 | 37,954 | 47.7 | 4.0 | 4.4 | 3.6 |
| New York | 90,448 | 122,419 | 157,301 | 73.9 | 5.7 | 6.2 | 5.1 |
| Pennsylvania | 50,236 | 68,626 | 86,104 | 71.4 | 5.5 | 6.4 | 4.6 |
| Midwest | 200,393 | 273,836 | 350,689 | 75.0 | 5.8 | 6.4 | 5.1 |
| East North Central | 138,314 | 190,778 | 239,339 | 73.0 | 5.6 | 6.6 | 4.6 |
| Illinois | 40,943 | 53,821 | 66,047 | 61.3 | 4.9 | 5.6 | 4.2 |
| Indiana | 18,669 | 23,839 | 28,941 | 55.0 | 4.5 | 5.0 | 4.0 |
| Michigan | 28,162 | 35,513 | 43,646 | 55.0 | 4.5 | 4.7 | 4.2 |
| Ohio | 34,131 | 52,808 | 65,454 | 91.8 | 6.7 | 9.1 | 4.4 |
| Wisconsin | 16,408 | 24,797 | 35,252 | 114.8 | 7.9 | 8.6 | 7.3 |

| | | | | | | | |
|---|---|---|---|---|---|---|---|
| West North Central | 62,079 | 83,058 | 111,350 | 79.4 | 6.0 | 6.0 | 6.0 |
| Iowa | 7,475 | 9,579 | 11,888 | 59.0 | 4.7 | 5.1 | 4.4 |
| Kansas | 5,900 | 7,753 | 10,347 | 75.4 | 5.8 | 5.6 | 5.9 |
| Minnesota | 17,872 | 26,043 | 36,575 | 104.6 | 7.4 | 7.8 | 7.0 |
| Missouri | 19,266 | 25,518 | 33,478 | 73.8 | 5.7 | 5.8 | 5.6 |
| North Dakota | 3,080 | 2,852 | 4,271 | 38.7 | 3.3 | −1.5 | 8.4 |
| Nebraska | 5,381 | 7,303 | 9,388 | 74.5 | 5.7 | 6.3 | 5.2 |
| South Dakota | 3,105 | 4,010 | 5,402 | 74.0 | 5.7 | 5.2 | 6.1 |
| South | 225,706 | 328,108 | 416,764 | 84.6 | 6.3 | 7.8 | 4.9 |
| South Atlantic | 138,484 | 203,630 | 259,963 | 87.7 | 6.5 | 8.0 | 5.0 |
| District of Columbia | 17,603 | 22,972 | 29,160 | 65.7 | 5.2 | 5.5 | 4.9 |
| Delaware | 1,835 | 2,723 | 3,175 | 73.0 | 5.6 | 8.2 | 3.1 |
| Florida | 30,975 | 46,994 | 61,753 | 99.4 | 7.1 | 8.7 | 5.6 |
| Georgia | 18,958 | 28,722 | 34,922 | 84.2 | 6.3 | 8.7 | 4.0 |
| Maryland | 19,523 | 29,809 | 37,046 | 89.8 | 6.6 | 8.8 | 4.4 |
| North Carolina | 19,961 | 28,548 | 36,498 | 82.8 | 6.2 | 7.4 | 5.0 |
| South Carolina | 5,573 | 8,306 | 10,902 | 95.6 | 6.9 | 8.3 | 5.6 |
| Virginia | 19,725 | 29,789 | 39,202 | 98.7 | 7.1 | 8.6 | 5.6 |
| West Virginia | 4,331 | 5,766 | 7,305 | 68.7 | 5.4 | 5.9 | 4.8 |
| East South Central | 32,080 | 46,154 | 58,706 | 83.0 | 6.2 | 7.5 | 4.9 |
| Alabama | 6,192 | 8,335 | 9,191 | 48.4 | 4.0 | 6.1 | 2.0 |
| Kentucky | 9,103 | 13,806 | 18,864 | 107.2 | 7.6 | 8.7 | 6.4 |
| Mississippi | 3,710 | 5,201 | 6,110 | 64.7 | 5.1 | 7.0 | 3.3 |
| Tennessee | 13,075 | 18,813 | 24,542 | 87.7 | 6.5 | 7.5 | 5.5 |

(continued)

**Table 5.29.** Change in Total Revenue for Reporting Public Charities by State, 2000, 2005, and 2010 *(continued)*

| | Total Revenue ($ millions) | | | Total % Change | Average Annual % Change | | |
| | 2000 | 2005 | 2010 | 2000–10 | 2000–10 | 2000–05 | 2005–10 |
|---|---|---|---|---|---|---|---|
| West South Central | 55,142 | 78,324 | 98,095 | 77.9 | 5.9 | 7.3 | 4.6 |
| Arkansas | 5,610 | 9,641 | 7,681 | 36.9 | 3.2 | 11.4 | -4.4 |
| Louisiana | 7,465 | 9,604 | 15,863 | 112.5 | 7.8 | 5.2 | 10.6 |
| Oklahoma | 6,535 | 7,961 | 9,186 | 40.6 | 3.5 | 4.0 | 2.9 |
| Texas | 35,532 | 51,117 | 65,365 | 84.0 | 6.3 | 7.5 | 5.0 |
| West | 154,923 | 235,426 | 319,273 | 106.1 | 7.5 | 8.7 | 6.3 |
| Mountain | 29,064 | 44,778 | 72,080 | 148.0 | 9.5 | 9.0 | 10.0 |
| Arizona | 8,510 | 14,951 | 30,836 | 262.3 | 13.7 | 11.9 | 15.6 |
| Colorado | 9,419 | 13,055 | 19,255 | 104.4 | 7.4 | 6.7 | 8.1 |
| Idaho | 1,090 | 1,981 | 3,337 | 206.1 | 11.8 | 12.7 | 11.0 |
| Montana | 2,227 | 3,316 | 3,859 | 73.3 | 5.7 | 8.3 | 3.1 |
| New Mexico | 2,661 | 3,693 | 4,630 | 74.0 | 5.7 | 6.8 | 4.6 |
| Nevada | 1,314 | 2,659 | 2,744 | 108.9 | 7.6 | 15.1 | 0.6 |
| Utah | 3,390 | 4,252 | 6,292 | 85.6 | 6.4 | 4.6 | 8.2 |
| Wyoming | 454 | 871 | 1,127 | 148.3 | 9.5 | 13.9 | 5.3 |
| Pacific | 125,860 | 190,648 | 247,193 | 96.4 | 7.0 | 8.7 | 5.3 |
| Alaska | 1,612 | 2,200 | 2,983 | 85.0 | 6.3 | 6.4 | 6.3 |
| California | 74,753 | 143,477 | 186,606 | 149.6 | 9.6 | 13.9 | 5.4 |
| Hawaii | 3,983 | 5,108 | 4,937 | 24.0 | 2.2 | 5.1 | -0.7 |
| Oregon | 29,517 | 15,281 | 21,526 | -27.1 | -3.1 | -12.3 | 7.1 |
| Washington | 15,995 | 24,582 | 31,141 | 94.7 | 6.9 | 9.0 | 4.8 |

*Sources:* Urban Institute, National Center for Charitable Statistics, Core Files (Public Charities, 2000, 2005, and 2010).
*Notes:* Subtotals may not sum to totals because of rounding. Total revenue figures are shown in current dollars and are not adjusted for inflation. Oregon's revenue decline in 2005 was the result of Kaiser Foundation Health Plan moving to California.

**Table 5.30.** The 10 States with the Highest Growth in Total Revenue Reported by Public Charities, 2000–10

| Rank | State | Total revenue for reporting public charities, 2000 ($ millions) | Total revenue for reporting public charities, 2010 ($ millions) | % change, 2000–10 | % change, 2000–10 (inflation adjusted) |
|---|---|---|---|---|---|
| 1 | Arizona | 8,510 | 30,836 | 262 | 181 |
| 2 | Idaho | 1,090 | 3,337 | 206 | 138 |
| 3 | California | 74,753 | 186,606 | 150 | 97 |
| 4 | Wyoming | 454 | 1,127 | 148 | 93 |
| 5 | Wisconsin | 16,408 | 35,252 | 115 | 67 |
| 6 | Louisiana | 7,465 | 15,863 | 113 | 65 |
| 7 | Nevada | 1,314 | 2,744 | 109 | 62 |
| 8 | Kentucky | 9,103 | 18,864 | 107 | 61 |
| 9 | Minnesota | 17,872 | 36,575 | 105 | 59 |
| 10 | Colorado | 9,419 | 19,255 | 104 | 59 |

*Sources:* Urban Institute, National Center for Charitable Statistics, Core Files (Public Charities, 2000 and 2010).
*Note:* Total revenue figures are shown in current dollars and are not adjusted for inflation.

117 percent (71 percent after adjusting for inflation). Arizona (195 percent), Idaho (164 percent), Wyoming (136 percent), California (113 percent), and Virginia (77 percent) saw the greatest increases in expenses after adjusting for inflation (table 5.34). Arkansas showed the slowest growth over the 10 years at 8 percent after adjusting for inflation.

Total assets for reporting public charities increased from $1.50 trillion in 2000 to $2.71 trillion in 2010 (table 5.35), an inflation-adjusted 43 percent increase. The West saw the greatest increase in assets, growing 104 percent (61 percent after adjusting for inflation). The top five states in asset growth are Louisiana (173 percent after adjusting for inflation), Delaware (152 percent), Arizona (152 percent), Wyoming (85 percent), and Utah (83 percent; table 5.36). Connecticut showed the least growth at 12 percent, −12 percent after adjusting for inflation.

Net assets (assets minus liabilities) of public charities grew by 60 percent (26 percent after adjusting for inflation) from 2000 to 2010 (table 5.37). The West saw the greatest increase by far at 93 percent (53 percent after adjusting for inflation). Louisiana (246 percent after adjusting for inflation), Arizona (124 percent after adjusting for inflation), Wyoming (95 percent after adjusting for inflation), Alaska (77 percent after adjusting for inflation), and Utah (73 percent after adjusting for inflation) saw the greatest growth in net assets among the states. Connecticut showed negative growth in net assets at −10 percent (−29 percent after adjusting for inflation) (table 5.38).

**Table 5.31.** Change in Public Support for Reporting Public Charities by State, 2000, 2005, and 2010

| | Public Support ($ millions) | | | Total % Change | Average Annual % Change | | |
|---|---|---|---|---|---|---|---|
| | 2000 | 2005 | 2010 | 2000–10 | 2000–10 | 2000–05 | 2005–10 |
| **United States** | **183,386** | **255,229** | **327,816** | **78.8** | **6.0** | **6.8** | **5.1** |
| Northeast | 54,009 | 73,202 | 93,457 | 73.0 | 5.6 | 6.3 | 5.0 |
| New England | 18,373 | 25,568 | 33,567 | 82.7 | 6.2 | 6.8 | 5.6 |
| Connecticut | 3,226 | 5,613 | 5,664 | 75.6 | 5.8 | 11.7 | 0.2 |
| Massachusetts | 11,913 | 15,679 | 23,038 | 93.4 | 6.8 | 5.6 | 8.0 |
| Maine | 867 | 1,113 | 1,185 | 36.7 | 3.2 | 5.1 | 1.3 |
| New Hampshire | 768 | 1,036 | 1,155 | 50.5 | 4.2 | 6.2 | 2.2 |
| Rhode Island | 1,034 | 1,535 | 1,810 | 75.0 | 5.8 | 8.2 | 3.4 |
| Vermont | 565 | 592 | 714 | 26.3 | 2.4 | 0.9 | 3.8 |
| Middle Atlantic | 35,636 | 47,634 | 59,890 | 68.1 | 5.3 | 6.0 | 4.7 |
| New Jersey | 4,132 | 5,399 | 6,618 | 60.2 | 4.8 | 5.5 | 4.2 |
| New York | 22,695 | 29,773 | 37,746 | 66.3 | 5.2 | 5.6 | 4.9 |
| Pennsylvania | 8,809 | 12,462 | 15,526 | 76.2 | 5.8 | 7.2 | 4.5 |
| Midwest | 35,837 | 46,839 | 55,686 | 55.4 | 4.5 | 5.5 | 3.5 |
| East North Central | 24,596 | 33,146 | 38,160 | 55.1 | 4.5 | 6.1 | 2.9 |
| Illinois | 8,074 | 10,320 | 13,236 | 63.9 | 5.1 | 5.0 | 5.1 |
| Indiana | 3,229 | 3,701 | 4,481 | 38.8 | 3.3 | 2.8 | 3.9 |
| Michigan | 4,376 | 5,357 | 6,032 | 37.8 | 3.3 | 4.1 | 2.4 |
| Ohio | 6,413 | 10,552 | 10,212 | 59.2 | 4.8 | 10.5 | −0.7 |
| Wisconsin | 2,504 | 3,216 | 4,200 | 67.7 | 5.3 | 5.1 | 5.5 |
| West North Central | 11,240 | 13,693 | 17,526 | 55.9 | 4.5 | 4.0 | 5.1 |
| Iowa | 1,317 | 1,466 | 2,097 | 59.3 | 4.8 | 2.2 | 7.4 |
| Kansas | 1,155 | 1,481 | 1,667 | 44.3 | 3.7 | 5.1 | 2.4 |
| Minnesota | 3,529 | 4,153 | 5,485 | 55.4 | 4.5 | 3.3 | 5.7 |
| Missouri | 3,660 | 4,414 | 5,473 | 49.5 | 4.1 | 3.8 | 4.4 |
| North Dakota | 251 | 332 | 441 | 75.9 | 5.8 | 5.8 | 5.8 |
| Nebraska | 939 | 1,294 | 1,640 | 74.6 | 5.7 | 6.6 | 4.9 |
| South Dakota | 389 | 553 | 722 | 85.7 | 6.4 | 7.3 | 5.5 |

*(continued)*

**Table 5.31.** Change in Public Support for Reporting Public Charities by State, 2000, 2005, and 2010 *(continued)*

| | Public Support ($ millions) | | | Total % Change | Average Annual % Change | | |
|---|---|---|---|---|---|---|---|
| | 2000 | 2005 | 2010 | 2000–10 | 2000–10 | 2000–05 | 2005–10 |
| South | 57,070 | 84,155 | 111,464 | 95.3 | 6.9 | 8.1 | 5.8 |
| South Atlantic | 38,080 | 58,008 | 74,967 | 96.9 | 7.0 | 8.8 | 5.3 |
| District of Columbia | 7,848 | 11,923 | 15,528 | 97.9 | 7.1 | 8.7 | 5.4 |
| Delaware | 448 | 630 | 940 | 110.0 | 7.7 | 7.1 | 8.3 |
| Florida | 7,479 | 12,137 | 15,810 | 111.4 | 7.8 | 10.2 | 5.4 |
| Georgia | 5,530 | 7,848 | 9,554 | 72.8 | 5.6 | 7.3 | 4.0 |
| Maryland | 3,963 | 5,715 | 8,526 | 115.1 | 8.0 | 7.6 | 8.3 |
| North Carolina | 4,838 | 7,380 | 9,202 | 90.2 | 6.6 | 8.8 | 4.5 |
| South Carolina | 1,256 | 1,813 | 2,369 | 88.6 | 6.6 | 7.6 | 5.5 |
| Virginia | 6,055 | 9,642 | 12,001 | 98.2 | 7.1 | 9.7 | 4.5 |
| West Virginia | 664 | 921 | 1,037 | 56.1 | 4.6 | 6.8 | 2.4 |
| East South Central | 6,818 | 9,038 | 12,373 | 81.5 | 6.1 | 5.8 | 6.5 |
| Alabama | 1,341 | 1,748 | 2,557 | 90.6 | 6.7 | 5.4 | 7.9 |
| Kentucky | 1,463 | 1,972 | 2,588 | 76.9 | 5.9 | 6.2 | 5.6 |
| Mississippi | 977 | 1,198 | 1,490 | 52.6 | 4.3 | 4.2 | 4.5 |
| Tennessee | 3,037 | 4,119 | 5,738 | 88.9 | 6.6 | 6.3 | 6.9 |
| West South Central | 12,172 | 17,109 | 24,124 | 98.2 | 7.1 | 7.0 | 7.1 |
| Arkansas | 922 | 1,334 | 1,908 | 106.9 | 7.5 | 7.7 | 7.4 |
| Louisiana | 1,311 | 1,802 | 2,960 | 125.8 | 8.5 | 6.6 | 10.4 |
| Oklahoma | 1,928 | 2,683 | 3,140 | 62.9 | 5.0 | 6.8 | 3.2 |
| Texas | 8,010 | 11,289 | 16,115 | 101.2 | 7.2 | 7.1 | 7.4 |
| West | 36,471 | 51,034 | 67,209 | 84.3 | 6.3 | 7.0 | 5.7 |
| Mountain | 7,505 | 10,834 | 15,630 | 108.3 | 7.6 | 7.6 | 7.6 |
| Arizona | 2,085 | 3,308 | 4,812 | 130.8 | 8.7 | 9.7 | 7.8 |
| Colorado | 2,627 | 3,683 | 5,269 | 100.6 | 7.2 | 7.0 | 7.4 |
| Idaho | 289 | 406 | 680 | 135.3 | 8.9 | 7.0 | 10.9 |
| Montana | 429 | 597 | 836 | 94.7 | 6.9 | 6.8 | 6.9 |
| New Mexico | 783 | 1,050 | 1,244 | 59.0 | 4.7 | 6.1 | 3.4 |
| Nevada | 434 | 693 | 998 | 130.1 | 8.7 | 9.8 | 7.6 |
| Utah | 639 | 726 | 1,312 | 105.3 | 7.5 | 2.6 | 12.5 |
| Wyoming | 220 | 370 | 479 | 118.3 | 8.1 | 11.0 | 5.3 |

*(continued)*

**Table 5.31.** Change in Public Support for Reporting Public Charities by State, 2000, 2005, and 2010 *(continued)*

| | Public Support ($ millions) | | | Total % Change | Average Annual % Change | | |
|---|---|---|---|---|---|---|---|
| | 2000 | 2005 | 2010 | 2000–10 | 2000–10 | 2000–05 | 2005–10 |
| Pacific | 28,966 | 40,199 | 51,579 | 78.1 | 5.9 | 6.8 | 5.1 |
| Alaska | 994 | 1,226 | 1,682 | 69.1 | 5.4 | 4.3 | 6.5 |
| California | 21,972 | 30,126 | 38,768 | 76.4 | 5.8 | 6.5 | 5.2 |
| Hawaii | 740 | 903 | 1,173 | 58.5 | 4.7 | 4.0 | 5.4 |
| Oregon | 1,678 | 2,613 | 3,339 | 98.9 | 7.1 | 9.3 | 5.0 |
| Washington | 3,581 | 5,332 | 6,617 | 84.8 | 6.3 | 8.3 | 4.4 |

*Sources:* Urban Institute, National Center for Charitable Statistics, Core Files (Public Charities, 2000, 2005, and 2010).
*Notes:* Subtotals may not sum to totals because of rounding. Public support figures are shown in current dollars and are not adjusted for inflation.

**Table 5.32.** The 10 States with the Highest Growth in Public Support Reported by Public Charities, 2000–10

| Rank | State | Public support for reporting public charities, 2000 ($ millions) | Public support for reporting public charities, 2010 ($ millions) | % change, 2000–10 | % change, 2000–10 (inflation adjusted) |
|---|---|---|---|---|---|
| 1 | Idaho | 289 | 680 | 135 | 86 |
| 2 | Arizona | 2,085 | 4,812 | 131 | 82 |
| 3 | Nevada | 434 | 998 | 130 | 82 |
| 4 | Louisiana | 1,311 | 2,960 | 126 | 78 |
| 5 | Wyoming | 220 | 479 | 118 | 72 |
| 6 | Maryland | 3,963 | 8,526 | 115 | 70 |
| 7 | Florida | 7,479 | 15,810 | 111 | 67 |
| 8 | Delaware | 448 | 940 | 110 | 66 |
| 9 | Arkansas | 922 | 1,908 | 107 | 63 |
| 10 | Utah | 639 | 1,312 | 105 | 62 |

*Sources:* Urban Institute, National Center for Charitable Statistics, Core Files (Public Charities, 2000 and 2010).
*Note:* Public support figures are shown in current dollars and are not adjusted for inflation.

**Table 5.33.** Change in Total Expenses for Reporting Public Charities by State, 2000, 2005, and 2010

| | Total Expenses ($ millions) | | | Total % Change | Average Annual % Change | | |
|---|---|---|---|---|---|---|---|
| | 2000 | 2005 | 2010 | 2000–10 | 2000–10 | 2000–05 | 2005–10 |
| **United States** | **749,866** | **1,077,696** | **1,454,753** | **94.0** | **6.9** | **7.5** | **6.2** |
| Northeast | 223,700 | 307,432 | 415,687 | 85.8 | 6.4 | 6.6 | 6.2 |
| New England | 71,687 | 98,021 | 142,952 | 99.4 | 7.1 | 6.5 | 7.8 |
| Connecticut | 13,794 | 19,598 | 23,985 | 73.9 | 5.7 | 7.3 | 4.1 |
| Massachusetts | 42,120 | 55,874 | 88,737 | 110.7 | 7.7 | 5.8 | 9.7 |
| Maine | 4,497 | 6,948 | 9,277 | 106.3 | 7.5 | 9.1 | 6.0 |
| New Hampshire | 4,013 | 6,164 | 8,449 | 110.5 | 7.7 | 9.0 | 6.5 |
| Rhode Island | 5,063 | 6,739 | 8,745 | 72.7 | 5.6 | 5.9 | 5.3 |
| Vermont | 2,201 | 2,698 | 3,760 | 70.8 | 5.5 | 4.2 | 6.9 |
| Middle Atlantic | 152,013 | 209,411 | 272,735 | 79.4 | 6.0 | 6.6 | 5.4 |
| New Jersey | 23,188 | 29,993 | 37,173 | 60.3 | 4.8 | 5.3 | 4.4 |
| New York | 82,127 | 115,366 | 152,390 | 85.6 | 6.4 | 7.0 | 5.7 |
| Pennsylvania | 46,698 | 64,052 | 83,172 | 78.1 | 5.9 | 6.5 | 5.4 |
| Midwest | 180,968 | 254,398 | 333,511 | 84.3 | 6.3 | 7.0 | 5.6 |
| East North Central | 124,284 | 177,542 | 227,180 | 82.8 | 6.2 | 7.4 | 5.1 |
| Illinois | 36,537 | 49,645 | 62,801 | 71.9 | 5.6 | 6.3 | 4.8 |
| Indiana | 15,503 | 22,061 | 26,987 | 74.1 | 5.7 | 7.3 | 4.1 |
| Michigan | 26,533 | 33,500 | 41,706 | 57.2 | 4.6 | 4.8 | 4.5 |
| Ohio | 30,820 | 49,572 | 62,417 | 102.5 | 7.3 | 10.0 | 4.7 |
| Wisconsin | 14,891 | 22,764 | 33,268 | 123.4 | 8.4 | 8.9 | 7.9 |
| West North Central | 56,684 | 76,856 | 106,332 | 87.6 | 6.5 | 6.3 | 6.7 |
| Iowa | 6,829 | 8,870 | 11,278 | 65.1 | 5.1 | 5.4 | 4.9 |
| Kansas | 5,394 | 7,039 | 9,978 | 85.0 | 6.3 | 5.5 | 7.2 |
| Minnesota | 16,157 | 24,303 | 35,094 | 117.2 | 8.1 | 8.5 | 7.6 |
| Missouri | 17,615 | 23,590 | 31,991 | 81.6 | 6.1 | 6.0 | 6.3 |
| North Dakota | 2,924 | 2,714 | 4,067 | 39.1 | 3.4 | −1.5 | 8.4 |
| Nebraska | 4,898 | 6,656 | 8,855 | 80.8 | 6.1 | 6.3 | 5.9 |
| South Dakota | 2,867 | 3,684 | 5,069 | 76.8 | 5.9 | 5.1 | 6.6 |

*(continued)*

**Table 5.33.** Change in Total Expenses for Reporting Public Charities by State, 2000, 2005, and 2010 *(continued)*

| | Total Expenses ($ millions) | | | Total % Change | Average Annual % Change | | |
|---|---|---|---|---|---|---|---|
| | 2000 | 2005 | 2010 | 2000–10 | 2000–10 | 2000–05 | 2005–10 |
| South | 203,702 | 299,429 | 398,891 | 95.8 | 7.0 | 8.0 | 5.9 |
| South Atlantic | 124,476 | 184,206 | 249,475 | 100.4 | 7.2 | 8.2 | 6.3 |
| District of Columbia | 16,126 | 20,496 | 26,898 | 66.8 | 5.2 | 4.9 | 5.6 |
| Delaware | 1,591 | 2,520 | 3,130 | 96.8 | 7.0 | 9.6 | 4.4 |
| Florida | 29,683 | 43,240 | 58,995 | 98.7 | 7.1 | 7.8 | 6.4 |
| Georgia | 16,823 | 25,670 | 33,946 | 101.8 | 7.3 | 8.8 | 5.7 |
| Maryland | 16,913 | 26,542 | 36,443 | 115.5 | 8.0 | 9.4 | 6.5 |
| North Carolina | 17,164 | 25,798 | 34,609 | 101.6 | 7.3 | 8.5 | 6.1 |
| South Carolina | 5,176 | 7,659 | 10,363 | 100.2 | 7.2 | 8.2 | 6.2 |
| Virginia | 16,926 | 26,755 | 37,893 | 123.9 | 8.4 | 9.6 | 7.2 |
| West Virginia | 4,074 | 5,527 | 7,198 | 76.7 | 5.9 | 6.3 | 5.4 |
| East South Central | 29,517 | 42,990 | 56,439 | 91.2 | 6.7 | 7.8 | 5.6 |
| Alabama | 5,799 | 7,615 | 8,950 | 54.3 | 4.4 | 5.6 | 3.3 |
| Kentucky | 8,473 | 12,993 | 18,284 | 115.8 | 8.0 | 8.9 | 7.1 |
| Mississippi | 3,302 | 4,837 | 5,757 | 74.4 | 5.7 | 7.9 | 3.5 |
| Tennessee | 11,943 | 17,545 | 23,448 | 96.3 | 7.0 | 8.0 | 6.0 |
| West South Central | 49,709 | 72,233 | 92,977 | 87.0 | 6.5 | 7.8 | 5.2 |
| Arkansas | 5,294 | 9,176 | 7,243 | 36.8 | 3.2 | 11.6 | −4.6 |
| Louisiana | 6,883 | 9,116 | 15,249 | 121.5 | 8.3 | 5.8 | 10.8 |
| Oklahoma | 5,824 | 6,985 | 8,599 | 47.6 | 4.0 | 3.7 | 4.2 |
| Texas | 31,707 | 46,957 | 61,887 | 95.2 | 6.9 | 8.2 | 5.7 |
| West | 141,496 | 216,437 | 306,664 | 116.7 | 8.0 | 8.9 | 7.2 |
| Mountain | 26,455 | 40,616 | 68,243 | 158.0 | 9.9 | 9.0 | 10.9 |
| Arizona | 7,944 | 13,584 | 29,648 | 273.2 | 14.1 | 11.3 | 16.9 |
| Colorado | 8,273 | 11,928 | 18,067 | 118.4 | 8.1 | 7.6 | 8.7 |
| Idaho | 953 | 1,808 | 3,188 | 234.7 | 12.8 | 13.7 | 12.0 |
| Montana | 2,062 | 3,078 | 3,642 | 76.6 | 5.9 | 8.3 | 3.4 |
| New Mexico | 2,487 | 3,401 | 4,379 | 76.1 | 5.8 | 6.5 | 5.2 |
| Nevada | 1,166 | 2,151 | 2,561 | 119.5 | 8.2 | 13.0 | 3.6 |
| Utah | 3,211 | 3,902 | 5,687 | 77.1 | 5.9 | 4.0 | 7.8 |
| Wyoming | 358 | 764 | 1,072 | 199.1 | 11.6 | 16.3 | 7.0 |

*(continued)*

**Table 5.33.** Change in Total Expenses for Reporting Public Charities by State, 2000, 2005, and 2010 *(continued)*

|  | Total Expenses ($ millions) | | | Total % Change | Average Annual % Change | | |
|---|---|---|---|---|---|---|---|
|  | 2000 | 2005 | 2010 | 2000–10 | 2000–10 | 2000–05 | 2005–10 |
| Pacific | 115,041 | 175,821 | 238,421 | 107.2 | 7.6 | 8.9 | 6.3 |
| Alaska | 1,427 | 2,094 | 2,762 | 93.6 | 6.8 | 8.0 | 5.7 |
| California | 66,688 | 132,157 | 179,796 | 169.6 | 10.4 | 14.7 | 6.4 |
| Hawaii | 3,025 | 4,366 | 4,704 | 55.5 | 4.5 | 7.6 | 1.5 |
| Oregon | 29,288 | 14,384 | 21,003 | −28.3 | −3.3 | −13.3 | 7.9 |
| Washington | 14,614 | 22,820 | 30,155 | 106.3 | 7.5 | 9.3 | 5.7 |

*Sources:* Urban Institute, National Center for Charitable Statistics, Core Files (Public Charities, 2000, 2005, and 2010).
*Notes:* Subtotals may not sum to totals because of rounding. Total expenses are shown in current dollars and are not adjusted for inflation.

**Table 5.34.** The 10 States with the Highest Growth in Expenses Reported by Public Charities, 2000–10

| Rank | State | Total expenses for reporting public charities, 2000 ($ millions) | Total expenses for reporting public charities, 2010 ($ millions) | % change, 2000–10 | % change, 2000–10 (inflation adjusted) |
|---|---|---|---|---|---|
| 1 | Arizona | 7,944 | 29,648 | 273 | 195 |
| 2 | Idaho | 953 | 3,188 | 235 | 164 |
| 3 | Wyoming | 358 | 1,072 | 199 | 136 |
| 4 | California | 66,688 | 179,796 | 170 | 113 |
| 5 | Virginia | 16,926 | 37,893 | 124 | 77 |
| 6 | Wisconsin | 14,891 | 33,268 | 123 | 76 |
| 7 | Louisiana | 6,883 | 15,249 | 122 | 75 |
| 8 | Nevada | 1,166 | 2,561 | 120 | 73 |
| 9 | Colorado | 8,273 | 18,067 | 118 | 72 |
| 10 | Minnesota | 16,157 | 35,094 | 117 | 72 |

*Sources:* Urban Institute, National Center for Charitable Statistics, Core Files (Public Charities, 2000 and 2010).
*Note:* Total expenses are shown in current dollars and are not adjusted for inflation.

**Table 5.35.** Change in Total Assets for Reporting Public Charities by State, 2000, 2005, and 2010

| | Total Assets ($ millions) | | | Total % Change | Average Annual % Change | | |
| --- | --- | --- | --- | --- | --- | --- | --- |
| | 2000 | 2005 | 2010 | 2000–10 | 2000–10 | 2000–05 | 2005–10 |
| **United States** | **1,500,161** | **2,065,822** | **2,708,905** | **80.6** | **6.1** | **6.6** | **5.6** |
| Northeast | 480,635 | 643,836 | 806,978 | 67.9 | 5.3 | 6.0 | 4.6 |
| New England | 200,704 | 275,674 | 334,457 | 66.6 | 5.2 | 6.6 | 3.9 |
| Connecticut | 60,124 | 63,399 | 67,056 | 11.5 | 1.1 | 1.1 | 1.1 |
| Massachusetts | 108,807 | 169,496 | 212,770 | 95.5 | 6.9 | 9.3 | 4.7 |
| Maine | 7,539 | 10,276 | 13,496 | 79.0 | 6.0 | 6.4 | 5.6 |
| New Hampshire | 10,986 | 14,907 | 19,699 | 79.3 | 6.0 | 6.3 | 5.7 |
| Rhode Island | 8,676 | 12,625 | 14,995 | 72.8 | 5.6 | 7.8 | 3.5 |
| Vermont | 4,572 | 4,971 | 6,440 | 40.8 | 3.5 | 1.7 | 5.3 |
| Middle Atlantic | 279,931 | 368,162 | 472,521 | 68.8 | 5.4 | 5.6 | 5.1 |
| New Jersey | 39,961 | 54,148 | 69,335 | 73.5 | 5.7 | 6.3 | 5.1 |
| New York | 148,763 | 193,697 | 249,685 | 67.8 | 5.3 | 5.4 | 5.2 |
| Pennsylvania | 91,208 | 120,317 | 153,501 | 68.3 | 5.3 | 5.7 | 5.0 |
| Midwest | 359,343 | 490,226 | 616,358 | 71.5 | 5.5 | 6.4 | 4.7 |
| East North Central | 247,662 | 332,620 | 412,402 | 66.5 | 5.2 | 6.1 | 4.4 |
| Illinois | 78,757 | 102,547 | 121,227 | 53.9 | 4.4 | 5.4 | 3.4 |
| Indiana | 36,325 | 45,028 | 56,289 | 55.0 | 4.5 | 4.4 | 4.6 |
| Michigan | 38,237 | 54,539 | 66,937 | 75.1 | 5.8 | 7.4 | 4.2 |
| Ohio | 69,526 | 91,624 | 112,854 | 62.3 | 5.0 | 5.7 | 4.3 |
| Wisconsin | 24,818 | 38,882 | 55,095 | 122.0 | 8.3 | 9.4 | 7.2 |
| West North Central | 111,681 | 157,606 | 203,956 | 82.6 | 6.2 | 7.1 | 5.3 |
| Iowa | 15,008 | 21,713 | 27,021 | 80.0 | 6.1 | 7.7 | 4.5 |
| Kansas | 9,367 | 12,502 | 16,917 | 80.6 | 6.1 | 5.9 | 6.2 |
| Minnesota | 30,881 | 47,135 | 63,041 | 104.1 | 7.4 | 8.8 | 6.0 |
| Missouri | 37,126 | 52,689 | 64,688 | 74.2 | 5.7 | 7.3 | 4.2 |
| North Dakota | 4,720 | 3,746 | 5,383 | 14.0 | 1.3 | −4.5 | 7.5 |
| Nebraska | 10,238 | 13,611 | 18,116 | 77.0 | 5.9 | 5.9 | 5.9 |
| South Dakota | 4,340 | 6,209 | 8,790 | 102.5 | 7.3 | 7.4 | 7.2 |

*(continued)*

Table 5.35. Change in Total Assets for Reporting Public Charities by State, 2000, 2005, and 2010 *(continued)*

| | Total Assets ($ millions) | | | Total % Change | Average Annual % Change | | |
|---|---|---|---|---|---|---|---|
| | 2000 | 2005 | 2010 | 2000–10 | 2000–10 | 2000–05 | 2005–10 |
| South | 422,855 | 594,083 | 802,711 | 89.8 | 6.6 | 7.0 | 6.2 |
| South Atlantic | 263,758 | 375,888 | 489,879 | 85.7 | 6.4 | 7.3 | 5.4 |
| District of Columbia | 26,618 | 35,267 | 43,701 | 64.2 | 5.1 | 5.8 | 4.4 |
| Delaware | 5,309 | 12,614 | 16,967 | 219.6 | 12.3 | 18.9 | 6.1 |
| Florida | 53,538 | 75,114 | 99,991 | 86.8 | 6.4 | 7.0 | 5.9 |
| Georgia | 37,286 | 51,715 | 67,599 | 81.3 | 6.1 | 6.8 | 5.5 |
| Maryland | 45,415 | 59,397 | 79,039 | 74.0 | 5.7 | 5.5 | 5.9 |
| North Carolina | 38,657 | 55,332 | 72,141 | 86.6 | 6.4 | 7.4 | 5.4 |
| South Carolina | 12,580 | 17,842 | 22,803 | 81.3 | 6.1 | 7.2 | 5.0 |
| Virginia | 38,493 | 60,830 | 77,948 | 102.5 | 7.3 | 9.6 | 5.1 |
| West Virginia | 5,863 | 7,776 | 9,689 | 65.3 | 5.2 | 5.8 | 4.5 |
| East South Central | 57,291 | 80,851 | 99,700 | 74.0 | 5.7 | 7.1 | 4.3 |
| Alabama | 11,523 | 14,139 | 16,377 | 42.1 | 3.6 | 4.2 | 3.0 |
| Kentucky | 15,117 | 20,859 | 25,112 | 66.1 | 5.2 | 6.7 | 3.8 |
| Mississippi | 6,580 | 8,808 | 10,571 | 60.6 | 4.9 | 6.0 | 3.7 |
| Tennessee | 24,070 | 37,044 | 47,640 | 97.9 | 7.1 | 9.0 | 5.2 |
| West South Central | 101,806 | 137,345 | 213,132 | 109.4 | 7.7 | 6.2 | 9.2 |
| Arkansas | 6,347 | 8,961 | 11,015 | 73.6 | 5.7 | 7.1 | 4.2 |
| Louisiana | 13,122 | 15,430 | 45,363 | 245.7 | 13.2 | 3.3 | 24.1 |
| Oklahoma | 11,934 | 16,206 | 22,690 | 90.1 | 6.6 | 6.3 | 7.0 |
| Texas | 70,404 | 96,748 | 134,063 | 90.4 | 6.7 | 6.6 | 6.7 |
| West | 237,328 | 337,677 | 482,857 | 103.5 | 7.4 | 7.3 | 7.4 |
| Mountain | 47,265 | 69,001 | 112,127 | 137.2 | 9.0 | 7.9 | 10.2 |
| Arizona | 11,651 | 18,243 | 37,109 | 218.5 | 12.3 | 9.4 | 15.3 |
| Colorado | 17,099 | 22,830 | 36,753 | 114.9 | 8.0 | 6.0 | 10.0 |
| Idaho | 2,369 | 3,174 | 5,196 | 119.3 | 8.2 | 6.0 | 10.4 |
| Montana | 3,585 | 5,779 | 6,856 | 91.2 | 6.7 | 10.0 | 3.5 |
| New Mexico | 4,543 | 5,947 | 8,936 | 96.7 | 7.0 | 5.5 | 8.5 |
| Nevada | 2,836 | 4,691 | 5,247 | 85.0 | 6.3 | 10.6 | 2.3 |
| Utah | 4,083 | 6,305 | 9,461 | 131.7 | 8.8 | 9.1 | 8.5 |
| Wyoming | 1,098 | 2,032 | 2,570 | 134.0 | 8.9 | 13.1 | 4.8 |

*(continued)*

**Table 5.35.** Change in Total Assets for Reporting Public Charities by State, 2000, 2005, and 2010 *(continued)*

| | Total Assets ($ millions) | | | Total % Change | Average Annual % Change | | |
|---|---|---|---|---|---|---|---|
| | 2000 | 2005 | 2010 | 2000–10 | 2000–10 | 2000–05 | 2005–10 |
| Pacific | 190,063 | 268,676 | 370,730 | 95.1 | 6.9 | 7.2 | 6.7 |
| Alaska | 1,895 | 2,981 | 4,044 | 113.4 | 7.9 | 9.5 | 6.3 |
| California | 127,581 | 202,468 | 281,307 | 120.5 | 8.2 | 9.7 | 6.8 |
| Hawaii | 10,737 | 13,121 | 15,119 | 40.8 | 3.5 | 4.1 | 2.9 |
| Oregon | 27,062 | 17,015 | 25,629 | −5.3 | −0.5 | −8.9 | 8.5 |
| Washington | 22,788 | 33,091 | 44,631 | 95.9 | 7.0 | 7.7 | 6.2 |

*Sources:* Urban Institute, National Center for Charitable Statistics, Core Files (Public Charities, 2000, 2005, and 2010).
*Notes:* Subtotals may not sum to the total because of rounding. Total assets are shown in current dollars and are not adjusted for inflation.

**Table 5.36.** The 10 States with the Highest Growth in Assets Reported by Public Charities, 2000–10

| Rank | State | Total assets for reporting public charities, 2000 ($ millions) | Total assets for reporting public charities, 2010 ($ millions) | % change, 2000–10 | % change, 2000–10 (inflation adjusted) |
|---|---|---|---|---|---|
| 1 | Louisiana | 13,122 | 45,363 | 246 | 173 |
| 2 | Delaware | 5,309 | 16,967 | 220 | 152 |
| 3 | Arizona | 11,651 | 37,109 | 219 | 152 |
| 4 | Wyoming | 1,098 | 2,570 | 134 | 85 |
| 5 | Utah | 4,083 | 9,461 | 132 | 83 |
| 6 | Wisconsin | 24,818 | 55,095 | 122 | 75 |
| 7 | California | 127,581 | 281,307 | 121 | 74 |
| 8 | Idaho | 2,369 | 5,196 | 119 | 73 |
| 9 | Colorado | 17,099 | 36,753 | 115 | 70 |
| 10 | Alaska | 1,895 | 4,044 | 113 | 69 |

*Sources:* Urban Institute, National Center for Charitable Statistics, Core Files (Public Charities, 2000 and 2010).
*Note:* Total assets are shown in current dollars and are not adjusted for inflation.

**Table 5.37.** Change in Net Assets for Reporting Public Charities by State, 2000, 2005, and 2010

| | Net Assets ($ millions) | | | Total % Change | Average Annual % Change | | |
|---|---|---|---|---|---|---|---|
| | 2000 | 2005 | 2010 | 2000–10 | 2000–10 | 2000–05 | 2005–10 |
| **United States** | **1,001,081** | **1,290,687** | **1,598,057** | **59.6** | **4.8** | **5.2** | **4.4** |
| Northeast | 335,266 | 413,534 | 488,290 | 45.6 | 3.8 | 4.3 | 3.4 |
| New England | 155,389 | 189,626 | 220,840 | 42.1 | 3.6 | 4.1 | 3.1 |
| Connecticut | 50,080 | 50,426 | 45,142 | −9.9 | −1.0 | 0.1 | −2.2 |
| Massachusetts | 83,204 | 110,136 | 141,129 | 69.6 | 5.4 | 5.8 | 5.1 |
| Maine | 4,936 | 7,092 | 8,876 | 79.8 | 6.0 | 7.5 | 4.6 |
| New Hampshire | 7,760 | 9,451 | 11,376 | 46.6 | 3.9 | 4.0 | 3.8 |
| Rhode Island | 6,255 | 9,158 | 10,173 | 62.6 | 5.0 | 7.9 | 2.1 |
| Vermont | 3,154 | 3,362 | 4,145 | 31.4 | 2.8 | 1.3 | 4.3 |
| Middle Atlantic | 179,876 | 223,908 | 267,449 | 48.7 | 4.0 | 4.5 | 3.6 |
| New Jersey | 25,497 | 32,819 | 39,844 | 56.3 | 4.6 | 5.2 | 4.0 |
| New York | 96,106 | 117,637 | 138,246 | 43.8 | 3.7 | 4.1 | 3.3 |
| Pennsylvania | 58,273 | 73,451 | 89,360 | 53.3 | 4.4 | 4.7 | 4.0 |
| Midwest | 236,593 | 299,603 | 357,245 | 51.0 | 4.2 | 4.8 | 3.6 |
| East North Central | 164,799 | 206,127 | 242,087 | 46.9 | 3.9 | 4.6 | 3.3 |
| Illinois | 52,900 | 63,405 | 69,099 | 30.6 | 2.7 | 3.7 | 1.7 |
| Indiana | 25,369 | 30,314 | 37,067 | 46.1 | 3.9 | 3.6 | 4.1 |
| Michigan | 23,242 | 30,697 | 38,160 | 64.2 | 5.1 | 5.7 | 4.4 |
| Ohio | 47,568 | 57,421 | 66,554 | 39.9 | 3.4 | 3.8 | 3.0 |
| Wisconsin | 15,720 | 24,291 | 31,207 | 98.5 | 7.1 | 9.1 | 5.1 |
| West North Central | 71,794 | 93,476 | 115,158 | 60.4 | 4.8 | 5.4 | 4.3 |
| Iowa | 8,830 | 12,522 | 15,292 | 73.2 | 5.6 | 7.2 | 4.1 |
| Kansas | 6,032 | 8,062 | 10,429 | 72.9 | 5.6 | 6.0 | 5.3 |
| Minnesota | 19,254 | 24,506 | 30,908 | 60.5 | 4.8 | 4.9 | 4.8 |
| Missouri | 24,478 | 32,336 | 37,120 | 51.6 | 4.3 | 5.7 | 2.8 |
| North Dakota | 2,750 | 2,273 | 2,900 | 5.5 | 0.5 | −3.7 | 5.0 |
| Nebraska | 7,692 | 9,995 | 13,188 | 71.4 | 5.5 | 5.4 | 5.7 |
| South Dakota | 2,758 | 3,783 | 5,322 | 93.0 | 6.8 | 6.5 | 7.1 |

*(continued)*

**Table 5.37.** Change in Net Assets for Reporting Public Charities by State, 2000, 2005, and 2010 *(continued)*

| | Net Assets ($ millions) | | | Total % Change | Average Annual % Change | | |
|---|---|---|---|---|---|---|---|
| | 2000 | 2005 | 2010 | 2000–10 | 2000–10 | 2000–05 | 2005–10 |
| South | 286,505 | 369,048 | 476,752 | 66.4 | 5.2 | 5.2 | 5.3 |
| South Atlantic | 180,901 | 235,181 | 280,571 | 55.1 | 4.5 | 5.4 | 3.6 |
| District of Columbia | 18,712 | 24,924 | 28,377 | 51.6 | 4.3 | 5.9 | 2.6 |
| Delaware | 3,563 | 4,456 | 4,821 | 35.3 | 3.1 | 4.6 | 1.6 |
| Florida | 34,365 | 45,444 | 55,349 | 61.1 | 4.9 | 5.7 | 4.0 |
| Georgia | 26,567 | 32,200 | 39,163 | 47.4 | 4.0 | 3.9 | 4.0 |
| Maryland | 31,263 | 38,572 | 43,212 | 38.2 | 3.3 | 4.3 | 2.3 |
| North Carolina | 26,954 | 37,288 | 45,719 | 69.6 | 5.4 | 6.7 | 4.2 |
| South Carolina | 7,956 | 9,532 | 11,927 | 49.9 | 4.1 | 3.7 | 4.6 |
| Virginia | 27,577 | 37,988 | 46,559 | 68.8 | 5.4 | 6.6 | 4.2 |
| West Virginia | 3,945 | 4,778 | 5,447 | 38.1 | 3.3 | 3.9 | 2.7 |
| East South Central | 36,450 | 46,030 | 55,931 | 53.4 | 4.4 | 4.8 | 4.0 |
| Alabama | 7,027 | 8,378 | 9,806 | 39.6 | 3.4 | 3.6 | 3.2 |
| Kentucky | 9,913 | 11,323 | 14,340 | 44.7 | 3.8 | 2.7 | 4.8 |
| Mississippi | 4,030 | 5,314 | 6,449 | 60.0 | 4.8 | 5.7 | 3.9 |
| Tennessee | 15,480 | 21,015 | 25,336 | 63.7 | 5.1 | 6.3 | 3.8 |
| West South Central | 69,154 | 87,837 | 140,249 | 102.8 | 7.3 | 4.9 | 9.8 |
| Arkansas | 4,586 | 6,682 | 7,997 | 74.4 | 5.7 | 7.8 | 3.7 |
| Louisiana | 8,219 | 9,459 | 36,030 | 338.4 | 15.9 | 2.9 | 30.7 |
| Oklahoma | 8,985 | 12,005 | 17,730 | 97.3 | 7.0 | 6.0 | 8.1 |
| Texas | 47,365 | 59,691 | 78,492 | 65.7 | 5.2 | 4.7 | 5.6 |
| West | 142,718 | 208,501 | 275,771 | 93.2 | 6.8 | 7.9 | 5.8 |
| Mountain | 28,231 | 43,721 | 60,591 | 114.6 | 7.9 | 9.1 | 6.7 |
| Arizona | 6,319 | 10,824 | 17,929 | 183.7 | 11.0 | 11.4 | 10.6 |
| Colorado | 10,261 | 15,610 | 20,574 | 100.5 | 7.2 | 8.8 | 5.7 |
| Idaho | 1,556 | 1,998 | 2,965 | 90.5 | 6.7 | 5.1 | 8.2 |
| Montana | 2,122 | 3,061 | 3,492 | 64.5 | 5.1 | 7.6 | 2.7 |
| New Mexico | 2,732 | 3,675 | 4,929 | 80.5 | 6.1 | 6.1 | 6.0 |
| Nevada | 1,985 | 3,266 | 3,371 | 69.8 | 5.4 | 10.5 | 0.6 |
| Utah | 2,545 | 3,977 | 5,576 | 119.1 | 8.2 | 9.3 | 7.0 |
| Wyoming | 711 | 1,309 | 1,755 | 147.0 | 9.5 | 13.0 | 6.0 |

*(continued)*

**Table 5.37.** Change in Net Assets for Reporting Public Charities by State, 2000, 2005, and 2010 *(continued)*

| | Net Assets ($ millions) | | | Total % Change | Average Annual % Change | | |
|---|---|---|---|---|---|---|---|
| | 2000 | 2005 | 2010 | 2000–10 | 2000–10 | 2000–05 | 2005–10 |
| Pacific | 114,487 | 164,781 | 215,180 | 88.0 | 6.5 | 7.6 | 5.5 |
| Alaska | 1,283 | 2,060 | 2,869 | 123.6 | 8.4 | 9.9 | 6.8 |
| California | 76,935 | 120,836 | 159,807 | 107.7 | 7.6 | 9.4 | 5.7 |
| Hawaii | 8,793 | 9,937 | 11,595 | 31.9 | 2.8 | 2.5 | 3.1 |
| Oregon | 13,142 | 11,341 | 14,997 | 14.1 | 1.3 | −2.9 | 5.7 |
| Washington | 14,334 | 20,606 | 25,912 | 80.8 | 6.1 | 7.5 | 4.7 |

*Sources:* Urban Institute, National Center for Charitable Statistics, Core Files (Public Charities, 2000, 2005, and 2010).
*Notes:* Subtotals may not sum to totals because of rounding. Net assets are shown in current dollars and are not adjusted for inflation.

**Table 5.38.** The 10 States with the Highest Growth in Net Assets Reported by Public Charities, 2000–10

| Rank | State | Total net assets for reporting public charities, 2000 ($ millions) | Total net assets for reporting public charities, 2010 ($ millions) | % change, 2000–10 | % change, 2000–10 (inflation adjusted) |
|---|---|---|---|---|---|
| 1 | Louisiana | 8,219 | 36,030 | 338 | 246 |
| 2 | Arizona | 6,319 | 17,929 | 184 | 124 |
| 3 | Wyoming | 711 | 1,755 | 147 | 95 |
| 4 | Alaska | 1,283 | 2,869 | 124 | 77 |
| 5 | Utah | 2,545 | 5,576 | 119 | 73 |
| 6 | California | 76,935 | 159,807 | 108 | 64 |
| 7 | Colorado | 10,261 | 20,574 | 101 | 58 |
| 8 | Wisconsin | 15,720 | 31,207 | 99 | 57 |
| 9 | Oklahoma | 8,985 | 17,730 | 97 | 56 |
| 10 | South Dakota | 2,758 | 5,322 | 93 | 52 |

*Sources:* Urban Institute, National Center for Charitable Statistics, Core Files (Public Charities, 2000 and 2010).
*Note:* Net assets are shown in current dollars and are not adjusted for inflation.

## Conclusion

While other chapters in this book have discussed the size of the nonprofit sector, this chapter focuses on the size and scope of public charities. In 2010, public charities accounted for almost 60 percent of all registered nonprofit organizations and represented nearly three-quarters of the revenue and expenses of the nonprofit sector in the United States. Many organizations saw growth slow in the second half of the decade when the recession hit the nonprofit sector. Overall, however, revenue for reporting public charities grew by 43 percent, expenses grew by 53 percent, and assets grew by 43 percent, after adjusting for inflation, between 2000 and 2010.

## Sources

American Hospital Association. 2010. AHA Annual Survey Database CD 2010.

Centers for Medicare & Medicaid Services, Office of the Actuary, National Health Statistics Group. 2010. "National Health Expenditure Accounts Data." http://www.cms.gov/NationalHealthExpendData/.

The Urban Institute, National Center for Charitable Statistics. 2000–10. "Core Files." Washington, DC: The Urban Institute.

———. 2000–10. "Public Charities Core Files." Washington, DC: The Urban Institute.

———. 2005. "Supplement Core Files." Washington, DC: The Urban Institute.

———. 2005–08. "IRS Statistics of Income Files." Washington, DC: The Urban Institute.

———. 2010. "IRS Business Master Files, Exempt Organizations." Washington, DC: The Urban Institute.

U.S. Census Bureau. 2000. *Statistical Abstract of the United States: 2000.* Section 1. Population. http://www.census.gov/prod/2001pubs/statab/sec01.pdf.

———. 2010. *Statistical Abstract of the United States: 2010.* Section 1. Population. http://www.census.gov/prod/2009pubs/10statab/pop.pdf

U.S. Department of Treasury, Internal Revenue Service. 2012. "Form 990 Series—Which Forms Do Exempt Organizations File? (Filing Phase-In)." http://www.irs.gov/charities/article/0,,id=184445,00.html.

# Technical Notes

For this chapter we used two primary datasets: the IRS Business Master Files of Tax-Exempt Organizations, and a special research version of the National Center for Charitable Statistics (NCCS) Core Files that excludes organizations marked as "out of scope" by the authors. Below are the descriptions of the datasets, methodology for estimated detailed revenue and expense breakdowns, and a description of the organizational classification system used throughout the chapter.

## IRS Business Master Files of Tax-Exempt Organizations, 1998–2011

The IRS Business Master Files (BMF) are cumulative files containing descriptive information on all active tax-exempt organizations. Data contained on the BMF are mostly derived from the IRS Forms 1023 and 1024 (the applications for IRS recognition of tax-exempt status). NCCS downloads these files monthly. Organizations must apply for recognition with the IRS to be included in the BMF unless they are religious congregations or have less than $5,000 in annual gross receipts.

Business Master Files were used for information on the number of nonprofits, filers and non-filers, contained in table 5.1. For each year reported, we used the BMF from the first month the data were available in the next year to ensure that organizations registering in December were included in the yearly counts. For example, for the 2005 total nonprofit number, we used the January 2006 BMF.

## NCCS Core Files

The NCCS Core Files are based on the Internal Revenue Service's annual Return Transaction Files (RTF), which contain data on all organizations that were required to file a Form 990 or Form 990-EZ and complied. It is important to note that the IRS does not keypunch financial data for approximately 80,000 organizations that filed Forms 990 but were not required to do so either because they are religious congregations or they received less than $50,000 in annual gross receipts for tax year 2010 ($25,000 for tax years before 2010). In addition, NCCS also excludes a small number of other organizations, such as foreign organizations or those generally considered part of government. These organizations are deemed out of scope.

The NCCS Core Files (1998–2010) contain a number of key financial variables from the Form 990, including contributions, program revenue, total revenue, total expenses, and assets.

# Estimates Methodology

Data from the Core Supplement Files, IRS Statistics of Income Samples Files, and the NCCS Digitized Data Files were used to produce the detailed revenue and expense breakdowns. While the NCCS Core Files served as the basis for these tables, these additional variables available in the Core Supplement, SOI, and Digitized Data files allow for more detailed financial analysis than the NCCS Core Files.

## Core Supplement

The Core Supplement Files includes select Forms 990 and Forms 990-EZ filed by 501(c)(3) organizations. To produce the Core Supplement Files, IRS Forms 990 and Forms 990-EZ received by the IRS are manually entered into a database. Most variables from the forms, schedules, and attachments are keyed by hand, and NCCS checks the financial variables for accuracy. The Core Supplement database contains over 100 variables from the balance sheet, statement of revenue, and functional expenses sections of the Form 990. The Core Supplement data include over 340,000 records covering tax years 2006 to 2011, with more than 28,500 records available for tax year 2010. The NCCS Core Supplement data accounts for 52 percent of total revenues and total expenses. For proportions coverage by the subsectors, see table 5.39.

## Statistics of Income

The Statistics of Income (SOI) Division of the IRS annually creates sample files of 501(c) organizations. These files, which are available from the IRS and NCCS, have included over 15,000 501(c)(3) filing organizations since 2000. Since 2000, SOI files for 501(c)(3) entities have included all organizations with $30 million or more in total assets ($10 million before 2000), plus a random sample of smaller organizations stratified and weighted by asset level. Thus, all organizations with total assets (end-of-year) of more than $10 million (before 2000 or 2001) or $30 million (more recent files) are

**Table 5.39.** Proportions of Revenue and Expenses Covered by NCCS Core Supplement Data

| Type of organizations | % of revenue | % of expenses |
|---|---|---|
| Arts, culture, and humanities | 44 | 44 |
| Education | 32 | 33 |
| Environment and animals | 52 | 53 |
| Health | 60 | 60 |
| Human services | 54 | 54 |
| International and foreign affairs | 51 | 52 |
| Other public and social benefit | 36 | 36 |
| Religion-related | 52 | 51 |

*Source:* Urban Institute, National Center for Charitable Statistics, Core Supplement Files, 2011.

included with a weight of 1. Weights for other organizations are designed to match populations of six other asset classes. The SOI file includes over 300 financial and programmatic variables from the Form 990.

## Digitized Data

The Digitized Data files include all Forms 990 and Forms 990-EZ filed by 501(c)(3) organizations that are required to file with the IRS. The forms received by the IRS were scanned and saved. Working with GuideStar and its contractors, most variables from the forms, schedules, and attachments were manually entered into a database. NCCS then checked the financial variables for accuracy and added organization-level descriptive variables such as NTEE classification codes and geographic identifiers such as county (FIPS) codes. The database includes all items in most financial sections and select nonfinancial items from tax years 1998–2003.

The detailed estimates were created as follows. Data from the Core Supplement database were used when the fiscal year was the same as the fiscal year in the Core File. Next, data from the SOI file was used when the fiscal year was the same as the fiscal year in the Core File. When the fiscal year information was not available, we assumed that the overall distribution of sources of revenue and types of expenses were similar in the previous or following fiscal year and used revenue and expense ratios from the datasets to estimate current figures. Ratios from the Digitized Data files were used when data from the Core Files or SOI files were not available. For any remaining organizations, an average based on the three-digit NTEE code and similar size were assigned.

# Classification of Organizations

Tables that group organizations into subsectors based on their primary activities use the National Taxonomy of Exempt Entities Core Codes (NTEECC). Both summary and detailed information on this classification system is available on the NCCS web site at www.nccs.urban.org. Also, a complete listing of the NTEE Core Codes used for each subsector breakout is available below.

While the vast majority of organizations are coded with a specific NTEE-CC code, a few organizations are coded as unknown. This code is normally temporary but may be permanent if no detailed information on the organization—a Form 990 with its program descriptions or a web site—is available.

## Arts, Culture, and Humanities

**Performing Arts Organizations**
A60—Performing Arts
A61—Performing Arts Centers
A62—Dance
A63—Ballet
A65—Theater
A68—Music
A69—Symphony Orchestra
A6A—Opera
A6B—Singing and Choral Groups
A6C—Bands and Ensembles
A6E—Performing Arts Schools

**Historical Societies and Related Organizations**
A80—Historical Societies and Related Historical Activities
A84—Commemorative Events

**Museums and Museum Activities**
A50—Museums and Museum Activities

A51—Art Museums
A52—Children's Museums
A54—History Museums
A56—Natural History and Natural Science Museums
A57—Science and Technology Museums

**Other Arts, Culture, and Humanities**
A01—Alliances and Advocacy
A02—Management and Technical Assistance
A03—Professional Societies and Associations
A05—Research Institutes and Public Policy Analysis
A11—Single Organization Support
A12—Fund Raising and Fund Distribution
A19—Support NEC
A20—Arts and Culture
A23—Cultural and Ethnic Awareness
A25—Arts Education
A26—Arts Councils and Agencies

A30—Media and Communications
A31—Film and Video
A32—Television
A33—Printing and Publishing
A34—Radio
A40—Visual Arts
A70—Humanities
A90—Arts Services
A99—Arts, Culture, and Humanities NEC

## Education

**Higher Education**
B40—Higher Education
B41—Two-Year Colleges
B42—Undergraduate Colleges
B43—Universities
B50—Graduate and Professional Schools

**Student Services**
B80—Student Services
B82—Scholarships and Student Financial Aid
B83—Student Sororities and Fraternities
B84—Alumni Associations

**Elementary and Secondary Education**

B20—Elementary and Secondary Schools
B21—Preschools
B24—Primary and Elementary Schools
B25—Secondary and High Schools
B28—Special Education
B29—Charter Schools

**Other Education**

B01—Alliances and Advocacy
B02—Management and Technical Assistance
B03—Professional Societies and Associations
B05—Research Institutes and Public Policy Analysis
B11—Single-Organization Support
B12—Fundraising and Fund Distribution
B19—Support NEC
B30—Vocational and Technical Schools
B60—Adult Education
B70—Libraries
B90—Educational Support
B92—Remedial Reading and Encouragement
B94—Parent and Teacher Groups
B99—Education NEC

## Environment and Animals

**Environment**

C01—Alliances and Advocacy
C02—Management and Technical Assistance
C03—Professional Societies and Associations

C05—Research Institutes and Public Policy Analysis
C11—Single-Organization Support
C12—Fundraising and Fund Distribution
C19—Support NEC
C20—Pollution Abatement and Control
C27—Recycling
C30—Natural Resources Conservation and Protection
C32—Water Resources, Wetlands Conservation and Management
C34—Land Resources and Conservation
C35—Energy Resources Conservation and Development
C36—Forest Conservation
C40—Botanical, Horticultural, and Landscape Services
C41—Botanical Gardens and Arboreta
C42—Garden Clubs
C50—Environmental Beautification
C60—Environmental Education
C99—Environment NEC

**Animals**

D01—Alliances and Advocacy
D02—Management and Technical Assistance
D03—Professional Societies and Associations
D05—Research Institutes and Public Policy Analysis
D11—Single-Organization Support
D12—Fundraising and Fund Distribution

D19—Support NEC
D20—Animal Protection and Welfare
D30—Wildlife Preservation and Protection
D31—Protection of Endangered Species
D32—Bird Sanctuaries
D33—Fisheries Resources
D34—Wildlife Sanctuaries
D40—Veterinary Services
D50—Zoos and Aquariums
D60—Animal Services NEC
D61—Animal Training
D99—Animal-Related NEC

## Health

**Nursing Services**

E90—Nursing
E91—Nursing Facilities
E92—Home Health Care

**Hospitals and Primary Treatment Facilities**

E20—Hospitals
E21—Community Health Systems
E22—General Hospitals
E24—Specialty Hospitals

**Outpatient Facilities**

E30—Ambulatory and Primary Health Care
E31—Group Health Practices
E32—Community Clinics

**Mental Health**

F01—Alliances and Advocacy
F02—Management and Technical Assistance
F03—Professional Societies and Associations
F05—Research Institutes and Public Policy Analysis

F11—Single-Organization Support
F12—Fundraising and Fund Distribution
F19—Support NEC
F20—Substance Abuse Dependency, Prevention, and Treatment
F21—Substance Abuse Prevention
F22—Substance Abuse Treatment
F30—Mental Health Treatment
F31—Psychiatric Hospitals
F32—Community Mental Health Centers
F33—Residential Mental Health Treatment
F40—Hotlines and Crisis Intervention
F42—Sexual Assault Services
F50—Addictive Disorders
F52—Smoking Addiction
F53—Eating Disorders
F54—Gambling Addiction
F60—Counseling
F70—Mental Health Disorders
F80—Mental Health Associations
F99—Mental Health NEC

**Disease-Specific**
G01—Alliances and Advocacy
G02—Management and Technical Assistance
G03—Professional Societies and Associations
G05—Research Institutes and Public Policy Analysis
G11—Single-Organization Support
G12—Fundraising and Fund Distribution
G19—Support NEC

G20—Birth Defects and Genetic Diseases
G25—Down Syndrome
G30—Cancer
G32—Breast Cancer
G40—Diseases of Specific Organs
G41—Eye Diseases, Blindness, and Vision Impairments
G42—Ear and Throat Diseases
G43—Heart and Circulatory System Diseases and Disorders
G44—Kidney Diseases
G45—Lung Diseases
G48—Brain Disorders
G50—Nerve, Muscle, and Bone Diseases
G51—Arthritis
G54—Epilepsy
G60—Allergy-Related Diseases
G61—Asthma
G70—Digestive Diseases and Disorders
G80—Specifically Named Diseases
G81—AIDS
G82—Alzheimer's Disease
G84—Autism
G90—Medical Disciplines
G92—Biomedicine and Bioengineering
G94—Geriatrics
G96—Neurology and Neuroscience
G98—Pediatrics
G9B—Surgical Specialties
G99—Diseases, Disorders, and Medical Disciplines NEC

**Medical Research**
H01—Alliances and Advocacy
H02—Management and Technical Assistance

H03—Professional Societies and Associations
H05—Research Institutes and Public Policy Analysis
H11—Single-Organization Support
H12—Fundraising and Fund Distribution
H19—Support NEC
H20—Birth Defects and Genetic Diseases Research
H25—Down Syndrome Research
H30—Cancer Research
H32—Breast Cancer Research
H40—Disease Specific Research
H41—Eye Diseases, Blindness, and Vision Impairments Research
H42—Ear and Throat Diseases Research
H43—Heart and Circulatory System Diseases and Disorders Research
H44—Kidney Diseases Research
H45—Lung Diseases Research
H48—Brain Disorders Research
H50—Nerve, Muscle, and Bone Diseases Research
H51—Arthritis Research
H54—Epilepsy Research
H60—Allergy-Related Diseases Research
H61—Asthma Research
H70—Digestive Diseases and Disorders Research
H80—Specifically Named Diseases Research
H81—AIDS Research

H83—Alzheimer's Disease Research
H84—Autism Research
H90—Medical Discipline Research
H92—Biomedicine and Bioengineering Research
H94—Geriatrics Research
H96—Neurology and Neuroscience Research
H98—Pediatrics Research
H9B—Surgical Specialties Research
H99—Medical Research NEC

## Other Health
E01—Alliances and Advocacy
E02—Management and Technical Assistance
E03—Professional Societies and Associations
E05—Research Institutes and Public Policy Analysis
E11—Single-Organization Support
E12—Fundraising and Fund Distribution
E19—Support NEC
E40—Reproductive Health Care
E42—Family Planning
E50—Rehabilitative Care
E60—Health Support
E61—Blood Banks
E62—Emergency Medical Transport
E65—Organ and Tissue Banks
E70—Public Health
E80—Health (General and Financing)
E86—Patient and Family Support
E99—Health Care NEC

# Human Services

## Crime and Legal-Related
I01—Alliances and Advocacy
I02—Management and Technical Assistance
I03—Professional Societies and Associations
I05—Research Institutes and Public Policy Analysis
I11—Single-Organization Support
I12—Fundraising and Fund Distribution
I19—Support NEC
I20—Crime Prevention
I21—Youth Violence Prevention
I23—Drunk Driving–Related
I30—Correctional Facilities
I31—Halfway Houses for Offenders and Ex-Offenders
I40—Rehabilitation Services for Offenders
I43—Inmate Support
I44—Prison Alternatives
I50—Administration of Justice
I51—Dispute Resolution and Mediation
I60—Law Enforcement
I70—Protection against Abuse
I71—Spouse Abuse Prevention
I72—Child Abuse Prevention
I73—Sexual Abuse Prevention
I80—Legal Services
I83—Public Interest Law
I99—Crime and Legal-Related NEC

## Employment and Job-Related
J01—Alliances and Advocacy
J02—Management and Technical Assistance
J03—Professional Societies and Associations
J05—Research Institutes and Public Policy Analysis
J11—Single-Organization Support
J12—Fundraising and Fund Distribution
J19—Support NEC
J20—Employment Preparation and Procurement
J21—Vocational Counseling
J22—Job Training
J30—Vocational Rehabilitation
J32—Goodwill Industries
J33—Sheltered Employment
J40—Labor Unions
J99—Employment NEC

## Food, Agriculture, and Nutrition
K01—Alliances and Advocacy
K02—Management and Technical Assistance
K03—Professional Societies and Associations
K05—Research Institutes and Public Policy Analysis
K11—Single-Organization Support
K12—Fundraising and Fund Distribution
K19—Support NEC
K20—Agricultural Programs
K25—Farmland Preservation
K26—Animal Husbandry
K28—Farm Bureaus and Granges
K30—Food Programs
K31—Food Banks and Pantries
K34—Congregate Meals
K35—Soup Kitchens
K36—Meals on Wheels

K40—Nutrition
K50—Home Economics
K99—Food, Agriculture, and Nutrition NEC

**Housing and Shelter**
L01—Alliances and Advocacy
L02—Management and Technical Assistance
L03—Professional Societies and Associations
L05—Research Institutes and Public Policy Analysis
L11—Single-Organization Support
L12—Fundraising and Fund Distribution
L19—Support NEC
L20—Housing Development, Construction, and Management
L21—Public Housing
L22—Senior Citizens' Housing and Retirement Communities
L25—Housing Rehabilitation
L30—Housing Search Assistance
L40—Temporary Housing
L41—Homeless Shelters
L50—Homeowners' and Tenants' Associations
L80—Housing Support
L81—Home Improvement and Repairs
L82—Housing Expense Reduction
L99—Housing and Shelter NEC

**Public Safety and Disaster Preparedness**
M01—Alliances and Advocacy
M02—Management and Technical Assistance
M03—Professional Societies and Associations
M05—Research Institutes and Public Policy Analysis
M11—Single-Organization Support
M12—Fundraising and Fund Distribution
M19—Support NEC
M20—Disaster Preparedness and Relief Services
M23—Search and Rescue Squads
M24—Fire Prevention
M40—Safety Education
M41—First Aid
M42—Automotive Safety
M99—Public Safety, Disaster Preparedness and Relief NEC

**Recreation and Sports**
N01—Alliances and Advocacy
N02—Management and Technical Assistance
N03—Professional Societies and Associations
N05—Research Institutes and Public Policy Analysis
N11—Single-Organization Support
N12—Fundraising and Fund Distribution
N19—Support NEC
N20—Camps
N30—Physical Fitness and Community Recreational Facilities
N31—Community Recreational Centers
N32—Parks and Playgrounds
N40—Sports Training Facilities
N50—Recreational Clubs
N52—Fairs

N60—Amateur Sports
N61—Fishing and Hunting
N62—Basketball
N63—Baseball and Softball
N64—Soccer
N65—Football
N66—Racquet Sports
N67—Swimming and Other Water Recreation
N68—Winter Sports
N69—Equestrian
N6A—Golf
N70—Amateur Sports Competitions
N71—Olympics
N72—Special Olympics
N80—Professional Athletic Leagues
N99—Recreation and Sports NEC

**Youth Development**
O01—Alliances and Advocacy
O02—Management and Technical Assistance
O03—Professional Societies and Associations
O05—Research Institutes and Public Policy Analysis
O11—Single-Organization Support
O12—Fundraising and Fund Distribution
O19—Support NEC
O20—Youth Centers and Clubs
O21—Boys Clubs
O22—Girls Clubs
O23—Boys and Girls Clubs
O30—Adult and Child Matching Programs
O31—Big Brothers and Big Sisters

O40—Scouting
O41—Boy Scouts of America
O42—Girls Scouts of
the USA
O43—Camp Fire
O50—Youth Development
Programs
O51—Youth Community
Service Clubs
O52—Youth Development,
Agriculture
O53—Youth Development,
Business
O54—Youth Development,
Citizenship
O55—Youth Development,
Religious Leadership
O99—Youth Development
NEC

**Children and Youth Services**
P30—Children and
Youth Services
P31—Adoption
P32—Foster Care
P33—Child Day Care

**Family Services**
P40—Family Services
P42—Single-Parent Agencies
P43—Family Violence
Agencies
P44—In-Home Assistance
P45—Family Services for
Adolescent Parents
P46—Family Counseling

**Residential and
Custodial Care**
P70—Residential Care
P73—Group Homes
P74—Hospice
P75—Senior Continuing
Care Communities

**Services Promoting
Independence**
P80—Centers to Support
the Independence of
Specific Populations
P81—Senior Centers
P82—Developmentally
Disabled Centers
P84—Ethnic and
Immigrant Centers
P85—Homeless Centers
P86—Blind and Visually
Impaired Centers
P87—Deaf and Hearing-
Impaired Centers

**Other Human Services**
P01—Alliances and Advocacy
P02—Management and
Technical Assistance
P03—Professional Societies
and Associations
P05—Research Institutes
and Public Policy Analysis
P11—Single-organization
Support
P12—Fundraising and
Fund Distribution
P19—Support NEC
P20—Human Services
P21—American Red Cross
P22—Urban League
P24—Salvation Army
P26—Volunteers of America
P27—Young Men's or
Women's Associations
P28—Neighborhood Centers
P29—Thrift Shops
P50—Personal Social Services
P51—Financial Counseling
P52—Transportation
Assistance
P58—Gift Distribution

P60—Emergency Assistance
P61—Travelers' Aid
P62—Victim's Services
P99—Human Service NEC

**International and
Foreign Affairs**
Q01—Alliances and Advocacy
Q02—Management and
Technical Assistance
Q03—Professional Societies
and Associations
Q05—Research Institutes and
Public Policy Analysis
Q11—Single-organization
Support
Q12—Fundraising and
Fund Distribution
Q19—Support NEC
Q20—Promotion of
International Understanding
Q21—International Cultural
Exchanges
Q22—International Student
Exchanges
Q23—International Exchanges
Q30—International
Development
Q31—International
Agricultural Development
Q32—International Economic
Development
Q33—International Relief
Q40—International Peace
and Security
Q41—Arms Control and Peace
Q42—United Nations
Associations
Q43—National Security
Q70—International Human
Rights
Q71—International Migration
and Refugee Issues

Q99—International, Foreign Affairs, and National Security NEC

## Other

### Civil Rights and Advocacy

R01—Alliances and Advocacy
R02—Management and Technical Assistance
R03—Professional Societies and Associations
R05—Research Institutes and Public Policy Analysis
R11—Single-Organization Support
R12—Fundraising and Fund Distribution
R19—Support NEC
R20—Civil Rights
R22—Minority Rights
R23—Disabled Persons' Rights
R24—Women's Rights
R25—Senior's Rights
R26—Lesbian and Gay Rights
R30—Intergroup and Race Relations
R40—Voter Education and Registration
R60—Civil Liberties
R61—Reproductive Rights
R62—Right to Life
R63—Censorship, Freedom of Speech and Press
R67—Right to Die and Euthanasia
R99—Civil Rights, Social Action, and Advocacy NEC

### Community Improvement

S01—Alliances and Advocacy
S02—Management and Technical Assistance
S03—Professional Societies and Associations
S05—Research Institutes and Public Policy Analysis
S11—Single-Organization Support
S12—Fundraising and Fund Distribution
S19—Support NEC
S20—Community and Neighborhood Development
S21—Community Coalitions
S22—Neighborhood and Block Associations
S30—Economic Development
S31—Urban and Community Economic Development
S32—Rural Economic Development
S40—Business and Industry
S41—Chambers of Commerce and Business Leagues
S43—Small Business Development
S46—Boards of Trade
S47—Real Estate Associations
S50—Nonprofit Management
S80—Community Service Clubs
S81—Women's Service Clubs
S82—Men's Service Clubs
S99—Community Improvement and Capacity Building NEC

### Philanthropy and Voluntarism

T01—Alliances and Advocacy
T02—Management and Technical Assistance
T03—Professional Societies and Associations
T05—Research Institutes and Public Policy Analysis
T11—Single-Organization Support
T12—Fundraising and Fund Distribution
T19—Support NEC
T20—Private Grantmaking Foundations
T21—Corporate Foundations
T22—Private Independent Foundations
T23—Private Operating Foundations
T30—Public Foundations
T31—Community Foundations
T40—Voluntarism Promotion
T50—Philanthropy, Charity, and Voluntarism Promotion
T70—Federated Giving Program
T90—Named Trusts and Foundations NEC
T99—Philanthropy, Voluntarism, and Grantmaking NEC

### Science and Technology

U01—Alliances and Advocacy
U02—Management and Technical Assistance
U03—Professional Societies and Associations
U05—Research Institutes and Public Policy Analysis
U11—Single-Organization Support
U12—Fundraising and Fund Distribution
U19—Support NEC
U20—General Science

U21—Marine Science and Oceanography
U30—Physical and Earth Sciences
U31—Astronomy
U33—Chemistry and Chemical Engineering
U34—Mathematics
U36—Geology
U40—Engineering and Technology Research
U41—Computer Science
U42—Engineering
U50—Biological and Life Sciences
U99—Science and Technology NEC

**Social Science**
V01—Alliances and Advocacy
V02—Management and Technical Assistance
V03—Professional Societies and Associations
V05—Research Institutes and Public Policy Analysis
V11—Single-Organization Support
V12—Fundraising and Fund Distribution
V19—Support NEC
V20—Social Science
V21—Anthropology and Sociology
V22—Economics
V23—Behavioral Science
V24—Political Science
V25—Population Studies

V26—Law and Jurisprudence
V30—Interdisciplinary Research
V31—Black Studies
V32—Women's Studies
V33—Ethnic Studies
V34—Urban Studies
V35—International Studies
V36—Gerontology
V37—Labor Studies
V99—Social Science NEC

**Other Public and Societal Benefit**
W01—Alliances and Advocacy
W02—Management and Technical Assistance
W03—Professional Societies and Associations
W05—Research Institutes and Public Policy Analysis
W11—Single-Organization Support
W12—Fundraising and Fund Distribution
W19—Support NEC
W20—Government and Public Administration
W22—Public Finance, Taxation, and Monetary Policy
W24—Citizen Participation
W30—Military and Veterans' Organizations
W40—Public Transportation Systems
W50—Telecommunications
W60—Financial Institutions

W61—Credit Unions
W70—Leadership Development
W80—Public Utilities
W90—Consumer Protection
W99—Public and Societal Benefit NEC
Z99—Unknown

**Religion-Related**
X01—Alliances and Advocacy
X02—Management and Technical Assistance
X03—Professional Societies and Associations
X05—Research Institutes and Public Policy Analysis
X11—Single-Organization Support
X12—Fundraising and Fund Distribution
X19—Support NEC
X20—Christian
X21—Protestant
X22—Roman Catholic
X30—Jewish
X40—Buddhist
X70—Hindu
X80—Religious Media and Communications
X81—Religious Film and Video
X82—Religious Television
X83—Religious Printing and Publishing
X84—Religious Radio
X90—Interfaith Coalitions
X99—Religion-Related NEC

NEC = not elsewhere classified

# Glossary

Some of these definitions have been taken from other publications, including the "Glossary of Philanthropic Terms" in Council on Foundations, *Corporate Philanthropy: Philosophy, Management, Trends, Future, Background* (Washington, DC: Council on Foundations, 1982); U.S. Census Bureau, *Statistical Abstract of the United States* (Washington, DC: U.S. Government Printing Office, 1985); and U.S. Census Bureau, *Social Indicators III* (Washington, DC: U.S. Government Printing Office, various years). We have revised many definitions from these publications to reflect their specific relationship to the independent sector. Other definitions of particular terms used to describe the functions of activities of this sector, such as *assigned value for volunteer time,* have been written by the authors.

**Adjusted gross income (AGI).** Total income as defined by the tax code, less statutory adjustments (primarily business, investment, or certain other deductions, such as payments to a Keogh retirement plan or an individual retirement account).

**Assets.** An organization's financial holdings, such as property or resources, cash, accounts receivable, equipment, and so on, and balances against liabilities.

**Assigned value for volunteer time.** The total number of hours formally volunteered to organizations in a year, multiplied by the hourly wage for nonagricultural workers for that year.

**Average.** A single number of values often used to represent the typical value of a group of numbers. It is regarded as a measure of the "location" or "central tendency" of a group of numbers. The *arithmetic mean* is the type of average used most frequently. It is derived by totaling the values of individual items in a particular group and dividing that total by the number of items. The arithmetic mean is often referred to as simply the "mean" or "average." The *median* of a group of numbers is the number or value that falls in the middle of a group when each item in the group is ranked according to size (from lowest to highest or vice versa); the median generally has the same number of items above it as below it. If there is an even number of items in the group, the median is the average of the two middle items.

**Average annual percentage change.** A figure computed by using a compound interest formula. This formula assumes that the rate of change is constant throughout a specified compounding period (one year for average annual rates of change). The formula is similar to the one used to compute the balance of a savings account that earns compound interest. According to this formula, at the end of a compounding period, the amount of accrued change (for example, employment or bank interest) is added to the amount that existed at the beginning of one period. As a result, over time (for example, with each year or quarter), the same rate of change is applied to an even larger figure.

**Charitable contribution.** A gift to a charitable cause that is allowed by the IRS as a deduction from taxable income. Both individual taxpayers and corporations can deduct contributions for charitable causes from their taxable incomes.

**Community foundation.** A public charity supported by combined funds contributed by individuals, foundations, nonprofit institutions, and corporations. A community foundation's giving is limited almost exclusively to a specific locale, such as a city, a county or counties, or a state.

**Constant-dollar estimate.** A computation that removes the effects of price changes from a statistical series reported in dollar terms. Constant-dollar series are derived by dividing current-dollar estimates by appropriate price indexes, such as the consumer price index, or by the various implicit price deflators for gross national product. The result is a series as it would presumably exist if prices remained the same throughout the period as they were in the base year—in other words, if the dollar had constant purchasing power. Changes in such a series would reflect only changes in the real (physical) volume of output. *See also* **Current dollars** *and* **Gross national product (GNP).**

**Consumption expenditure.** Expenditures for goods and services purchased by individuals; operating expenses of nonprofit institutions; the value of food, fuel, clothing, and rental of dwellings; financial services received in kind by individuals; and net purchases of used goods. All private purchases of dwellings are classified as gross private domestic investment. Per capita personal consumption expenditures are total personal consumption expenditures divided by the appropriate population base. Per capita components of personal consumption expenditures are derived in the same way. *See also* **Per capita.**

**Contributions deduction.** Taxpayers can deduct from their taxable income contributions made to certain religious, charitable, educational, scientific, or literary 501(c)(3) organizations. These could be in the form of cash, property, or out-of-pocket expenses incurred while performing volunteer work.

**Corporate contribution.** A general term referring to charitable contributions by a corporation. The term usually describes cash contributions only but may also include other items, such as the value of loaned executives, products, and services.

**Corporate foundation.** A private philanthropic organization set up and funded by a corporation. A corporate foundation is governed by a board that may include members of the corporation board and contributions committee, other staff members, and representatives of the community.

**Corporate social responsibility program.** A philanthropic program operated within a corporation. The program may be managed through a department of its own or through a community affairs (or similar) department.

**Current dollars.** The dollar amount that reflects the value of the dollar at the time of its use. *See also* **Constant-dollar estimate.**

**Current operating expenditures.** All expenses included in the Statement of Revenue, Expenses, and Changes in Net Assets on Form 990, except grants and allocations, specific assistance to individuals, and benefits paid to or for members. Among current operating expenditures are such components as wages and salaries, fringe benefits, supplies, communication charges, professional fees, and depreciation and depletion charges. *See also* **Form 990** *and* **Total expenses.**

**Earnings.** All cash income of $1 or more from wages and salaries and net cash income of $1 or more from farm and nonfarm self-employment.

**Employment.** See **Labor force.**

**Endowment.** Stocks, bonds, property, and funds given permanently to nonprofit entities, primarily to foundations, hospitals, or schools, so nonprofit entities may produce their own income for grantmaking or operating purposes.

**Form 990.** The annual tax return that tax-exempt organizations with gross revenues of more than $50,000 must file with the IRS. The Form 990 is also required by many state charity offices. This tax return includes information about the organization's assets, income, operating expenses, contributions, paid staff and salaries, names and addresses of persons to contact, and program areas. *See also* **Form 990-PF** *and* **Form 990-N.**

**Form 990-N.** The annual informational return that tax-exempt organizations with gross revenues of less than $50,000 must file with the IRS. The Form 990-N is also known as the e-postcard and contains basic information about an organization, such as name, address, and officer name.

**Form 990-PF.** The annual information return that must be filed with the IRS by private foundations and nonexempt charitable trusts that are treated as private foundations by the IRS. This form replaced Form 990-AR circa 1981.

**Foundation.** A nongovernmental nonprofit organization with funds and a program managed by its own trustees and directors, established to further social, educational, religious, or charitable activities by making grants. A private foundation receives its funds from, and is subject to control by, an individual, family, corporation, or other group consisting of a limited number of members. In contrast, a community foundation receives its funds from multiple public sources and is classified by the IRS as a public charity. *See also* **Community foundation** *and* **Public charity.**

**Full-time employment.** Full-time workers are those who usually work 35 hours or more in a given week, regardless of the number of hours worked in the reference week.

**Full-time-equivalent volunteer.** A figure derived from an estimation procedure used to transform total hours formally volunteered to an organization into a figure equivalent to the value of full-time paid employment. The total annual volunteer hours are divided by 1,700 (which is a reasonable approximation of actual hours worked by a full-time worker during a year).

**Gross national product (GNP).** GNP is the total national output of final goods and services valued at market prices. *See also* **National income.**

**In-kind contribution.** See **Noncash (in-kind) contribution.**

**Independent sector.** The portion of the economy that includes all 501(c)(3) and 501(c)(4) tax-exempt organizations as defined by the IRS, including all religious institutions (such as churches and synagogues) and all persons who give time and money to serve charitable purposes. The independent sector is also referred to as the voluntary sector, the nonprofit sector, and the third sector. *See also* **Section 501(c)(3)** *and* **Section 501(c)(4).**

**Labor force.** The civilian labor force is the sum of employed and unemployed civilian workers. The total labor force is the sum of the civilian labor force and the armed forces. "Employed" persons are all people age 16 and older in the civilian noninstitutional population who, during the reference week, worked at all (as paid employees, in their own business or profession, or on their own farm) or who worked 15 hours or more as unpaid workers in an enterprise operated by a family member. For purposes of this profile, the full-time-equivalent employment of volunteers has been added to the traditional definition of the labor force. Also included are workers who were not working but who had jobs or businesses from which they were temporarily absent because of illness, vacation, bad weather, labor-management dispute, or personal reasons, whether or not they were paid for the time off or were seeking other jobs. Each employed person is counted only once. Workers holding more than one job are counted in the job at which they worked the most hours during the reference week. *See also* **Full-time-equivalent volunteer.**

**National income.** The earnings of the private sector plus compensation (wages, salaries, and fringe benefits) earned by government employees during a specified period. Earnings are recorded in the forms in which they are received, and they include taxes on those earnings. Earnings in the private sector consist of compensation of employees, profits of corporate and incorporated enterprises, net interest, and rental income of persons. National income is a component of gross national product and is less than gross national product, mainly because it does not include capital consumption (depreciation) allowances and indirect business taxes. *See also* **Gross national product (GNP).**

**National Taxonomy of Exempt Entities–Core Codes (NTEE-CC).** A classification system for tax-exempt nonprofit organizations, consisting of 26 major groups under 10 broad categories. (See the NCCS web site, http://nccs.urban.org/, for further details.)

**Noncash (in-kind) contribution.** An individual or corporate contribution of goods or commodities as distinguished from cash. Noncash contributions from individuals can include such items as clothing, works of art, food, furniture, and appliances. Noncash contributions from corporations may also take various forms, such as donation of used office furniture or equipment, office space, or the professional services of employees. Although noncash contributions from individuals are tax deductible, noncash contributions from corporations generally are not. *See also* **Corporate contribution.**

**Nonprofit.** A term describing the IRS designation of an organization whose income is not used for the benefit or private gain of stockholders, directors, or any other persons with an interest in the company. A nonprofit organization's income is used to support its operations. Such organizations are defined under section 501(c) of the Internal Revenue Code. Nonprofit organizations that are included in the definition of the independent sector are nonprofit, tax-exempt organizations that are included in sections 501(c)(3) and 501(c)(4) of the code. *See also* **Section 501(c)(3)** *and* **Section 501(c)(4).**

**Nonprofit institutions serving households (NPISH).** The nonprofit sector as defined by the Bureau of Economic Analysis. This definition includes tax-exempt organizations providing services in religion and welfare, medical care, education and research, recreation, and personal business, such as labor unions, legal aid, and professional associations. The category excludes nonprofits—such as chambers of commerce, trade associations, and homeowners' associations—that serve businesses rather than households; it also excludes nonprofits that sell goods and services in the same way as for-profit businesses, such as tax-exempt cooperatives, credit unions, mutual financial institutions, and tax-exempt manufacturers, such as university presses.

**North American Industry Classification System (NAICS).** NAICS was the system used by the 1997 Economic Census. Earlier censuses had used the SIC system. Although many individual NAICS industries correspond directly to industries in the SIC system, most higher-level groupings do not. As such, data comparison between the two systems should be done carefully. *See also* **Standard Industrial Classification (SIC).**

**Operating foundation.** A private foundation that devotes most of its earnings and assets directly to the conduct of its tax-exempt purposes (for example, operating a museum or home for the elderly) rather than making grants to other organizations for these purposes.

**Operating organization.** An operating organization engages in various activities, such as producing information or delivering services and products to its members and the public, in contrast to other entities that function as sources of financial support by raising funds and delivering them. Examples of operating organizations are museums, colleges, universities, and social services agencies.

**Out-of-scope organization.** An organization identified as either foreign in origin or a governmental or supporting government entity (such as a public or state college); it has been excluded from the IRS file of tax-exempt organizations for purposes of the *Almanac.*

**Outlay.** How a nonprofit organization uses its funds: whether it spends them, gives them away, or invests them.

**Part-time employment.** Part-time workers usually work less than 35 hours a week (at all jobs), regardless of the number of hours worked in the reference week.

**Per capita.** A per capita figure represents an average computed for every person in a specific group (or "population"). It is derived by taking the total of an item (such as income, taxes, or retail sales) and dividing it by the number of people in the specified population.

**Personal income.** Income received by persons from all sources. Personal income is the sum (less personal contributions for social insurance) of wage and salary disbursements, other labor income, proprietors' income, rental income, dividends, personal interest income, and transfer payments. Per capita personal income is total personal income divided by the appropriate population base. *See also* **Per capita.**

**Pretax income.** A corporation's annual income before it has paid taxes. The IRS allows corporations to deduct up to 10 percent of their taxable income as contributions to charitable organizations and to carry forward such contributions in excess of 10 percent over a five-year period. Corporations do not usually release information on their taxable income, however, and data collected by groups such as the Conference Board are based on income before calculation of income taxes. Taxable income and income before taxes may be similar or very different, depending on the industry and the corporation's tax structure.

**Public charity.** The largest category of 501(c)(3) organizations, which serve broad purposes, including assisting the poor and the underprivileged; advancing religion, education, health, science, art, and culture; and protecting the environment, among others. A public charity that is identified by the IRS as "not a private foundation" (as defined in section 509(a) of the Internal Revenue Code) normally receives a substantial part of its income, directly or indirectly, from the general public or from government sources, which a private foundation does not. The public support must be fairly broad and not limited to a few individuals or families. Only public charities and religious organizations can receive tax-deductible contributions.

**Reporting public charity.** Public charities that report to the IRS on Form 990. Charities that do not have to file Forms 990 are religious organizations and congregations and charities with less than $50,000 in annual gross receipts.

**Section 501(c)(3).** The Internal Revenue Code section that defines tax-exempt organizations organized and operated exclusively for religious, charitable, scientific, literary, educational, or similar purposes. Contributions to 501(c)(3) organizations are deductible as charitable donations for federal income tax purposes.

**Section 501(c)(4).** The Internal Revenue Code section that defines tax-exempt organizations organized to operate as civic leagues, social welfare organizations, and local associations of employees. These organizations are included in the independent sector.

**Standard Industrial Classification (SIC).** The classification system and definition of industries in accordance with the composition of the economy. Although this classification is designed to cover all economic activity in the United States, government statistical collections emanating from this classification system do not distinguish between private nonprofit organizations and private for-profit organizations. This system was replaced by the NAICS starting in 1999.

**Support organization.** Support organizations collect funds and distribute them primarily to operating organizations. Support organizations usually do not operate service delivery programs. Examples include federated fundraising organizations such as United Ways or Catholic Charities. *See also* **Operating organization.**

**Tax exempt.** A classification granted by the IRS to qualified nonprofit organizations that frees them from the requirement to pay taxes on their income. Private foundations, including endowed company foundations, are tax exempt; however, they must pay a 1 or 2 percent excise tax on net investment income. All 501(c)(3) and 501(c)(4) organizations are tax exempt.

**Total expenses.** All current operating expenditures plus grants and allocations, specific assistance to individuals, benefits paid to or for members, and payments to affiliates. *See also* **Current operating expenditures.**

**Transfer payments.** Funds transferred from nonprofit institutions serving households to households. *See also* **Nonprofit institutions serving households (NPISH).**

**Transfer receipts.** Funds that nonprofit institutions serving households receive from private and public sources, such as donations and grants. *See also* **Nonprofit institutions serving households (NPISH).**

**Volunteer.** A person who gives time to help others for no monetary pay. *Formal volunteering* is defined as giving a specified amount of time to organizations such as hospitals, churches, or schools. *Informal volunteering* is ad hoc and involves helping organizations as well as individuals, including neighbors, family, and friends.

**Volunteer hours.** The average number of hours a week volunteered and the total number of hours volunteered by the population in a particular year. To calculate the average hours volunteered a week, volunteer hours are estimated using information on volunteering reported for the most recent period (such as three months or one week) in a particular survey by activity area (such as health or religion). These hours are then totaled and multiplied by the percentage of people in the population in that period who reported volunteering in that area. Total volunteer hours are calculated by multiplying the percentage of the population volunteering in each activity area specified in Gallup surveys (health, education, and so on) by the average volunteer hours worked in each area. Then, all figures for these areas are summed to get the total number of hours per period. If the particular period is three months, these totals would then be multiplied by four to arrive at the total hours volunteered in a particular year. *See* also **Volunteer.**

# About the Authors

**Katie L. Roeger** is assistant program director of the National Center for Charitable Statistics, a program of the Center on Nonprofits and Philanthropy at the Urban Institute. She manages the NCCS database of nonprofit organizations and integrates business, Census, and other survey data. Ms. Roeger transforms raw data into research reports that inform policymakers, the general public, and students about the tax-exempt sector. She also provides statistical support for surveys and other research studies. Recently completed research projects include the revocation of nonprofit organizations, nonprofit-government contracts, domestic and international charitable giving, education support organizations, and diversity in nonprofit leadership. Ms. Roeger's studies have been cited in the national media, and she has been quoted in the *Chicago Tribune, Star Tribune* (MN), and the *New York Times*. Before joining the Urban Institute, Ms. Roeger worked as a mathematical statistician with the U.S. Census Bureau, where she evaluated the accuracy of economic indicators and conducted research to improve statistical methodologies.

**Amy S. Blackwood** is a consultant with the Urban Institute's National Center for Charitable Statistics, working on various nonprofit research projects. Before her consultancy, she was a research associate at NCCS and worked as a policy analyst at the Corporation for National and Community Service. Ms. Blackwood's work with NCCS has focused on examining public charities in the health and education subsectors. She holds a master's degree in public service and administration from Texas A&M University.

**Sarah L. Pettijohn** is a research associate in the Center on Nonprofits and Philanthropy, where she serves as a project team member on various studies. In addition to her research work, Ms. Pettijohn is a Ph.D. candidate and adjunct faculty member at American University in the Department of Public Administration and Policy. She holds an M.P.A. and graduate certificate in nonprofit management from the University of Texas at Dallas. Ms. Pettijohn was named an emerging scholar by the Association for Research on Nonprofit Organization and Voluntary Action in 2011 and a Founders Forum fellow in 2010 by the American Society for Public Administration.

# Index

Tables and figures are referred to by "*t*" and "*fig*" after the page number.